Medieval Literature
and Civilization

Medieval Literature and Civilization

Studies in Memory of
G. N. GARMONSWAY

edited by
D. A. PEARSALL
and
R. A. WALDRON

UNIVERSITY OF LONDON
THE ATHLONE PRESS
1969

Published by
THE ATHLONE PRESS
UNIVERSITY OF LONDON
at 2 Gower Street London WC1
Distributed by Constable & Co Ltd
10 *Orange Street London* WC2

Canada
Oxford University Press
Toronto

U.S.A.
Oxford University Press Inc
New York

485 11101 2

Printed in Great Britain by
WESTERN PRINTING SERVICES LTD
BRISTOL

In Memoriam
GEORGE NORMAN GARMONSWAY

An Acclamation

Green wave-hills, heavers, wedge on wedge rising,
Rear, curve, smite with cold shine on stone cliffs.
Bide
where the sea-mark stands.
    Loud is the swan-way.
        Under star-bright heaven
           Hold to the south;
Then west.
           Mark under swan-way the keels of the sea-kings
Studding the sunrise, shield-rim of morning.
Far-wandering sea-ravens, shearing deep water, they
Mingle with storm, harsh blades of the bitter wind.
Swiftly the sea-wolves run, gathering to foam; on
Wide wings, the mild havens darkening, ride.

Bent under world's-work, land-dwellers, waking,
Rise to the onslaught, raise the iron spear:
'Here stands, unfearing, an earl with his fighting-men,
On the watch; homeland warding and keeping—
This earth of Ethelred, land of my lord,
His folk and his fields.'
           Hark as the breakers roar;
Hear the flood thunder.
           Doomed, by the hunters felled,
from that far overwhelming they still send their answer:
'Higher shall the spirit be; sterner the heart;
Stronger the mind as our strength falls away.'
Those peoples, long blended, attackers, defenders,
What are they to us, the remote men of Maldon?
We have seen dragons, burning our land, our home,
Struck from the skies. They lay broken over meadow.

In our time the kraken is rising from slumber.
Where are they now, those steadfast companions?
The sheaf after reaping is gone from its setting.
How far now is Leif? He is further than Vineland.
How is it with Gunnar? The fair fields of home
Called him home from exile: he fell to his enemies.
How is it with Njál?
                    'Our land shall be settled
with law; and with anarchy ravaged and wrecked.'
He was old; he was wise. They burnt him, of course.
Yet, seeing their mind, he said:
                    'God is merciful.
He won't let us burn in both this world and next.'

These were ourselves. The far-seeing. The slayers. For the burners had,
Like us, a keen sense of duty. Life's potence the Light-dweller
Binds into earth-form; sets the flame flowering;
Sheds the husk, shrivelled; frees again, harvesting,
Coarse, fair and fine. These are ourselves; these
Urbanely, with humour, he, vigilant scholar,
Drew for us clearly, in their full humanity.

                    Set here the sea-mark.
            Silent the golden swan-way.

                                        Michael Mason

Preface

THIS volume was planned in 1965, when Norman Garmonsway retired from the Chair of English which he occupied at King's College in the University of London. It was to be a collection of essays representative of the core of scholarly interests of a widely-cultivated friend and colleague, and our intention was to present it to him upon his seventieth birthday in May, 1968. His sudden death in February 1967, while he was in the midst of his second post-retirement teaching session at the University of Toronto, has deprived us of our hope of pleasing him with a tribute to his own learning from some of those who shared his concerns.

These original contributions to the study of medieval literature and civilization in Britain and Scandinavia are now published as an appropriate memorial to him. From the first, the aim has been to offer to the public a book of essays which have a direct bearing upon his central academic interests and which is thus structured, in some measure, after the pattern of his mind. In the world of learning he controlled a province like that of the king whom he made the subject of his Dorothea Coke Memorial Lecture in 1963: 'an extensive empire across the northern seas'. Like his master H. M. Chadwick, he saw the study of the language and literature (together with the history and archaeology) of early Britain and Scandinavia as forming a single coherent discipline and this conception of unity in diversity can be glimpsed both in the range of matters which he chose to write upon and in many of his individual pieces.

At the same time, we hope that these essays will reach the interested non-specialist. For Norman Garmonsway was, despite his erudition and his skill in the several learned roles of philologist, textual critic, editor, historian, and literary critic, the very antithesis of the remote and secluded scholar. He was a channel of communication between exact scholarship and a wider public. It was altogether fitting that his felicitous translation of the *Anglo-Saxon Chronicle*, invaluable as it is both to the historian and to the student of literary history, should have been published in Dent's Everyman's Library and that his last major literary task was the revision of the popular *Penguin English Dictionary*, which he compiled with Miss Jacqueline Simpson. Moreover, he generously devoted a great part of his energies, through more than forty-five years as an active teacher, to the direct communication of his knowledge and enthusiasm to generations of students. It is as much through these rich personal contacts of classroom and study as through his published works that his influence will live and continue to bear fruit.

Those who worked with him, especially those who had the good fortune to take up their first university appointment in his department at King's, will remember him as the most benign and kindly of colleagues. He would never interfere, but was always ready to help. Even the preliminary interview soon lost the character of an ordeal and became, under his guidance, a friendly discussion about books and scholarship—or so it seemed to the candidate. To watch him, later, conducting interviews of applicants for admission, or of graduates, was to see how the confidence he inspired brought out the best in even the most diffident or self-conscious of students. Other professors of English may have had more to do in the day-to-day running of their departments but none could have claimed that Norman's benevolent regime of trust, loyalty and affection was not effective.

His work at King's, in fact, was only part of his contribution to the academic life of the University of London. As a member of the Board of English Studies for twenty years and as member of numerous academic and advisory committees, he had the opportunity to bring the same qualities, the same generous and leisurely wisdom, to a much wider range of concerns and at a time, moreover, when the London English syllabus was in the throes of a radical reappraisal. His academic visits as external examiner or visiting lecturer, to universities throughout Britain, as well as in the United States and Canada, extended still further the sphere of his influence and gained him the respect and affection of all those he met.

To accommodate essays from all those colleagues and former pupils who would, no doubt, have wished to contribute to this token of esteem would have required a much larger volume. We would like, however, to thank the many who have taken a close interest in the progress of the book. The help and advice of the officers of the Athlone Press in bringing our plans to physical realization is gratefully acknowledged.

D.A.P.
R.A.W.

Contributors

S. A. J. BRADLEY
Lecturer in English, University of York

GEOFFREY BULLOUGH
Emeritus Professor of English Language and Literature,
University of London

A. C. CAWLEY
Professor of English Language and Medieval English Literature,
University of Leeds

PETER CLEMOES
Elrington and Bosworth Professor of Anglo-Saxon,
University of Cambridge

NORMAN DAVIS
Merton Professor of English Language and Literature,
University of Oxford

BRUCE DICKINS
formerly Elrington and Bosworth Professor of Anglo-Saxon,
University of Cambridge

NORMAN E. ELIASON
Professor of English, University of North Carolina

P. G. FOOTE
Professor of Old Scandinavian, University College,
University of London

GEORGE KANE
Professor of English Language and Medieval Literature,
King's College, University of London

CONTRIBUTORS

WILLIAM MATTHEWS
Professor of English,
University of California at Los Angeles

† FREDERICK NORMAN
Emeritus Professor of German, University of London

R. I. PAGE
Fellow of Corpus Christi College, Cambridge, and University
Lecturer in Anglo-Saxon

ROBERT R. RAYMO
Professor of English, New York University

G. H. RUSSELL
Professor of English, Australian National University, Canberra

G. V. SMITHERS
Professor of English Language and Medieval Literature,
University of Durham

E. G. STANLEY
Professor of English, Queen Mary College,
University of London

BEATRICE WHITE
Professor of English, Westfield College,
University of London

DOROTHY WHITELOCK
formerly Elrington and Bosworth Professor of Anglo-Saxon,
University of Cambridge

DAVID M. WILSON
Reader in Archaeology of the Anglo-Saxon Period,
University College, University of London

R. M. WILSON
Professor of English Language, University of Sheffield

Contents

CONTENTS

ILLUSTRATIONS

GEORGE NORMAN GARMONSWAY was born on 6 May 1898 at Hartlepool, Co. Durham. From the Henry Smith School there, he went as a Scholar to St Catherine's College, Cambridge, and after a distinguished undergraduate career, interrupted between 1917 and 1919 by commissioned service in the Royal Garrison Artillery, he was awarded First Class Honours in both parts of the English Tripos in 1921, one of his examiners being Professor Bruce Dickins, who has contributed a paper to the present volume. His career as a university teacher of English began at the University College of Wales at Aberystwyth, where he taught from 1921 to 1930; he went then to King's College, London, where he was successively Lecturer, Reader, and (from 1956) Professor of English Language and Medieval Literature. He was elected Fellow of the Royal Historical Society in 1954 and Fellow of the Society of Antiquaries in 1960. His work at King's was interrupted by a second period of war service between 1939 and 1945, this time with the Ministry of Food. After the war he spent two short periods in the United States as Visiting Professor of English in the University of California at Los Angeles (1955) and the University of North Carolina (1962) and again on his retirement in 1965 he crossed the Atlantic to take up a similar post in the University of Toronto; it was there that he died on 28 February 1967.

His principal publications are *An Early Norse Reader* (Cambridge University Press, 1928), *Ælfric's Colloquy* (An edition of the Latin and English Texts. Methuen, 1939), *The Anglo-Saxon Chronicle* (Translated with an Introduction. Foreword by Bruce Dickins. Dent, 1954), *Canute and His Empire* (The Dorothea Coke Memorial Lecture in Northern Studies, University College, London. H. K. Lewis, 1963), *The Penguin English Dictionary* (With Jacqueline Simpson. Penguin Books, 1965), and numerous reviews and articles, among them: 'A note on a passage in

Beowulf', *Aberystwyth Studies*, 1922; 'Gíslasaga', *Saga-Book of the Viking Society*, xi, 1935; 'Eyrbyggja Saga', *Saga-Book of the Viking Society*, xii, 1937; the chapters on Old English literature for 1939–41 in *The Year's Work in English Studies*, xx, xxi, xxii, 1941–43; 'Old Norse Jarðarmen', *The Early Cultures of North-West Europe* (H. M. Chadwick Memorial Studies. Edited by Sir Cyril Fox and Bruce Dickins. Cambridge University Press, 1950); 'Anna Gurney: Learned Saxonist', *Essays and Studies* (The English Association. John Murray, 1955); (With R. R. Raymo) 'A Middle-English Prose Life of St. Ursula', *The Review of English Studies*, New Series, ix, 1958; (With R. R. Raymo) 'A Middle English Metrical Life of Job', *Early English and Norse Studies* (Presented to Hugh Smith in honour of his sixtieth birthday. Edited by Arthur Brown and Peter Foote. Methuen, 1963); and 'Anglo-Saxon Heroic Attitudes', *Franciplegius: Medieval and Linguistic Studies in Honor of Francis Peabody Magoun, Jr.* (Edited by J. B. Bessinger, Jr. and R. P. Creed. New York University Press and Allen and Unwin, 1965).

I

The Early Germanic Background of Old English Verse

FREDERICK NORMAN

PERHAPS, in the title, there should have been a reference to 'secular' verse for it is with secular, or rather non-Christian, aspects that we are here concerned. However, can *Beowulf* by any stretch of the imagination be called secular?—though it is indeed predominantly so even if the overriding idea may be Christian. And much of the religious verse, quite apart from metaphor, diction and presentation, which naturally enough show much traditional Germanic influence, has strong secular elements. After all, the happy blend of Christian sentiment and traditional method in the telling of a story is a distinctive characteristic of Old English literature. The only truly secular narrative preserved is *The Battle of Finnsburgh*. There is no reference to the Deity, or to any deity, and in the paraphrase of part of the action given in *Beowulf* there is no such reference, either. In *The Battle of Maldon* there is proper contempt for the heathen Viking, and we never lose sight of the fact that this is also a clash between heathen and Christian; Byrhtnoth's final pious words would suggest that the author was a cleric. There is less Christian evidence in the ferocious gloating over the bloodshed to which we are treated in *The Battle of Brunanburh*, and the reference to the sun, God's candle, is singularly inappropriate in the context in which it is placed. The *Charms* are partly Christian, partly they pay lip-service to Christianity. Even when they are not Christian they are hardly secular, their primitive magic is embedded in religious notions.

The odd heathen line, handed down from some very early context, may have survived here and there, particularly in the

Charms. Apart from that, all Old English verse is produced by professed Christians, and most of it by trained clerics. God is never very far from their thoughts even when they are dealing with essentially non-religious matters.

Not all the Germanic tribes indulged in literary composition; or if they did no traces have reached us. Nor is it by any means certain or even necessary to assume that all tribes, at some early stage or other, have possessed what we should regard as a literary culture. By the time that the tribes came into contact with Rome one must take it for granted, from their general state of culture, that there was religious observance together with some remembered and formalized verbal utterance, and there presumably existed, on analogy with what we learn from other relatively primitive cultures, simple magical incantation and charms. All of these must stem to begin with from a priestly caste. We know almost nothing of secular poetry produced outside this priestly cultural environment.

The famous short account in the *Germania* of Tacitus proves that the tribes of which he knew had no developed form of writing, that they had cosmological poetry handed down orally, and that they used the alliterative line as a formal principle of composition. Except for some later groupings of lines into stanzaic forms the alliterative line was to remain the fundamental unit in Germanic verse until Romance forms, at different times in different Germanic cultures, ousted the older inherited type which had ruled unchallenged for many centuries. The Tacitean Ingaevones, (H)erminones and Istaevones cannot have been three tribes; they must have been three tribal groupings, as is indeed obvious from the account given. We are not entirely justified in equating the groups with a later division based on linguistic and partly geographical considerations into North-, East- and West-Germanic. We are, however, on safe ground when we believe that there was a religious tradition common to a large number of tribes which spoke of Tuisto and his son Mannus. Knowledge of both of them has vanished completely and it is unwarranted to

4

establish any sort of connection between, for instance, late Scandinavian accounts of the creation and the tantalizingly brief reference by the Roman historian.

In Chapter xl of the *Germania* we receive further information on Germanic religion in the account of the rites connected with the Earth goddess Nerthus. Seven tribes, which are named by Tacitus, belong to the Nerthus confederation. They are all situated in the North, in Schleswig-Holstein, possibly in Jutland, and in the off-shore islands. Only three of these tribes are mentioned in late sources. *Widsith* refers to the Varini, Aviones and, most doubt-fully, to the Eudones. The Reudigni, the Suardones and the Nuithones have vanished without a trace. It is here that we hear for the first time the name of the Anglii. They occur in the third place in Tacitus's list of seven, and there is nothing to single them out from the others. From later developments it is, however, clear that they either were or soon became the dominant tribe, and we may assume that they ultimately incorporated most of the rest. Whilst we are not definitely told, we cannot credit that the procession of the goddess was a dumb show. It would be against all probability not to be convinced that there was some sort of verbal accompaniment, and from the evidence quoted above we may take it that there existed a set composition in alliterative form, a eulogy of the goddess intoned by priests, acolytes and possibly the general population.

The goddess Nerthus does not seem to have disappeared as completely as Mannus and Tuisto. We know from Adam of Bremen of the cult of the male fertility-deity Freyr, son of Njorðr, at Uppsala. The informant of Adam, though he pretends to some knowledge, is unfortunately too horrified to report it. Njorðr and Nerthus are exact linguistic parallels. The former, indeed, is masculine, the latter feminine; that, however, cannot impugn the linguistic correspondence. Both were clearly deities connected with fertility rites.

As for secular verse: in the *Annals* Tacitus reports that Arminius, slain by relatives in A.D. 17, was still celebrated in song. Tacitus is writing about eighty years after the killing so that here we have evidence of secular composition and of the survival of the composition for two or three generations. Whilst we know nothing of the type of composition it is likely to have been encomiastic, which would include the recounting of warlike exploits; it may also have been threnodic. Tacitus's wording, unfortunately, does not allow us to conclude whether he had heard of one song or of more. Again, all traces of this poetry have been lost. Later Germanic poetry knows nothing of Arminius or of anybody else in those early days. In the nineteenth century Arminius became an early German hero, and much ink has been spilt by some German scholars arguing learnedly and irrelevantly some connection with the Sigfried story. The arguments have proved nothing, and they cannot. It is normal for Germanic chieftains to be slain by relatives, and treacherously to boot.

The culture of the early Germanic tribes as depicted by Tacitus has been used time and again to explain later patterns in Germanic history which are removed from the Roman author by hundreds of years, and frequently by well over a thousand! Not only that: the tribes about whom Tacitus collected most information—he was never an eyewitness—were to a large extent wiped out in the struggle to keep them out of the empire. What the Roman tells us for instance about the loyalty of the retainer to the chief is a common characteristic in aggressive, marauding cultures. It is meaningless when commenting on the loyalty unto death of most of Byrhtnoth's retainers to refer back to the behaviour of the *comitatus*. Much can obviously be gleaned from a perusal of the *Germania*, though we need not believe everything we are told about these noble savages and much which is undoubtedly true is not particularly Germanic.

For several hundred years after the death of Tacitus there is not a shred of evidence in any classical writer that will tell us anything about literary composition amongst the Germanic tribes. Our first real break comes with the Byzantine writer Priskos, and what he has to tell us refers to Huns and not, as is still frequently stated, to Goths. Priskos was writing in the middle of the fifth century, he was an eyewitness and a trained observer, he had visited the court of Attila, and he had attended a banquet given by the scourge of God at which there was some sort of heroic recitation, probably of an encomiastic kind. Now it is certain that by this time similar recitations might have been heard at some of the Germanic courts, and it is likely enough that Hunnish and Germanic poetry dealt in a similar manner with similar themes, and may well have influenced one another in ways we can no longer tell, yet the poetry which Priskos describes was not Germanic poetry.

We are justified in assuming that by the time of Priskos secular poetry, both encomiastic and straightforward heroic narrative, was cultivated by the scop who was attached to the court, who was so to speak the historical heroic memory of the tribe, and who enshrined the warlike aspirations of chief and retainers in song. Tacitus gives us a careful description of the set-up at the court of a Germanic warrior-chief; such information was vital intelligence for the Romans and we must assume that had there been a person with anything like the functions of the later Germanic scop, he would have heard and we should have been told. A linguistic parallel to the lack of information on this point in the *Germania* would be the lack of a common Germanic word for poet. We might assume that *scop* was the common word, and that this word was supplanted in the North by *skald*, a word that was most likely borrowed together with some poetic practices from the Irish by early Vikings. The latter assumption is indeed arguable, and very likely true; it cannot prove the former. There was, however, a common word for a poetic composition: Gothic **liuþ*,[1] Old Norse *ljóð*, Old High German *liod*, Old Saxon *lioth*, Old English *leoþ*. The word can mean slightly different types of poetic composition in the different languages yet there can be no doubt that there was a common Germanic word for 'song' even if there was no common word for the poet.

Few early Germanic heroic lays have been preserved, and all of

---

[1] *Liuþ* is not preserved as a simplex in Gothic. The word can be inferred with certainty from *liuþon*: 'to praise', *awiliuþ*: 'thanksgiving' and *liuþareis*: 'singer'. Venantius Fortunatus (b. about 530, d. after 600) supplies the latinized *acc. pl. leudos* which to him are *barbara c rmina*, referring to Frankish recitation.

them are fragmentary or corrupt or both. Scandinavia, in very late copies, supplies a lay on the *Wounding of Ermanaric* (originally Gothic), a *Wayland-lay* (originally Anglian or Saxon), a fragment of an old *Sigurd-lay* (originally Frankish), an old *Attila-lay* (originally Burgundian, and then incorporated in Frankish traditions when the Franks overran the Burgundians in the sixth century), and the fragmentary *Battle of Goths and Huns* (originally Visi-Gothic?); Germany contributes the fragmentary *Hildebrand-lay*, written down *c.* 815 and showing insular influence in the writing, in the Anglo-Saxon foundation Fulda (originally Langobard); England produces the fragmentary *Battle of Finnsburgh* (Anglian?, later Danish?). The prototype of the *Ermanaric-lay* must have existed *c.* 400; the *Wayland-lay* is very early but undatable; *Sigurd-lay*, *Attila-lay*, and the *Battle of Goths and Huns* should not be later than 500; *Hildebrand-lay* and *Battle of Finnsburgh* may be tentatively dated early in the seventh century. All these lays, except possibly that on Hildebrand for which we have no actual documentary proof,[1] were known in England, and many more besides to which we frequently have obscure allusions; obscure because there was no need to be explicit! The habit of composing heroic lays seems to have ceased in Southern Germania not later than 700; in Northern Germania, where small courts survived far longer, it was carried on a good deal later though with the introduction of the skaldic manner the old-fashioned style went out of favour. In the South the decay of the heroic lay was undoubtedly partly connected with the spread of Christianity; in the North composition of the old style of lay seems to have ceased before large-scale christianization had taken place.

Germanic heroic poetry deals largely with historical characters. Frequently we can identify them, many are plainly historical though there is no strict proof. Some characters are of mythical or semi-mythical origin and this is a realm where conjecture inevitably enters: it is hardly possible to prove the 'age' of a mythical character. The earliest historical characters known to us from song

---

[1] Nothing can be deduced from the late reference to an 'Ildebrand', in company with Wade, and various sprites and demons that live near water.

are the Anglian Offa and the Ostro-Gothic Ermanaric. For the former there is no record outside song and genealogies, though exist he undoubtedly did; the latter is amply attested in historical writing. The latest to occur in Southern Germania is Alboin the Langobard, murdered in the year 572 in Italy by his wife and her paramour in a classical manner reminiscent of Agamemnon and Clytemnestra. Where, in the South, we can infer the existence of an historical prototype the dates lie between about 350 and 572. It is reasonable to assume that the early heroic lay does not introduce historical characters (whose historicity we happen not to be able to prove) who would not fit into the above scheme. This should mean that a body of verse was created at a certain time, under certain conditions, and that when these conditions changed the lays were indeed remembered and handed on, though composition in the old style ceased. It is to be noted that Scandinavian rulers who occur in *Beowulf* all flourish before the death of Alboin; the extreme dates for Danes, Geats and Swedes seem to lie between 470 and at the latest 550. Here there is, however, a difficulty. Whilst some of the Scandinavian material clearly goes back to heroic lays the historical canvas in some of the material adduced would seem to burst the bounds of any early lays as we know them. The information in *Beowulf* is puzzling, it is also reasonably precise, and it could without difficulty go back to the recollections of one man. The real crux remains: why was an Anglian audience in the middle of the eighth century content to listen to a poem that produced such a wealth of subsidiary Scandinavian material unless the audience was fairly familiar with the background? No really satisfactory answer has yet been given.

Nothing is to be learnt for our purpose from the actual remains of the Gothic language. Indirect evidence is supplied by Jordanes in the middle of the sixth century in his History of the Goths. Had the earlier work by Cassiodor, which Jordanes must have used extensively, or that of the wholly unknown Ablabius, been preserved we should undoubtedly have known more. Jordanes presents us with a version of the *Wounding of Ermanaric*, partly sober history, partly based on poetic tradition; he also mentions various Gothic heroes who are remembered in song. Of two of them we know nothing further, one, Fridigern, occurs in classical historical contexts as a tough, resolute and able leader, the fourth, Vidigoia, is almost certainly the hero known in English literature as Wudga or Widia, at a later date turned into the son of Weland and Beadohild. In another section Jordanes refers to an account of the death of Vidigoia at the hands of treacherous Sarmatians. This short reference is embedded in a quotation from Priskos; it is almost certain that the passage about Vidigoia which is an obvious gloss and has nothing to do with the context was added by Jordanes, and that makes the first occurrence of Vidigoia mid-sixth rather than mid-fifth century. The Gothic historian also mentions the threnodies intoned when the Visi-Goths bore their slain king from the battlefield in 451; these were presumably extempore productions though based on familiar models;[1] anyhow, there is no later echo. A later Gothic hero of whom much is told is Theodoric, the Ostro-Gothic king in Italy who died in 526. Hama and a number of other 'Gothic' heroes cannot be proved to be historical. How much of this Gothic material was current in the Gothic tongue we do not know. It is likely that much of it, including a great deal of the matter ascribed to Theodoric, owed its existence and certainly its preservation to the Langobards, the immediate and rather more fortunate successors of the Ostro-Goths in Italy.

Old High German literature offers a little more though not much. It contains about 300 lines of alliterative verse, much of it preserved in a most unsatisfactory state. The *Hildebrand-lay*, of Langobard origin, is the supremely important survival; unfortunately it is a fragment. Far more, however, was known, was kept alive tenaciously in oral tradition, and appears in written form in the twelfth and thirteenth centuries.

---

[1] Cf. the extempore poem on Beowulf's victory over Grendel, *Beow.* 871–4. True, the poet quickly passes on to a lay of Sigmund of which we are told a great deal more. Did the author not wish to repeat himself (though he is hardly averse to repetition)?

There is nothing really helpful in Old Saxon though some Latin chronicles give hints and preserve scraps.

Indigenous Scandinavian heroic traditions are far too late to convey to us any reliable information about early Germanic literature. Where we do have early traditions, as in the various accounts of Danes, Geats and Swedes in *Beowulf*, the English poem is in fact the primary literary source.[1]

Thus, in the end, if we wish to study the development of early Germanic literature, we inevitably turn to the rich store preserved in Old English.

Regard for their mother-tongue led the Germanic invaders of England to use their own language in contexts that in Germany for instance, and certainly in Merovingian France, would have demanded Latin. This is perfectly intelligible in the case of the Western Franks though West-Frankish must have been known and understood amongst, at the very least, the Frankish nobility until the disappearance of the Carolingian dynasty. We are not concerned here with the reasons why a strong vernacular tradition failed to arise in Germany proper.[2] In England there is good evidence to show that at the very beginning of christianization in the early seventh century the Kentish king prevailed upon the foreign monks to write down the traditional law of the land in English. And thus the tradition continued. Whilst naturally

[1] The frequent discrepancies, not only between the saga-accounts and *Beowulf* but also between the various Northern sources themselves, cannot be dealt with here. We must assume that the saga-accounts stem largely from early poetic traditions. The poems ought to have been current round about 600, or a little earlier. We just do not know in what form, how, and how early they reached Northern England. None of this Scandinavian material, as far as we can judge, reached Germany. The answer ought to be that the Anglians, both on the Continent and in their new island home, remained on friendly terms with at the very least the Danes and possibly with Geats who escaped death or subjugation by the ultimately victorious Swedes.

[2] The Frank Otfrid did his best, and with great determination, to establish the 'Frankish tongue', as he called it, as a respectable literary medium. His Gospel Harmony, in rhymed verse, gruesome as much of it may be to us, was a remarkable and considerable achievement by an incredibly industrious, devoted and modest scholar and teacher.

Latin was much used, whilst at a comparatively early date Aldhelm produced polished Latin verse,[1] whilst a magnificent early culture expressed almost exclusively in Latin arose in Northumbria in the latter half of the seventh century, side by side with this flowering of Latin there continued the literary cultivation of the mother-tongue. In the case of the larger religious epics in the vernacular, some of which should still be eighth century or a little later, we must assume that there were written copies; no such assumption need be made for shorter secular verse and certainly not for heroic compositions of *The Battle of Finnsburgh* type: such poetry lived far from books, and the preservation of any of it is a fortunate accident. Indeed, Charlemagne is said to have ordered a collection of the *antiquissima carmina*—largely for historical reasons be it noted—which, if it ever existed, has vanished without a trace, and King Alfred is reported to have been well acquainted with secular vernacular poetry, and to have loved it. We know that, like Charlemagne, he collected learned men around him wherever he could find them. He himself wrote an introduction to the Dialogues of Gregory the Great, the translation of which he had entrusted to Werferth, and together with the Welshman Asser he translated Boethius. The metres of Boethius were certainly translated by Alfred into Old English prose, and there is no compelling reason why we should not ascribe the metrical version to him as well since he can be presumed to be the author of the occasional verses in the *Cura Pastoralis*. The great codices which preserve Old English poetry for us were written well after the time of Alfred, largely round about the year 1000; the impetus and tradition for making such collections we must ascribe to Alfred and his circle. There is nothing strictly speaking 'heroic' in any of these collections, and it is exceedingly doubtful whether, with all his love and knowledge, it would have occurred to the king to have such traditional poetry written down.

---

[1] How much truth there may be in the account that Aldhelm entertained passers-by with vernacular poetry, accompanying himself on a stringed instrument, we cannot tell. We can, however, be certain that he knew much of it and was competent to compose in the vernacular manner.

12

Old English literature preserves over 30,000 lines of alliterative verse, which is almost three times as much as the rest of the Germanic tribes have handed down, and a vast amount of religious and historical prose. The prose, as we should expect, is by and large later. Until the time of the Danish invasions the cultural centres were in the North; ruthless pillage and destruction made any sustained intellectual activity impossible, the scholars who survived largely migrated to the South, and the South also suffered grievously. Life became relatively normal again under Alfred and his successors, though the glories of Northumbria were gone for good. The Danish dynasty which took over in the eleventh century had little learning itself but was not inimical to indigenous scholarship. However, the final and deadly blow came in 1066. The Norman invasion killed Old English literary culture, and killed it for good. The twelfth century produced great literature in England, and intellectual England was in the forefront of Europe. But it was a Latin culture that owed almost nothing to native English sources and talent, and in so far as it was vernacular it was Anglo-Norman. When English, much altered, re-emerges as a literary tongue, the alliterative measure, though remarkably changed and no longer obeying earlier rules, has been stubbornly preserved. This preservation in itself shows that at a humble and non-literary level a great deal was remembered and some new material was produced. There was, however, no real life left in the native tradition, and except for isolated themes and hints the new literature really is new, and owes almost nothing to the England before the Norman conquest.

Scholarship in Old English and in Anglo-Saxon culture generally has of late years tended to concentrate far more on the actual Old English problems than on the wider Germanic and early European background. This has led, most advantageously, to an examination of the internal problems of Old English literature in a detailed and intensive manner, and it has brought us much new information, particularly by the meticulous comparison of extant texts. Such a method of study naturally eschews too much speculation about ultimate origins: it doubts the value of and frequently it scorns literary constructs and purely theoretical reconstructions. This intimate way of looking at Old English poetry is at its best when dealing with such elegiac productions as *The Seafarer*, *The Wanderer*, or *The Ruin*, or when considering the Old English elegiac contribution in much of the Biblical verse. This English elegiac mood (an early importation into Northumbria by Irish Christians?) is of course found in Scandinavian, and in particular in Icelandic literature and there, possibly like the habit of prose saga, it may also go back to Celtic influence. It is not an attitude one normally associates with early Germanic verse though even here one must be cautious when one remembers how King Gelimer, a Vandal of all people, asked his Byzantine conquerors in North Africa for a harp so that he might bewail his fate. And encomiastic verse in praise of the dead leader, a type we know existed in early Germania though we have no actual very early example in any vernacular, is bound to become reminiscent and reflective. So even the elegiac note, frequently regarded as a particularly Anglo-Saxon attitude and then explained as due almost entirely to Christian influences, may well have affinities with earlier melancholy reflections of pensive Teutonic warriors, improbable and perhaps startling as that may appear to us.

The reflective note creeps into the off-shoots of heroic verse as well. It is strangely intermingled in *Deor*, it is present in the *Waldere*-fragments, though that may merely be caused by the fact that a speech by Hildegyð, reminiscent and encouraging, has been preserved, and it is part of the texture of *Beowulf*. There is only a faint trace of it in *The Battle of Maldon* and, significantly enough, it is entirely absent in the *Finnsburgh*-fragment; we are unable to ascertain how much of the elegiac mood that pervades Hildeburh's reflections in the famous paraphrase penned for us by the *Beowulf*-poet was present in the original heroic poem.

When the heroic remains and allusions in Old English literature were first being studied there was a tendency to disregard the rights and values of Old English literature itself and to use it merely as a means of discussing origins in distant times. It was assumed that there was a vast store of traditional verse more or less common to all the Germanic peoples, and problems of transmission thus were not unduly troublesome. Nowadays we are indeed troubled, nor are we capable of accounting satisfactorily for the very large dose of Scandinavian material contained in *Beowulf*. Whatever theory of origin is proposed, ultimately we are inevitably faced by the central problem: how can we account for the well-informed interest taken by a Northern English Anglian audience—most probably a Mercian audience in the middle of the eighth century—in a poem the central theme of which is the exploits of a Geatish hero at a Danish court, the fight of this same hero, when king of the Geats, against a dragon, the introduction, remarkably accurate in a work of imagination not purporting to be sober history, of stories concerning several generations of Danish, Geatish and Swedish kings, and a number of allusions to Scandinavian tales which we can piece together more or less by patient search and persistent study? Unless we wish to postulate that the audience was either half-asleep or not listening, or content not to understand, all of which are quite impossible assumptions, we must conclude, on the available evidence, that there was indeed an attentive and reasonably knowledgeable audience. More than that: the poet was a cleric, and for his time a learned man: he wrote his poem, and for that he needed leisure and the necessary material. A patron must have supplied him with this, and the patron will have had some idea of what the poet was going to produce, and must have approved. It is tempting, though highly conjectural, to regard Offa of Mercia as the patron. But this brings us back to the original query; what earthly interest could Offa have had in this particular theme? Even if we assume, which is probable enough, that whilst the Anglians were still in continental Anglia there was an alliance and a firm friendship between Danes and Anglians, even if we assume that this friendship continued as the Anglians migrated to England, rather more gradually than we are led to expect from Bede's account, and as the Danes moved south from Jutland and ultimately into and

15

even beyond continental Anglia, what possible interest could there be in Geatish-Swedish wars?

Scholars of our older literature in England and in the United States have become somewhat impatient of too much theorizing in a country where there are few signposts and where one is apt to become hopelessly lost. Few can still be found who are willing to venture out into the territory of *Widsith* scholarship where audacious conjecture, though fascinating and brilliant, is still the rule, and many are at long last becoming resigned to the fact that nothing certain is to be known and that it is therefore more sensible to turn to other matters. Yet whilst it is true that no certainty can be reached and that we cannot hope to reconstruct a factually completely reliable literary history of any one of the early Germanic tribes we can, though with considerable misgivings, say more about the Anglians than about the rest of them, even the Goths, of whose literary development we know far less than we care to imagine. This may well be due to an historical accident. The Anglians kept out of imperial politics and the alluring South, and they went to England instead, where they were able to settle down and to preserve their own individuality, character and identity. The Ostro-Goths vanished as a nation in the middle of the sixth century, though large numbers of them and of their relatives, the Gepids, became absorbed by the equally able and determined Langobards, who then took over and developed further their store of story; the Visi-Goths were overrun in the first quarter of the eighth century, by an alien Arab culture. Neither branch of the Gothic family thus had the chance to take part in later literary developments. Paul the Deacon and Gregory of Tours give us much information from which we can gather something of the literary life of Langobards and Western Franks; both nations settled on Roman soil and the indigenous culture though much altered by the Germanic invaders proved far more durable in the end. Germany was again different. Christianity came relatively late. Whether the Church stamped as vigorously as is often asserted on the old heathern culture, whether the ruling classes themselves turned away from their old traditions: the older way of life and the stories associated with it failed to become acceptable in the new Christian society.[1] It is perfectly true that a great deal survived for hundreds of years but it survived at a sub-literary level. Indeed the Anglians were fortunate.

We can postulate the following for all early Germanic tribes: alliteration, as the universal and only method of composing verse; religious verse which could well include some historical reminiscences, which would be produced by the priests and which would be in their keeping; simple charms using magical formulae, which would undoubtedly stem from the priest-caste as well though such charms would be apt to slip away from priestly control; occasional verse, frequently one line only, claiming ownership of an article, laying claim to property, giving the name of the maker of an article, and similar matters. The last-named could only occur amongst tribes who had developed or received some form of writing. The *notae* mentioned by Tacitus may well imply runic characters. However that may be, a runic alphabet must have been in existence not later than the middle of the second century A.D., and many scholars would place its origin much earlier than that. Every Germanic tribe ultimately learnt to handle runes; invention of the alphabet must have happened in one place, certainly somewhere where Mediterranean influence could make itself felt, but how quickly this knowledge then spread we have no means of telling. It was a cumbrous form of writing, its use on parchment is late, the bulk, in early days, must have been incised into wood and, except for chance survivals due to special chemical conditions in the soil, runes on wood must inevitably have perished. Unfortunately there are few early inscriptions on less perishable material.

None of the above material will have been of great literary merit, and our own interest is naturally centred on any evidence

[1] The one serious attempt at a higher literary level to use native material was the monkish *Waltharius*. Whilst it is totally dependent on classical models—mainly Virgil and Statius—it does show complete familiarity with the details of the old lay. This is not surprising. The author was a cleric, and Benedictine monks were recruited almost exclusively from the ranks of the landed aristocracy, the very class in which we should expect such knowledge.

of heroic poetry. Now whilst more primitive forms of verse can indeed be presumed for all the Germanic tribes, that does not permit us to credit them with more developed forms without further ado. Heroic poetry, judged by what has survived and from what can be reconstructed from other sources, arose during the age of the migrations, probably during the second half of the fourth century. It concerned chieftains and their immediate following, and in almost every case—Wayland is an exception and even then not entirely so—we are dealing with family feuds. Women sometimes play a more active role, as is the case with the Burgundian Guðrun and to a certain extent with the Frankish Brynhild; normally their role is more passive: they are the link formed by marriage between two clans, and they stand helpless between the warring factions.[1] The poetry is in a sense parochial, and closely bound up with the everyday life and struggle within and without the tribe. All the characters are Germanic, including Attila who, from the point of view of Germanic heroic poetry, is a Germanic chieftain. His ruthlessness, which is then frequently stated to be 'non-Germanic', has been much exaggerated. In that respect, there is little to choose between Attila and Ermanaric! Rome and the Roman Empire, the place where almost every Germanic chieftain hoped to be able to loot, is of no account and Caesar is merely mentioned as the incredibly wealthy Southern potentate whose gold and treasure one covets. At its lowest the poetry is therefore concerned with the lust for gold and plunder of a closely-knit, marauding band of warriors, controlled by an autocratic chief. It is therefore in a sense 'court' poetry. From this it should follow that, to begin with at any rate, such poetry would only be found in places where a 'court' had developed. Kingship was widely spread amongst the Germanic tribes; it was not the invariable form of organization, and where there was no chief there was little incentive to produce this type of poetry for poets did not produce unless there was an audience to listen, and if appropriate, to reward. And even where there were 'courts' we

---

[1] The Scandinavian battle-maiden Hild who eggs on her father Hǫgni and her lover Heðinn is part of a late and typically Northern tradition.

need not assume, unless we have good evidence, that heroic poetry necessarily flourished.

It is one of the puzzles of Germanic heroic verse that praise of heroic deeds is not by any means always bound up with the tribe whose heroes are celebrated. From this it has been rather incautiously assumed that tribal affinities were not of any great moment in the composition of heroic poetry. This cannot possibly be true. To begin with an heroic poem must have dealt with a real or a presumed event within the tribe. Later a scop might well carry the poem to another tribe and there it might well become a favourite. Such transposition from one court to another we know of, and in the fictional account of *Widsith* we see this presented in an idealized way. This report is fiction; yet it cannot have departed too violently from a possible reality. All our evidence is late, and in our late evidence it is rare that a tradition is recorded which actually belongs to the area where we first hear of it. Thus we have Anglian traditions of the continental Offa, and that is where they belong. In Danish heroic tradition Offa has of course been danicized. The heroes of the earliest Edda poems are not Icelanders or even Norwegians; it is not obvious at first glance that there is anything other than Offa in Anglian heroic tradition that is truly Anglian, preposterous as such a notion must seem. No tribe would have produced one heroic poem, and one poem only! Many further examples could be adduced.

Now if we could be certain that the tribal affinity of a hero had not been changed during the wanderings of his story it would be a simple matter to discover the ultimate origin. Frequently, no such certainty is possible, and this uncertainty is particularly troublesome in the case of the Anglians. Whilst it is likely enough that they had a hand in the development of stories concerning Ingeld, Finn, Wayland and the abduction of Hild by Heoden, to mention only a few, there is nothing approaching hard proof, and the interpretation of the circumstantial evidence must remain a matter of opinion.

It was stated above that the oldest historical characters that we meet in heroic poetry are Offa the Anglian and Ermanaric the

Ostrogoth, the former in a famous story that unfortunately defies completely convincing reconstruction, the latter in an historical context that is tolerably well known. Ermanaric died round about 370, Offa possibly a little earlier. It all depends how one interprets later genealogies. Poems praising the two (though Ermanaric is hardly praised! The scop and his audience must have belonged to the anti-Ermanaric party that was making common cause with the Hun Balamber) must have been current not later than 400. As far as we are able to tell, the factual historical element in both these poems is still very much to the fore; there is little evidence of the inner conflict with which we are confronted in later poems and it would appear, in both cases, that we are dealing with the beginnings of the development of the *genre*. Priority has normally been accorded to the Goths, particularly as the evidence in Priskos has been consistently misinterpreted and as the great heroic figure of Theodoric has overshadowed the discussion. Poetry concerning the Goth Theodoric can, however, hardly have existed until after the middle of the sixth century, far too late to tell us anything about origins, and it must anyway owe its development to the Langobards. Heroic poetry cannot have started to develop suddenly amongst a number of tribes. Either we date its origin amongst the Germanic peoples far back, in which case it may well have existed at our critical date of 400 in a large number of tribes controlled by chieftains, or we date its origin in the time of the migrations. If we follow the latter course, and that certainly fits our available evidence best, then we have to look for a definite place. The Gothic hypothesis cannot be proved, and the Anglians must remain serious competitors. At this time we have no evidence for any court poetry in Scandinavia; it is almost certain that there was none.

The North seems to become interested in Southern heroic poetry some time during the latter half of the fifth century. News, and that must mean news in poetic form, reached Scandinavia of Ermanaric, Attila, the Burgundian Guðere, the Franks Sigmund and Sigfried. Stories of Wayland the Smith and of Hild, the daughter of Hagena, must have travelled north round about the same time. And to these we must add, among others, Offa and Ingeld. How do these stories reach Scandinavia? The usual theory makes the 'Gothic' material retrace the steps of the original Goths who went south and east in the second century, travel down the Vistula and thus across to Sweden. This route will naturally not do for Burgundian and Frankish material and quite certainly not for Wayland, Hild, Offa and Ingeld which all originate in the north of Germany. So the Frankish material is frequently said to go by sea—perhaps carried back by Beowulf when he swam home?— and the rest, which is true enough, via Jutland and the Danish isles. Perhaps another piece of evidence will help to clear up the problem. Importation of heroic song from the South into Scandinavia seems to have ceased a little after 500. Iring, both Theodoric the Goth and Theodoric the Frank, Waldere, Hildebrand, and Alboin, to name only a few and the most famous, remain completely unknown.[1] All of the earlier heroes are of course known to the Anglians in England, and this knowledge must have travelled over the water with them from their continental home in poetic form. The migration must have lasted a good many years; there is evidence that the kings of Anglia did not leave the continent until well after 500. We can therefore assume that a royal court continued to exist in continental Anglia where, in a manner not so very different from that described by the Anglian poet of *Beowulf* at the court of Hrothgar a little over two hundred years later, heroic recitation could be heard. Any scop at the court would know all the early lays that have been mentioned, and friendly Danish visitors will have learnt them and taken them home with them. As for the later lays: they reached the Anglians in England directly from the continent, and they were not transmitted to Scandinavia. Continental Anglia, according to the testimony of the Anglian Bede, was still waste land at the beginning of the eighth century. Whether we can take this information quite

[1] Theodoric the Goth occurs in a demonstrably late story in the Edda in which he is falsely accused of adultery with the wife of Attila; a confused memory of Hildebrand occurs in a late saga preserved in a fourteenth-century copy. Neither can possibly have reached Scandinavia until centuries later than the time which we are considering here. Knowledge of Hildebrand in England is at best doubtful.

literally or not there was obviously no centre from which the poetic productions of the South could be handed on.

It is widely held that early Old English literature was predominantly produced, and here one is almost tempted to say 'written', after about 700, in Anglian territory, and that its preservation was due to the careful manner in which it was collected in Saxon England. Doubts have of late been cast on the very simplicity of this pattern, and it must be admitted that the linguistic evidence, in very many cases, is far from convincing. Texts were so thoroughly saxonized that few Anglian traces remained. Yet it is unlikely that the general truth of the statement will be successfully assailed, and the Anglians, who also gave their name to England, rather than the Saxons, will continue to be regarded as the main poetic force in early English literature.

Nothing definite can be said about poetry amongst the continental Anglians though even here all is not darkness. We have referred above to the Nerthus cult described by Tacitus and we surmised that a religious procession without some sort of verbal accompaniment was unthinkable. The Anglians were part of the confederation which practised this cult. They are the only tribe of which, later, we have detailed knowledge, and it is reasonable to assume that they absorbed all the others and became the dominant political factor in the area. At the time of Offa they seem still to have been consolidating their power. They had, by then, spread right across the neck of the peninsula west of Sleswig, controlled the land 'between the two seas' and occupied the narrow ridge, easily defended, that was later to be fought over tenaciously between Saxon and Dane. Their home base was presumably Land Angeln though they must have spread considerably beyond this relatively small territory which could never have held all the Anglians who migrated to the new island home.

Right in the centre of Land Angeln, about twelve miles north-east of Sleswig, there is a large village known as Süder-Brarup. A large proportion of the inhabitants have Danish names though no one talks Danish as a first language. The village boasts an enormous almost square common, traditionally supposed to have been a meeting-place in Anglian days, and this is likely enough. Close to the common there is a peat-bog which was excavated in the middle of the nineteenth century. A very large collection of weapons, utensils, articles of clothing, personal ornaments and coins was brought to the surface. The coins were Roman, dating from Nero to Septimius Severus, i.e. up to A.D. 194. Before they were immersed in the bog most of the articles had been broken or otherwise made useless, by deliberate damage. They were intended as ritual offerings to some deity or other. Whilst there may be some articles which were not of Anglian manufacture—obviously the Roman coins were not—the majority of the articles should be Anglian. A few have inscriptions on them; two of these present us with a runic sequence of which one is reasonably intelligible.

There is an inscription on the inside of a bronze shield-buckle. This was nailed to the wooden shield in such a way that the inscription could not normally be seen. We have to read from right to left, on account of the shape of the A-rune, and we obtain AISGRH. Nobody has been able to make sense of this.

A circular bronze ferrule that was used to protect the lower end of a wooden sheath yielded a longer inscription. The runes run from left to right and can be read without difficulty. They read: OWLÞUÞEWARNIWAJEMARIR which should be read as: O WLÞUÞEWAR NI WAJE MARIR. There is a clearly noticeable gap between the first two letters, and the O must stand for OÞALA: 'property'. This abbreviation O for 'property' is frequently found in runic inscriptions, and this sense of the rune O was so well known that it was sometimes even taken over into book-writing. Thus in *Waldere* I.31a the scribe wrote *ealdne* ᛟ instead of *ealdne eðel*. In the second word the rune-master forgot a U and the word should be *wulpuþewar*. The first element could be compared to Gothic *wulpus*: 'glory', or the North Germanic god Ullr; it should be noted however that this would constitute the only evidence for the knowledge of this god in the South. 'Servant of the god Ullr' has been suggested; one could also interpret: 'glorious servant', then perhaps referring to the sword but this is equally problematic. The *ni* is the negative, *waje* should be a verb, and formally it would appear to be a third person singular present subjunctive. There is reasonable evidence for a meaning 'spare'. The last word *marir* means 'the famous one' and ought to refer to the weapon. If we take *wulþuþewar* to be a personal name, and that, on the scanty evidence, is the most likely solution, the meaning of the whole inscription would be: 'Property. Wulþuþewar (owns me). May the famous one not spare (the enemy)'. The date of the inscription is said to be 250/300 A.D. There are no Anglian peculiarities in the language nor would we, at this date, expect any or even be able to spot them with precision.

Now there is no doubt that the place where all these objects were found is right in the centre of Anglian territory. Since most of the objects underwent ritual destruction before they were immersed some religious significance must be attached to this activity. Whenever objects were dumped, and there is proof that the bog was used in this manner on a number of occasions, there must have been a public religious ceremony. Now and again there may well have been friendly neighbours present from other tribes but by and large the actors concerned must have been Anglians. That is as far as one can go with safety except that one could regard the inscription as a long line alliterating on *w*, in which case we may here have the earliest line of English verse.

In 1639, a large golden horn was dug up near Gallehus, about three miles north-west of Tönder, just north of the present German-Danish border. A somewhat smaller horn, about twenty inches long, was dug up close to the earlier find in 1734. Both horns were preserved in the Royal Art Gallery at Copenhagen, both were stolen on 4 May 1802, and they were probably melted down immediately. Fortunately, very careful drawings had been made. The smaller horn has an inscription in runic characters which can be read without difficulty. We have a long alliterative line in which a person claims to have made an article: EK HLEWAGASTIR HOLTIJAR HORNA TAWIDO: 'I Hlewagast, the son of Holta, made the horn'. Holtijar could also conceivably mean the 'wood-dweller'. The meaning is far clearer than that of the earlier line discussed above though again we cannot say with certainty whether we are dealing with a North Germanic or with an Ingwaeonic text. Again, we can only offer a suggestion based on provenance. The horns were found on what was certainly Anglian territory at the time. They were ritual objects made of (looted?) gold. If they were of local manufacture they were then buried somewhere near their place of origin; if they came from further afield they might have come from anywhere in Germania. A slight hint may be contained in the form *holtijar*. If this means *holt-saete* that could be interpreted not only as 'wood-dweller' but also as 'person from Holstein'. Holstein lies immediately south of Anglia, and the northern part of it may well have been in Anglian occupation at the time. Most scholars would consent to a date round about A.D. 400. At that time no Danes were settled in the district, and if the horns are North Germanic they must have been taken there. This is indeed possible but it is simpler to assume that the horns were buried reasonably near to the place where they were made, and in that case we can regard the inscription as Anglian.[1]

At the time when the horns were made there existed at least one poem which was concerned with an exploit of the young Offa. This poem was so well known that it travelled along with other heroic verse to the Danish court, and at a later date when the Danes were engaged in similar battles very near to the spot where Offa had fought they turned him into a Dane. This cannot have been before the latter half of the seventh century so that the Danes sang of Offa the Anglian for well over two hundred years before they danicized him.

We know that a rich store of story went over to England with the Anglians, we know that they continued to collect heroic material from the continent, we know that in the eighth century they are possessed of an astonishing amount of information, in

---

[1] No references to the literature of the subject are here given. They will be found in my article 'The Continental Background of Early Anglian Literature', *Proceedings of the University of Durham Philosophical Society*, i (1959), 38 ff.

story form, from Scandinavia, we know that they are responsible for at the very least the bulk of early English literature, we know that their relations with the Danes who had gradually occupied deserted continental Anglia remained friendly and intimate for a long time after they had settled in England, we have seen that whilst there is no conclusive evidence—how could there be?—there are good grounds for arguing that from the time of Tacitus onwards, round about A.D. 100, the Anglians became the dominant partners in the Nerthus confederation,[1] we have seen that there is no good reason for denying that the objects found in the peat-bog at Süder-Brarup and the Golden Horns of Gallehus were of Anglian provenance, and we thus have evidence of cultural activity, slender though it inevitably be, which begins at a time when we know almost nothing of any other Germanic tribe.

It would lead too far if an attempt were here made to marshal the evidence for ascribing a good deal of early heroic material to the Anglians. Whether we believe that the Anglians were originally responsible for the stories of Hild, Wayland, Finn, Ingeld, to name only a few, they certainly had a hand in developing and propagating the material very much in the way that their original southern neighbours, the Langobards, worked up Gothic and Gepid material. Their honourable place in early Germanic literature is assured.

The earliest reference to the Danes in Anglian literature occurs in the paraphrase of a poem on the youthful exploit of Offa of which we have a fuller though not necessarily more original version in Saxo Grammaticus. Offa is here compared to a powerful Danish king, Alewih, of whom we know nothing. Alewih is stated to have been a most redoubtable hero and yet he could not match the prowess of Offa. It is not absolutely certain but the reference appears to be friendly. Anglians and Danes can thus be assumed to have been friendly allies in the latter half of the fourth

[1] The Swaefe, i.e. the Swabians settled along the Eider, had clearly been incorporated by the time of Offa, and seeing that Widsith purports to be a Myrging we may assume that the Myrgings also, who must have sat south of the Eider, became part of the Anglian community either during the reign of Offa or shortly afterwards.

century. We know that Saxo Grammaticus preserves a good deal of material which was originally demonstrably Anglian, we can judge from this and from the Old English material that Anglian and Danish heroic traditions were closely allied, and we need indeed look no further than the beginning of Saxo's History of the Danes where he states:

Now Dan and Angul, with whom the stock of the Danes begins, were begotten by Humble, their father, and were the governors and not merely the founders of our race. . . . And these two men, though by the wish and favour of their country they gained the lordship of the realm, and, owing to the wondrous deserts of their bravery, got the supreme power by the consenting voice of their countrymen, yet lived without the name of king: the usage whereof was not then commonly resorted to by any authority among our people. Of these two, Angul, the fountain, so runs tradition, of the beginnings of the Anglian race, caused his name to be applied to the district which he ruled. This was an easy kind of memorial wherewith to immortalize his fame: for his successors a little later, when they gained possession of Britain, changed the original name of the island for a fresh title, that of their own land.

2

Runes and Non-Runes[1]

R. I. PAGE

THE STUDY of Anglo-Saxon runes has long been bedevilled by the admission to the corpus of doubtful and even clearly non-runic inscriptions and incised objects. There are good semantic and historical reasons for this. Since their first appearance in the language in the seventeenth century, the words 'rune' and 'runic' have acquired wide ranges of meaning, and the adjective has been applied to things on which there are no runes, or even inscriptions at all, as, for example, the Sandbach and Blackwell crosses.[2] The more emotive meanings of the words have attracted mystics, muddlers and cranks, who have enthusiastically discovered runes where none exist,[3] while the epigraphical examples of the Laird of

[1] Many scholars have helped with this paper, and I should like to express thanks to Mr C. E. Blunt, Rev. I. H. Bowman, Mr R. S. L. Bruce-Mitford, Dr J. C. Corson, Mr P. Grierson, Mr D. Hamer, Mr H. Hargreaves, Dr E. Okasha, Mr P. S. Peberdy, Mr P. K. Roberts-Wray, the late Professor A. H. Smith and Dr D. M. Waterman; and to the staffs of the National Museum of Ireland, the Birmingham and Brighton Public Libraries, the library of the Society of Antiquaries of London, and the Royal Library, Stockholm, from whose collection of Stephens papers (dep. 189) all quotations from unpublished letters to that scholar are taken.

[2] F. H. Crossley, *Cheshire* (London, 1949), p. 228; W. Stephenson, 'Blackwell, and its sculptured cross', *Journal of the Derbyshire Archæological and Natural History Society*, xxxix (1917), 79. These two examples are of unequal value. No inscription has ever been recorded on the Blackwell cross. Of Sandbach, the Elizabethan antiquary, William Smith, writing before the crosses were thrown down and damaged in the Civil War, reported, 'In the market place do stand hard together two square *Crosses* of *Stone*, on steps, with certain Images and Writings thereon graven; which, as they say, a man cannot read, except he be holden with his head downwards' (W. Smith and W. Webb, *The Vale-Royall of England* . . . (London, 1656), part i, p. 46).

[3] Witness here C. Roach Smith's ready identification of a lost 'helmet with letters upon it which nobody could read' as 'probably a bronze dish inscribed

Monkbarns and Mr Pickwick have been earnestly followed in the runic field. Some artefacts on which runes might be expected are so poorly preserved that chance surface marks have been seen as runic letters, letters indeed whose very forms make them easily confused with scratches, plough-marks, damaged decorative motifs and the like.[1] There seems too to be a primary epigraphical law by which characters which cannot be identified as anything else are called runes.

The present paper has two aims: to prune the corpus of some texts which have been wrongly or doubtfully listed as runic, and tentatively to suggest a few additions. Professor H. Marquardt's invaluable *Bibliographie der Runeninschriften nach Fundorten* (1961) has done much towards the first of these, and my study is intended rather as a development than as a criticism of that distinguished scholar's work. The *Bibliographie* is not ruthless enough. Though she listed inscriptions 'die in der Literatur als "runisch" gedeutet worden sind, deren runischer Charakter aber zweifelhaft ist', Professor Marquardt failed to show just how doubtfully runic some of them were, or how slight the basis of identification. In dealing with the lost stones from Amesbury, for example, she queries *'Mit Runen?'* The Amesbury stones owe their inclusion in the bibliography to G. Stephens's citation of them in the introduction to the English section of *The Old-Northern runic monuments of Scandinavia and England . . .* (London–Copenhagen–Lund, 1866–1901), i–ii, p. 360. Stephens derives his material from R. C. Hoare, *The ancient history of South Wiltshire* (London, 1812), p. 198, and Hoare in turn quotes John Aubrey, who is thus our sole authority, and one not noted for scholarly precision. Even Aubrey

with runes' (*Collectanea antiqua* (London, 1857), iv, appendix, p. 34), and, in two letters, dated 12 February and 15 April 1868, to G. Stephens, J. Brent's jubilant cry, 'Rejoice! Rejoice! I have got a small piece of Samian Ware . . . inscribed with six Runes!' followed by the crestfallen admission that they had proved 'cursive Roman'.

[1] See, for example, D. M. Wilson's comment on possible runes on a silver plate associated with an Anglo-Saxon sword from Långtora, Uppland, Sweden ('Some neglected late Anglo-Saxon swords', *Medieval Archaeology*, ix (1965), 38).

only says, "Tis said here there were some letters on these stones, but what they were I cannot learne', so the evidence for Amesbury runes is slight indeed. An example of different treatment in the *Bibliographie* is the golden armlet found at Aspatria, Cumberland, in 1828, on which Marquardt records '5 *Zeichen, von W. Hamper als Runen gelesen*'. This is true as far as it goes, though we note that Hamper's interpretation (*Archæologia Æliana*, ii (1832), 267–8) and its accompanying illustration derive, not from the armlet, but from a drawing of it. The seven relevant *Bibliographie* entries which follow Hamper's all either ignore the runes or dispute their existence. The armlet is still extant, in the British Museum (inv. no. 1904, 11–2, 1), and is neither runic nor Anglo-Saxon.

A key figure in the present discussion is inevitably George Stephens, whose four monumental, enthusiastic and extravagant volumes contain the nearest thing to a corpus of Anglo-Saxon runic inscriptions that we yet possess. Four groups of objects in Stephens's collection require notice.

(1) Those which Stephens never thought to be runic, since he included them only as parallel illustrative examples: the Aldborough sundial, the memorial stone fragments from Dewsbury, Yarm, Wycliffe (then lost but since recovered), and Thornhill, Yorks (W.R.) (not to be confused with the rune-stones from the same church), and the Cuxton disc-brooch with its owner formula *Ælfgivv me ah*. Of these Dewsbury and Yarm contrive to get into the *Bibliographie*, but only because they were wrongly listed among the English rune-stones by H. Arntz in his *Die Runenschrift* (1938), p. 89 and elsewhere.

(2) Four inscriptions which Stephens, in some cases in common with other scholars, wrongly called runic; the Brough-under-Stainmoor stone, correctly identified as Greek by A. H. Sayce and G. F. Browne independently;[1] the Chertsey bowl, which Stephens,

[1] See the story as told by G. F. Browne in *The recollections of a bishop* (London, 1915), p. 204. Announcing Sayce's identification to Stephens in a letter dated 27 June 1884, J. T. Fowler commented, 'the wonder to me now is that anyone could ever suppose it to be anything else' and added the warning which all runologists would do well to remember, 'My good friend, doth not much O.N. learning make you to see everything through O.N. spectacles?'

following the great J. M. Kemble, thought to be in 'mixt Runes and decorated Uncials', though he subsequently reported that it had been read as modern Greek ('this piece therefore *goes out*'); the St Andrews ring, which is probably late medieval and certainly not runic; and the Roman pig of lead from Truro on which Stephens found the runic letter *stan*.

The inscriptions in these two groups can be easily disposed of, as can some others of the same sort not in Stephens but in the *Bibliographie*: the Beckermet stone, with its virtually unreadable but certainly not runic text, and the Great Edstone sundial whose Old English inscription, + *Loðan me wrohtea*, contains, contrary to Marquardt's statement, no runes other than *wynn*.

The last two groups, however, need detailed examination.

(3) Inscriptions found on objects which are still known, but which now have no visible texts; one of the two Sandwich stones (*Sandwich B* in the *Bibliographie*), the Kirkdale slab and the Irton cross: perhaps too the Bingley font. Further, Stephens records more extensive texts than can now be read on a number of other objects, such as the Bewcastle cross, the Falstone 'hogback' and the Gilton pommel.

(4) Inscribed objects now lost, and known only from early references, sometimes supported by drawings:[1] the Hoddam and Leeds stones, the brooch from a collection in the north of England, listed by Stephens under Northumbria, the so-called pocket sundial from Cleobury Mortimer, the 'owi'[2] ring of unknown provenance, Here also may be included the coin found at Wijk-bij-Duurstede, Netherlands, which could, from Stephens's reproduction of the runic forms, be either Anglo-Saxon or Frisian.

From group 3 the Sandwich B stone can be removed at once,

---

[1] I omit here the Bewcastle cross head which Stephens mentioned (*Old-Northern runic monuments*, i-ii, p. 398) and reproduced without knowing what it was (*The runes, whence came they?* (London, 1894), pp. 58–9, listed under 'England, Northumbria'). On this fragment see my 'The Bewcastle cross', *Nottingham Mediaeval Studies*, iv (1960), 54–6.

[2] Runes are transliterated according to B. Dickins, 'A system of transliteration for Old English runic inscriptions', *Leeds Studies in English*, i (1932), 15 ff.

for nobody has yet read runes on it though both D. H. Haigh and Stephens list it among the runic monuments, and Stephens argues that a pagan inscription was cut away from its surface in Christian times. The other items in the group call for a discussion of the runic work of Haigh, who is a key witness in every case. That of the Kirkdale inscription is confused by the existence of a double find report. Two versions, referring to the one stone, have been listed as separate items: they are given in Stephens, *Old-Northern runic monuments*, iii, pp. 184, 214. The first records Haigh and J. T. Fowler's examination of 'part of a coffin-slab . . . on which was cut a Latin Cross Quadrate. . . . On the 4 ends of this Cross were Old-English runes, slightly carved.' Haigh read 'kyni | ŋœþi | lwal | dæg', which Fowler could not support, for though he agreed that 'runes *were* there', he 'could not make anything out of them'. Stephens adds that deterioration of the stone had now left 'not one distinct stave'. The second report also derives from Haigh and Fowler, describing how they took casts of a 'ruined *Runic Cross* at Kirkdale' in or about 1870. Fowler stated, 'The staves are I fear hopelessly gone, only just enough is left to see that there *were* runes; one is ᚷ ['ŋ']'.[1] These are certainly two versions of the same record of the cross-inscribed flat stone known as 'King Ethelwald's grave-slab', still preserved inside Kirkdale church.[2] Stephens thought of two stones, a cross and a slab, and recorded them as such in his *Handbook* and in *The runes, whence came they?* Such later writers as W. Viëtor and W. G. Collingwood followed him, and Marquardt lists two in her *Bibliographie*. Apart from Haigh, the only investigator to have read an extensive runic inscription on the Kirkdale slab was G. F. Browne. In 1885 he commented, 'Now only one rune can be seen, though others are

---

[1] The original letter, dated 21 June 1870, survives, showing Stephens to be a fairly inaccurate copyist.

[2] This is shown by Fowler's extant letters. Stephens was worried by the Kirkdale material for he asked Fowler about it several times. Three of Fowler's replies survive, from 1870 (quoted above), from 1880 and from 1891. It is sufficiently clear from them that Haigh and Fowler made only a single common visit to Kirkdale. In 1870 Fowler said the runes were on a cross, in 1880 on a cross on a coffin-slab and in 1891 on a cross-shaft.

detected in a careful rubbing.'¹ His illustration to the Disney
lectures given in 1888, nos. 1–2, fig. 11, shows a clear 'kuni |
ŋœþi | lwal | dæg', which seems to be an imaginative reading of a
rubbing, helped by memories of Haigh's interpretation, though
Browne's runes are set, not at the four ends of the cross, but above
and below its horizontal arms. Otherwise, as has been seen, Fowler
as early as 1870, and several writers since, have found little or
nothing legible on the Kirkdale slab.² Even Fowler's 'ŋ' is suspect,
for this form could easily be part of a decorative interlace or other
pattern misread as a rune, as has happened, for example, on some
of the *Wigræd* sceattas.³

For the Irton cross inscription too, we are reliant upon Haigh,
who reported, in a panel on its west side, three lines of letters, very
much worn, but with several runes preserved, notably 'ḡ', 'þ', 'f',
'm' and 'æ'. These he first reconstructed as *gibidæþ foræ . . .*
(*g = gar*), but later, in a paper presented in 1870, completed the
text '+ḡebiddæþ | foræḡodm | undæssawle', marking the first
twelve characters as distinct.⁴ This inscription has not been remarked by anyone else, neither by earlier recorders of the cross,
such as the Lysons brothers (1816) and Jefferson (1842), nor by a
later investigator such as J. Romilly Allen who reported in 1880
that there was '*absolutely no trace of letters of any kind*'.⁵ Viëtor
thought he saw fragments of 'b' where Haigh read 'þ', but otherwise only horizontal incisions to mark a three-line text.⁶

¹ ' "Scandinavian" or "Danish" sculptured stones found in London . . .',
Archaeological Journal, xlii (1885), 256. Yet in a letter to Stephens, dated 2 January
1884, Browne remarked that a rubbing of the slab 'does not shew the slightest
trace of letters'.
² See, for example, W. Viëtor, *Die northumbrischen Runensteine* (Marburg, 1895),
p. 19; W. G. Collingwood, 'Anglian and Anglo-Danish sculpture in the North
Riding of Yorkshire', *Yorkshire Archæological Journal*, xix (1907), 278.
³ P. Grierson, *Sylloge of coins of the British Isles. I, Fitzwilliam Museum . . .*
(London, 1958), nos. 235–6.
⁴ Stephens, *Old-Northern runic monuments*, i–ii, p. 469; D. H. Haigh, 'The runic
monuments of Northumbria', *Proceedings of the Geological . . . Society of the West
Riding of Yorkshire*, v (1870), 217 and fig.
⁵ D. and S. Lysons, *Magna Britannia. iv, Cumberland* (London, 1816), p. cci;
S. Jefferson, *The history and antiquities of Cumberland*, ii (Carlisle, 1842), p. 207 and
fig.; Stephens, *Old-Northern runic monuments*, iii, p. 200.
⁶ *Die northumbrischen Runensteine*, p. 16.

Haigh's runic work is, like so much of the same date, idio-
syncratic. It is uneven in quality, occasionally recording with
apparent accuracy data of importance.[1] But in general it shows the
same tendency towards extensive reading of faint and weathered
texts as do the examples already discussed. On the Collingham
stone where only the remains of two words, 'æft [.] | [.] swiþi', can
now be seen, Haigh read an elaborate memorial text containing
several odd Old English forms, *Œonblæd this settæ æfter gisibæ ymb
Auswini cyning gicegæth thær sawle*, this being a version, amended
and completed from the study of casts and rubbings, of an earlier
attempt.[2] On the Bewcastle cross, Haigh, in company with several
of his contemporaries, read a number of lines of runes certainly
not there now, and we have an admittedly unfriendly account by
the rival antiquary, J. Maughan, of Haigh's methods of obtaining
and treating his evidence.[3] The Bingley font inscription, now
completely illegible except for a very few scattered and doubt-
fully identifiable runes, received a long and elaborate interpretation, based partly on photographs, casts and rubbings,[4] while on a
part of the Alnmouth cross where now only V, E, and H can
be read Haigh confidently found [HL]VDWYG·MEH·FEG
[DE].[5]

In two cases Haigh's results can be checked fairly closely, the
Gilton sword-pommel and the Falstone 'hogback'. In 1872 Haigh
reported runes on both sides of the pommel, reading ICU IK
SIGI MUARNUM IK WISA on that where a confused text is still
clear, and DAGMUND (i.e. *Dægmund*) 'nearly effaced' on the

[1] As, for example, in his drawing of the badly-damaged runic face of the
Hackness cross ('The monasteries of S. Heiu and S. Hild', *Yorkshire Archæological
Journal*, iii (1875), pl. 3 no. 4).

[2] 'Runic monuments of Northumbria', pp. 199–202.

[3] D. H. Haigh, 'The Saxon cross at Bewcastle', *Archæologia Æliana*. N.S. i
(1857), 152 ff., figs. 3–13; J. Maughan, *A memoir on the Roman station and runic
cross at Bewcastle* (London, 1857), pp. 31–8.

[4] 'Runic monuments of Northumbria', p. 206. See the variant reading in
'Yorkshire runic monuments', *Yorkshire Archæological Journal*, ii (1871–2), 254.

[5] 'Saxon cross at Bewcastle', p. 186 and fig. 18; but cf. J. Stuart's drawing in
The sculptured stones of Scotland (Edinburgh, 1856–67), ii, pl. cxvii, which shows the
stone in much its present condition.

other, where no traces now remain.[1] No runes are shown on the
earliest drawings of this side in T. Wright, *The archaeological album*
(1845), p. 204, or J. Y. Akerman, *Remains of pagan Saxondom*
(1854), pl. xxiv, while Haigh's earliest published account of the
pommel, in 1861, also ignores them.[2] From the date it was first
recorded until the present the Gilton pommel has been in various
antiquarian collections, and there is no reason to believe that its
condition has deteriorated since 1872, or indeed that the runes of
one side have been lost and those of the other preserved. Of the
Falstone 'hogback' a very detailed and convincing drawing
accompanies the find-report of 1822.[3] This makes it clear that the
condition of the stone has altered little since the early years of the
nineteenth century. Yet in 1857 Haigh published a transcript of
the texts showing them to be considerably more complete than
now.[4] Almost identical readings were given by Stephens, *Old-
Northern runic monuments*, i, p. 456, on the basis of a cast in the
National Museum, Copenhagen. This cast still survives, and gives
the runes in very much their present state.

From this discussion of Haigh's runic work it is clear that the
Irton inscription was a figment of Haigh's fertile imagination, and
Kirkdale may be the same, though Fowler's evidence gives some,
if very little, support to that text. Fowler was a careful epigraphist
as his treatment of the sadly deteriorated runes of the Crowle stone
shows.[5]

Of the inscriptions in group 4 pictures exist of the Leeds,
Cleobury Mortimer, 'owi' and Wijk inscriptions. The Leeds rune-
stone was one of a number of early carved stones found when the
old parish church was demolished in 1837–8. A year or two later
the architect responsible, R. D. Chantrell, lectured on his finds to

---

[1] 'Notes in illustration of the runic monuments of Kent', *Archæologia Cantiana*,
viii (1872), 259–60.

[2] *The conquest of Britain by the Saxons* (London, 1861), pp. 51–2.

[3] J. Wood, 'Some account of a Saxon inscription, on a stone found near
Falstone . . .', *Archæologia Æliana*, i (1822), 103–4.

[4] 'Saxon cross at Bewcastle', p. 155 and fig. 15.

[5] *Proceedings of the Society of Antiquaries of London*, 2 Ser. iv (1867–70),
187–90.

the Institute of British Architects and the Leeds Philosophical and Literary Society, though I know of no record of this discourse. At about the same time, according to G. F. Browne in a letter to Stephens on 9 November 1882, he made full-scale drawings of the material, but there was no publication until 1856,[1] and we do not know where the rune-stone was then. The fragments of the great Anglo-Saxon cross now in Leeds parish church were removed by Chantrell and ultimately put in his garden at Rottingdean, Sussex, not being returned until the 1870's. The rune-stone may have gone south with them, though it is then surprising that it did not return with the great cross. More probably it was among the mass of ancient material taken by Leeds citizens from the site of the old church, as its historian, R. W. Moore, tells.[2] Thus the 1856 publication may have been based on a sketch made nearly twenty years before. Other pictures of this monument derive from Chantrell's early drawing. The most prolific and influential writer on the subject, once again D. H. Haigh, worked only from the architect's version, and did not see the original himself,[3] nor is there sign that the Leeds stone was examined by later writers. According to Chantrell it was fragmentary, with parts of two lines of runes, 'cuni-' (? 'cunl-') and 'onlaf'. Though Haigh's interpretation of this as *cyning Onlaf*, 'king Olaf', can be rejected out of hand, there is nothing improbable in either the letter forms illustrated or their sequence. Indeed, 'cun' could be part of the word *becun*, 'cross, monument', often found in memorial inscriptions, while 'onlaf' may be the OE personal name *Onlaf* (*becun æfter Onlafe*, 'memorial for Onlaf', with the first letter of the preposition fragmentary), or could contain the common noun *laf*, 'relict, widow' or perhaps 'remains, corpse'. It is likely, then,

---

[1] D. H. Haigh, 'On the fragments of crosses discovered at Leeds in 1838', *Proceedings of the Geological . . . Society of the West Riding of Yorkshire*, iii (1856–7), 502 ff.

[2] *A history of the parish church of Leeds . . .* (Leeds, 1877), p. 56. See also Chantrell's remarks, *Proceedings of the Geological . . . Society*, iii, 537.

[3] This is indicated by Haigh's 'When the fragment can be examined by an experienced eye, I suspect that the second character will prove to be Y', 'Runic monuments of Northumbria', p. 214.

36

that Chantrell drew an accurate picture of a genuine runic find.

The Cleobury Mortimer 'pocket sundial' and its two accompanying stone discs were found in 1816 but not published until 1868, when the 'dial' was accurately described as an 'uncertain stone implement'.[1] It was last recorded in the collection of a Dr E. Whitcombe of Birmingham—presumably the Edmund Bancks Whitcombe, native of Cleobury Mortimer, who died in Birmingham in 1911—towards the end of the nineteenth century. A drawing of one side of the 'dial' accompanied the find-report, and was repeated in ?1869 when the well-known antiquary Albert Way first publicized du Noyer's identification of it as a sundial.[2] In 1879 Haigh produced new drawings of both 'dial' and discs, recording runes on the latter.[3] On one he shows a retrograde, roughly radial inscription in which 'l', 'a', 'æ', 'i' and 'w' are clear and the early 'c' form ⟨ and a damaged 'œ' are possible. On the other Haigh found 'æo', worn and only faintly traceable. No other drawings of these characters are known, so that, until the 'sundial' is rediscovered, Haigh remains our only authority for them, which is unfortunate in view of the speciousness of his other work in the field. However, there is nothing fundamentally unlikely about the runes Haigh drew, except perhaps for the archaic 'c'. South Shropshire is rather an unusual place to find runes though there are occasional West Midlands examples, and, since the uncertain stone object is also a portable one, the place of discovery may be far from the place where the inscription was cut.

The only drawing of the 'owi' ring seems to be that given in W. Jones, *Finger-ring lore* (1877), p. 421, whence derives the

[1] J. W(ilson), 'Uncertain stone implement', *Archæologia Cambrensis*, 3 Ser. xiv (1868), 446–8. The identification as a sundial was suggested in G. V. du Noyer, 'Uncertain stone implement explained', *Archæologia Cambrensis*, 3 Ser. xv (1869), 87–8.

[2] 'Ancient sun-dials', *Archaeological Journal*, xxv (1868), 222–3. There is a dating discrepancy here. Way's article was published after, though it is dated before, du Noyer's, which derives from a letter written in December 1868.

[3] 'Yorkshire dials', *Yorkshire Archæological Journal*, v (1879), 201–3.

illustration in Stephens, *Old-Northern runic monuments*, iii, p. 213. Though the runes shown certainly read 'owi', the ring is suspect, and was, for example, intentionally omitted from D. M. Wilson's handlist of material outside the British Museum in his catalogue, *Anglo-Saxon ornamental metalwork 700–1100 in the British Museum* (1964). Jones's book gave no details of the ring at all, apart from a title to the illustration, which, as we shall see, is suspect too. According to Stephens, 'The engraving was lent to Mr Jones . . . by one of the English learned societies. But unhappily no note was made of it, and he cannot say whence it came or where it is publisht and described.' This seems a delicate rewording of Jones's more forthright account in a pair of letters written to Stephens in May 1877. Jones investigated the source of the illustration which had, at the publishers' request, been hastily added to make the book ready for the season. 'The cut you particularly mention . . . was . . . merely inscribed "A new Year's ring", though why and wherefore I cannot tell . . .' 'The artist engaged upon that work informs me that he does not remember whence the copy was taken', though Jones thought that the source was probably the *Archaeological Journal* where, however, I have been unable to find it. Jones added the opinion of a friend, an expert on rings, who dated this example to the early modern period. Unless Stephens had further information, which does not survive, from Jones, he was, to say the least, disingenuous in his treatment of the story of this illustration. The picture shows a slim ring with an oval or circular bezel which bears a fairly convincing 'owi', though the shape of 'o' is slightly irregular and the other two symbols are not exclusively runic. The general effect is not unlike one of the fifteenth- and sixteenth-century signet rings with merchants' marks which survive in quite large numbers,[1] and it may have been one of these that the original artist copied.

The silver coin found at Wijk in 1836 is recorded in Stephens, *Old-Northern runic monuments*, i–ii, pp. 563–4, and also in D. H. Haigh, 'Miscellaneous notes on the Old English coinage', *Numis-*

---

[1] See, for example, O. M. Dalton, British Museum *Catalogue of the finger rings . . .* (London, 1912), nos. 356, 423, 559.

matic Chronicle, N.S. ix (1869), 192 and pl. v, which presumably derives from Stephens. The original is lost, apparently destroyed in the German advance on Louvain in August 1914. Stephens's picture was taken from a copy of a copy (by the careful van der Chijs) of an original whose silver was 'in very poor condition', so there is likely to be error in it, particularly since it hardly indicates the state of the coin. Stephens shows a radial legend of runes and rune-like forms, mostly with bases towards the centre, and with no indication of the beginning. The sequence 'x' (or 'k' inverted), 'l' (inverted), ?'u', 'læ', 'n' or 'g', 'au' and an obscure form ?'s' can be seen. The reverse has a monogram which Stephens identified as *Ecgberht*. As illustrated, the coin does not fit into any known Anglo-Saxon series. Its weight as given by Stephens is aberrant. The use of the monogram is a non-English feature and Stephens's confident reading of it is dubious. The forms of the runes—if they are correctly drawn—are not characteristically Anglo-Saxon (unless one is in fact 'k'), nor does their sequence give any Anglo-Saxon word. Unless another coin of this type appears we can never know (a) whether the legend has been accurately copied, and was in fact runic, (b) whether the coin was Anglo-Saxon or Continental Germanic.

Of the Northumbrian brooch we have no drawings, only a transcript of the runes in Stephens, *Old-Northern runic monuments*, i–ii, pp. 386–7. This reproduces the inscription from a letter written by J. M. Kemble to J. J. A. Worsaae in 1847. Kemble had not seen the text, but Worsaae, to whom the piece had been shown by 'a gentleman in Northern England', had sent him details for his opinion on them. The brooch has never been traced despite a certain amount of nineteenth-century publicity, nor do I know of either Kemble's or Worsaae's original letter. Stephens's version is in two lines and divided into individual words, though this may be Kemble's arrangement. The runes he gives are 'judrd mec worh[t] | e ælchfrith mec a[h]', 'c' being Ⱦ throughout. Kemble added the two bracketed runes. He interpreted the text as a maker and owner formula similar to those on the Sittingbourne scramasax and the Lancashire ring, 'Guthrid made me. Ælchfrith owns me'. There are, however, formidable runological problems. The Scandinavian type 'c' is suspect. 'j' is not elsewhere used for OE back *g*. A vowel must be supplied in *Guthrid*, which is presumably a form of *Guðred*. The spirant spellings in 'd', 'th' and 'ch' are unusual in Anglo-Saxon runic usage.

Finally, in the case of the Hoddam stone we have no extant reproduction, only a description by a single authority, C. K. Sharp, who reported that 'in the ancient church of Hoddam, a sculptured stone, which was built into the wall, bore an inscription of some length, in Runic characters'.[1] The old church was demolished in 1815, and the stone has not been noted since. There are three difficulties here. We do not know what Sharp meant by 'Runic', for he may, as will be seen later, have used the term loosely to mean something like 'archaic', 'mysterious'.[2] If he used the word precisely, to mean 'drawn from the runic alphabet', his identification of the characters may or may not have been correct. If his identification was correct, the runes may have been either Scandinavian or Anglo-Saxon. Hoddam is, of course, within the Anglo-Saxon runic area, situated not far from Ruthwell and Bewcastle. It is also in the coastal region of north-west England and south-west Scotland where Scandinavian runes were used, as on the Hunterston brooch, the Bridekirk font and the wall of Carlisle cathedral.

Thus of the nine inscriptions in groups 3 and 4, one, Leeds, is probably genuinely runic: two, Cleobury Mortimer and Wijk, may be: five, Sandwich B, Kirkdale, Irton, Northumbria, and 'owi' are strongly suspect: and of one, Hoddam, there is inadequate evidence. Marquardt lists Leeds, Sandwich B, Irton, Northumbria, and 'owi' as *Inschriften in angelsächsischen (anglischen) Runen*, Cleobury Mortimer and Hoddam as *Inschriften mit runenähnlichen Zeichen*. Kirkdale appears twice, once (A) in

---

[1] D. Wilson, *The archæology and prehistoric annals of Scotland* (Edinburgh, 1851), p. 550.

[2] Wilson himself warns against the unclear use of 'runic' (*Archæology and prehistoric annals*, pp. 542–3). He also notes a stone in Anwoth parish, Kirkcudbrightshire, with marks which some antiquaries 'suppose to be Runic inscriptions'.

the first list, once (B) in the second. Wijk is intentionally omitted.

Before leaving Stephens's work I must consider two inscriptions whose interpretations are still in doubt; the cryptic text of the Sutton, Isle of Ely, brooch, and the 'æniwulufu' legend of a coin in the British Museum. When Stephens wrote on the Sutton brooch it was known only from Hickes's engraving.[1] In 1951, however, the piece came to light again after an interval of two and a half centuries, and it was then possible to establish the high degree of accuracy of the *Thesaurus* picture. Scratched round the rim of the brooch back is an OE text, comparatively easy to interpret, in Roman characters. A strip of metal is riveted to the back of the brooch, and on this is inscribed a second text, this time not in Roman letters. Stephens thought they were 'stave-runes, several runes on the same stave',[2] here following Hickes who had called them '*Runæ* sive potius *Runarum* jugationes'. In fact, as I have noted elsewhere, these symbols bear only a slight similarity to Anglo-Saxon, or indeed any other, runes. They are probably a cryptic script, perhaps contrived for magical use. What they say I have no idea.

In the case of the 'æniwulufu' coin (listed by Marquardt as *England B*) there is doubt both as to the correct identification of the characters and as to the authenticity of the specimen. This gold coin, of the module of a tremissis, has an obverse legend +CNYM1NꝲI+ꝲ LIO and a reverse VENA with scattered letters elsewhere in the field. For the obverse Haigh suggested the reading 'æniwulufu', retrograde and set within another legend, CLIO, which he explained variously as *gliw*, 'wise', and *hleo*, 'protector'. This reading of the runes has been commonly followed, save by Stephens who read *Æniwulu ku(nung)* (= Anwulf king) and Hempl who preferred the absurd *æniþu lufu*, 'unity (and) love'.[3]

---

[1] A. Fountaine, *Numismata Anglo-Saxonica & Anglo-Danica breviter illustrata* (Oxford, 1705), p. 186, in Hickes's *Thesaurus*.

[2] *Old-Northern runic monuments*, i-ii, p. 292.

[3] D. H. Haigh, 'Miscellaneous notes on the Old English coinage', *Numismatic Chronicle*, N.S. ix (1869), 172-3; Stephens, *Old-Northern runic monuments*, iii,

The legend certainly resembles 'æniwulufu', with two, though unimportant, epigraphical difficulties. The fourth character, ᚦ, could be read with Hempl 'þ', though 'w' is probably equally possible. The penultimate, ᚠ, is only 'f' if it is a blundered form omitting the lower arm of that rune. Otherwise it should be 's', as on St Cuthbert's coffin and the Greymoor Hill amulet ring. It is tempting to take, with Haigh, the legend as the common OE personal name *Eanwulf*, though the final 'u' is as embarrassing as it is in other runic inscriptions—the *skanomodu* solidus text and the words 'flodu', 'giuþeasu' on the Franks casket. A first element *Æni-* could be paralleled in the occasional form *Ænheri* of the Moore and Leningrad manuscripts of Bede's *Historia ecclesiastica*, where it is presumably related to the CGerm *Auni-*, having early *æ* for the reflex of WGerm *au . . . i*.[1] Unless the coin is very early, the medial *-i-* could hardly be the original unstressed vowel, but must be an intrusive one, perhaps due to the simplex *Eni* and influenced by such common variant pairs as *Cyn-/Cyni-*, *Sig-/Sige-*. *-wuluf* would show an intrusive vowel of the common type which developed between *l* and a following consonant, as in the Whitby comb 'h/e/lipæ'.

There are, however, difficulties over identifying this coin as runic. It was given to the British Museum by Count de Salis, who bought it in 1856 and was told it was found in England early in the nineteenth century. But there is doubt if this specimen is genuine. The compilers of the British Museum catalogue of Anglo-Saxon coins intentionally omitted it, and Sutherland rejects it.[2] It may in fact be a cast, as casts of this or similar coins are known to have circulated in the early nineteenth century. The reverse type, with its two figures holding up grotesquely large hands, is unusual, but appears on two related coins, probably genuine. The first, in the

pp. 236–41; G. Hempl, 'Old-English runic *ænipu lufu*', *Transactions of the American Philological Association*, xxvii (1896), Proceedings, lxiv–vi.

[1] H. Ström, *Old English personal names in Bede's history* (Lund, 1939), p. 114; O. S. Anderson, *Old English material in the Leningrad manuscript of Bede's Ecclesiastical History* (Lund, 1941), p. 104.

[2] C. H. V. Sutherland, *Anglo-Saxon gold coinage in the light of the Crondall hoard* (Oxford, 1948), p. 49, note 4 and refs.

Royal Coin Cabinet, The Hague, which can be traced back to the collection of J. L. Kuijt of Leiden, has a similar reverse with the legend ᚣEN F-SI/// and an obverse with the text + CORNILIO, clearly related to the C. . . .LIO of the British Museum example.[1] The second, in the collection of Mr P. Grierson of Cambridge, has the reverse legend VEN/TA and other scattered letters, and on the obverse + CΛÞΛINDI+ FILIO. This is the specimen illustrated in A. de Belfort, *Description générale des monnaies mérovingiennes* (Paris, 1892–5), iii, no. 4731, where it is ascribed to Winchester, and by Ponton d'Amécourt in 1883, and it can be traced back to the Norblin collection in the 1830's.[2] A further coin, or perhaps the British Museum specimen, was found at Folkestone and exhibited to the Society of Antiquaries of London on 24 February 1736–7.[3] Its legend is recorded in the minute book as +CΠᚣΠΠDI+ᚴLIO, which is remarkably like that of the British Museum example, though the exhibitor's transcript, + CUÞUÞUDI CHRISTI FILIO, shows distinctive resemblances to the Grierson coin. Clearly the legends of the British Museum and Grierson pieces are closely related, deriving from a common original. On the whole it is likely that this original was in Roman characters. The resemblance to a retrograde 'æniwulufu' is then chance, but it is so striking as to suggest that the die-cutter knew runes and was experienced in cutting them.

Five stone inscriptions, unnoticed by Stephens, are listed in the *Bibliographie*, three fragments from Whitby, and the sundials of Darlington and Old Byland. The three Whitby stones are now in the British Museum. One is part of a cross-head whose inscription was first cautiously recorded by W. G. Collingwood: 'the lettering, incised in a frame . . . has the look of runes; one might even imagine "[Ky]niswith." '[4] The text is repeated, queried, in the

---

[1] Stephens, *Old-Northern runic monuments*, iii, pp. 241–2.

[2] See *British Numismatic Journal*, xxxi (1962), 171–2 and refs.

[3] See D. M. Metcalf, 'Eighteenth-century finds of medieval coins from the records of the Society of Antiquaries', *Numismatic Chronicle*, 6 Ser. xviii (1958), 87–8.

[4] 'Anglian and Anglo-Danish sculpture in the East Riding, with addenda to the North Riding', *Yorkshire Archæological Journal*, xxi (1911), 302; also the same journal, xxiii (1915), 290.

same writer's catalogue of Anglo-Saxon inscriptions in Yorkshire, while the *Victoria County History* lists it as a 'worn inscription'.[1] Baldwin Brown is positive: 'A plain strip runs across the face of the transom with an inscription in runes, but nothing can be made of the few surviving characters.'[2] In 1943, however, C. A. R. Radford rejected this 'inscription' in terms which certainly now apply to the stone. 'The parallel lines . . . have been thought to contain a Runic inscription. I can find no trace of this. The lines are not horizontal and I consider that they represent damage at a later date.'[3] In the same article Radford himself published two inscribed stones and identified them as runic: no. 14 (= W. 6 in the British Museum), with an 'Illegible Runic inscription', and no. 21 (= W. 8) with a 'Runic inscription with an initial cross'. The characters on stone 14, though much weathered, do not resemble runes in the least. They are much more like one of the minuscule scripts, perhaps even post-Conquest, in which case the stone has been reused at a later date. Only a fragment of the beginning of the stone 21 inscription remains, the bases of most letters lost. Some of the characters look like runes: the first (after the clear initial +) could be a serifed 'u', the second 'w' or 'þ' (though these two are not confined to runic alphabets), and the fourth 'l'. Other letters, however, are clearly non-runic, being made up of curling lines which rune-masters usually avoid. Too little of this stone remains for us to be able to make any constructive comment on its text.

Fowler was the first to notice, in 1863, the early double-sided sundial at Darlington. He sent a rubbing to Haigh who included an account and a drawing of one side in his article on Yorkshire sundials, apparently without having seen the original himself.[4] Haigh showed unusual caution in describing a mark 'almost effaced, something like the rune **Dæg** . . . indicating the **dæg-**

---

[1] *VCH Yorkshire*, ii, p. 128.

[2] G. B. Brown, *The arts in early England* (London, 1903–37), vi, p. 100.

[3] Sir Charles Peers and C. A. R. Radford, 'The Saxon monastery of Whitby', *Archaeologia*, lxxxix (1943), 37. Similar parallel grooves run obliquely across another Whitby fragment, Radford no. 15 (= W. 11).

[4] 'Yorkshire dials', pp. 154–5.

mæl point'. His drawing shows a clear form, indeed rather like a widened 'd', set radially between two of the rays. Unfortunately Haigh's hesitancy was fruitless, for in the *Victoria County History* Hodges, who was confused about the two sides of the dial, spoke firmly about 'the rune',[1] and Marquardt listed the stone, '*Mit D-Rune zur Bezeichnung des "dæg-mæl-point"* (?), *heute nicht mehr sichtbar*'. This comment is ambiguous, suggesting at least the possibility that a genuine rune had deteriorated and become lost, so it is worth recording what can actually be seen on the Darlington stone. Its two dials are cut on the two faces of a flat slab which is broken at one edge. One has eight concentric circles, the other six, in each case divided into sectors by the rays. Both sides of the slab are weathered and abraded, the eight-circle side the more so, and on it no runes are visible nor (despite Hodges) have any ever been found there. On the six-circle side, at the point where Haigh saw the rune-like form, the surface is damaged and there are two fairly straight lines crossing. These are almost certainly accidental, and are only remotely like 'd'. As Marquardt noticed, a shape like the rune 'd' is shown in a similar, though not identical position, on Haigh's drawing of the Anglo-Saxon sundial at Old Byland.[2] Accordingly she listed this '*Mit D-Rune?*' though no previous scholar had made the identification. The Old Byland sundial is both difficult of access and badly weathered. It is doubtful if in fact the letter 'd' is there.

A mixed group of objects remains to be disposed of. The weight from Ahlheden, Jutland, now in the National Museum, Copenhagen, on which F. Magnussen identified 'œui', was rejected even by the eclectic Stephens: 'It is not sure that the strokes are runes at all.'[3] The brooch from the Bateman collection (British Museum 93, 6–18, 32), traditionally associated on slender grounds with Kent, has an undoubted but uninterpreted runic inscription which could be either Anglo-Saxon or Continental Germanic. Two urns,

---

[1] *VCH Durham*, i, p. 240.
[2] 'Yorkshire dials', p. 141, taken from a cast, though Haigh saw the origina himself.
[3] *Old-Northern runic monuments*, i-ii, p. 160.

one from Lackford and one from Loveden Hill, have rune-like symbols, which may show an inadequate knowledge of runes on the part of their cutter.[1] D. M. Wilson has pointed out a group of fakes, copies of the amulet ring from Kingmoor, now in the British Museum (see *England D* in the *Bibliographie*).[2] Finally in this section we must note that there are modern inscriptions in Anglo-Saxon runes which will never—it is to be hoped—get into the runic corpus. Two examples serve to illustrate. In the church at Great Ormside, Westmorland, is a lectern, apparently local work from or after the restoration of 1885, on whose pedestal are cut the runes 'i·s·x·'. I do not know the explanation of these: the sequence suggests an attempt at the name of Christ (cf. 'ihs $\overline{xps}$' on St Cuthbert's coffin), but the use of points may indicate initials, perhaps those of J. S. Twigge, the early twentieth-century antiquarian parson, with 'x' in error for the similar 't'. In the garden at Grove Place, Nursling, Hampshire, stand two statues, probably eighteenth- or nineteenth-century, each with a runic title on the plinth. These read 'þunr' and 'wodn'. From the context—the figures are crowned, one sceptred as Jove, the other armed as Mars—these are obviously *Þunor* and *Woden*, the first confirmed by a symbol containing 'thunder-flashes' above the name.

On the positive side there are a number of new inscriptions, recently found or published, to be added to Marquardt's catalogue: the Monkwearmouth, Orpington and Lindisfarne rune-stones, the Leningrad Gospels, the Loveden Hill urns, the Dover brooch, the Welbeck Hill bracteate and the Sarre pommel, together with rune-like characters on the Hunstanton brooch and on pommels from Faversham and Gilton.[3]

Not included in the *Bibliographie* and indeed not generally known, though details of them have long been published, are the inscriptions of York and Hamwih, Southampton. The first of

---

[1] T. C. Lethbridge, *A cemetery at Lackford, Suffolk* (Cambridge, 1951), p. 20 and fig. 27; *Illustrated London News* for 31 August 1963, pp. 320–1.

[2] 'A group of Anglo-Saxon amulet rings', *The Anglo-Saxons* (ed. P. Clemoes), pp. 168–70.

[3] For details of these finds see S. C. Hawkes and R. I. Page, 'Swords and runes in south-east England', *Antiquaries Journal*, xlvii (1967), 1–26.

these is on a wooden spoon, now in the Yorkshire Museum (register no. C 628), which was recorded first in J. Raine, *Yorkshire Museum: Handbook to the antiquities* (1891), p. 218, and then in D. M. Waterman, 'Late Saxon, Viking, and early medieval finds from York', *Archaeologia*, xcvii (1959), 85–6, where the runes are accurately delineated. According to Raine the spoon was discovered, with a large number of other objects, 'in 1884 in Clifford street whilst rebuilding the place of worship, etc., belonging to the Quakers'. He included it in a group of 'Scandinavian curiosities'. Waterman expresses no opinion as to whether the spoon is Scandinavian or English, though he dates it later than the Danish occupation of the city—to the tenth or eleventh century. The runes are ᚳᚣ, almost certainly to be read that way up: they are presumably the Anglo-Saxon 'cx', though they could perhaps be Scandinavian *um*.

The Hamwih inscription, the runes 'catæ' scratched on the foot-bone of a cow, was discovered during the 1951 excavations of the storage pits related to the Anglo-Saxon settlement site of Southampton. It was in pit 66A, in Grove Street. The related finds have not been analysed in detail, and only a provisional report of the runes has yet appeared, in *The Archaeological News Letter*, iv (1951–3), 62. The bone is preserved, with the other Hamwih material, in the City Museums, Southampton.

The only other commonly unknown object for which we have some positive runic evidence is the lost Anglo-Saxon stone fragment from Norham, Northumberland. This was still in existence in 1776 when Hutchinson recorded its inscriptions, which seem to have been in Roman characters save for a runic 'm' in an uncertain context.[1] By 1852 the stone had been lost and has not since been seen, so we must rely on Hutchinson's illustration, reluctantly since it gives a most un-Anglo-Saxon impression. It is likely that the letter in question was a damaged or weathered Roman M, but the north-east occasionally evidences mixed inscriptions of runic and Roman forms, such as the Alnmouth

---

[1] W. Hutchinson, *A view of Northumberland . . .* (Newcastle, 1778), ii, p. 25. See also J. Raine, *The history and antiquities of North Durham* (London, 1852), p. 259.

cross and the Chester-le-Street stone. Moreover, 'm' is one of the runes which sometimes intrudes into non-runic texts, as in the archangel's name [R]VmIA[EL] on St Cuthbert's coffin, in the Chester-le-Street name EADmVnD, and in a number of coin legends.[1]

A painting of a rune-stone otherwise unknown forms part of the portrait of Humphrey Wanley now in the library of the Society of Antiquaries of London, a picture which dates from 1711.[2] This shows the scholar surrounded by the treasures of the Harley collection of which he was keeper. In the foreground is an antique vase which elsewhere appears in a portrait of Edward Harley, and on the table rests the Guthlac roll, while Wanley holds up a Greek manuscript of St Matthew's gospel, wrongly described by the Society's historian as 'a book with Anglo-Saxon runes'.[3] In the left foreground stands a rune-stone, shown as a sort of pillar, square in cross-section and with a rather rounded top on which marks which may be runes can just be traced. On one face of the pillar is a panel formed in incised lines, framing an inscription of six runes, upside down, the first two retrograde. The runes are 'þrxfds', the letters clearly cut and well preserved. Since other objects in the picture are genuine, this stone should be genuine too, though it resembles none now known and the only rune-stones to be connected with Wanley reached Harley's collection in 1721, as will be seen below. In fact, however, this is unlikely to be a picture of a real stone in view of the inverted and (in some cases) retrograde setting of the characters, and in view of the sequence of the

[1] For example, in the royal name, abbreviations of *moneta(rius)* and *me fecit* on coins of Eadmund of East Anglia and on his memorial coinage, *BMC*, i, p. 92, 68; p. 102, 178; p. 112, 327; p. 115, 381; p. 119, 426.

[2] The back of the picture bears a note giving the date 1711, but this is a copy of an earlier document, and it has been suggested that 1711 is an error for 1717, since the painter, Thomas Hill, made other portraits of Wanley in 1716 and 1717.

[3] J. Evans, *A History of the Society of Antiquaries* (Oxford, 1956), pl. iv. Unfortunately this plate cuts out the corner with the rune-stone. The picture is no. II in G. Scharf, *A catalogue of the pictures belonging to the Society of Antiquaries . . .* (Bungay, 1865), which contains a detailed account with the rune-stone described as 'An oriental inscribed stone of the cushion form.'

runes. The picture is probably imaginary, designed to illustrate one further aspect of Wanley's antiquarian interests.

When a reference to a runic object is unsupported by any drawing we are faced with the difficulties I have mentioned in discussing the Hoddam stone, primarily the problem of the meanings to ascribe to the words 'runic' and 'rune'. *OED* gives the following relevant meanings and dates: for 'runic', A. I, consisting of runes (as in 'runic characters'), 1662; Ib, carved or written in runes, 1685; Ic, inscribed with runes, 1728; 2, of poetry, etc., such as might be written in runes, especially ancient Scandinavian or Icelandic, 1690; 3, belonging to ancient Scandinavia or the ancient North, 1665; 3b, of ornament, of the interlacing type which is characteristic of rune-bearing monuments, 1838: for 'rune', I, a letter of the earliest Teutonic alphabet, 1685/90; 2a, an incantation or charm denoted by magic signs, 1796. This is useful as an indication of the danger of accepting early uses of the words at their face value, though the *OED* articles on these words are by no means complete and in most of the references can be readily antedated. For example, the editors of the dictionary made no use of the endearingly eccentric work, *Britannia antiqua illustrata* by the seventeenth-century Cambridge antiquary, Aylett Sammes, who used 'rune' in sense I ('the Ancient *Getes* or *Saxons* nam'd their Characters, *Runes*') and 'runic' in sense Ib ('their *Runick* or Magical Writings'),[1] while some years earlier still, in 1668, Junius used 'runic' in sense Ib and probably Ic ('the Runike inscription left with him', 'manie Runike monuments').[2] Sammes often connects 'runic' with 'magical', explaining that the 'Character [*sic*] . . . called *Runick* . . . were made use of by *Woden*, not only

---

[1] *Britannia antiqua illustrata* (London, 1676), pp. 440, 434. Those who delight in antedating *OED* will rejoice in Sammes's book which contains such examples as: *Berserker* (*OED* 1822), 'this sort of furious Onset was called Berserker', p. 438; *Edda* (*OED* 1771), 'To begin then with this EDDA, concerning the Expedition of WODEN out of *Asia*', p. 431; *Skald* (*OED* 1763), 'the Founder of that Tribe called Scalders, which . . . made it their business to set forth in Verses' (elsewhere *Skaldi, Skaldri*), p. 438.

[2] W. Hamper, *The life, diary, and correspondence of Sir William Dugdale, knight* (London, 1827), pp. 384-5.

for Inscriptions, but Magical Charms and Imprecations'. There is clearly here a connection with meaning 2a of 'rune' which can thus hardly be as late as 1796.[1] Certainly 'runic' was in use as one of the Gothick words of the eighteenth and early nineteenth centuries, contrasting with the staider 'Roman' and having such connotations as 'magical', 'mysterious', 'sinister', 'eerie'. It is thus that Scott overworked the word in *The Pirate*. At the same time the history of runic studies in England explains the intimate association of the word 'runic' with 'Scandinavian'. Probably the most important stimulus to the development of runic scholarship in this country was the work of the Dane, Ole Worm, whose books *Runer, seu Danica literatura antiquissima* (Amsterdam, 1636), *Danicorum monumentorum libri sex* (Copenhagen, 1643) and *Specimen lexici runici* (Copenhagen, 1650) were avidly read here and often quoted. Worm's *Monumenta* is abundantly illustrated with woodcuts of rune-inscribed monuments from Norway, Sweden and Denmark. His *Specimen* is an Old Norse-Latin dictionary, the catch-words given in both runic and Roman script. Not surprisingly 'runic' came to be used of both the epigraphical script of the monuments and the medieval Scandinavian language of Worm's lexicon and the literature written in it. The preponderance of Scandinavian runic remains over those of other countries and in other tongues, and the eagerness with which runic studies were pursued in the North, has resulted in the word being associated with Scandinavia down to the present day, and the confusion between script and language lasted at any rate into the nineteenth century, despite the attempts of scholars like Hickes to make a clear distinction between the two. Thus right from the seventeenth century, when they first appeared in English, 'rune'

---

[1] *Britannia antiqua illustrata*, p. 439. Sammes may, in fact, use 'rune' in sense 2a in 'These Runes our Ancestours set up against the Enemies', p. 442, though it is just possible that he refers here to the letters rather than the import of the text. See also W. Nicolson, *The English historical library* (London, 1696-9), i, p. 132: 'The Characters themselves were first . . . call'd *Runer*; tho afterwards that word came to acquire some new significations: As, I. *Enchantments* . . .' For further discussion of 'rune', 'runic' see H.-G. Goetz, *Geschichte des Wortes 'rūn (rune)' und seiner Ableitungen im Englischen* (Göttingen, 1964), pp. 72 ff.

and 'runic' were used with a wide range of meanings, so that any reference to a runic monument must be regarded with suspicion. Just as writers have sometimes been baffled by the form of 'runic' —witness Thoresby's 'Ruinick'[1]—so they have often been ignorant of any proper meaning for it, and the alert reader will often spot such absurdities as 'The vignette represents a Runic or Buddhist cross near Ramsey Bay, Isle of Man' or such misrepresentations as 'stones inscribed with the runic alphabet known as Ogham'.[2]

A very early and undoubted allusion to a lost rune-stone, though there is no way of knowing what sort of runes it displayed, is the unidentified Westmorland place-name *Runcrosbanc* 1286.[3] Most references are much later, from or after that great period of learning in the late seventeenth century when amateurs up and down the country were on the look-out for Anglo-Saxon antiquities. From these more modern times come a number of accounts of runic objects now lost or unidentifiable, but only when a reference is given by a scholar skilled in the script and precise in his language can we think it likely that the object actually was inscribed in runic characters. Such a scholar was Wanley who mentions four examples, all of which he had seen himself. In his journal which lists his dealings on Harley's behalf (Lansdowne MS 771, in the British Museum) Wanley notes for 16 February 1720/1, 'My Lord [Harley] sent in an antient Gold Ring found at Newbury in Berkshire, which the Lord Bathurst gave him yesterday. There are some Runic Letters discernable upon it.' His entry for 25 November 1721 records 'two stones with Runic Letters, and another with the Armes of Courtney, found by Mr Auditor Harley in the Church of [*blank space*] in Northamptonshire, in an heap of Rubbish'.[4] Presumably all three came from Northamptonshire,

---

[1] R. I. Page, 'Ralph Thoresby's runic coins', *British Numismatic Journal*, xxxiv (1965), 29.

[2] E. Forbes, *A history of British starfishes, and other animals of the class echinodermata* (London, 1841), p. 230; J. M. White, 'Tristan and Isolt', *Myth or Legend?* (London, 1955), p. 73.

[3] A. H. Smith, *The place-names of Westmorland* (Cambridge, 1967), ii, p. 187.

[4] C. E. and R. C. Wright, *The diary of Humfrey Wanley 1715–1726* (London, 1966), i, pp. 87 and 123. The latter are presumably among the 'divers pieces of

though Wanley may mean only that the heraldic stone did. Neither Berkshire nor Northamptonshire is a known runic area. Wanley's fourth reference to a runic monument is in Bodley H.9.5 Art., a copy of the second edition of W. Nicolson's *The English historical library* (London, 1714) with manuscript annotations. Apropos of a note on runes Wanley wrote: 'When Sir Andrew Fountain was in Ireland, he met with and bought [*sic*] to London a Wooden Hand or Scepter of an Irish or Danish King with many Runic Letters on it.' This must be the 'old Irish Hand, Scepter, or Mace, which I borrowed of him [Fountaine]' mentioned in Wanley's journal for 10 September 1720, though without reference to any runes.[1] It could be—though the dates make this rather doubtful—the object commented on by William Nicolson, bishop of Carlisle, in a letter to Lhuyd (Bodleian MS Ashmole 1816, fo. 515, undated, but *c.* 1701), 'your Irish Inscription (which, tho' it seems somew^t to counterfeit a Runic Motto, I take to be no more than a casual and insignificant flourish)'. It may also, though this is even more doubtful, be intended by Stephens's obscure entry, 'Dublin Museum, Ireland. The *later* runes. On a wooden Cavel. Apparently only a scribble. Cannot be further dated',[2] though this again could be the 'little stick' which, according to a letter in the Royal Library, Stockholm, G. M. Atkinson sent to Stephens on 21 June 1872 with the remark, 'This is the only relick of the Rune staff I have seen in Ireland.' None of these can be traced further. The 'sceptre' is not listed in the Fountaine sale catalogue (1889). The National Museum of Ireland knows nothing of Stephens's cavel.

There is no point in listing in detail the poorly authenticated references to runic objects. A pair of examples will stress the difficulties. Lot 87 in the sale catalogue of the collection of John White of Newgate Street (1778) is described as 'An antient Runic ring, found near the Picts Wall, 1773', with the tantalizing addition

Antiquity' which Wanley proposed to send to Wimpole on 1 December 1721 (ibid., ii, p. 434). No rune-stones are mentioned in the Harley sale catalogue (1742).

[1] Wright, *Diary of Humfrey Wanley*, i, p. 68.
[2] *The runes, whence came they?*, p. 58.

'*See the account with it.*' This lot was sold to Tyssen for £1 13*s*. 0*d*., though it does not appear in the Tyssen sale catalogue (1802). Besides the usual problems of identification here there is a further cause for suspicion. White was a well-known dealer in antiquities, which he sometimes made himself. This ring could well be a fake, and Tyssen an innocent dupe. The account of the Abbotsford stone, given in Mrs Hughes's *Letters and recollections of Sir Walter Scott* (ed. H. G. Hutchinson, London, n.d.), p. 100, makes specific mention of a runic inscription, yet probably wrongly. The entry for 5 May 1824 begins, 'Walked again to the stone in memory of Kerr of Cessford and looked at the large stone with a Runic inscription which is in the adjoining plantation.' The stone examined by Mrs Hughes can only be identified with a Pictish cross slab, uninscribed, now in the National Museum of Antiquities of Scotland, Edinburgh. This elaborately sculptured stone was discovered in the old castle of Woodray, Aberlemno, Forfarshire, and was presented to Scott who put it up on his estate.[1] The stone is runic in sense 3b only, and it is curious that this lady, so well-informed and under Sir Walter's tutelage, should have referred so explicitly to an inscription.

I have tried in this paper to define some difficulties of establishing the Anglo-Saxon runic corpus. Inevitably a few hard cases remain for extended discussion elsewhere—the Bury St Edmunds lead plate, with its quotation from Ælfric following a ?runic title; the Rome bronze fragment, with its Anglo-Saxon runic alphabet which, however, uses a Scandinavian 'c'; the Coquet Island ring, which has now collapsed into a greyish powder; a dubiously Anglo-Saxon sword of unknown provenance with ?runes engraved on its tang and perhaps inlaid in its blade;[2] the Gandersheim (Brunswick) casket, of walrus ivory, with a metal plate inscribed with runes stuck to its base—a genuine casket with a suspect inscription;[3] a number of urns which have rune-like symbols

[1] Stuart, *Sculptured stones of Scotland*, i, p. 31, pl. xcviii, xcix.

[2] R. E. Oakeshott, *The sword in the age of chivalry* (London, 1965), p. 32, pl. 4A.

[3] A. Fink, 'Zum Gandersheimer Runenkästchen', *Karolingische und Ottonische Kunst* (Wiesbaden, 1957), pp. 277–81.

of uncertain interpretation; sceattas with blundered legends which may derive from genuine runic ones which have not survived incorrupt. Inevitably, too, this study can only present a provisional statement. We may confidently expect fresh runic inscriptions in the coming years while lost ones may be rediscovered, and further material recovered from early records newly identified or studied.

3

Deor—a Begging Poem?

NORMAN E. ELIASON

IN A PAPER entitled 'Two Old English Scop Poems'[1] I advanced the view that *Deor* as well as *Widsith* is a begging poem. This view, a novel one of *Deor* though not of *Widsith*, gains strength from the comparison I there made of the two poems, which share certain features suggesting that the purpose of both is the same. For *Widsith* a plausible case can be made out that begging is its purpose. For *Deor* the case is trickier. This is why the title of my present paper,[2] which is concerned with *Deor* alone, ends with a question mark.

Instead of rehearsing the rather involved argument of my *PMLA* paper and all its ramifications or treating matters of detail, textual and otherwise, that are dealt with there and elsewhere,[3] I shall here consider more broadly two basic questions: What is there in *Deor* that suggests it is a begging poem? What is gained by construing it thus?

The first, establishing the fact or even the likelihood that *Deor* is a begging poem, is difficult. The difficulty is inherent in the very nature of the case, for two factors are involved, neither of which can be relied on to provide proof or even reasonable assurance of what I am trying to establish. One of these factors is begging. Of begging, the one thing we cannot expect is the truth—certainly not always the whole truth and often not any truth at all. We

---

[1] *PMLA*, lxxxi (1966), 185–92.

[2] Originally presented at the MLA meeting, Chicago, 28 December 1965, in essentially the same form as here.

[3] 'The Story of Geat and Mæðhild in Deor', *SP*, lxii (1965), 495–509, and 'The Thryth-Offa Digression in *Beowulf*' in *Franciplegius: Medieval and Linguistic Studies in Honor of Francis P. Magoun, Jr.* (New York, 1965), pp. 124–38.

expect instead and almost invariably get some sort of cock-and-bull story which, stripped of its embellishments, is usually reducible to three essentials: (1) a subterfuge of some kind enabling the beggar to disclaim that he is begging, (2) an exaggerated claim of his need and merit, and (3) a canny reluctance to specify exactly what he wants or hopes to get.

When, as here in *Deor*, the begging is not that of a mere beggar but of a poet or, as he labels himself, a scop, a second and even more unreliable factor must be reckoned with. A scop, a professional entertainer with a reputation for being clever with words and skilled in the telling of tales, might reasonably be counted on for something better than simply a hard-luck yarn or a wheedling plea for a handout. His audience—the court, the king, or whomever else he was addressing—would expect to be entertained rather than pestered. And the scop, even though obliged to beg, would presumably have had enough professional pride not to descend to outright begging nor resort to the cajolery of ordinary begging.

If, then, there is begging in *Deor* we ought not to expect it to be palpable, nor should we be surprised if it is somewhat adroit.

The begging becomes evident only in the last eight lines of the poem, where the scop, instead of citing further instances of misfortunes suffered by others long ago and far away, tells of his own misfortune. He had once been the court scop of the Heodenings, he says, and there had been highly regarded and richly rewarded but had been supplanted in this lucrative post by another scop named Heorrenda. Clearly this account is not what it purports to be, for the tale is neither true nor plausible—as the audience must have perceived, of course, since they knew that the scop who was addressing them there in person could not possibly have served at the court of the Heodenings, a people as remote from them in time and place as the Goths or Mærings were. The tale, though seemingly devised only to resemble the misfortunes he has previously cited,[1] is really a pure cock-and-bull story, I think,

---

[1] The sole grounds on which its incredibility can be excused: 'The heroic setting which the *Deor* poet gives to his own fictitious career was evidently chosen

concocted by the scop so that he can tell of the fame and fortune
once enjoyed but later lost by a scop in the distant past and then
claim these as his own by the pretence that he himself is this
ancient scop. This ruse is curious, for since the claim is preposterous,
it is an utterly transparent ruse—unaccountably inept, it would
seem, or simply stupid. Actually it is a clever subterfuge, enabling
the scop to exaggerate his merit and need and in the same breath
to disavow that he is doing anything of the kind. If the ruse were
less transparent, if it contained even a trace of plausibility, it could
be construed as a guileless ruse of a mere beggar—an impression
which he, as a scop, was trying to avoid. Perhaps in his attempt to
be adroit here he overreached himself, leaving his audience as
mystified about the purpose of his tale as modern scholars have
been.

His audience would have got the point, I should think, at the
conclusion at any rate, where for the sixth time he repeats the
refrain *þæs ofereode, þisses swa mæg*. At the beginning of the poem,
where it occurs after the allusions to the misfortunes of Welund
and of Beadohild, the refrain seems only to mean, 'Just as their
dreadful but long since past misfortunes finally came to an end, so
also eventually will *this*'—the *this* signifying misfortune in general
or any particular misfortune that anyone in the audience might be
thinking of. But by the end, coming as it there does after the tale
of his own misfortune—a misfortune so patently fictional that it
cannot be taken in earnest—the refrain acquires a less serious and
less general sense, particularly the *this*, which, as its deictic force
implies and as its reiteration keeps suggesting, must signify something specific—his own misfortune, evidently, which unlike the
other has not yet been assuaged. Thus the refrain, instead of a
murky offer of consolation for any or all who suffer misfortune,
seems to be a pretty pointed plea for relief of his own.

Precisely what the scop wanted is, of course, not clear. That his
misfortune was great, that he had lost his post as court scop as his

in order that his last example of misfortune outlived might harmonize in tone and
general atmosphere with his five other examples.' Kemp Malone, *Deor*, 3rd ed.
(London, 1961), p. 16.

yarn might seem to suggest, or that he had any hopes of rich recompense, seems altogether unlikely from the flip manner of his begging. Whatever need prompted him to compose his poem is unknown to us, though very likely not to his audience, and whatever reward he expected for it is unspecified. Like any beggar he was canny enough not to say and, as a scop, clever enough to say it in a cunningly cryptic and tantalizing way.

The point I have been making is not that *Deor* is obviously a begging poem but rather that, if it is, there are reasons why this should not be readily apparent and some grounds for suspecting that it is. Thus, however dubious it may seem at first, the view that *Deor* is a begging poem would seem to be a tenable assumption, worthy of serious consideration if it enables us to explain and vindicate what is otherwise inexplicable or indefensible in the poem.

Immediately preceding the tale of the scop's misfortune and apparently separating it awkwardly from the five other instances of misfortune he has previously cited are some general reflections on misfortune. These reflections, together with the refrain, are the basis for the view that *Deor* is a consolation poem. Although doubts have been voiced about this from time to time—usually only nagging little ones—the view has long prevailed and is still generally accepted. Viewed thus, the poem exhorts us by precept and example to endure misfortune as best we can because, as the refrain suggests, it will eventually pass and, as the reflections gloomily remind us, it stems from God. The consolation is surely neither very comforting nor really clear. We are evidently to take our choice between the devil-may-care hope that our lot may somehow improve or Christian resignation to it. The Christian resignation, moreover, is not wholly gloomy, for we are reminded that, though the Lord allots misfortune to some, He allots favour and prosperity to others. It is no wonder, therefore, that these reflections have proved troublesome to scholars, who have either rejected all or some of these seven lines (28–34) as interpolations or have tried to reconcile the contradictions there somewhat more effectively than the poet seemed capable of.

The poet's audience, I suggest, would not have found these lines so troublesome. However piously and wholeheartedly they may have subscribed to the sombre Christian platitude expressed there, they could be counted on to sense its less sombre and more immediate application. Misfortune and its relief ultimately depend on the Lord God, to be sure, but sometimes—especially if the misfortune is slight and easily remedied—it is to a lord nearer at hand that the audience would naturally look, particularly when they were virtually invited to do so by the poet's designation of the lord simply as *dryhten*, a term as apt to suggest their king as their God. Instead of an awkwardly placed and confusing comment on misfortune in general, the passage seems to me deftly inserted at the very place where the scop wants to shift attention from the misfortune of others to his own and to remind the king that it is not to God alone that he, the scop, is appealing for relief.

If the scop's intent was to offer consolation, urging the audience to bear their misfortunes with Christian fortitude or Boethian stoicism and holding forth the small comfort that, like the misfortunes of others, theirs would somehow subside, then the examples he cites are incomprehensible. This is certainly true of his own misfortune, a palpable and trivial fiction placed at the end of the poem as a foolish afterthought. It is equally true of the other five misfortunes, where his choice, treatment, and arrangement are utterly inexplicable. One or two of them are not represented as misfortunes at all. In none is the poignancy of the suffering, or the fortitude with which it was endured, adequately stressed. The order in which they are arranged is senseless.

If, however, the scop's intent was to beg, his handling of these five misfortunes is explainable. Not surprisingly, in view of his oblique way of begging, he begins far afield, citing the grievous but remote misfortunes of Welund and of Beadohild. Next he cites the misfortune of Mæðhild which, if I have correctly identified it, is neither so grievous, for it had a happy ending, nor so remote. The story, an unsavoury one involving Offa, king of the Angles in the fifth century, was still vitally interesting to an eighth-century Mercian audience because of its contemporary pertinence. Offa the Angle was the most illustrious ancestor of their own king, Offa of Mercia. The scop, by his impudence in alluding to this story and having thus directed the audience's attention to contemporary affairs, has prepared them to grasp the significance of the two other misfortunes he then cites. These misfortunes, of the Mærings and of the Goths, are notable because they are not depicted as misfortunes at all—an oddity that I think the audience were expected to note and to resolve by construing them as thinly veiled references to their own situation. Like the Mærings under Theodric, the Mercians had been ruled for a remarkably long time by Offa—thirty years if the reference in line 18 is significant—and like the Goths under Eormanric their own domain had been vastly extended under their remarkably able king, whose success and ruthlessness undoubtedly caused some murmurings of dissatisfaction.

The impudence of the scop in voicing such current complaints about Offa's reign is not at all surprising, I think, for at court the position of a scop was a privileged one. Much like the later court fool, he was allowed to say things no one else dared to, provided he did so with enough circumspection or wit to mollify the royal ear.

It is not my purpose here to defend anew these interpretations of the Mæring, Goth, and Mæðhild passages but simply to show that, when they are interpreted thus, the poet's handling of the five misfortunes is justifiable. Nor has it been my purpose to substantiate my claim that the poem was composed in Mercia during Offa's reign or to vindicate my assumption that it was to him that the poet was addressing his appeal. For all of this, the evidence, which I have presented elsewhere,[1] is, I readily admit, suggestive rather than compelling. But where conclusive evidence is lacking, as it is here and in much else of concern in Old English studies, it is futile to insist on proof. Unless we are to throw up our hands in despair, we have to indulge in speculation or assumption.

The view that *Deor* is a consolation poem is also an assumption, taking its cue from the way the poem begins and succeeding well

[1] In the three papers cited above.

enough for thirteen lines but then failing because thereafter the poem falls apart. The assumption that it is a begging poem accounts for all of it, enabling us to see how everything there fits together in a conscious and artful design. *Deor*, it seems to me, is either a very bad consolation poem or a remarkably adroit begging poem.

Its most remarkable feature is not its felicitous and unique refrain but the design of the poem, which is craftily contrived so that the scop can conceal his purpose at first, teasing us along to the end, where it is finally revealed. The scop is not a craven beggar but a clever one, indirect in his approach and employing wit and impudence rather than whining humility.

In the wit and impudence, in the refrain, and especially in the artfully contrived design qualities are displayed rarely found in Old English poetry and nowhere else there so effectively combined. This is not surprising. Qualities such as these were evidently confined to scop poetry, of which very little survives, perhaps only *Deor* and *Widsith*. These two poems, the source of most of our information about scops, have been wrongly interpreted, I think, and as a consequence we have in the past greatly overrated the professional status of scops and underrated their skill. On both scores *Deor* helps to set us right, for, if forced to beg, the scop can hardly be credited with a highly honoured or esteemed calling and, if capable of begging so cleverly, his skill was considerable.

If *Deor* is a begging poem we not only need to revise our conception of Old English scops but to this particular scop we ought to grant his proper due, for though his is not the first such poem in the English language—an honour that belongs to *Widsith*—it is, I believe, the best.

4

Mens absentia cogitans in
The Seafarer and *The Wanderer*

PETER CLEMOES

THE MIND thinking intensely of distant things is a powerful motif in both *The Seafarer* and *The Wanderer*. In the former the mind is in a state of excitement; in the latter it is in the grip of painful memories. In each case the concept gives rise to some of the keenest imagining and the most expressive writing in these poems. In patristic writings it is an established topic that this consciousness of objects beyond immediate physical surroundings is of the essence of mental activity. Two of the passages in which this view is expressed are likely to have influenced *The Seafarer* and *The Wanderer*. To realize the nature of this influence is to recognize more clearly what part this attribute of the mind plays in these poems.

The relevant passage in *The Seafarer* is the following:

> Forþon nu min hyge hweorfeð   ofer hreþerlocan,
> min modsefa   mid mereflode,
> ofer hwæles eþel   hweorfeð wide,
> eorþan sceatas;   cymeð eft to me
> gifre ond grædig,   gielleð anfloga,
> hweteð on hwælweg   hreþer unwearnum
> ofer holma gelagu . . .[1]

Ideas present in these lines are present also in part of Alcuin's *De*

---

[1] Lines 58–64a. 'Now my mind roams beyond the breast that confines it, my spirit roams widely with the ocean flood across the domain of the whale, across the surface of the earth; the solitary flier returns to me filled with eagerness and desire, calls, urges my heart irresistibly on to the whale's path across the expanse of ocean . . .'

Animae ratione liber,[1] a letter which he addressed to an educated, religious lady at Charlemagne's court and which is a short treatise, homiletic in tone, on the human soul in relation to God, to the body it occupies and to the material world.[2] In the light of his belief that the soul's intellectual faculty, *mens*, is in the image of God, Alcuin exclaims at one point:[3]

Nec etiam aliquis potest satis admirari, quod sensus ille vivus atque cœlestis, qui mens vel animus nuncupatur, tantæ mobilitatis est, ut ne tum quidem, cum sopitus est, conquiescat: tantæ celeritatis, ut uno temporis puncto cœlum collustret, et si velit, maria pervolet, terras et urbes peragret: omnia denique, quæ libuerit, quamvis longe lateque submota sint, in conspectu sibi ipse cogitando constituat. Et miratur aliquis, si divina mens Dei, universas mundi partes simul, et semper præsentes habeat, quæ omnia regit ubique præsens, ubique tota; cum tanta sit vis ac potestas mentis humanæ intra mortale corpus inclusæ, ut ne septis quidem gravis hujus ac pigri corporis, quo illigata est, coerceri ullo modo possit, quominus liberam cogitandi facultatem, quietis impatiens habeat.[4]

---

[1] *PL*, ci, 639–50.

[2] This tract was known in Anglo-Saxon England—at any rate at a later period—for it was used as a main (though not direct) source for two closely related Christmas homilies by Ælfric, *Ælfric's Lives of Saints*, ed. W. W. Skeat (EETS, 1881–1900), item I, and *Twelfth Century Homilies in MS Bodley 343*, ed. A. O. Belfour, i (EETS, 1909, repr. 1962), item IX. These homilies partly differ from one another and partly are verbally identical (if allowance is made for Bodley 343's twelfth-century language), each being a variant rendering of a Latin homily which has survived in a manuscript of the first half of the eleventh century, Boulogne-sur-Mer MS 63, fols. 13–18. This Latin homily is in part a sequence of sentences selected from Alcuin's *De Animae ratione* and reordered, their wording being mostly unchanged but sometimes slightly modified. Skeat I and Belfour IX are verbally identical almost throughout their rendering of that part of the Latin homily which is derived from Alcuin. On problems of authorship of the Latin homily, see *Homilies of Ælfric: A Supplementary Collection*, ed. J. C. Pope, i (EETS, 1967), 4 and nn. 2 and 3. I hope to publish a study of it later.

[3] *De Animae ratione*, c. viii, op. cit., 642D–3A.

[4] 'Nor furthermore can one sufficiently admire the fact that this living and divine faculty which is called *mens* or *animus* is of such mobility that it does not become inactive even when it is asleep, of such speed that at one moment of time it surveys the sky and, if it wishes, flies across seas, traverses lands and cities, in short, by thinking, it, of itself, sets before its view all things it chooses, however far and wide they may be removed. And yet some people marvel if the divine

And again, in one of the two poems incorporated in the tract towards its end, he says in praise of the soul ennobled by its ability to acknowledge its creator:

> Quæ [*scil.* anima sagax] mare, quæ terras, cœlum quæ pervolat altum,
> Quamvis sit carnis carcere clausa suæ.[1]

In both *The Seafarer* and Alcuin's treatise the mind ranges widely beyond the confines of the body in which it is shut up,[2] flying[3] across sea and land (referred to in the same relative order). There is an especially clear-cut likeness between *The Seafarer* and Alcuin's verse, for in Alcuin's poem, as compared with his prose, the mind's flight is not subordinated to the idea that it moves instantly; there is a sharper impression of the mind flying, because the verbs *collustrare* and *peragrare* do not occur; sea and land are referred to more prominently, before, not after, the sky; cities are not mentioned; and the contrast between the mind's freedom of movement and its confinement within the body is expressed more pointedly. The correspondence, plainest between the two poems, does not consist merely of sharing the same general view of mental activity; there are more definite likenesses than that: in both cases no particular object of thought is specified, distance is

mind of God keeps all parts of the universe simultaneously and always present to it—God's mind which rules all things, everywhere present and everywhere whole —when the strength and power of the human mind shut up within a mortal body is so great that it cannot be restrained at all even by the confines of this heavy and sluggish body to which it is tied, from having the free power of thinking without tolerating rest.'

The relevant passage in Ælfric's homilies—here identical to one another in wording—is: 'Uton nu behealden þá wundorlican swyftnysse þære sawle. heo hæfð swá mycele swyftnysse þæt heo on ánre tíde gif heo swá wyle. besceawað heofonan and ofer sǽ flyhð. land. and burga geondfærð. and ealle þas þing mid geþohte on hire sihðe gesæt' (Skeat no. 1, lines 122–6).

[1] Op. cit., 647C. 'Which flies across sea, lands and lofty sky, although it is shut in the prison of its body.'

[2] In *The Seafarer* it is the second element of *hreþerlocan* that expresses the confinement of the mind in the body. From this the preposition *ofer* acquires the sense of opposition that is expressed in the Latin poem by *quamvis*.

[3] I find Sieper's suggestion, accepted by Mrs I. L. Gordon (*The Seafarer* (London, 1960), note to line 62b), that the *anfloga* refers to the cuckoo and not to the speaker's spirit wholly unsatisfying imaginatively.

conceived of spatially, not temporally, and the means used to represent the mental process are the same. Closeness of this kind is likely to be due to some specific connection: both Alcuin and the *Seafarer* poet may have been indebted to a common source; either Alcuin or the *Seafarer* poet may have been indebted to the other. Alcuin owed his ideas in *De Animae ratione* mainly to Augustine and partly to Cassian.[1] No other authority has been detected. Alcuin himself excludes certain of Augustine's writings as sources.[2] The works by Augustine from which Werner[3] cites source-passages are *Enarrationes in psalmos, Soliloquia, De Trinitate* and *De Genesi ad litteram*. Typically Alcuin re-expresses the thought of these passages: there is a word-for-word borrowing only once. But there is no sign anywhere of an intermediate source. Werner includes among Alcuin's debts to Augustine the reference to the power of the human mind to think instantly of distant things, but he cites no source-passage. Probably Augustine did not provide one;[4] but Alcuin's understanding of the concept may have been formed partly by such pronouncements as this in *De Genesi ad litteram*:

Nec illud alterum [*scil.* visio spiritalis], quo absentia corporalia cogitantur, insinuare difficile est: ipsum quippe cœlum et terram, et ea quæ in eis videre possumus, etiam in tenebris constituti cogitamus; ubi nihil videntes oculis corporis, animo tamen corporales imagines

[1] See K. Werner, 'Der Entwickelungsgang der mittelalterlichen Psychologie von Alcuin bis Albertus Magnus', *Denkschriften der Kaiserlichen Akademie der Wissenschaften. Philosophisch-historische Classe*, xxv (Vienna, 1876), 69–150, the part concerning Alcuin's tract being pp. 70–7.

[2] He says (c. xiii, op. cit., 645C): 'Fecit quoque idem doctor [*scil.* Augustinus], ut in libris Retractationum ejus legitur, alia de ratione animæ opuscula, id est, *de Quantitate animæ librum unum; de Immortalitate animæ lib. unum; de Duabus Animabus librum unum; de Immortalitate animæ, et ejus origine libros quatuor*, qui necdum inventi sunt a nobis.' *De Anima et eius origine* is clearly intended by the last-named. Of Jerome's reply to an inquiry by Augustine concerning the origin of the soul Alcuin says (ibid.): 'in patria legimus, sed hic nobiscum non reperitur.'

[3] See above, n. 1.

[4] This is the opinion kindly communicated to me by the Rev. Professor J. Burnaby. Here I want to record my gratitude to the Rev. Professor D. E. Nineham (formerly a colleague of Professor Garmonsway's at King's College, London) who has helped my investigations in a number of ways.

intuemur, seu veras, sicut ipsa corpora videmus, et memoria retinemus; seu fictas, sicut cogitatio formare potuerit. Aliter enim cogitamus Carthaginem quam novimus, aliter Alexandriam quam non novimus.[1]

Outside Augustine's works, however, there is a passage that is close enough to Alcuin's to suggest that it was a specific source. This occurs in the *Hexaemeron* of Ambrose.[2] In expounding the phrase *ad imaginem Dei* Ambrose first specifies various limitations of the human body and then continues:

Non ergo caro potest esse ad imaginem Dei, sed anima nostra quæ libera est, et diffusis cogitationibus atque consiliis huc atque illuc vagatur, quæ considerando spectat omnia. Ecce nunc sumus in Italia, et cogitamus ea quæ ad Orientales aut Occidentales partes spectare videntur, et cum illis versari videmur qui in Perside sunt constituti, et illos videmus qui degunt in Africa, si quos cognitos nobis ea terra susceperit: sequimur proficiscentes, inhæremus peregrinantibus, copulamur absentibus, alloquimur separatos, defunctos quoque ad colloquium resuscitamus, eosque ut viventes complectimur et tenemus, et vitæ officia his usumque deferimus. Ea igitur est ad imaginem Dei, quæ non corporeo æstimatur, sed mentis vigore: quæ absentes videt, transmarina visu obit, percurrit aspectu, scrutatur abdita, huc atque illuc uno momento sensus suos per totius orbis fines et mundi secreta circumfert . . .[3]

---

[1] Lib. XII, c. vi, *PL*, xxxiv, 458. 'Nor is it difficult to introduce the second [i.e. the spirit's vision], by means of which absent material objects are thought of: indeed we think about the sky itself and the earth and everything which we can see in them even when we are in the dark; where, seeing nothing with the eyes of the body, we yet with the mind look at images of material things, whether they are true, as we see the objects themselves and retain in the memory, or imaginary, as thought may have fashioned them. For we think in one way of Carthage which we have known and in another of Alexandria which we have not known.'

[2] This passage was known to me only in the form that it takes in a late compilation (*De Spiritu et anima liber unus, PL*, xl, 781) until Professor J. E. Cross identified the original. I am greatly indebted to him for this valuable piece of information, particularly valuable in relation to *The Wanderer* (see below).

[3] Lib. VI, c. viii, *PL*, xiv, 275. 'Therefore the flesh cannot be after the image of God, but our soul which is free and in widespread thoughts and deliberations roams hither and thither, which in considering looks at everything. Behold we are now in Italy and we think of those things which seem to look towards eastern or western parts and we seem to live with those who are placed in Persia and we see those who live in Africa if that land has received any who are known

Ambrose's theme is sufficiently akin to Alcuin's to make it likely
that Alcuin would recall this passage and be influenced by it when
writing his own: Ambrose makes the point that man's likeness to
God lies in his soul, and not in his body, because of the soul's
power to range throughout the world in thought; Alcuin makes
the point that the soul's power to range throughout the world in
thought, in spite of being confined within its body, is so wonderful that it is no marvel that God has the power to know everything all the time. Both Ambrose and Alcuin demonstrate the
soul's power to think freely by referring to its ability to see what is
absent, to cast its gaze upon things across the sea and to range
throughout the world instantaneously.

Much of this common ground is shared by *The Seafarer* too.
But, since we find the mind's escape from the body and flight in
thought across sea and land integrated and expressed as a single
idea only in Alcuin's poem and *The Seafarer*, it seems to me
probable that one of these two is indebted to the other rather than
both, independently, to Ambrose. If *The Seafarer* influenced
Alcuin it acted upon both his prose and his poem. But on general
grounds it seems unlikely that Alcuin's expository, essentially
intellectual prose, emphatic in expression though it is, should have
admitted influence from such an imaginative source as *The Seafarer*. And there would have to be positive evidence if the view
that it did were to prevail against the various indications that *The
Seafarer* is a ninth-century (or possibly later) poem[1] and was thus
too late to be known to Alcuin. On the other hand it is highly
probable that the *Seafarer* poet's imagination should have been
stimulated by Alcuin's concept of the mind escaping from the

to us: we follow them when they are setting out, we keep with them when they
are journeying, we are united with them when they are absent, we speak to them
when they are separated, even when they are dead we revive them to talk to, and
we embrace and hold them as we would living people and accord them the
courtesies and usage of life. The soul therefore is after the image of God, being
measured not by bodily but by mental activity, for it sees those who are absent,
casts its gaze upon things across the sea, scans them with its glance, examines what
is hidden, and hither and thither in a single moment makes its perceptions range
throughout the limits of the world and the secrets of the universe . . .'
[1] See Gordon, op. cit., pp. 29–31.

body and flying in thought over sea and land: Alcuin's poetic statement would have presented it to his mind as a sharply defined thought and the prose statement of it would have impressed him with the idea's significance. Here was exactly the kind of idea to activate a sensibility that is exemplified by the vivid apprehension of the cries of seabirds earlier in the poem. What is more likely than that this poet should actualize *pervolare*[1] as a calling bird in order to depict a disturbed, urgent state of mind in the context of his poem? Both the unique word *anfloga*[2] and the strikingly realistic verb *gielleð* suggest that his imagination was keenly engaged. Alcuin's wording would have given him a powerful nucleus round which to crystallize his portrayal. That he should have been helped associatively by various elements in Christian and Christianized pagan thought is probable too.[3] Such basic symbols as the dove representing the Holy Spirit at Christ's baptism and St John's eagle may have been not without influence. So may patristic exegesis of biblical reference to birds, such as Augustine's interpretation of the psalm verses

Concupiscit et deficit anima mea in atria Domini. Cor meum et caro mea exultaverunt in Deum vivum. Nam et passer invenit sibi domum, et turtur nidum sibi, ubi ponat pullos suos, altaria tua, Domine virtutum, rex meus et Deus meus

in which 'heart' is linked with 'sparrow' and 'flesh' with 'turtle-dove', various correspondences between them being set forth.[4] More immediate in impact may have been bird imagery in combination with the belief, accepted throughout medieval

[1] The relative uncommonness of this word (as against *volare*) may have helped to attract his attention to it.

[2] See the discussion by V. Salmon at p. 2 of ' "The Wanderer" and "The Seafarer" and the Old English Conception of the Soul', *MLR*, lv (1960), 1–10.

[3] Such influence is demonstrable, for there is no reference anywhere in *De Animae ratione* to the breast as the location of the mind.

How far the *Seafarer* poet was aware of the pagan antecedents in using the poetic word *hyge* as an equivalent of *mens* or *animus* or *sagax anima* is doubtful; see the discussion by V. Salmon, loc. cit., pp. 5–6. The ordinary prose word would have been *mod*, which, for example, Ælfric uses to render both *animus* and *mens* at Skeat no. 1, lines 184–5.

[4] *Enarratio in psalmum LXXXIII*, n. 7, *PL*, xxxvii, 1060–1.

Christian tradition, that the soul, normally invisible, could become visible at the moment of death, for there is a known example relatively close to hand in the late-seventh- or early-eighth-century *Life of St Gregory* by a Whitby monk, in which it is related that Paulinus's soul 'migrated to the heavens, when he died, in the form of a white bird, great like a swan, and very beautiful.' This is a story for which, as Dr B. Colgrave has helpfully pointed out to me, the author is likely to have taken his precedent from Gregory's *Dialogues*—a book well known to him —where[1] it is told that the soul of a certain Abbot Spes at his death issued from his mouth in the form of a dove and, after the roof had parted miraculously, flew off into the heavens. Still more relevant, since it associates bird imagery with a process of development in the mind's conscious thought, is a passage in Boethius's *De Consolatione philosophiæ*, in which Philosophy says:

Pennas etiam tuae menti, quibus se in altum tollere possit, adfigam, ut perturbatione depulsa sospes in patriam meo ductu, mea semita, meis etiam vehiculis revertaris.

And continues in the following Metre:

Sunt etenim pennae volucres mihi,
quae celsa conscendant poli;
quas sibi cum velox mens induit,
terras perosa despicit,
aeris immensi superat globum
nubesque postergum videt . . .[2]

While Alcuin's wording, especially in his poem, remains closer than any other to that of *The Seafarer*, influence from these or

---

[1] Lib. iv, c. x, *PL*, lxxvii, 336A and B.

[2] Lib. iv, end of pr. i and beginning of m. i. 'Wings too I shall fix to your mind, with which it may lift itself up on high, so that, with all confusion removed, you may return safe into your native land, under my leadership, by my way and by my means of conveyance also.' 'For my wings are swift, that they may mount the heights of the heavens; when the quick mind has donned them it looks down upon lands, detesting, rises above the globe of the immense air and sees clouds behind . . .'

I owe this reference and some other most helpful suggestions to Mr M. R. Godden of Pembroke College, Cambridge.

similar sources may well have played its part. Similarly, Old English poetic tradition entered into the *Seafarer* poet's treatment of the bird symbol in his use of the epithets *gifre ond grædig* with reference to the returning mind.[1]

I believe, then, that the idea of the mind escaping from the body and flying in thought across sea and land came to the *Seafarer* poet probably from Alcuin's *De Animae ratione*—from the poem, but against the background of the corresponding passage in the prose[2]—and that he vivified it by the working of his imagination in association with elements of Christian, or Christianized, thought and in relation to traditional Old English poetic expression. If that is so, this is the first known connection with another work that provides a clear-cut *terminus a quo* for the poem: a debt to *De Animae ratione* means that *The Seafarer* could not have been composed before the ninth century, for it is believed to have been in about 799 or soon afterwards that Alcuin wrote his tract.[3]

If the *Seafarer* poet was influenced by Alcuin's prose as well as by his verse, probably he knew the tract as a whole, since the relevant passage of prose and the poem are not adjacent and we have no reason to suppose that their influence came to him through an intermediary. That is not without interest for our estimate of his intellectual calibre. It also prompts the question whether it is probable that any other part of the tract influenced him when he was writing his poem. Man, says Alcuin,[4] comprises soul and body. The origin of the soul is to be left to the knowledge of God

---

[1] For other examples of these adjectives as a pair, always in a bad sense, see Bosworth-Toller and supplement, s.v. *gífre* and *grǽdig*.

[2] Apart from the general influence which I think Alcuin's prose had in impressing the *Seafarer* poet with the significance of the thought that he took over, the symbolization of the returning mind as a calling bird may owe something to Alcuin's words 'omnia denique, quæ libuerit, . . . in conspectu sibi ipse cogitando constituat', for it forcefully combines the process to which these words refer and the effect which the thoughts have on the thinker in the poem.

[3] See E. S. Duckett, *Alcuin, Friend of Charlemagne* (New York, 1951), p. 271. On the dating of *The Seafarer*, see Gordon, op. cit., pp. 27–32.

[4] My summary does not retain the order in which the ideas are propounded in the original.

alone. All Catholic writers agree, however, that it is made by God but is not part of the nature of God. Christ assumed full humanity in both body and soul. The soul is endowed by its Creator with eternal life and with blessedness. It cannot lose eternal life; the soul is the spirit of life which, if lived here according to the command of its Creator, will in future be that of angels, though less now. Blessedness is to have God in it by being just, merciful, good, holy and loving, as God is. It is akin to God in its higher part, *mens*, which bears the image of the Trinity in having one substance but three interrelated powers, those of understanding, will and memory. The soul's supreme function is to love the absolute good, namely God. Love of God crowns its outstanding virtues of prudence, righteousness, temperance and fortitude. Its beauty is the study of the wisdom through which God is loved, and true wisdom is to act in accordance with this knowledge.

As God is the life of the soul, so is the soul the life of the body. It can be separated from its body only by the will of its Creator: it will be separated unwillingly to be reunited on the Day of Judgment. Nobility in the soul is to love God and rule the flesh. The soul rules the body through the senses but is not of them. Incorporeal and invisible, its relationship with its body is through the media of light and air. Virtue is its beauty and vice its deformity. It has free will to choose between them. It should regulate the body's members rationally. The soul has the three elements of desire, reason and anger in its nature. Animals share with man the first and third, but in man the second should rule the other two. Reason's four outstanding virtues are prudence, righteousness, temperance and fortitude. Corrupt desire produces gluttony, lust and avarice; corrupt anger produces sadness and sloth; and corrupt reason produces pride and vainglory.

While remaining in itself, the soul, with wonderful speed, forms figures (*figuras format*) of things felt by the senses, stores them in the memory, recalls them and forms figures of unknown things by relating them to comparable things that are known (*ex notis enim speciebus fingit ignota*). The speed with which the soul

71

operates gives us some inkling of the wonderful power of God, for whereas the human mind can think of only one thing at a time God knows everything always. The soul is given names according to its various functions—*anima, spiritus, sensus, animus, mens, ratio, voluntas* and *memoria.*

Clearly the tract and *The Seafarer* have common ground: for instance, the latter expresses aspirations towards God; the inter-related powers of memory, will and understanding play a part in it; the phrase *modes lust* (line 36) refers to a concept not unlike Alcuin's desiring part of the soul.[1] But there is no necessary connection at any point, and there are recognizable differences: for instance, *The Seafarer* does not elevate reason above desire and anger,[2] and the tract has none of *The Seafarer*'s preoccupation with the transitoriness and decay of life in this world. What we can say is that they are in harmony: the statement by the speaker in *The Seafarer* that the direction of his thoughts is as described in lines 58–64a

> forþon me hatran sind
> Dryhtnes dreamas   þonne þis deade lif
> læne on londe[3]

depends on the belief that the mind which ranges the world as his does will lead him to God, and this is the point that Alcuin's tract as a whole expounds. More specifically, a probable link between Alcuin's tract and *The Seafarer*—in lines 58–62 and possibly more generally—is opposed to Professor G. V. Smithers's view, based partly on the manuscript reading *wælweg* in line 63, that in lines 58–64a we have a description of the launching of the soul on 'the

---

[1] 'Concupiscentia', Alcuin says (*De Animae ratione*, c. iv, op. cit., 640C), 'data est homini ad concupiscenda quæ sunt utilia, et quæ sibi ad salutem proficiant sempiternam.'

[2] Alcuin owed this proposition to Cassian, for he has it in the form which the latter had given to an idea which was ultimately Platonic; see Werner, loc. cit., p. 73.

Ira ('anger') he refers to as follows (op. cit., 640C): 'data est ad vitia cohibenda, ne impiis, id est, peccatis, homo serviat dominis.'

[3] Lines 64b–66a. '. . . because the joys of the Lord are dearer to me than this dead, transitory life on land.'

road taken by the dead' or 'the road to the abode of the dead' and that the seafaring theme is an allegory of death,[1] for the relevant passages in the prose and verse of the tract depict the mind leaving the body in thought and not in death and death enters very little anywhere into Alcuin's account of the soul's relationship with God.

The anguish caused to a solitary man by keen memories of the friendly comradeship he has lost is vividly portrayed in *The Wanderer* in perhaps the poem's most moving passage (lines 29b–57). The portion of Ambrose's *Hexaemeron* which I have quoted[2] may well have been an influence here, rather than Alcuin. The emphasis that Ambrose lays on familiar persons and on what they do in his depiction of distant objects of thought; his implication that we think of these persons to compensate for their absence from our actual surroundings; his supposition that they are separated from us by the sea or by death; his portrayal of the directness and intensity with which we associate ourselves with them in our imagination: all these have their counterparts in the poem. In particular,

þinceð him on mode   þæt he his mondryhten
clyppe ond cysse   ond on cneo lecge
honda ond heafod   swa he hwilum ær
in geardagum   giefstolas breac[3]

could have been indebted to the suggestive power of *eosque* (i.e. the dead) *ut viventes complectimur et tenemus, et vitæ officia his usumque deferimus.* And

---

[1] See 'The Meaning of *The Seafarer* and *The Wanderer*', *Medium Ævum*, xxvi (1957), 137–53 and xxviii (1959), 1–22. The arguments concerning *wælweg* occur at xxvi, 137–40 and 152. For some valid objections to Smithers's view, see Gordon, op. cit., pp. 8–10 and 42 (note to line 63).

[2] Above, p. 66. In sending me the reference to this passage (see above, p. 66, n. 2), Professor Cross saw, as I do, that it is relevant to *The Wanderer*.

[3] Lines 41–4. 'It seems to him in his mind that he embraces and kisses his liege lord and lays his hands and head on his lord's knee just as in days gone by he used to enjoy the gift-seat.'

Cearo bið geniwad
þam þe sendan sceal   swiþe geneahhe
ofer waþema gebind   werigne sefan[1]

could be in a similar relationship to Ambrose's reference to the mind crossing the sea in thought. In my view this amounts to evidence of a link. There are important differences: Ambrose's thoughts about those from whom he is separated are partly concerned with what they are doing in the present, whereas the exile is thinking exclusively about the past; Ambrose does not refer to dreaming in sleep as the wanderer does. But these differences result from the process by which Ambrose's passage of general application has been made specific to the poem, in that the exile is inevitably absorbed in the past, and dreaming, rather than controlled thinking, reflects the compelling nature of his situation. The topic of the mind haunted by its memories receives more extended treatment than any other in the poem; the degree of amplification seems to me due to Ambrose's example.

A comparison of lines 55b–57 with the equivalent reference in the *Hexaemeron* draws our attention to the active role that the thinker's mind has. This in turn affects our interpretation of the immediately preceding, difficult lines 50b–55a,[2] for lines 55b–57 serve as a climax to them. If lines 51–55a are thought to refer, as they are by Leslie,[3] to an hallucination—an otherwise attractive hypothesis—this sort of delusion would be too passive a state of mind to herald the verb *sendan* in line 56, with its implication of volition. Memory, rather than involuntary hallucination, seems to me to be the theme of lines 51–55a—memory made poignant (lines 49–50a) by dreaming (lines 39–48). If that is so, the likelihood is that in lines 51–2

þonne maga gemynd   mod geondhweorfeð,
greteð gliwstafum,   georne geondsceawað . . .

[1] Lines 55b–57. 'Sorrow is renewed for one who has to send a weary mind repeatedly across the expanse of the waves.'

[2] If, that is, 50b is regarded as an introduction to 51 onwards, as it is, rightly in my view, in R. F. Leslie's edition, *The Wanderer* (Manchester, 1966).

[3] Ibid., p. 9.

mod, and not *gemynd*, is the subject of *geondhweorfeð* and hence of the two verbs in the next line as well.[1] The verb *geondhweorfeð* would then have its literal sense 'wanders throughout' and the two lines would be translated 'when the mind wanders throughout its memories[2] of kinsmen, greets them[3] joyfully [cf. Ambrose's *defunctos quoque ad colloquium resuscitamus*], scans them eagerly [cf. Ambrose's *percurrit aspectu*] . . .' It would follow that *mod* is also the subject of *bringeð* in line 54b:[4]

no þær fela bringeð
cuðra cwidegiedda.[5]

'Sorrow would be renewed' (line 50b) because of the limitations of memories, perhaps—if the obscurities of lines 53–54a would support such an interpretation—because they are fading. The pathos of the inadequacy of memory would indeed contribute to the sadness of repeatedly sending a weary mind in loneliness across an expanse of ocean.

Memories, not of happiness that has been lost, but of the event that has caused loss of happiness, are a prominent theme earlier in the poem. The *eardstapa* ('wanderer') who speaks his mind is

earfeþa gemyndig,
wraþra wælsleahta,   winemæga hryre.[6]

What he then says (lines 8–29a) seems to me to be to the effect that perseverance—in his case in his search for a new lord—depends on not giving way to one's sense of calamity. General probability has to provide the grounds for this interpretation, since the allusive,

---

[1] Cf. Leslie's discussion, op. cit., p. 76 (note to line 52). His suggestion that the recollection of kinsmen eagerly surveys the imagination seems to make poor sense.

[2] See Bosworth-Toller supplement, s.v. *ge-mynd*, IVa.

[3] The obscure *secga geseldan* in line 53a may be the object of *greteð* and *geondsceawað*.

[4] See Leslie's note to this line, op. cit., p. 79.

[5] '. . . does not bring there many familiar sayings.'

[6] Lines 6b–7. '. . . mindful of hardships, of fierce slaughters, of the fall of dear kinsmen.'

generalized terms that the poet is using preclude precise intellectual definition. To suppose that in lines 11b–14 the wanderer is making a virtue out of the necessity of his complete isolation by proclaiming the nobility of taciturnity seems to me much less satisfactory than to suppose that, cut off from communication with his fellow men, he is reminding himself of the virtue of mental discipline:

> Ic to soþe wat
> þæt biþ in eorle   indryhten þeaw
> þæt he his ferðlocan   fæste binde,
> healde his hordcofan.[1]

Line 14b then introduces the reason why it is essential to keep thoughts in check:

> Hycge swa he wille,
> ne mæg werigmod   wyrde wiðstondan
> ne se hreohyge   helpe gefremman.[2]

To dwell on disaster is merely to incapacitate the mind. Presence of mind is the means of survival. In this grim realization, the wanderer, like all *domgeorne* ('those eager for glory',[3] line 17), has

---

[1] Lines 11b–14a. 'I know as a truth that it is a very noble custom in a man to bind fast the breast that shuts in his mind, keep control of the place where his thoughts are stored.'
Likewise in *Homiletic Fragment II*, lines 3–4a, where the phraseology is similar, the advice may well be to keep the mind concentrated (on God), and, again, in *Maxims I*, line 121, the point is probably control of thought rather than of speech.

[2] Lines 14b–16. 'Think as he will, a man exhausted in mind cannot withstand fate or the man troubled in mind effect help.'
The association of line 14b with what follows represents a change from recent editorial practice. It is immaterial that the manuscript has no point between the halves of line 14 and that it does not begin *hycge* with a capital, for it never has any punctuation or capitalization in the middle of a line in this poem, even, for instance, in line 29 or line 55, in each of which there is a clear break in the sense mid-line. Likewise it is of no significance that the manuscript has a point at the end of line 14 and begins the first word of line 15 with an enlarged minuscule letter, for precisely the same features occur at the end of line 65 and the beginning of line 66 although *Wita* in line 65b is the implied subject of *sceal* in line 66a.

[3] Can *dom* be God's favourable judgment—and hence His mercy—rather than men's?

had to keep a firm grip on his mind many a time throughout years of searching, desolate as he has been.

If this view of lines 8–29a be accepted, a line of thought which runs through the poem as far as line 57 is that the possibility of God's mercy remains for someone to whom misfortune has come, however long he has had to endure, and that to endure one must not give way to despair, although there is no escaping the poignancy of remembering lost happiness. The further step of advocating control over *speech* is taken later, in lines 66b and 70–2. Such control is one of the marks of a wise man. It rests, we are told, on the ability first to bring one's thoughts under control:

> Beorn sceal gebidan þonne he beot spriceð
> oþþæt collenferð cunne gearwe
> hwider hreþra gehygd hweorfan wille.[1]

Ambrose's *Hexaemeron* does not seem to have had any influence on *The Wanderer* other than in its description of the mind thinking of those that are at a distance, for Ambrose's development of the relationship between God and the human soul is quite different from the poem's line of thought. The influence may not have been a direct one; a homily, for instance, may have acted as intermediary. However that may be, the poet unites Christian intellectualism, the strength of heroic emotions, realism and a traditional, generalized mode of expression in a profound portrayal of the mental experience of loneliness. The combination of mental wandering and physical wandering gives to the symbolism of this part of the poem a fundamental inclusiveness.

[1] Lines 70–2. 'A man must wait, when he utters a vow, until, firm of mind, he knows clearly where the thought of his breast will roam.'

77

5

William of Malmesbury
on the Works of King Alfred

DOROTHY WHITELOCK

WILLIAM OF MALMESBURY is the first person to give a list of the
writings of King Alfred; he is the first person to attribute to the
king a translation of Orosius and of part of the Psalter, and to claim
that Asser helped the king to translate Boethius; and he gives us
certain information on the authority of what he believed to be
King Alfred's Handbook. It may be of interest, therefore, to consider the possible sources of his knowledge.

He tells us himself that in his search for materials for the history
which he is writing he had travelled far and wide, and several
passages in his works show that this was no empty boast. He made
a long stay at Glastonbury, where he studied the archives;[1] he saw
documents preserved at Muchelney[2] and at St Frideswide's,
Oxford;[3] he mentions the archives of St Oswald's, Worcester.[4] He
visited Hereford, where he made copies of inscriptions on a tomb
and a cross;[5] he saw at Sherborne a church which he believed to
have been built by St Aldhelm,[6] and he received information
from an old brother at Sherborne about the earlier history of that
house.[7] He was himself a witness of a miracle at St Ives, Hunting-

---

[1] See his *De antiquitate Glastoniensis ecclesiae*.

[2] Hugh Farmer, 'William of Malmesbury's Life and Works', *Journal of
Ecclesiastical History*, xiii (1962), 42, from the evidence of a passage in some
manuscripts of the B recension of *De gestis Regum Anglorum* (henceforward cited
as G.R.).

[3] G.R., i, ed. W. Stubbs, p. 213.

[4] *Gesta Pontificum Anglorum* (henceforward cited as G.P.), ed. N. E. S. A.
Hamilton, p. 293.

[5] G.P., p. 299.   [6] G.P., p. 378.   [7] G.P., p. 179.

donshire,[1] presumably when he was visiting the fenland monasteries, Thorney, where he admired the beauty of the site, and where he saw a charter of immunity for that abbey,[2] and Crowland, where he received information from its prior.[3] He probably journeyed to the north, for he describes the desolation of York, resulting from the Conqueror's harrying (adding that the dialect of Northumbria, and especially of York, is unintelligible to 'us southerners');[4] and he speaks of an inscription in a *triclinium* at Carlisle.[5] He is unlikely to have failed to visit Durham, if he went from York to Carlisle. He speaks with admiration of the stained glass at Rochester;[6] he had met Archbishop Anselm,[7] and he had heard a monk of Christ Church, Canterbury, relate a miracle of St Dunstan.[8] Presumably it was at Winchester that he saw a blind man healed by the merits of St Swithin;[9] in any case he is unlikely to have been unfamiliar with this place.[10] It is important for our study that he visited Worcester, where he learnt various matters about St Wulfstan from Nicholas, who was prior about 1113 to 1124.[11] We have no right to assume that he had not visited other places even if he does not say or imply this in his work. He would naturally know the churches not far from Malmesbury, especially his own diocesan see of Salisbury. He would hardly have confined himself on his visit to the eastern counties to Thorney and Crowland; his interest in St Ive is likely to have been aroused at Ramsey, and he probably went to some at least of the abbeys of Peterborough, Ely and Bury St Edmunds. When he was as near to Abingdon as Oxford, he would surely not fail to pay it a visit.

When one examines the sources he used for his historical writings, one sees that he had access to a large number of works and documents: among others, we may mention a version of the

---

[1] G.P., p. 320.　　　[2] G.P., pp. 326 f.　　　[3] G.P., p. 322.
[4] G.P., pp. 208 f.　　　[5] G.P., p. 208.　　　[6] G.P., p. 138.
[7] G.P., p. 121.　　　[8] G.P., p. 31.　　　[9] G.P., p. 168.
[10] Eadwulf, abbot of Malmesbury, 1109–18, had been a monk at Winchester.
[11] See *The Vita Wulfstani of William of Malmesbury*, ed. R. R. Darlington, p. ix. William's work is mainly based on a lost vernacular *Life of Wulfstan* by the Worcester monk Coleman, but he mentions Nicholas as his authority in Book III, cc. 9, 10, 13 and 17.

Anglo-Saxon Chronicle of the E type, that is, the type which was at Canterbury at any rate as late as the end of the eleventh century, when the compiler of F used it, and probably later.[1] He knew Bede's *Ecclesiastical History*, Nennius's *Historia Brittonum*, Eddi's *Life of St Wilfrid*, as well as the tenth-century *Life* of this saint by Frithegod, and other hagiographical sources including the *Life of St Æthelwold*, by Wulfstan, precentor of Winchester Cathedral, along with a lost work by the same writer called *De Tonorum Harmonia*;[2] also the chronicle of Æthelweard, some letters of Boniface and of Alcuin, the works of Aldhelm, and a number of minor records such as the letter of Radbod to King Athelstan, found in a shrine at Milton Abbas, Dorset.[3] During the course of his work he came across a Latin poem on King Athelstan, for which he is the only authority.[4] He had access to the collection of letters and other documents preserved in Cotton Tiberius A.xv, probably a Canterbury collection, and it would be at Canterbury that he found the letter of Pope Formosus (in a form tampered with in the Canterbury interests) which survives, apart from his work, only in a Canterbury register.[5] His use of post-Conquest Latin writers, such as Osbern of Clare, Gotselin and the Canterbury historian Eadmer, is well known. It is obvious that William had made good use of his opportunities of examining and collecting sources during his travels, for it is improbable that he found many of these works in his own library. His collection need not have been exhaustive, however. He shows no sign of having used the other versions of the Anglo-Saxon Chronicle, such as the C version at Abingdon or the D version, probably by his time at Worcester, which place, indeed, seems to have had a collection of

---

[1] See *The Anglo-Saxon Chronicle: A Revised Translation*, by D. Whitelock, with D. C. Douglas and S. I. Tucker (London, 1961), pp. xvi and xx–xxi. The surviving E manuscript, Bodleian MS Laud. Misc. 636, is a copy made at Peterborough, probably after 1116.

[2] G.R., i, p. 167.

[3] G.P., pp. 399 f. On William's sources see also Stubbs's edition of G.R., i, pp. xx f.

[4] See D. Whitelock, *English Historical Documents c. 500–1042* (London, 1955), pp. 277–83.

[5] Ibid., pp. 820 f.

versions of the Chronicle for the use of the writer of the *Chronicon ex Chronicis* which goes under the name of Florence of Worcester. Whether or not William had seen a manuscript of Asser's *Life of King Alfred* is a matter which we shall discuss later.[1]

William was not only a historian: he had wide intellectual interests, in Latin literature, in philosophy, in canon law.[2] It is to be regretted that we have no early catalogue of the library of Malmesbury, where he was himself librarian, to tell us what he could find there. William speaks appreciatively of the zeal of Abbot Godfrey (1091–1109) in adding to and arranging the library, and he is also proud of his own efforts in this respect: 'I have come short of none of our ancestors: nay . . . I have far outstripped them all . . . I have collected much material for reading, emulating in this the prowess of the memorable man of whom I speak.'[3] Abbot Godfrey's additions would be Latin manuscripts, and we know something of what were William's interests because his handwriting has been identified in several manuscripts.[4] Of these, the most interesting in connection with the present paper is Trinity College, Cambridge, MS O.5.20 (1301), which includes the *De Divisione Naturae* of Johannes Scottus. Yet all we can discover of the pre-Conquest contents of this library is that it had a manuscript of the Old and New Testaments which was believed to have been purchased by St Aldhelm at Dover;[5] and that Dr Ker has been able to assign to Malmesbury a Prudentius, written about 1000. With less certainty a manuscript of the West Saxon Gospels, Cotton Otho C.i, part 1 is attributed

[1] See pp. 91–3 below.

[2] See the introductions by Stubbs to both volumes of his edition of G.R., and also the article by Hugh Farmer cited p. 78, n. 2, above.

[3] Stubbs's rendering in G.R., i, p. xvi of a passage in G.P., p. 431.

[4] See N. R. Ker, 'William of Malmesbury's Handwriting', *English Historical Review*, lix (1944), 371–6, and Hugh Farmer, op. cit. The manuscripts with this hand include, in addition to the work of Johannes Scottus, works of Bede on *Proverbs*, Jerome on *Ecclesiastes*, both Origen and Bede on the *Song of Songs*, Paul the Deacon's *Life of Gregory I*, a collection of patristical commentaries on the sapiential books, Martianus Capella, *De Nuptiis Philologiae et Mercurii*, works of Vegetius, Frontinus and Eutropius, and a collection of canon law, councils, papal constitutions and the sermons of St Leo.

[5] G.P., pp. 376–8.

to Malmesbury. If William knew this work, it would show that he did not automatically assume that any translation into Old English emanated from King Alfred.

We should not be justified in assuming that William had by him all the works which we know him to have used; he may in some cases have merely taken notes when he visited other places. Yet it is clear that we must pay careful heed to anything which he tells us about the works of King Alfred, seeing how much opportunity he had to look at manuscripts in many religious houses. When he tells us what we should not otherwise have known, we must consider whether his information comes from lost manuscripts.

Yet one cannot outrule the possibility of oral tradition. One must glance at what else he has to say about the king, and at the sources of this information. He had, as we have seen, an E-type version of the Anglo-Saxon Chronicle, but he also has details which come from Asser's *Life*, whether directly or not.[1] Thus he sends Alfred to Rome a second time, in 855,[2] and gives the account of how Alfred had to begin the fighting at Ashdown alone, because his brother would not leave divine service.[3] His account of Alfred's wife and family goes back to Asser, with some differences that may simply be error,[4] but William adds some later history, the marriage of one of the daughters (whom he calls wrongly Ethelswitha, instead of Ælfthryth) to Baldwin of Flanders, to whom she bore sons.[5] From Asser also come the accounts of the foundation of Athelney and Shaftesbury,[6] of Alfred's invention of a method of telling the time, of the division of his revenues,[7] and of the translation at the king's order of Gregory's *Dialogues* by Werferth, bishop of Worcester.[8] Since neither Asser nor the E

---

[1] See pp. 91–3 below.　　　[2] G.R., i, p. 109.　　　[3] G.R., i, p. 123.

[4] G.R., i, p. 129, with which compare Asser, cc. 29 and 75; William alters the order and adds an extra daughter, so that for Asser's Æthelgeofu he has two names, Ethelswitha and Elfgifu.

[5] G.R., i, p. 133.　　　[6] G.R., i, pp. 130 f.　　　[7] G.R., i, p. 133.

[8] G.R., i, p. 131. It is probable that this information comes from Asser, for though William may have seen a manuscript of the work, no extant manuscript mentions Werferth's authorship.

version of the Chronicle records Alfred's later campaigns, these are missing from William's work; but the E version did contain the entry at annal 883 which tells of Alfred's sending alms to India, which is not in the Parker manuscript, nor in Asser. William identifies the Sigehelm who took the alms thither with a bishop of Sherborne[1]—wrongly, for Sigehelm was undoubtedly a layman, and Sigehelm, bishop of Sherborne, attests charters from 925-32. Yet I do not believe that this identification was first made by William: he was told at Sherborne that this church still had in its possession some rare gems brought back from India by Bishop Sigehelm on this occasion. Neither William nor the monks at Sherborne had the apparatus for seeing how far out chronologically this identification was; but either they or William omitted in the list of Sherborne bishops three names which should come between Asser and Sigehelm, in order to bring Sigehelm into Alfred's reign. William's text of the Anglo-Saxon Chronicle, being of the E type, did not enter Asser's death (909 or 910 in other manuscripts); if it had, he might have had qualms about the identification of Sigehelm. This same error was known to the compiler of the *Chronicon ex Chronicis*, who enters the expedition to India in his annal for 883, declaring that the alms were taken by a bishop of Sherborne who had succeeded Asser.[2] But he gives his name as Suithelmus (a name unknown in the Sherborne lists), and he cannot be the source for William's statement. It was the monks of Sherborne who had a motive for the faulty identification, to bring honour on a bishop of their own, and I do not doubt that it was there that William picked it up.[3]

It was not only at Sherborne that William found legendary material. He tells the Durham story of how Alfred was visited by St Cuthbert when he was in distress at Athelney, and was promised victory by the saint.[4] This tale occurs in an anonymous work of the middle of the eleventh century, *Historia de Sancto Cuthberto*,[5]

[1] G.P., p. 177.   [2] Ed. B. Thorpe, I, pp. 98 f.
[3] See also p. 93 below.   [4] G.P., i, pp. 125 f.
[5] Ed. T. Arnold, *Symeonis Monachi Opera Omnia*, I, pp. 204 f.

and William may have seen this, or have heard the legend, if he visited Durham. If he knew the story which gives the credit for this victory to St Neot—and in his visit to the eastern monasteries[1] he may well have heard of it, for it is found already in the eleventh-century Old English *Life of St Neot*[2]—he may have rejected it. It is difficult to have two saints receiving the sole credit for the same victory, and, moreover, the *Life of St Neot* attributes to Alfred youthful passions and misdeeds in order to let St Neot have the honour of bringing about a reform. William might have tacitly rejected this slander. However, he did accept the Abingdon account that, after their abbey had been destroyed by the Danes, Alfred took for his own use its lands and what belonged to them, *malorum præventus consiliis*.[3] It was probably from Winchester that William received, with some scepticism (*si famæ creditur*), the story that Bishop Denewulf had been a swineherd whom Alfred met in the woods when expelled from his kingdom, had had educated and eventually raised to episcopal office.[4] It may have been a Winchester legend that Alfred bought the place for his burial at the price of a mancus of gold for a foot of land.[5]

William has other legends about Alfred which cannot be assigned to any source. He says that he entered the enemies' camp before the battle of Edington in the guise of a minstrel,[6] which was perhaps a floating tale which could be attached to any leader. William himself relates something similar about Olaf Sihtricson before the battle of Brunnanburh.[7] He says also that Alfred created such peace in his kingdom that no one dared to touch gold bracelets which he had ordered to be hung at crossroads.[8] This is a variant of popular ways of describing the peace created by a famous king. If it owes anything to Bede's account of the peace in

[1] See p. 79 above. St Ives is not far from St Neots.
[2] Ed. R. P. Wülcker in *Anglia*, iii, 102 ff. and by G. C. Gorham, *The History and Antiquities of Eynesbury and St Neots*, pp. 256–61.
[3] G.P., p. 191. [4] G.P., p. 162.
[5] G.R., i, p. 134. [6] G.R., i, p. 126.
[7] G.R., i, pp. 142 f. [8] G.R., i, p. 130.

Edwin's reign,[1] it is an inferior imitation, for the copper-cups which no one dared to remove from beside the springs were placed there for the use of travellers, whereas Alfred's gold bracelets are pointless. Without historical justification, William ascribes to Alfred the creation of hundreds and tithings.[2]

It is possible that William was the first to attach some of these tales to Alfred, yet there is no reason to doubt that in his day a considerable amount of oral tradition and legend was current about this king. William was no doubt speaking truly when he said that the places where Alfred had suffered ill-fortune and poverty were still shown by the natives.[3] He would probably have known that Alfred was credited with the authorship of books, even before he came across manuscripts of any of them; for the chronicle of Æthelweard, which William used, speaks of an unknown number, specifying only the *Boethius* by name, the author of the *Life of St Neot* knew that Alfred wrote many books, and the king's reputation for learning and wisdom continued into the Middle Ages.

When William begins the well-known passage[4] in which he enumerates the works of King Alfred with the flamboyant claim: *plurimam partem Romanæ bibliothecæ Anglorum auribus dedit*, he could be repeating a tradition, and have called the works he then proceeds to name 'the principal works' in the belief that his list was not necessarily complete. He lists the *Orosius*, Gregory's *Pastoralis*, Bede's *Gesta Anglorum*, Boethius's *De Consolatione Philosophiæ*, and 'a book of his own which in the native language is called *Encheridion*,[5] *id est manualem librum*'. He says he began to

---

[1] *Historia Ecclesiastica*, Book II, c. 16. Cf. also the praise of the reigns of William I and Henry I in Anglo-Saxon Chronicle, s.a. 1087, 1135; lines 462–5 of Book II of Wulfstan the precentor's poem on St Swithin (ed. A. Campbell, *Frithegodi Monachi Breuiloquium vitæ beati Wilfredi et Wulfstani Cantoris Narratio Metrica de Sancto Swithuno*), where part of Bede's account is used in praise of King Edgar; and lines 45–50 of the Middle English *Lay of Havelok the Dane*.

[2] G.R., i, p. 129.   [3] G.R., i, p. 129.   [4] G.R., i, p. 132.

[5] Some manuscripts of the second recension read *Handboc*, which fits the words *patria lingua*, whereas the phrase as given above is exactly that used by Asser.

translate the Psalter, but died before he had hardly finished the first part.

It is certain that he had seen a copy of Alfred's *Cura Pastoralis*, for he refers expressly to its prologue, quoting, inaccurately, some of its contents. When William says that Alfred's intention is that the English may read hastily what, if peace return, they will be able to read in Latin, one wonders if he has misunderstood Alfred's direction, after outlining his programme of education in English, that 'one may teach further in the Latin language those whom one wishes to teach further and to bring to higher [i.e. ecclesiastical] orders'. But misunderstanding would not account for William's claim that the preface ascribes the decay in learning to the fact that everyone was more concerned to save his life than to read books. One gets the impression that William is quoting carelessly, possibly from memory, adding a surmise of his own into the text. He is closer to this when he mentions the circulation to all principal sees; he interprets the *æstel* as a *pugillaris* (writing-tablet) but he says it had on it one mancus of gold, instead of fifty;[1] he names correctly Alfred's four helpers, without at this point referring to his own identification of *Johannes presbyter* with Johannes Scottus.

William appears to be referring to this same preface in another place. He believed that Johannes Scottus was the same person as a *sanctus sophista* Johannes, whose four-line epitaph, which was once on the left of the main altar in the church of Malmesbury, William quotes both in his *Gesta Regum* and his *Gesta Pontificum*.[2] This epitaph shows that this Johannes died as a martyr. As W. H. Stevenson suggests,[3] he is to be identified with *Iohannes se wisa*, who is named in the text known as the *Resting-Places of the English Saints*, which was drawn up in the late tenth century, as being buried at Malmesbury.[4] William identified this Johannes with

---

[1] This error suggests that the manuscript he used had the numeral *l* instead of *fiftegum* and that he misread it as 'one'; or William could have misread a note he had made on the passage.

[2] G.R., i, p. 132; G.P., p. 394.

[3] *Asser's Life of King Alfred*, pp. 335 f.

[4] F. Liebermann, *Die Heiligen Englands*, p. 17.

Johannes Scottus, and claimed that he came to England at Alfred's invitation and was placed at Malmesbury.[1] His authority for this he gives in a letter to his friend Peter, where he says: *cujus* [Alfred's] *munificentia illectus et magisterio ejus ut ex scriptis ejus intellexi sullimatus, Malmesberiæ resedit.*[2] The writings here referred to must be the preface to the *Cura Pastoralis*, for it is the only work of Alfred's with a reference to 'John my priest'—unless, of course, William found something in what he calls the Handbook, but if so, he would have been likely to say so. To account for the martyrdom,[3] William tells a tale of Johannes Scottus being murdered by his pupils, with their styles, a tale previously told of St Cassianus and found, among other places, in the entry for this saint in the Old English *Martyrology*.[4] We cannot know for certain that William was the first to tell this story of Johannes Scottus, about whose death there seem to be no known details; if it was already part of a legend about him, this would help to explain William's identification of him with the martyred *sophista* Johannes; but perhaps it is more likely that William, in his eagerness to believe that a saint buried in his house (and accorded honours only second to St Aldhelm)[5] was the philosopher whose work he so greatly admired,[6] told this story in order to account for the martyrdom mentioned in the epitaph. His belief in this identity prevented William from connecting the priest John in Alfred's preface with John the Old Saxon, whom he mentions as abbot of Athelney in a passage based on Asser.[7] We must leave it an open question whether he knew Asser's account of how this John was attacked and wounded by inmates of his monastery, but survived;[8] it is not a very similar tale to that told of the murder of Johannes Scottus,

---

[1] G.R., i, pp. 131 f.; G.P., p. 394.

[2] Printed by Stubbs in his edition of G.R., i, pp. cxlv f.

[3] W. H. Stevenson suggests that the *sophista* Johannes had been slain by the Danes.

[4] Ed. G. Herzfeld, p. 146 (13 August). It is in the martyrology attributed to Bede. The story occurs in Prudentius, *Peristephanon*, c. IX.

[5] G.P., p. 421.

[6] See p. 81 above, and the account of Johannes Scottus given G.P., pp. 392–4.

[7] G.R., i, p. 130.   [8] Asser, cc. 95–7.

but it could have reminded William of this tale. It is a coincidence, at least, to read of two scholars called John, both contemporaries, both set on by members of their own monastery.

When William includes Bede's *Ecclesiastical History* among the works translated by Alfred, he may be repeating a tradition; Ælfric also regarded this as Alfred's work.[1] Yet it is highly probable that William had seen at least one manuscript of a work fairly widely known.[2] If on a visit to Worcester he had seen their manuscript, now in the Cambridge University Library, which contains after Bede's preface a West Saxon genealogy and regnal list, ending with Alfred,[3] any previous conviction he may have had concerning Alfred's authorship would have been reinforced.[4]

William is the first person to assign to Alfred the translation of Orosius. He may have seen the manuscript, since lost, which was at Glastonbury in the Middle Ages,[5] for he stayed a considerable time there. The two extant manuscripts (which come from Winchester and Abingdon)[6] have no preface, nor anything to connect them with Alfred beyond the statement that the account of Ohthere's voyages which is inserted into Orosius's geographical

[1] *Catholic Homilies*, ed. B. Thorpe, II, 116 ff.

[2] There are five extant manuscripts: Cotton Otho B.xi (mainly burnt, but known from a transcript), which was written at Winchester (C); Tanner 10 (T), from Thorney; Corpus Christi College, Cambridge, MS 41 (B), one of Leofric's gifts to Exeter; Corpus Christi College, Oxford, MS 279, part ii (O), of unknown provenance; and Cambridge University Library, MS Kk.3.18 (Ca), from Worcester. The scheme of transmission implies lost manuscripts. Medieval catalogues mention copies at Canterbury, Durham and Burton-on-Trent. The work was available at either Canterbury or London about 900, when extracts were copied into Domitian ix.

[3] This could have been in O, the exemplar of Ca, but O has lost all the beginning section of the work. It is not in B or C, and was not in T (defective at the beginning), unless we assume that B, closely linked with T, and C, which belongs to the other branch, omitted it independently.

[4] On the question of authorship of this translation, which is not now usually thought to be by Alfred, see D. Whitelock, 'The Old English Bede', *Proc. Brit. Acad.*, xlviii (1962).

[5] *Johannes Glastoniensis Chronica*, ed. T. Hearne, p. 434.

[6] British Museum, Additional MS 47967 (Lauderdale or Tollemache) and Cotton Tiberius B.i.

chapter was given to 'his lord King Alfred'. This could have seemed to William, as it has to some later scholars, sufficient evidence for Alfred's authorship.[1] The fact that William considered Alfred's translation of the Psalter to be incomplete, suggests that it was not because of a vague tradition that he thought Alfred translated the psalms, but that he had seen a prose translation of the first of the three divisions into fifty psalms into which the Psalter was often divided, similar to that which survives in the manuscript of the Paris Psalter.[2] This contains no indication whatever of authorship, but the manuscript seen by William may have had something, rubric or preface, which made him think it Alfred's; there is no other instance of his claiming a work as by Alfred without evidence of any kind.[3]

He would have known that Alfred translated Boethius's *De Consolatione Philosophiæ* from the statement of Æthelweard, whose chronicle he knew. It is not William's attribution to Alfred which interests us, for the work is clearly shown to be his by its preface; it is some additional information which he gives, which is found nowhere else. In two places[4] he says that Asser explained the sense of the work to the king in simpler terms. This is the more interesting since there is no doubt that Alfred did use a Latin commentary on Boethius's work. But this, which was clearly related to one now normally ascribed to Remigius of Auxerre, can hardly be described as an explanation in simpler terms.[5] William could have seen a manuscript of the Latin text of the *De Consolatione Philosophiæ* with some glosses, for such were not uncommon; yet he would

---

[1] The question of authorship is discussed by D. Whitelock, 'The Prose of Alfred's Reign', in *Continuations and Beginnings: Studies in Old English Literature*, ed. E. G. Stanley (London, 1966), pp. 89–93.

[2] Bibliothèque Nationale, MS fonds latin 8824. A version of this prose translation was available at Winchester to the writer of Vitellius E.xviii in the eleventh century.

[3] On the question of Alfred's authorship see Whitelock, 'The Prose of Alfred's Reign', pp. 94 f., and works there cited.

[4] G.R., i, p. 131; G.P., p. 177.

[5] On the commentaries to the *De Consolatione Philosophiæ*, see D. Whitelock, 'The Prose of Alfred's Reign', pp. 82 f., and the fuller discussion by K. Otten, *König Alfreds Boethius* (Tübingen, 1964).

hardly have made the factual claim which he does, unless it contained something to connect it with Asser, or, at least, with Alfred; if he knew the part of the *Life of King Alfred* in which Asser describes how he and the king read works together, he might have concluded that a glossed text had been produced by Asser for the king's use. It is also possible that he saw a note to this effect in some lost manuscript of the Old English work.[1] Yet he may merely be repeating a tradition, and, if so, the place where he learnt it would surely be Sherborne, where, as we have seen, he picked up information redounding to the honour of another bishop of that see.[2] We may wonder why, in that case, he does not also mention that Asser wrote a *Life* of the king, but a possible explanation of this omission is given below.[3]

William certainly had a copy of a book which he thought was the Handbook, i.e. the *Enchiridion* described by Asser. From it he corrects the statement that Aldhelm's father was brother of King Ine;[4] this suggests that the book included a West Saxon royal genealogy and regnal list, and it may be the same book known at Worcester as the *Dicta* of King Alfred,[5] for this is mentioned as having a list of West Saxon kings. William's 'Handbook' also supplied information about St Aldhelm, about his composition of native poetry, and his use of this art to attract an audience when wishing to instruct them.[6] And the *Dicta* known at Worcester also contained an anecdote of a saint, this time Jerome, who was slighted by Pope Siricius and avenged long after by Pope Gregory's order that no lights should be burnt at Siricius's tomb.[7] I have

---

[1] Apart from a fragment, only two manuscripts survive, the mid-tenth-century Cotton MS Otho A.vi, with the verse rendering of the *Metres* and the early-twelfth-century Bodley MS 180, entirely in prose. Their provenance is unknown. A manuscript of this work was given by Leofric to Exeter (A. J. Robertson, *Anglo-Saxon Charters*, p. 228), and there was one at Canterbury in the Middle Ages.

[2] See p. 83 above.　　　　[3] See p. 93 below.　　　　[4] G.P., p. 332.

[5] *Florentii Wigorniensis Monachi Chronicon ex Chronicis*, ed. B. Thorpe, I, p. 272.

[6] G.P., p. 336.

[7] This is added from *Angulsaxonum regis Ælfredi veredictis dictis* in the margins of Cambridge University Library MS Kk.4.6, a Worcester manuscript containing a lot of material used by William of Malmesbury.

suggested elsewhere[1] that if William knew the passage in which Asser describes the *Enchiridion* as a collection of *flosculos*, culled from various masters, and then came across a manuscript which included (perhaps as the first item) the Old English work which we call the *Soliloquies of St Augustine*, he might have been misled by its preface, which describes the selecting of extracts from the works of various Fathers, and by its being called *þa blostman* at the end of Book I and the beginning and end of Book II, into believing that he had found the *flosculos* of the *Enchiridion*. Similarly, if the same manuscript was available to the Worcester writers, they may have called it the *Dicta* of King Alfred because he himself calls this work *þa cwidas* at the beginning and end of Book III. The material which William uses from what he thinks is the Handbook, and that used at Worcester from the *Dicta*, would come from other sections of the manuscript. One should note that a West Saxon genealogy, and anecdotes about St Aldhelm, are not what Asser's description would have led us to expect in the *Enchiridion*; nor does it seem to me very probable that a book compiled only for Alfred's private use would be available. Certainty is not possible, but unless the *Soliloquies* were in what William took to be the Handbook, he missed this work altogether.

The argument that William may have wrongly identified a manuscript containing the *Soliloquies* with the *Enchiridion* described by Asser depends on the assumption that he knew this part of Asser's *Life*. More than once in this paper the possibility that William knew this work has been mentioned, and it is now time to consider it more fully. W. H. Stevenson[2] thought that all the parts in William's works which go back to Asser could have been taken from Florence of Worcester. When Stevenson was writing, it was believed that the *Chronicon ex Chronicis* was the work of Florence, who died in 1118, and that the rest of the work was a continuation by his fellow-monk John. But Professor Darlington has since then produced strong arguments for assigning the whole *Chronicon* up to 1140 to John,[3] in which case it cannot have been

---

[1] 'The Prose of Alfred's Reign', pp. 71–3.
[2] Asser's *Life of King Alfred*, pp. lx–lxiii.
[3] *The Vita Wulfstani of William of Malmesbury*, pp. xvi–xviii.

available to William in 1125. Professor Darlington also, in agreement with a view expressed by Stubbs,[1] rejects the idea that William was dependent on the *Chronicon* in other places where there are agreements between his work and that of the Worcester historians. If we accept his view on William's independence, we require another explanation of the agreement between him and the *Chronicon* in their selection from the *Life*.[2] Both authors may be indebted to an abridged version of the *Life*, made by someone about to write a history, and hence excluding matter not directly germane to his purpose. It could have been part of the preparations for the *Chronicon* and have been seen by William at Worcester, where, as Professor Darlington says: 'Not improbably William had seen John at work on the preliminary matter.'[3] Such an abridgement could have included the account of the *Enchiridion*, which was not used by the author of the *Chronicon*, who was less interested than was William in Alfred's literary achievements. Stevenson had to explain William's knowledge of the *Enchiridion* as obtained solely from a manuscript of it, and to regard William's use of the exact words of Asser: *Enchiridion . . . id est manualem librum*[4] as a not impossible coincidence.

Yet, even if William did avail himself of a ready-made selection, it does not follow that he had no acquaintance with the complete *Life*. His knowledge of the *Enchiridion* could have come from this, and there is a possibility, though by no means a certainty, that he knew how Asser had read books with the king,[5] and knew the tale of the attack on John, abbot of Athelney.[6] We should not lay great stress on his failure to mention the source of his information; he does not always name his authorities. What at first sight seems more extraordinary, if he knew the whole *Life*, is that he does not mention that Asser was the author of a *Life* of King Alfred when he tells us how he helped Alfred with the *Boethius*, especially in

---

[1] G.R., ii, pp. cxxviii–cccxxxi.

[2] There is no question of the use of William's work by the *Chronicon* in regard to the use of Asser, for the former gives the incidents in his own words, and the latter quotes Asser literally, and has a great deal which is omitted by William.

[3] Op. cit., p. xviii, n. 2. [4] See p. 85, n. 5, above.
[5] See p. 90 above. [6] See p. 87 above.

the rather fuller reference when in the *Gesta Pontificum* he speaks about the bishops of Sherborne. But, as we have already seen,[1] what William had learnt at Sherborne had convinced him that a bishop who follows Asser in the episcopal lists had taken alms of King Alfred to India in 883. Now Asser's *Life of Alfred* deals with events later than 883, and in *c.* 91 Asser says he is writing in the forty-fifth year of King Alfred. A historian of William's acuteness could not fail to see that this was incompatible with the journey of his successor to India in 883.[2] Since he would regard the gems alleged to have been brought back from this expedition as evidence for the accuracy of the information, he would not be able to accept an attribution of the *Life* to Asser. William's silence is no certain proof that he was unaware of the work, and it should not be used to shed doubt on the authenticity of the *Life*. We cannot prove beyond doubt that he did know the complete work; however, we may note that his dealings with Worcester would give him an easy opportunity to see the manuscript of the *Life* which lies behind the *Chronicon*.[3]

---

[1] See p. 83 above.

[2] Though William did not use a version of the Anglo-Saxon Chronicle which recorded Asser's death in 910, the author of the *Chronicon* did; his omission of this entry must have been deliberate, to avoid clashing with his annal for 883, with its wording *Assero Scireburnensi episcopo defuncto.*

[3] This manuscript shared errors with the Cotton MS Otho A.xii, which survived until 1731 and is the basis of all editions. Stevenson (p. xlvii) thinks the Worcester historian used the Cotton MS. There was also a rather better manuscript, used in the *Historia Regum* attributed to Symeon of Durham, on which see P. Hunter Blair, 'Some Observations on the *Historia Regum* attributed to Symeon of Durham', *Celt and Saxon*, ed. N. K. Chadwick (Cambridge, 1963), pp. 99–102. Another manuscript was used by the *Annals of St Neots*, and was probably the one from which entries were made at Bury St Edmunds into Bodley MS 297 of the *Chronicon ex Chronicis*, on which see Stevenson, p. 101. Like the Durham manuscript, it avoided an error common to Cotton Otho A.xii and the *Chronicon*. See also D. Whitelock, *The Genuine Asser* (The Stenton Lecture 1967), pp. 17–20.

6

Old English '-calla', 'ceallian'

E. G. STANLEY

THE WORD *hildecalla* (*Exodus* 252) has received considerable attention, usually together with *ceallian* of line 91 of *The Battle of Maldon*:

ongan ceallian þa   ofer cald wæter.

That *hildecalla* is written -*calla*, and not *-*cealla*, could be explained either on the grounds that this hapax legomenon is part of the Old English poetic vocabulary with its probably conscious retention of Anglian features, or on the grounds that the second syllable of a compound does not bear the stress, or on the grounds that both these factors are working together. It is clear, therefore, that initial /k/ in itself 'is no test of loan' from Scandinavian.[1] Hofmann, however, can see no compelling reason for regarding the word *hildecalla* as a native word; and in support of the Scandinavian

---

[1] Thus, correctly, E. Björkman, 'Scandinavian Loan-Words in Middle English', Part II, *Studien zur englischen Philologie*, XI (1902), p. 214; though Björkman was aware of the possibility that in late Old English texts (such as the English texts in the lost manuscript of *The Battle of Maldon*, MS Cotton Otho A.xii, may be assumed to have been) superficial West-Saxonization might lead to *al*+consonant being written *eal*+consonant even after *c*, he makes no attempt to distinguish West-Saxonization by a West Saxon translating into his own language from West-Saxonization by an Anglian turning out a piece of acceptable late old English *Schriftsprache*. The form -*calla* in Book I of MS Junius 11 could well be the conscious retention of a poetic Anglianism, much like the form *cald* common in verse; or it could be the result of developments in the reduced stress of the second element of a compound. On the other hand, it could be the result of an Anglian speaker's reluctance to extend the letter sequence *eal* to syllables beginning with *c*, where *ceal*- would be read /tʃal/; this explanation is unlikely in the context of Book I of MS Junius 11. Similarly, a West Saxon turning **ceallian* into his dialect (if we may assume that it did not exist in his dialect) would be less likely to jib at *ceallian* than an Anglian speaker.

origin of the word he alleges, 'Nordischer Einfluss lässt sich auch sonst für die Exodus vermuten'.[1] Unfortunately he does not reveal on what he bases his surmise that *Exodus* shows other signs of Norse influence. The dating of Old English verse is a notoriously difficult business; *Exodus* has perhaps been accepted too readily, still under the influence to some extent of modified Cædmonian theories,[2] as an early poem. Nevertheless, we seem to have no surer sign of Norse influence than is provided by *hildecalla*, and, though it might not be wise to date the poem as early, it would certainly be folly to date it as late on the basis of the Norse element in it. We know that native words which do not occur in prose survived in verse; not a few of these words come only once. *Exodus* is a text in which not a few words are the only occurrences in the language; no reason has been adduced by Hofmann that might make one depart from the accepted view that *hildecalla* is one of these words, and is, like the rest of them, of native origin.

If this is the correct view of *hildecalla*, there is nothing impossible about the assumption that *ceallian* is of native origin also.[3] The Middle English distribution of the word *calle* does not support the view that ME *calle* is of Scandinavian origin, though clearly, if *ceallian* and **callian* were native words rare in Old English, the existence of a cognate in Norse (cf. OIcel *kalla*), close in form to the Anglian **callian* and in common use, is sure to have had an influence on the revival in late Old English and later English of **callian*. The absence of *calle* in southern Middle English texts (e.g. the Kentish Sermons, *Ayenbite of Inwyt*, *The Owl and the Nightingale*, *Poema Morale*) might seem to lend support to the theory of Scandinavian origin; but the word does not come in

---

[1] 'Nordisch-englische Lehnbeziehungen der Wikingerzeit', *Bibliotheca Arnamagnæana*, XIV (1955), §291. Cf. R. Cleasby and G. Vigfusson, *An Icelandic-English Dictionary*, 1874 (and 1957), s.v. *kalla*. Scandinavian influence on *The Battle of Maldon* is discussed in detail (not always convincingly) by Hofmann, pp. 193–9; see also Dame Bertha S. Philpotts, *MLR*, xxiv (1929), 172–90.

[2] See, for example, E. B. Irving's edition, *Yale Studies in English*, CXXII (1953), pp. 27 f.

[3] See E. V. Gordon, *The Battle of Maldon* (1937), p. 49; cf. A. Campbell, *Old English Grammar*, p. 221 n. 3.

the *Ormulum*, where, if in Orm's time *callen* had been a common
loan-word, one might have expected the alliterative phrase *clepe and
calle* so common in many Middle English dialects; and Laʒa-
mon does not use the word either. The word is rare in the vocabulary of the *Ancrene Wisse* and MS Bodley 34, though it comes, for
example, in *St Marharete* (once only?) and in *The Wooing of
Our Lord*. On the other hand it comes in the lyric *Moder milde flur
of alle* written in a Gloucestershire manuscript probably by a
Gloucestershire man;[1] the word comes several times in MS Harley
2253, probably a Herefordshire manuscript,[2] indeed, the only time
the word comes in *King Horn* is in the version contained in this
manuscript (line 907), so that it seems likely to have been in use in
Herefordshire, and that is supported by William Herebert's use of
the word.[3] The word is specially common, among early texts, in
Genesis and Exodus and in the *Bestiary*, but does not occur at all in
Vices and Virtues; and the word is very common indeed in northern
texts, especially *Cursor Mundi*, in *Havelok*, and Robert of Brunne.
We may safely assume the northern word to have been in such
common use because of the existence of the Scandinavian word;
it could well be a straightforward loan-word. The same could be
true of the East Midlands, though it is difficult to account for
Orm's failure to use the word. It is difficult to understand the
distribution in the rest of the Midlands. There could have been a
word of native origin in Herefordshire and Gloucestershire: on the
other hand, Scandinavian loan-words are not so rare in this area
for Norse derivation to be ruled out in this case.

There is some evidence for the existence of a Middle English
word *callen* in the area of Essex, Middlesex, London, an area where
we may assume *The Battle of Maldon* to have been written (though

---

[1] Carleton Brown, *English Lyrics of the Thirteenth Century*, no. 61, and cf.
p. xxvii; cf. also N. R. Ker, *Medieval Libraries of Great Britain* (1964), p. 112, on
the provenance (Lanthony, near Gloucester) of MS Corpus Christi College, Oxford, 59.

[2] See Theo Stemmler, *Die englischen Liebesgedichte des MS. Harley 2253* (1962),
pp. 26–9; N. R. Ker, *Facsimile of British Museum MS. Harley 2253*, EETS 255
(1965), pp. xxii f.

[3] e.g. Carleton Brown, *Religious Lyrics of the Fourteenth Century*, 17.6, 21.8.

it is possible that Ely might have been the place of composition).[1] It may be a coincidence, but it is worth recording that in this area the word is used in a way described by G. V. Smithers as 'probably peculiar to the K[yng] A[lisaunder] group'.

> Ac Tholomeu, tofore hem alle,
> Loude on heiȝ he gan hem calle.
>
> (*Kyng Alisaunder*, 3647 f.[2])

> Þe king he fond in his halle.
> On þis maner he gan him calle.
>
> (*Arthour and Merlin*, 1373 f.)

> Þer he was among hem alle,
> Þis wise he gan hem calle.
>
> (Ibid., 2785 f.)

Smithers notes 'not merely the unusual syntax of *calle* . . . but also the association with *gan*. Here *calle* refers to the shouting of taunts in battle'.[3]

The line in *The Battle of Maldon* does not make the same syntactical use of *ceallian*; but the sense is the same, and the association with *ongan* is identical with that using ME *gan*.[4] This is not proof that *ceallian* is a word of native origin. However, it is sure that the auxiliary use of *gin* in Middle English is not due to Norse influence: we seem to be dealing with a set phrase *he gan* (. . .) *calle* derived from OE *ongan ceallian*, for which mixed origin is possible but not likely.

OE *ceallian* seems to have had the specialized sense found only in descriptions of battles—cf. the meaning of *hildecalla*. We can

---

[1] See E. V. Gordon, op. cit., pp. 38–40. Jordan, *Mittelenglische Grammatik*, p. 10, lists texts which he thinks are from Essex or Middlesex (London in some cases); the reason for this ascription varies from text to text; in some cases it is the evidence of rhymes, in others of the whole text (or of one manuscript of a text). There are good reasons for not following him in several of his ascriptions. For a fuller discussion see G. V. Smithers, *King Alisaunder*, ii, EETS 237 (1957), pp. 40 ff. and p. 58 on the Norse element.

[2] See Smithers, op. cit., p. 113.

[3] *MED*, s.v. *callen* 1.(a), shows that similar locutions may have existed in other parts of the country; cf. *Sir Gawain and the Green Knight*, 2212.

[4] See T. Mustanoja, *A Middle English Syntax*, Part I (1960), pp. 610 ff.

ignore the fact that *Vices and Virtues* does not contain a Middle English form of the word: as in the *Ormulum*, *clepien* (Orm's *clepenn*) is used for Modern English 'to call', and there is no more occasion for using the battle word derived from *ceallian* in *Vices and Virtues*, than in the *Ormulum*. The form of OE *ceallian* is what we should expect for Essex;[1] we should have to explain **callian*, if that form had been in the text of *The Battle of Maldon*, as a sign that the word was part of the Anglian poetic vocabulary. The spelling *ceallian*, perhaps supported by the distribution of ME *he gan* (. . .) *calle*, makes that less likely, in spite of the evidence of the spelling of *hildecalle* (which could in any case be explained either as the result of reduced stress or as part of the Anglian element in the poetic material). The spellings of *The Battle of Maldon* are characteristic late West Saxon, with *baldlice* (*-licost*), *cald*, *waldend* but *wealdan* and *geweald*.[2] The form *gealgean* for *ealgean*[3] is a south-eastern characteristic, probably not Essex—though the evidence of late Old English sporadic forms of this kind is insufficient for us to be sure that such forms are impossible in Essex.[4] As E. V. Gordon[5] has pointed out, the form *gofol* for *gafol* is characteristic of Essex and the East Midlands in Middle English, but also Kent in Old English. The *on* in *formoni* (*pace* Gordon, p. 38) is not a satisfactory distinguishing mark of any late Old English dialect;[6] and altogether there seems nothing in the language of the text to allow us to assume for it an area of origin other than Essex and the

[1] See E. Ekwall, 'Contributions to the History of Old English Dialects', *Lunds Universitets Årsskrift*, N. F. Avd. 1, vol. xii, no. 6 (1917), pp. 15, 31, and H. Hallqvist, *Studies in Old English Fractured 'ea'* (1948), pp. 67, 115 f., for such Essex place-names as *Chalvedon* (<OE *cealfa-dūn*).

[2] I discuss the distribution of *eal*+consonant especially after *w* in a forthcoming study.

[3] See E. V. Gordon, op. cit., p. 46.

[4] See W. Heuser, *Altlondon*, 1914, p. 35, for an etymology of *Yeldham* (Essex) <OE **eald ham*, doubted by Ekwall (op. cit., p. 15) and rejected by A. H. Smith, *English Place-Name Elements*, vol. i, English Place-Name Society, xxv (1956), p. 201.

[5] Op. cit., p. 47.

[6] See Luick, *Historische Grammatik der englischen Sprache*, §§112 Anm., 367 Anm. 2.

south-east.[1] And it looks as if *ceallian*, a lexical survivor from the heroic age, was indigenous in south-east England in Byrhtnoth's day.

[1] The association of the lost manuscript, MS Cotton Otho A.xii, with Worcester, stressed by Gordon, op. cit., pp. 33, 39 f., need not extend to the part containing *The Battle of Maldon*; cf. N. R. Ker, *Catalogue of Manuscripts Containing Anglo-Saxon*, pp. 221 f.

7

Comedy of Character in the Icelandic Family Sagas

R. M. WILSON

SINCE IDEAS of what constitutes humour may vary from age to age, we are often left uncertain whether what seems to us comic in the literature of a particular period was so regarded by its contemporaries. The stock jokes of the time are perhaps recognizable by their recurrence, but apart from these we may often see humour where none was intended, or fail to notice it when it is there, especially if it involves word-play or puns in a language imperfectly known to us, as the language of an earlier age must always be. We can be fairly certain that some of the episodes and characters in the family sagas were intended to be humorous, but it is unlikely that we can appreciate fully all the lighter touches that are present in them. Often the only evidence available consists in the reactions of the characters themselves; from these we can sometimes see what kinds of things provoked laughter, but if there is no audience there will be no reaction which can be used as evidence. Not that laughter by itself necessarily implies the existence of comedy; in times of danger both Víga-Glúmr and his son Vigfúss are subject to a kind of nervous hysteria which results in laughter, but there is no indication that the events in question were regarded by anyone as being at all humorous.

The family sagas contain perhaps rather more comedy than might have been expected from their subjects. But, apart from *Bandamanna saga*, humour is always a subsidiary factor, appearing sporadically and contributing only in a very general way to the effect of the saga as a whole. Moreover, it is almost always a grim humour, based on facts which in themselves are unpleasant.

Friendly laughter, such as that found among Kjartan's companions in *Laxdæla saga*, or friendly joking, as in Egill Skallagrímsson's remarks on hearing that Einarr had visited Borg in Egill's absence,[1] are rare, and even then the humour in both cases is based on the unpleasant facts of mutilation and death. The typical humour of the family sagas is perhaps best illustrated by the appearance of what may be called the heroic jest, a humorous or deprecating remark by someone in deadly danger or at the point of death. The best-known example comes from *Njáls saga*, when Thorgrímr is sent forward by the attackers to find out whether Gunnarr is at home. As he climbs over the roof of the house Gunnarr thrusts at him with his halberd, whereupon he returns to his companions:

Gizurr leit við honum ok mælti: 'Hvárt er Gunnarr heima?'
Þorgrímr svarar: 'Vitið þér þat, en hitt vissa ek, at atgeirr hans var heima.'
Síðan fell hann niðr dauðr. (I.S., xi, p. 172.)

Gizurr looked at him and said: 'Well, is Gunnarr at home?'
Thorgrímr answered: 'Find that out for yourselves. All I know is that his halberd is.'
Then he fell down dead.

However, this is only one of a number of such scenes. In *Grettis saga*:

Í því bili snaraði Þorbjörn fram fyrir dyrrnar ok lagði tveim höndum til Atla með spjótinu á honum miðjum, svá at stóð í gegnum hann.
Atli mælti við, er hann fekk lagit: 'Þau tíðkast nú in breiðu spjótin,' segir hann.
Síðan fell hann fram á þresköldinn. Þá kómu fram konur, er í stofunni höfðu verit. Þær sá, at Atli var dauðr. (I.S., vi, p. 144.)

Just then Thorbjörn stepped quickly in front of the door, and with both hands thrust his spear into Atli's middle, so that it pierced him through.

---

[1] *Íslendinga Sögur*, ed. Guthni Jónsson (Reykjavík, 1946-9), iv, pp. 151-2; ii, pp. 282-3. Unless otherwise stated, all references are to this edition of the family sagas.

Atli said, when he received the wound: 'These broad-bladed spears are all the fashion nowadays.'
Then he fell forward on to the threshold. The women who were inside the house came out, and they saw that Atli was dead.

Again, with the death of Helgi Droplaugarson:

Ok í því hjó Hjarrandi til Helga, en hann brá við skildinum, ok hljóp af sverðit í andlit honum ok kom á tanngarðinn ok af vörrina neðri.
Þá mælti Helgi: 'Aldri var ek fagrleitr, en lítit hefir þú um bætt.'
(I.S., x, p. 148.)

With this Hjarrandi cut at Helgi who raised his shield so that the sword glanced off it into his face and against his lower teeth, cutting off his bottom lip.
Then said Helgi: 'I never was very handsome, and you have certainly not improved my looks now.'

In *Vatnsdæla saga* Hrolleifr throws a spear which transfixes Ingimundr:

Ok er hann fekk lagit, reið hann aftr at bakkanum ok mælti: 'Þú sveinn, fylg mér heim.'
Hann hitti eigi sonu sína, ok er þeir kómu heim, var mjök liðit á aftaninn.
Ok er Ingimundr skyldi af baki fara, þá mælti hann: 'Stirðr em ek nú, ok verðum vér lausir á fótum inir gömlu menninir.'
Ok er sveinninn tók við honum, þá þaut í sárinu. Sá sveinninn þá, at spjótit stóð í gegnum hann. (I.S., vii, p. 56.)

When he received the wound he rode back to the bank and spoke: 'You, boy, come home with me.'
He didn't meet his sons, and when he and the boy arrived home it was well on to evening.
When Ingimundr came to dismount, then he said: 'I am feeling stiff now, and we get very bad on our feet, we old men.'
As the boy helped him, there was a sucking noise from the wound, and the boy saw that there was a spear through him.

A more developed example of the same kind of thing comes from *Njáls saga*:

Kolskeggr brást við fast ok óð at honum ok hjó með saxinu á lærit ok undan fótinn ok mælti: 'Hvárt nam þik eða eigi?' 'Þess galt ek nú', segir Kolr, 'er ek var berskjaldaðr',—ok stóð nökkura stund á hinn fótinn ok leit á stúfinn. Kolskeggr mælti: 'Eigi þarft þú at líta á, jafnt er sem þér sýnist, af er fótrinn.' Kolr fell þá dauðr niðr. (I.S., xi, p. 146.)

Kolskeggr turned fiercely and rushed at him [i.e. Kolr]; he struck him on the thigh with his sword and took the leg off. Kolskeggr said: 'Well, did I hit you or not?' 'I'm paying now', said Kolr, 'for not covering myself with my shield', and he stood for a time looking at the stump. 'You don't need to look! It's just as you thought, the foot is off', said Kolskeggr. Then Kolr fell down dead.

No doubt the heroic jest became a convention, and one that may perhaps be satirized in *Bandamanna saga* in the last words of Hermundr:

... ok er hann kemr, þá mátti Hermundr ekki mæla, ok var prestr þar hjá honum. Ok einn tíma, er prestr lýtr at honum, þá lætr í vörrunum; 'Tvau hundruð í gili, tvau hundruð í gili'; ok síðan andask hann.

... and when [the priest] came, then Hermundr could not speak, and the priest remained with him. On one occasion when the priest bent over him, then he murmured with his lips: 'Two hundred in the gully, two hundred in the gully', and afterwards he died. (This version of the saga from *Íslenzk Fornrit*, ed. Guthni Jónsson (Reykjavík, 1936), vii, p. 361.)

But the very fact that such a convention could develop in the family sagas is significant of the usual type of humour to be found in them. At other times it makes its capital out of humiliation, suffering, illness, or old age. In *Eyrbyggja saga* the idea that Thórarinn has himself accidentally cut off his wife's hand is treated as a joke, though admittedly by his enemies (I.S., iii, p. 32); illness is a matter for laughter in *Thorsteins saga hvíta* (I.S., x, p. 5) and in *Víga-Glúms saga* (I.S., viii, p. 7); while even so great a man as

103

Egill Skallagrímsson discovers that all his fame does not save him from jokes aimed at the infirmities of age (I.S., ii, pp. 306 ff.). The use of such subjects for comedy no doubt owes something to a different sense of humour in a different age and a rougher environment, and perhaps also to the fact that a more gentle humour might have weakened the heroic atmosphere which the authors of the family sagas were trying to convey. The purely comic characters in the family sagas are almost invariably the minor ones. They usually take part only in a single brief episode, but may occasionally appear more frequently and even have some influence on the plot. In the main they are used to satirize the particular vices which are especially despised in a heroic society such as that represented in the family sagas; cowardice, avarice, boasting, and stupidity. Such characters are often serfs, and a good example of the type is Thórthr inn huglausi in *Gísla saga*. Gísli, suspecting an ambush by his enemies, persuades Thórthr to exchange cloaks with him:

Þá mælti Gísli: 'Ef svá berr til, at nökkurir menn kalla á þik, þá skaltu þess mest gæta at svara aldrigi, en ef nökkurir menn vilja þér mein gera, þá haltu til skógarins.'
En þat var mjök jafnfært um vit ok hugrekki, því at hvártki var neitt til. Gísli leiðir nú eykina. Þórðr var mikill maðr vexti, ok bar hann hátt í sleðanum. Hrósaði hann sér ok heldr ok þóttist vegliga búinn. (I.S., v. p. 46.)

Then Gísli said: 'If it should happen that anyone calls to you, you must be careful not to answer, and if anyone tries to harm you, then run off to the woods.'
The fellow had as much sense as he had spirit, since he had nothing of either. Gísli now leads the oxen. Thórthr was a big man, and he sat high on the sledge. He plumed himself rather, and thought he was very splendidly dressed.

As a result of the exchange Thórthr is killed by Thorgrímr the Norwegian in mistake for Gísli. Because of his stupidity and self-importance Thórthr is easily deceived by Gísli, and so also is Egill by Thormóthr in *Fóstbrœðra saga*:

Egill hét húskarl þeira Skúfs. Hann var mikill maðr vexti ok sterkr, ljótr yfirlits, ófimr ok óvitr. Hann átti kenningarnafn ok var kallaðr Fífl-Egill.

Egill was the name of one of Skúfr's servants. He was a big and strong fellow, ugly, clumsy, and stupid. He had a nickname and was called Silly-Egill . . .

Thormóthr takes Egill with him to the Thing. Egill there hears Thorgrímr telling of the killing of Thorgeirr and informs Thormóthr, whereupon they go there:

Þormóðr gerði ýmisst, at hann horfði í himininn upp eða niðr í jörðina fyrir sik.
Egill mælti: 'Hví lætr þú þann veg?'
Þormóðr svarar: 'Þanninn er himinninn í at sjá ok svá jörðin sem þá, er vábrestir verða.'
Egill mælti: 'Fyrir hverju er vant at verða vábrestir?'
Þormóðr svarar: 'Fyrir tíðendun verða vábrestir ávallt. Nú ef svá kann at berast, at þú heyrir vábrestinn, þá forða þú þér, sem þú mátt, ok hlaup heim til búðar sem skjótast ok gæt þín þar.'

Thormóthr kept looking alternately up at the sky and then down at the ground in front of him.
Egill said: 'Why are you behaving like that?'
Thormóthr replied: 'Because both the sky and the ground look as though there were a big crash coming.'
Egill said: 'And why should there be a big crash?'
Thormóthr answered: 'Such a big crash always comes just before great events happen. Now if you hear a great crash, then take care of yourself as well as you can, run back to the booth as quickly as possible, and take shelter there.'

Thormóthr then kills Thorgrímr:

En er Egill heyrir brestinn, er Þormóðr vann á Þorgrími, hljóp hann þá heim til búðar Skúfs. Menn geta at líta, hvar maðr hljóp, ok ætluðu, at sá myndi valda áverkum við Þorgrím. Egill varð stórum hræddr, er hann sá manna för eftir sér ok með vápnum. Ok er hann var handtekinn, þá skalf á honum leggr ok liðr sakar hræðslu. En þegar er þeir kenndu Egil, þá þóttust þeir vita, at hann myndi eigi hafa unnit á Þorgrími. Rann hræðsla af honum sem hita af járni. (I.S., v, pp. 295–300.)

When Egill heard the sound of the blow which Thormóthr had dealt Thorgrímr, he ran back to the booth of Skúfr. The men saw someone running, and thought that it must have been the man who had killed Thorgrímr. Egill was terrified when he saw them coming after him with weapons, and when they caught him he was trembling all over from fear. But as soon as they recognized Egill, then they felt sure that he could not have been the man who had killed Thorgrímr. Then his fear left him as heat leaves the iron.

In fact the cowardice of thralls seems to have become a convention which may be used rather crudely in some of the sagas. This is certainly the case in *Eyrbyggja saga* when Arnkell, surprised by his enemies, sends two of his serfs for help:

Ok er Arnkell hafði þetta mælt, hófu þrælarnir á rás, ok varð Ófeigr skjótari. Hann varð svá hræddr, at hann gekk náliga af vitinu, ok hljóp í fjall upp ok þaðan í fors einn ok týndist, ok heitir þar Ófeigsfors. Annarr þræll hljóp heim á bæinn, ok er hann kom til hlöðunnar, var þar fyrir félagi hans ok bar inn heyit. Hann kallar á þann þrælinn, er hljóp, at hann skyldi leggja inn heyit með honum, en þat fannst á, at þrælnum var verkit eigi leitt, ok fór hann til með honum.

As soon as Arnkell had said that, the two thralls took to their heels. Ófeigr was the swifter of the two, and was so terrified that he nearly lost his wits; he ran up onto the mountain and fell into a waterfall where he was drowned, so that the place is now called Ófeigr's Fall. The other thrall ran back to the farm, and when he came to the barn he found there another thrall who was carrying in the hay. The latter called to the thrall who came running up to help him with the hay, and he soon discovered that this one was not afraid of work, for he started in straight away. . . .

Having finished with the hay,

. . . þeir gengu inn, þá er þeir höfðu inn borit heyit, ok fóru af skinnstökkum sínum. Þá vöknuðu fylgðarmenn Arnkels ok spurðu, hvar hann var.

Þá var sem þrællinn vaknaði af svefni, ok svarar: 'Þat er satt,' segir hann, 'hann mun berjast inn a Örlygsstöðum við Snorra goða.' (I.S., iii, pp. 99–101.)

After they had carried in the hay, they went into the house, took off their jerkins. Then Arnkell's followers woke up and asked where he was. Then it seemed as if the thrall had just awakened from sleep, and he answered: 'That's true', he said, 'he must be fighting with Snorri gothi at Örlygsstathr.'

Even when the character is not a serf we may find a similar rather implausible treatment, as with Nagli in the same saga:

Í þessu kómu þeir Þórarinn eftir ok var Nagli skjótastr. En er hann sá, at þeir ofruðu vápnunum, glúpnaði hann ok hljóp um fram ok í fjallit upp ok varð at gjalti. . . . Ok er þeir kómu í túnit, sá þeir, at Nagli var kominn fram um garðinn ok stefndi inn til Búlandshöfða . . . Þar fengu þeir Þórarinn tekit Nagla, því at hann var náliga sprunginn af mæði. (I.S., iii, pp. 32–3.)

With this Thórarinn and his company, with Nagli at their head, were upon them. But when Nagli saw them brandishing their weapons, then he was terrified, and ran past them up onto the mountain, out of his wits with fear. . . . And when they came to the homefield, they saw that Nagli had got past the outer fence and was making for Búland's Head. . . . There Thórarinn and his company overtook Nagli because he was nearly dead from his exertions.

In a man of higher birth it may be that the cowardice is only hinted at. This is the case with Björn the White in *Droplaugarsona saga*, whose very nickname may perhaps be an indication of his lack of courage:[1]

Björn hét maðr, er bjó á Mýrum fyrir vestan Geitdalsá. Hann var kallaðr Björn inn hvíti. Hann átti dóttur Helga Ásbjarnarsonar.

Björn was the name of a man who lived at Mýrar to the west of the Geitdale river. He was called Björn the White, and was married to the daughter of Helgi Ásbjarnarson. . . .

In support of Helgi Ásbjarnarson he is involved in a fight with Helgi Droplaugarson:

[1] Cf. Lee M. Hollander, *The Sagas of Kormák and The Sworn Brothers* (Princeton, 1949), p. 124: 'He was called Helgi the White, nor was that nickname given to him in contempt but because he was a handsome man with beautiful hair of light blond colour.' But it is not easy to find firm evidence in the sagas for such a meaning of *hvítr*.

... en Helgi Droplaugarson skaut í knéskel honum [i.e. Helgi Ásbjarnarson], ok renndi ofan í legginn, klofnaði til leggrinn ok svá niðr í gegnum ristina, ok varð Helgi Ásbjarnarson þegar óvígr. Þá settist Björn hvíti undir herðar honum, ok barðist hvárrgi þeira um daginn.

Helgi Droplaugarson wounded him [i.e. Helgi Ásbjarnarson] in the kneecap, and the spear glanced off and split the shin-bone right down to the instep, so that Helgi Ásbjarnarson was then out of the fight. Then Björn the White supported him with his shoulder, and neither of them fought any more that day. . . .

Helgi is later stabbed in his bed by Grimr, and most of the household pursue the killer:

Nú koma heim flestir ór leitinni, ok lifði Helgi þá ok spurði, hvárt þeir Björn væri aftr komnir ok Hjarrandi.
'Hér er ek', kvað Björn.
'Svá er ok', kvað Helgi, 'at Hjarrandi lýsir enn mestan drengskap við mik.'
Nú andast Helgi. (I.S., x, pp. 127, 146, 156.)

Now most of them returned from the search. Helgi still lived, he asked whether Björn and Hjarrandi were back.
'Here I am', said Björn.
'It's still true then', said Helgi, 'that Hjarrandi shows more courage in support of me.'
Then Helgi died.

The cowardice of Björn is clear, though the nearest that this comes to being openly stated is in the last remark by Helgi. Mörðr in *Njáls saga* is a more complex figure, and it is probably as much envy as cowardice that stops him from interfering in a fight when told about it by a woman:

Kona hljóp heim, er sá, ok sagði Merði ok bað hann skilja þá.
'Þeir einir munu vera', segir hann, 'at ek hirði aldri, þó at drepist.'
'Eigi munt þú þat vilja mæla', segir hon, 'þar mun vera Gunnarr, frændi þinn, ok Otkell.'
'Klifar þú nökkut jafnan, mannfýla þín', segir hann, ok lá hann inni, meðan þeir börðust. (I.S., xi, p. 127.)

A woman who saw the fight ran home and told Mörthr, and begged him to separate them.

'It seems likely', he said, 'that they are only the kind of people who can kill each other for all I care.'

'You can't mean that', she said, 'Gunnarr, your kinsman, and Otkell are there.'

'Must you always be chattering, you silly woman', he said, and he stayed lying in bed whilst they fought.

Boastfulness may also be the distinguishing quality of a comic character. This is sometimes combined with cowardice, as with the Narfi of *Kormáks saga* (I.S., vi, pp. 309 ff.). At other times the boaster may be brave enough, as is Hrappr in *Laxdæla saga*, whose boastfulness is comic even though it results in his death:

Hann kveðst Hrappr heita ok vera breiðfirzkr at móðurkyni,—'ok þar hefi ek upp vaxit. Hefi ek nafn Víga-Hrapps ok þat með nafni, at ek em engi dældarmaðr, þó at ek sjá lítill vexti . . . en ek hefi þat af nafni, at ek vil ekki sitja mönnum slíkar hneisur. . . .'

Hrappr segir margt, en spurði fás, en þó varð hann brátt varr, at þeir ætluðu at stefna at Helga, ok lét hann vel yfir því ok sagði, at hans skal eigi á bak at leita.

. . . Hrappr hleypr þegar upp á selit ok spurði, hvárt skolli væri inni.

Helgi svarar: 'Fyrir þat mun þér ganga, sem sá sé nökkut skæðr, er hér býr inni, at hann muni bíta kunna nær greninu.' Ok þegar lagði Helgi spjóti út um selsglugginn ok í gegnum Hrapp. Fell hann dauðr til jarðar af spjótinu. (I.S., iv, pp. 196, 197.)

He said he was called Hrappr and his mother's people came from Breithafjörthr,—'and there I grew up. I am called Killer-Hrappr, and am just as the name suggests, since I am not an easy man to deal with, even if I'm not very big. . . . I don't have that name for nothing, and I don't take abuse from anyone. . . .'

Hrappr talked a lot, and asked few questions, but he soon found out that they intended to attack Helgi, and he approved of that, and said that they wouldn't have to look in the rear for him. . . .

Hrappr jumped right up onto the roof of the hut, and asked whether the old fox was at home.

Helgi answered: 'You'll soon find out that the one who lives here is rather ugly and can bite if anyone gets too near his lair.' With that Helgi thrust his spear through the roof-opening and through Hrappr. He fell dead off the spear and down to the ground.

Stinginess, coupled with timidity, is characteristic of Thorkell in *Fóstbræðra saga*, compelled against his will to entertain the two ruffians Butraldi and Thorgeirr:

Þorkell hét maðr, er bjó í Gervidal. Hann var vel fjáreigandi, en lítill í þegnskap, en eirinn í skaplyndi, huglauss í hjarta. . . .

There was a man called Thorkell who lived in Gervidalr. He was well-off, but not very generous, slow to take offence and timid in his heart. . . .

Butraldi comes and is received without enthusiasm:

Ok í því bili heyrir hann, at drepit er á dyrr, ok batnar honum ekki við þat, gengr hann fram ok til dura ok lýkr upp hurðunni ok sér einn mikinn mann standa með vápnum fyrir durunum. Þorkell spyrr þann mann at nafni. Hann nefndist Þorgeirr. Þorkell spyrr, hvers sonr hann væri. Hann kveðst vera Hávarsson. Þá kemr æðra í brjóst Þorkatli, ok dattaði hjarta hans við.

Þorkell mælti þá: 'Hér er kominn Butraldi við þriðja mann, ok veit ek eigi, hvern frið hann býðr þér. Hygg ek, at hann hafi illan hug á þér, því at hann er vinr Vermundar, óvinar yðvars, en ek má eigi manns blóð sjá, ok mun ek í öngvit falla, ef þér berizt á.' (I.S., v, pp. 224–5.)

Just then he heard someone knock at the door, and that didn't make him feel any better. He went to open the door and saw a big man all armed standing outside. Thorkell asked the man his name. He said that he was called Thorgeirr. He asked whose son he was, and was told that he was the son of Hávarr. Then Thorkell became afraid and his heart sank.

Thorkell said: 'Butraldi and two other men are staying here, and I don't know how you will get on with them. I don't think that he'll care much for you since he's a friend of Vermundr your enemy. But I can't bear the sight of blood and would faint if you started fighting.'

There follows an amusing description of the way in which the two are entertained—after a fashion—by Thorkell.

Avariciousness and over-confidence appear in the Eyjólfr of *Njáls saga*:

> Eyjólfr var virðingamaðr mikill ok allra manna lögkænastr, svá at hann var inn þriði mestr lögmaðr á Íslandi. Hann var allra manna fríðastr sýnum, mikill ok sterkr ok it bezta höfðingjaefni. Hann var fégjarn sem aðrir frændr hans. (I.S., xi, p. 340.)

Eyjólfr was a very distinguished man and excellently skilled in law, so that he was the third best lawyer in Iceland. He was the most handsome of men, tall and strong, and the best of chieftains. But like all his kindred he was greedy for money.

Bjarni and Flosi know that Eyjólfr's intelligence is undermined by avarice. He himself is completely unaware of his weakness, and it is this lack of self-knowledge that makes him susceptible to comic treatment in a skilfully worked-out scene. At first Bjarni speaks as man to man, but soon introduces flattery, which Eyjólfr pretends to ignore. Flosi realizes that it is a waste of time beating about the bush, since after all Eyjólfr is no fool, so he takes over the discussion and makes concrete proposals. Eyjólfr begins with a fine display of moral indignation, but is eloquently silent while Flosi, Bjarni, and Hallbjörn go through the elaborate gesture of presenting him with a gold ring, and his next speech is a self-satisfied contradiction of all he has previously said. After warning the others to take care, for bribery is illegal, Eyjólfr goes off to Snorri's booth, presumably feeling that after such a manœuvre he is now on a level with Snorri gothi himself. But Snorri knows all the answers, so that Eyjólfr soon comes to realize that neither truth, lies, nor silence will do any good, and only now does he realize that he has been tricked. The end of the incident is tragedy, since Eyjólfr's acceptance of the defence results in his death, but the comedy lies in the fact that until almost the very end it is Eyjólfr who considers himself to be in full control.

Particularly interesting is the character of Kaupa-Hethinn, invented by Njáll as a cover for Gunnarr in his dealings with Hrútr. Kaupa-Hethinn is the supremely self-satisfied man who knows everything, and rather prides himself on being something of a rough diamond. There is no self-righteousness about him, and he is quite prepared to live and let live so long as his own outstanding merits are properly recognized:

> Hann er maðr skapillr ok margmæltr, þykkist einn vita allt. Hann rekr aftr kaup sín oftliga ok flýgr á menn, þegar eigi er allt gert sem hann vill. (I.S., xi, p. 49.)

> He is a bad-tempered and talkative man, who thinks he knows everything. He often snatches back what he is selling, and flies at people if things are not being done as he wants.

His disdain at the idea that there could possibly be any great men in his own district or in Reykjadalr confirms Hrútr in the opinion that Kaupa-Hethinn need not be taken seriously, and the very naïveté of the latter tricks the easygoing Hrútr into expecting some easy amusement from leading him on. His opinion that Kaupa-Hethinn is merely a self-confident blunderer is confirmed when the latter is unable to repeat the summons correctly, since to be incompetent in a legal matter was a particular cause for derision,[1] and all the more comic in Kaupa-Hethinn's case because of his confidence in his own ability. But though we laugh with Hrútr at Kaupa-Hethinn, we also laugh at Hrútr himself, since his own laughter shows how completely he is being deceived. The satire on typical saga vices is of little importance here, and our laughter is directed, not at the character of Kaupa-Hethinn, but at the way in which Hrútr is taken in.

This is a more sophisticated comedy than is usual in the sagas, but there are other instances where a rather more complex humour seems to be aimed at. A not very successful attempt to depict a stock comic character, but one who deceives our expectations, is that of Atli in *Hávarðar saga*:

> Atli hét maðr, er bjó í Otradal ok átti systur Steinþórs á Eyri, er Þórdís hét. Atli var manna minnstr ok vesalligastr, ok svá er sagt, at þar eftir væri skaplyndi hans, at hann var inn mesti vesalingr.

> Atli was the name of a man who lived in Otradalr, and was married

---

[1] Cf. *Droplaugarsona saga*, I.S., x, p. 139.

to Thórdís, the sister of Steinthórr of Eyrr. Atli was the smallest of men and most wretched looking, and it was said that his mind was like his body and he was the puniest of wretches.

One morning, rising early, he sees Steinthórr on his way to the farm, and in an attempt to avoid the obligations of hospitality, immediately hides himself in a heap of hay, clad only in his nightshirt. Thórdís gives Steinthórr the provisions he needs, and is then persuaded to hide him behind the hangings whilst his men ride away. The frozen Atli creeps out of the hay, discovers that his storeroom is bare, and begins to revile Steinthórr, unaware of his presence in the room. However, warmed in Thórdís's bed, Atli realizes that Steinthórr is not so bad after all, whereupon Steinthórr steps forward, and they agree to let bygones be bygones. And indeed, when we later find Atli helping Hávarthr, he is a very different man, brave, strong, and generous. He agrees to entertain Hávarthr and his followers, and shows great bravery and leadership in helping them against the Dyrafjörthr men led by Thorgrímr:

Hlaupast menn nú at, svá sem ætlat var. Þat var it fyrsta athlaup, at Atli inn litli hljóp at Þorgrími ok hjó til hans tveim höndum með sverðinu, ok beit eigi á. . . .
Atli sér, at eigi mun svá búit hlýða, kastar síðan sverðinu ok hleypr undir Þorgrím ok rekr hann niðr við völlinn. Nú er eigi vápnit hjá honum, en hann veit, at liðsmunr er mikill. Verðr honum þat fyrir, at hann greyfist niðr at honum Þorgrími ok bítr sundr í honum barkann, dregr hann síðan þangat til, er sverð hans var, ok sníðr af honum höfuðit. . . .
Atli settist niðr ok bað þá leiða fyrir sik. Hann rak af þeim hárit ok gerði þeim koll ok bar í tjöru eftir. Síðan tók hann kníf sinn ór skeiðum ok rak af þeim öllum eyrun ok bað þá svá markaða fara á fund Dýra ok Þórarins, kvað þá heldr muna mega, at þeir hafði fundit Atla inn litla. (I.S., v, pp. 180, 190–2.)

The men now attacked as had been planned, and at the first onslaught Atli the Little ran at Thorgrímr. He struck at him two-handed with his sword, but it would not bite on him. . . .
Atli saw that he could not succeed in this way, so he threw his

sword down, ran under Thorgrímr's guard, and threw him down to the ground. Now there was no weapon near, and he knew that the odds were great against him, so he threw himself down on Thorgrímr and bit his throat in two. He then dragged him to where his sword lay, and cut his head off. . . .
Atli sat down and had the men brought before him. He cut their hair off, shaved their heads, and then tarred them. Next he drew his knife from the sheath, cut off their ears, and bade them marked in this way to go and find Dýri and Thórarinn, saying that they would now remember how they had come across Atli the Little.

But the change is too great; the earlier Atli is the traditional type of minor comic character, with nothing about him to suggest the later metamorphosis. He has received the traditional treatment: his appearance lacks dignity and his mind is as mean as his body, whilst in addition he is the greatest of misers, and his early actions completely fulfil our expectations. The author has described too well the conventional comic character, and without a clearer indication of something below the surface we cannot accept the later Atli as having any real connection with the earlier one. No doubt the author was trying to create something more complex than the conventional minor comic character, but this necessitated a modification of the traditional technique which he was either unable or unwilling to make.

On the other hand the character of Björn in *Njáls saga* is a much more successful attempt at the same kind of thing. His first appearance in the saga prepares us in the conventional way for the usual comic character:

. . . maðr, er Björn hét ok var kallaðr Björn hvíti . . . Björn átti þá konu, er Valgerðr hét . . . Björn var maðr sjálfhælinn, en húsfreyju hans þótti þat illt. Hann var skyggn ok skjótr á fæti.

. . . a man called Björn who was nicknamed Björn the White . . . Björn was married to a woman called Valgerthr . . . Björn was given to praising himself, and his wife didn't care much for that. He was keen-eyed and quick of foot. . . .

His nickname perhaps carries the implication of cowardice, and when Kári asks for his help, Björn's wife is soon warning Kári against him:

'Hvárki frý ek mér', segir Björn, 'skyggnleiks né árædis eða nökkurrar karlmennsku . . . Skal ek víst verða þér at liði öllu, því sem þú beiðir.'

Húsfreyja hans mælti: 'Tröll hafi þitt hól', sagði hon, 'ok skrum, ok skyldir þú eigi mæla ykkr tál báðum ok hégóma í þessu. En gjarna vil ek veita Kára mat ok aðra góða hluti, þá er ek veit, at honum má gagn at verða. En á harðræði Bjarnar skalt þú ekki treysta, því at ek uggi, at þér verði at öðru en hann segir.'

'I don't deny', said Björn, 'that I am keen-sighted, nor am I lacking in courage to do brave deeds . . . I shall certainly help in everything you ask.'

His wife spoke: 'The devil take your bragging and boasting', she said. 'Don't make yourself or him believe such nonsense. I will gladly give Kári food and other good things which I know will be useful to him. But never trust to Björn's courage, since I'm afraid you'll find things turn out very differently from what he says.' . . .

He manages to trick the sons of Sigfúss, but no sooner has he done so than he boasts more than ever:

Kári kvað hann hafa sýnt í þessu mikla trúligleika við sik.

Björn mælti: 'Þat ætlaða ek hættara nökkurum manni en mér, ef ek héta trausti mínu eða umsjá, at þeim skyldi mun í fara.'

Húsfreyja hans mælti: 'Fyrr væri illa en þú værir dróttinssviki.'

Kári said that in this he had shown great loyalty to him.

Björn said: 'I think there is greater risk of other people being untrustworthy rather than that I should be, once I had promised protection and help.'

His wife said: 'You are bad enough as it is without becoming a traitor as well.' . . .

Kári wishes to leave and asks Björn to accompany him:

Björn mælti: 'Þetta er hættuför mikil, ok munu fáir hafa hug til nema þú ok ek.'

Húsfreyja mælti: 'Ef þú fylgir Kára illa, þá skalt þú þat vita, at þú skalt aldri koma í mína rekkju sinn síðan. Skulu frændr mínir gera fjárskipti með okkr.'

'Þat er líkara, húsfreyja', segir hann, 'at fyrir öðru þurfi ráð at gera en þat beri til skilnaðar okkars, því at ek mun mér bera vitni, hverr garpr eða afreksmaðr ek em í vápnaskipti.'

Björn said:' That is a very risky journey, and apart from us two very few would have the courage to undertake it.'

His wife said: 'If you don't give Kári good support, you had better know that you shall never get into bed with me again, and my kinsmen will see to the division of property between us.'

'It's more likely, wife', he said, 'that you will have to find some other reason than this for a divorce, since I shall show how brave and dauntless I am when it comes to fighting.' . . .

Kári makes plans to deal with an assault by the sons of Sigfúss:

. . . ok hafði Björn í sínu orði hvárt, at hann vildi flýja sem harðast, eða hitt, at hann vildi bíða ok taka í móti, ok þótti Kára at þessu allmikit gaman.

. . . and one minute Björn was all for running away, and the next he was all for fighting, and Kári thought it all very amusing. . . .

So far Björn has been little more than a source of amusement to Kári and he should now become a liability. That he does not do so is surprising, but in fact when the sons of Sigfúss do appear there is no mention of flight, and Björn turns out to be courageous enough, though never recklessly so:

[Kári] bað Björn standa at baki sér ok hafa sik eigi allmjök frammi,— 'en ger mér gagn, slíkt er þú mátt.'

'Hitt hafða ek ætlat', segir Björn, 'at hafa engan mann at hlífiskildi mér, en þó er nú þar komit, at þú munt ráða verða. En með vitsmunum mínum ok hvatleika má ek þó verða þér at gagni, en óvinum okkrum ekki óskeinisamr.' . . .

Maðr einn skauzt at ok ætlaði at höggva fót undan Kára ok komst á hlið honum. Björn hjó af þessum manni höndina ok skauzt aftr síðan at baki Kára, ok fengu þeir honum engan geig gervan. . . .

Björn hafði særða þrjá menn, þá er ætlat höfðu til at vinna á Kára, ok var þó aldri svá frammi, at honum væri nein raun í.

[Kári] asked Björn to defend his back, and not to press too far forward,—'but give me what help you can.'

'I never expected to use anyone as a shield', said Björn, 'but as things are, I suppose you must have your own way. But with my good sense and quickness I may still be able to help you and do our enemies plenty of damage.' . . . A man rushed forward intending to cut off Kári's foot. He came at his side, but Björn cut off the man's arm and immediately got back behind Kári so that no one could do him any harm. . . . Björn had wounded three men who were attacking Kári, but he was never himself so far forward that he was in any danger. . . .

They report the deaths:

Björn kvaðst eigi nenna at drepa hann [i.e. Gunnarr], en kvað hann þó þess makligan, en þeir, er svöruðu, kváðu fá fúnat hafa fyrir honum. Björn kvað nú kost vera, at fúnaði svá margir af Síðumönnum sem hann vildi. Þeir sögðu þá ill at vera.

Björn said that he hadn't had the heart to kill him [i.e. Gunnarr], although he had deserved it. Those who answered said that it was likely that few were dead because of Björn. Björn said that he was now in a position to kill as many of the men of Sítha as he wished. They said that that would indeed be bad. . . .

The irony of the reply shows that no one really believes in Björn's courage. From the beginning he is described as a braggart, and he remains one. But he has qualities that do not appear in other such characters. He is astute enough, never short of a ready answer, and only at the end, when his wife has come to realize that she has misjudged him, do we realize that his nickname does not necessarily indicate cowardice:

Húsfreyja spurði þá tíðenda ok fagnaði þeim vel.
Björn svaraði: 'Aukizt hafa heldr vandræðin, kerling.'
Hon svarar fá ok brosti at. Hon mælti þá: 'Hversu gafst Björn þér, Kári?'
Kári svarar: 'Berr er hverr at baki, nema sér bróður eigi, ok gafst Björn mér vel. Hann vann á þrimr mönnum, en er þó sárr sjálfr, ok var hann mér inn hallkvæmsti í öllu því, sem hann mátti.' (I.S., xi, pp. 397–409.)

Björn's wife welcomed them home and asked for news.

Björn answered: 'Things are getting worse and worse, lass.'
She spoke little, but smiled. Then she said: 'How did Björn behave,
Kári?'
Kári answered: 'Bare is the back without a brother! Björn did well.
He wounded three men, and was wounded himself, and in everything
he was as useful to me as he could be.'

There is no exaggeration here, and we can believe of Björn, as we
cannot of Atli, that he is the same man throughout. No doubt he
will later boast of the deeds that he and Kári did, but if he exag-
gerates them, there will at any rate be a good foundation of fact in
his assertions. The real comedy here is in the apparent reversal of
values which occurs when Björn is revealed as more than a stock
figure, and its success is due to the skill of the author in the depiction of a character varying slightly but significantly from the
conventional type.

Such figures as these necessarily lack the elaboration of fully
defined characters, otherwise they would upset the balance of the
plot. The major characters are naturally more complex, and since
they reflect the heroic virtues, any comedy connected with them
must be very different. Atli and Björn represent attempts to
bridge the gap, the former only partially successful, the latter
wholly so. Not all the major characters have comic elements, and
in the case of those who have, since they are fully rounded characters, comedy can only be a single and comparatively minor element in them.

Much of the comedy connected with Snorri gothi is probably
traditional, since he appears in a number of sagas and his character
is much the same in all of them. He is above all a complete master
of intrigue, though never merely the cunning rascal. His schemes
always result in profit to himself, if to no one else, but though
important we feel that this is not really the main point—he plots
because he enjoys it, and any incidental profit is merely a bonus.
He dislikes an open quarrel, and always tries to avoid being involved in one: his enemies are rarely openly struck down, but more
frequently cunningly ensnared by their own folly. He refuses to
be goaded into half-measures; he bides his time until he can

strike a decisive blow, and then he is ruthless. He is a man of peace—when it suits his purposes—but certainly does not lack physical courage, and on occasion has a dry wit:

> Þessi tíðendi kómu til búðar Snorra goða, at Þorgils Hölluson var veginn.
> Snorri segir: 'Eigi mun þér skilizt hafa. Þorgils Hölluson mun vegit hafa.'
> Maðrinn segir: 'Enda fauk höfuðit af bolnum.'
> 'Þá má vera, at satt sé', sagði Snorri. (I.S., iv, p. 206.)

The news that Thorgils Hölluson had been killed came to the booth of Snorri gothi.
Snorri said: 'You must have misunderstood. It must have been Thorgils Hölluson who did the killing.'
The man said: 'All the same his head flew from his body.'
'Then perhaps it's true', said Snorri.

He can foresee every likely development, deduce the outcome of any feud or lawsuit, know the exact moment at which to put his plotting into operation, and when to join the winning side so as to get the maximum credit:

> Snorri var vitrastr maðr á Íslandi, þeira er eigi váru forspáir. Hann var góðr vinum sínum, en grimr óvinum. (I.S., xi, p. 264.)

Snorri was the wisest man in Iceland of all those who did not possess second sight. He was good to his friends but fierce to his enemies. . . .

Snorri figures most prominently in *Eyrbyggja saga*, where we find the fullest description of him:

> Snorri var meðalmaðr á hæð ok heldr grannligr, fríðr sýnum, réttleitr ok ljóslitaðr, bleikhárr ok rauðskeggjaðr. Hann var hógværr hversdagliga. Fann lítt á honum, hvárt honum þótti vel eða illa. Hann var vitr maðr ok forspár um marga hluti, langrækr ok heiftúðigr, heilráðr vinum sínum, en óvinir hans þóttust heldr kulða af kenna ráðum hans. Hann varðveitti þá hof. Var hann þá kallaðr Snorri goði. Hann gerðist þá höfðingi mikill, en ríki hans var mjök öfundsamt, því at þeir váru margir, er eigi þóttust til minna um komnir fyrir ættar sakar, en áttu meira undir sér fyrir afls sakar ok prófaðrar harðfengi. (I.S., iii, p. 22.)

Snorri was a man of medium height and rather slender, handsome in appearance, with regular features, a fair complexion, fair hair, and a red beard. He was usually of even disposition, but it was difficult to tell from his appearance whether he thought well or ill of anything. He was wise and foreseeing in many things, implacable and revengeful. He gave good advice to his friends, but his enemies thought they felt the coldness of his counsel. He had charge of the temple, and so was called Snorri gothi. He became a great chieftain, but was much envied because of his power since there were many who thought themselves not inferior to him in birth, and they considered themselves superior in strength and proven courage.

He first reveals his abilities at the age of fifteen when he deceives the admittedly rather stupid Börkr (I.S., iii, pp. 30–1). The long-term cunning of his scheme here is matched by several instances of quick-wittedness, such as that shown in the fight at Álftafjörðr (I.S., iii, pp. 122–3). With Snorri we can always expect a contradiction between the apparent and the real meaning of speech and behaviour. In pursuit of his ends he is willing to accept apparent humiliation, and he can play any part which suits his purpose. In *Heiðarvíga saga* he is the guileless admirer of Thorgils's oratorical ability in his truce-speech, and persuades him to recite it before Thorgils realizes that it will cover Barthi and his party who have joined them in the dark (I.S., vii, pp. 288–91).

Although much of the comedy associated with Snorri is likely to be traditional, the way in which it is worked into any particular saga must depend on the individual author. Snorri is at his most masterly in the scenes at the All-Thing in *Njáls saga*, as is shown by the way in which he crushes Eyjólfr (I.S., xi, pp. 340–5). But his ability is not extended here, and his masterpiece is the management of the interview with Gizurr and Ásgrímr (I.S., xi, pp. 348–50). Snorri takes complete charge of the conversation and wins them round to his own way of thinking by a well-judged mixture of flattery and practical advice. He convinces them that he is doing them a good turn—as indeed he is, but he is doing an even better one for himself. He manages to avoid both an open alliance with them and the disadvantages of neutrality, and since he is made chief arbitrator in the final awards and receives gifts for his services, the practical results to himself are evident enough. The smooth assurance of his handling of Gizurr and Ásgrímr gains emphasis from the contrast with their previous interview with Skafti, since the latter has a blunt directness with which they are better able to cope than with Snorri's evasions.

Other characters in the sagas have something of Snorri's qualities. Ófeigr, in *Bandamanna saga*, by astutely playing on the weaknesses of the chieftains combined against his son, splits the confederation and changes threatened defeat into ultimate victory. Similarly, Helgi Droplaugarson is in some ways an early sketch of Snorri, while in *Vatnsdæla saga* Thorsteinn is the diplomat of the family who does well for them and even better for himself. But Snorri's pre-eminence is evident from the fact that we judge them by comparison with him. He is the master of them all, and the comedy lies in the smooth and practised way in which he gets the better of his opponents and feathers his own nest at the same time.

Much of the rather boisterous humour connected with Grettir may also be traditional, more particularly his scornful verses and frequent apposite use of proverbs. On the other hand, the humorous conversation with his brother Thorsteinn, and the joking with Sveinn (I.S., vi, pp. 135 ff., 147 ff.), are perhaps due rather to the author, as also Grettir's remark about the way in which he was entertained at Reykjahólar:

Var hann spurðr at, hversu honum hefði líkat vistargerðin eða vetrvistin á Reykjahólum.
Hann svarar: 'Þar hefi ek svá verit, at ek hefi jafnan mínum mat orðit fegnastr, þá er ek náða honum.' (I.S., vi, p. 162.)

He was asked whether he had enjoyed the entertainment or the winter quarters at Reykjahólar.
He answered: 'I was entertained there in such a way that I enjoyed the food very much—when I could get any.'

No doubt the wry sense of humour and jesting pleasure in his own ugliness, shown by Egill Skallagrímsson in his poems and verses, also owes something to tradition. On the other hand, the author of the saga is probably to be credited with some of the comic elements in Egill's character. These arise mainly from the fact that with all his greatness he has one of the basic vices of heroic society—he is incurably avaricious. Since Egill is also essentially unselfconscious the author can make the avarice humorous by the casual air with which at various times he makes the point. When Egill and his party are captured by the Kurlanders, they escape from their fetters, get hold of as much plunder as possible, and make for the woods, Egill carrying a large meadcask. The incident has other comic features, but its main interest lies in the light it throws on Egill, and as usual the main point is made at the end:

Sagði Egill, at mjöðdrekku þá vill hann hafa at afnámsfé, er hann fór með, en hon var reyndar full af silfri. (I.S., ii, p. 117.)

Egill said that he would take as his share of the plunder the meadcask that he had carried off, and it turned out to be full of silver.

Elsewhere, as here, the success of the author's method lies essentially in the timing. So, for example, with the two chests of silver given to Egill by King Athelstan when his brother is killed. The king makes it clear that the silver is to be shared between his father and his other kin. Egill leaves England, goes to Norway where he secures a large inheritance, and only then returns to Iceland:

Váru þeir með Skalla-Grími um vetrinn. Egill hafði þar ógrynni fjár, en ekki er þess getit, at Egill skipti silfri því, er Aðalsteinn konungr hafði fengit honum í hendr, hvárki við Skalla-Grím né aðra menn. (I.S., ii, p. 153.)

They remained with Skalla-Grímr during the winter. Egill had plenty of money, but we are not told that he shared the silver which King Athelstan had entrusted to him either with Skalla-Grímr or with anyone else.

The effect of this remark is due entirely to its position in the narrative. In the first place we have now completely forgotten about the silver, and in the second Egill has by this time acquired a comfortable fortune, so that only his incurable avarice leads him to keep the silver which does not belong to him.

Egill's desire for money is that of the miser; he loves it for its own sake, for the mere pleasure of possessing it. To be sure, he later makes a half-hearted offer of the silver to his father:

> Ok er Egill var búinn, þá gekk Skalla-Grímr út með honum ok hvarf til hans, áðr Egill steig á bak, ok mælti: 'Seint þykkir mér þú, Egill, hafa greitt fé þat, er Aðalsteinn konungr sendi mér, eða hvernig ætlar þú, at fara skyli fé þat?'
>
> Egill segir: 'Er þér nú féfátt mjök, faðir? Ek vissa þat eigi. Þegar skal ek láta þik hafa silfr, er ek veit, er þú þarft, en ek veit, at þú munt enn hafa at varðveita eina kistu eða tvær, fullar af silfri.'
>
> 'Svá þykkir mér', segir Skalla-Grímr, 'sem þú munir þykkjast skipt hafa lausafé með okkr. Muntu láta þér vel hugna, at ek gera slíkt, er mér líkar, af því, er ek varðveiti.'
>
> Egill segir: 'Þú munt engis lofs þykkjast þurfa at biðja mik um þetta, því at þú munt ráða vilja, hvat sem ek mæli.' (I.S., ii, p. 177.)

When Egill was ready, then Skalla-Grímr went outside with him. He took leave of Egill before he mounted his horse, and said: 'You seem to have been very slow in paying over, Egill, the money which King Athelstan sent to me. What do you mean to do with it?'

Egill said: 'Are you really short of money, father? I didn't know that. Any time I know that you need it, I will gladly let you have some money. But I suspect that you still have a chestful or two of silver in safe keeping somewhere.'

'It seems to me', said Skalla-Grímr, 'that you think you have already divided up between us what money there is. I hope it won't trouble you if I do as I like with that which is still mine.'

Egill said: 'You will certainly not think that you need to ask my agreement for that, since you will surely do as you like, whatever I may say.'

Had the offer been accepted, we can feel certain that Egil would have found perfectly good reasons for delaying the fulfilment of it. In return, Skalla-Grímr thereupon takes a chest of money away and hides it, so anticipating Egill's later disposal of King Athelstan's treasure, then returns home and is found dead:

COMEDY OF CHARACTER IN ICELANDIC SAGAS

Lét Egill þar gera haug á framanverðu nesinu. Var þar í lagðr Skalla-Grímr ok hestr hans ok vápn hans ok smíðartól. Ekki er þess getit, at lausafé væri lagt í haug hjá honum. Egill tók þar við arfi, löndum ok lausum aurum. (I.S., ii, p. 179.)

Egill had a grave-mound made there on the point of the headland. Skalla-Grímr was placed inside it with his horse, his weapons, and his smith's tools, but we are not told that any loose money was laid in the barrow with him. Egill took possession of his inheritance, the land and the gold.

Even to honour his father, Egill could not bear to part with actual money, and certainly neither Skalla-Grímr nor any of his kin ever got any of King Athelstan's silver.

Other incidents help to emphasize Egill's avarice; his annoyance when King Hákon refuses him the estates he had won in a holmgang, and his undisguised pleasure when Arinbjörn quite unnecessarily makes up for this by presenting him with a large sum of money (I.S., ii, pp. 223, 224). Similarly, the fate of the magnificent shield given to him by Einarr is only what we have now come to expect:

Þá var spillt skildinum ok kastat í sýruker. En síðan lét Egill taka af búnaðinn, ok váru tólf aurar gulls í spöngunum. (I.S., ii, p. 284.)

Then the shield was spoiled and thrown into a whey-tub. But Egill first had the decorations stripped off, and there were twelve ounces of gold on the cross-pieces.

Throughout the saga such incidents accumulate, and as a result Egill's last wish—to take King Athelstan's chests of silver to the All-Thing, scatter the money on the Law-Hill, and enjoy the sight of everyone fighting for it—and his last action in disposing of it in such a way that, if he could not do what he liked with it, then no one else should have it, are both convincing. His avarice is thus seen to be the most deeply-rooted of all his characteristics, and the author's recurrence to it has the effect of showing Egill to us as a complete and complex character, a great man who is as great in his defects as in his virtues.

Perhaps the major character who shows most clearly the comic intention of an individual author is the Skarphethinn of *Njáls saga*. Not that there is anything comic about him either in appearance or in behaviour. The first description of him shows that his appearance is odd and perhaps rather frightening (I.S., xi, p. 58); it is certainly not ludicrous, and if it were no one would dare laugh. Skarphethinn is not comic for any of the usual reasons, but simply because of his attitude of mind. Njáll, his father, has a divine wisdom which can accept the things of this world when he cannot change them. Kári, his brother-in-law, is more human and concerns himself solely with practical matters. Skarphethinn is in between: lacking wisdom, perhaps unconsciously he despises practical ability in worldly matters, and the fact that he has all the attributes needed for success in a heroic society only makes his position more frustrating. Because of this he has an attitude of scorn and aloofness which finds expression in continual sarcasm, irony, and the use of understatement. So with his first appearance in the saga:

Skarpheðinn spyrr: 'Hvat fé er þat, faðir?'
'Hér er fé þat, er Gunnarr greiddi mér fyrir heimamann várn.'
'Koma mun þat til nökkurs', sagði Skarpheðinn ok glotti við. (I.S., xi, p. 83.)

Skarphethinn asked: 'What money is that, father?'
'This is the money that Gunnarr paid me for our servant.'
'It will come in useful', said Skarphethinn, and he smiled as he said it.

Skarphethinn knows very well the way things are turning, but he always refuses to become emotionally involved in any situation, and the very quietness of his remark carries with it a sense of inevitability. Almost immediately Kolr, the slayer of Svartr, is himself killed, and again Skarphethinn supplies the appropriate comment:

Skarpheðinn mælti: 'Miklu eru þrælar atgerðameiri en fyrr hafa verit. Þeir flugust þá á, ok þótti þat ekki saka, en nú vilja þeir vegast',— ok glotti við. (I.S., xi, p. 85.)

Skarphethinn spoke: 'Thralls are fiercer now than they were. They used to fly at each other before, and no one bothered much about that, but now they want to be killing',—and he smiled as he said it.

Out of the mounting tragedy Skarphethinn makes a kind of game which has the result of heightening the tension. Not that this is Skarphethinn's intention; his smile shows that his amusement is real enough—and he often smiles, though the smile is far from promoting ease of mind in others. It seems rather to reflect a detached amused judgement on the general folly of mankind which gives his humour a universal quality. Nothing is too much for him, and on occasion this gives him full control of a situation (e.g. I.S., xi, pp. 213–14). But it is rare for him to make any practical use of his power; he is more concerned with asserting his own independence than with controlling a situation. The irresponsibility of his wit, shown best perhaps in his jeers when Ásgrímr and the sons of Njáll are seeking support from other chieftains at the Thing (I.S., xi, pp. 273 ff.), only emphasizes the grim undertones. Skarphethinn's remarks to his father as he leaves to kill Thrainn are jocular enough, but the real meaning is clear:

Njáll kallar á Skarpheðin: 'Hvert skal fara, frændi?'
'I sauðaleit', sagði hann.
'Svá var eitt sinn fyrr', segir Njáll, 'ok veidduð þér þá menn.'
Skarpheðinn hló at ok mælti: 'Heyrið þér, hvat karlinn segir. Eigi er hann grómlauss.' (I.S., xi, p. 218.)

Njáll called to Skarphethinn: 'Where are you going, son?'
'To look for sheep', he said.
'That happened once before', said Njáll, 'and it was men that you hunted.'
Skarphethinn laughed at that, and said: 'Do you hear what the old man says? He must suspect something.'

Skarphethinn never runs the risk of involving himself; the only time he is stung into anything like directness is in the scene when Flosi repeats the old insult about Njáll's beardlessness (I.S., xi, pp. 289–91), but he soon regains his poise, and at the burning makes light of the whole affair:

Þeir tóku nú eld ok gerðu bál mikit fyrir durunum.

126

Þá mælti Skarpheðinn: 'Eld kveykvið þér nú, sveinar, hvárt skal nú búa til seyðis?'
Grani Gunnarsson svaraði: 'Svá skal þat vera, ok skalt þú eigi þurfa heitara at baka.' (I.S., xi, p. 304.)

They now took fire and made a great blaze in front of the doors. Then Skarphethinn spoke: 'Hello, boys, you are lighting a fire now; have you taken up cooking?'
Grani Gunnarsson answered: 'That is what is going to happen, and you won't need to be better done.'

He even makes light of the death of his father:

Skarpheðinn hafði sét, er faðir hans hafði niðr lagizt ok hversu hann hafði um sik búit. Hann mælti þá: 'Snemma ferr faðir várr í rekkju, ok er þat sem ván er, hann er maðr gamall.' (I.S., xi, p. 307.)

Skarphethinn had seen, when his father lay down, how he had prepared himself. Then he said: 'Our father is going to bed early, but that's not surprising since he is an old man.'

In his final remarks we have all the easy jesting and fantastic understatement which are characteristic of him, but the matter-of-factness of his final remark about Njáll shows an unexpected tenderness which by its very sobriety helps to heighten the tragedy:

Þá fellu ofan stórviðirnir ór ræfrinu.
Skarpheðinn mælti: 'Nú mun faðir minn dauðr vera, ok hefir hvárki heyrt til hans styn né hósta.' (I.S., xi, p. 307.)

Then the great beams fell from the roof.
Skarphethinn said: 'Now my father must be dead, and I have heard neither groan nor cough from him.'

Skarphethinn is far from being a comic character in the usual sense of the term, nor is he ever connected with comic situations. He appears only in the tragic sections of the saga, and since he has the 'ill-luck' typical of the doomed saga hero, he could much more easily be regarded as a tragic character. But this would ignore Skarphethinn's sense of humour and the use of it made by the author. The wry matter-of-factness and grim jocularity give us the temper of the man and the situation, so that whenever he appears

127

the typical comment is expected, however apprehensively. Because of this it is not easy to believe in the crosses found branded on him after his death:

Þá var Skarpheðinn flettr af klæðunum, því at þau váru ekki brunnin. Hann hafði lagit hendr sínar í kross ok á ofan ina hægri. Tvá díla fundu þeir á honum, annan í millum herðanna, en annan á brjóstinu, ok var hvárrtveggi brenndr í kross, ok ætluðu menn, at hann myndi sik sjálfr brennt hafa. Allir menn mæltu þat, at betra þætti hjá Skarpheðni dauðum en þeir ætluðu, því at engi maðr hræddist hann. (I.S., xi, p. 320.)

Then Skarphethinn was stripped of his clothes, since they were not burned. He had placed his hands crosswise, with the right one over the left. They found two marks on him, one between the shoulders and the other on the chest, both in the shape of a cross, and they thought that he must have branded them on himself. Everyone said that it seemed better to be with the dead Skarphethinn than they had expected, for no one was afraid of him.

We never laugh at Skarphethinn, but there is certainly a strand of humour, however grim, in his characterization, and it is this peculiar sense of humour that is the key to his character.

8

Þrándr and the Apostles

P. G. FOOTE

IN THE *Saga of the Faroe Islanders* Þrándr í Götu is forcibly converted to Christianity. Later on, as part of a settlement between him and the family of Sigmundr Brestisson, he takes young Sigmundr Leifsson as his foster-son. Circumstances then make it imperative for Leifr and Þóra, the boy's parents, to reclaim their son, so that he may not be put in a perilous position as a hostage. They decide to visit Þrándr, and when they arrive, Þóra and the boy, now nine years old, are put in a room together. The text then goes on:

modir hans spurde huat Þrandr hefde kent honum. en hann kuezst numit hafua allar saksoknir at sækia ok rettarfar sitt ok annarra. la honum þat græitt firir. þa spyrr hon huat fostri hans hefde kent honum j helgum frædum. Sigmundr kuezst numit hafa pater noster ok kredduna. hon kuezst heyra vilia ok hann gerde suo ok þotti henni hann syngia pater noster til nockurrar hlitar. en kredda Þrandar er a þessa læid.

> Gangat ek æinn ut
> fiorir mer fylgia
> fim guds æinglar
> ber ek bæn firir mer
> bæn firir Kristi
> syng ek salma .vij.
> siai gud hluta minn.

ok j þessu kemr Þrandr j stofuna ok spyrr huat þau tale. Þora suarar ok segir at Sigmundr son hennar hafui flutt firir henni fræde þau er hann hafde kent honum ok þiki mer æingi mynd a segir hon a kredo. Þui er suo hattat sem þu uæitzst segir Þrandr at Kristr atti .xij. læri-suæina edr flæire ok kunne sina kreddu huerr þeirra. nu hefi ek mina kreddu en þu þa er þu hefir numit ok erv margar kreddur ok er sligt segir hann æigi a æina lund rett. Skilia nu tal sitt.[1]

The last chapters of *Færeyinga saga*, like some earlier bits of it, are now preserved only in *Flateyjarbók* from the end of the fourteenth century. There is no reason to suppose that the passage quoted here is a novelty or interpolation and it must thus have been originally written about the year 1200 or soon afterwards. As we shall see, there are also some general considerations which make it seem appropriate to assign it to such an early date.

The verse in the passage has often been cited as one of the oldest recorded variants of a very popular form of prayer, known in old and young instances as a morning or going-out prayer but chiefly in use in modern Europe as a night-prayer or sleep-charm for children.[2] It is sometimes called the 'angel-prayer', and the

---

[1] *Flateyjarbók*, ed. Guðbrandur Vigfússon and C. R. Unger (1860–8), ii, pp. 400–1. The following translation is by Professor George Johnston of Carleton University, Ottawa, and I am very grateful to him for letting me use it:

His mother asked what Thrand had taught him, and he says he has found out how to prosecute all law cases, and what his own legal rights are and the rights of others—this was all in front of his nose. Then she asks what his foster-father has taught him of sacred learning. Sigmund says he has learnt the pater-noster and the creed. She says she wants to hear, and he did as she asked, and she thought he could chant the paternoster more or less right, but Thrand's creed goes like this: I go not out alone: / follow my footing / five of God's angels; / I pray a prayer for myself, / prayer before Christ; / I sing seven psalms, / may God watch over my lot. And with this in comes Thrand into the room and asks what they are talking about. Thora answers and says that Sigmund has recited the learning for her which he has taught him—'and to me there seems no shape to it,' says she, 'not to the creed.' 'It happens this way as you know,' says Thrand, 'that Christ had twelve disciples, or more, and each knew his own creed; now I have my own creed and you the one that you have learnt, and there are lots of creeds, and in such a thing,' says he, 'one way has not got all the right.'

The second line of the verse here is a translation of the variant line found in the Faroese version recorded by J. C. Schrøter, *ferðum mínum fylgja*, see *Færeyinga saga*, ed. C. C. Rafn (1832), p. iv.

[2] Konrad Maurer, 'Ein altes Kindergebet', *Germania*, xii (1867), 235–7; J. Fritzner, *Ordbog over det gamle norske Sprog* (1883–96), ii, pp. 342–3; *The Tale of Thrond of Gate*, englished by F. York Powell (1896), pp. xiii n. 1, xxxviii; F. Ohrt, *Gamle danske Folkebønner* (Studier fra Sprog- og Oldtidsforskning, nr.

English examples best known today have the introduction, 'Matthew, Mark, Luke, and John / Bless the bed that I lie on'.[1] Much could be said about the verse itself and its parallels and analogues, but in this note I wish only to comment on some features of the anecdote in which it is set.

The word *kredda* has not been found in any other early Icelandic text.[2] In modern Icelandic it may be used neutrally of 'belief' in general, but equally or more often it seems to have a pejorative sense, though a tolerant tone, and be used to mean 'superstitious, irrational, obstinate belief'.[3] This is well covered by the gloss given by Jón Ólafsson of Grunnavík (1705–79), 'Credo, f. confessio, Isl. alias Kredda, præsertim cum vana qvædam vel futilia credenda indigitare volumus.'[4] One may think that it is likely that the

149, 1928), p. 56; idem, in *Folketro*, ed. Nils Lid (Nordisk Kultur, xix, 1935), p. 90; *Handwörterbuch des deutschen Aberglaubens*, ii (1929–30), pp. 837–9.

[1] On this type of prayer see the works cited in note 2, p. 130 and the pioneer collections of R. Köhler, 'Ein altes Kindergebet', *Germania*, v (1860), 448–56, xi (1866), 435–45, 'Italienische Nachtgebete', *Jahrbuch für romanische und englische Literatur*, viii (1867), 409–17 (all reprinted in his *Kleinere Schriften*, iii (1900), 320–51); E. Carrington, 'A note on the "White Paternoster"', *The Folk-lore Record*, ii (1879), 127–34; I. and P. Opie, *The Oxford Dictionary of Nursery Rhymes* (1951), pp. 303–5 (it seems undesirable to use the term *lorica* of this kind of prayer-charm as the Opies and York Powell, loc. cit., do); Hamish Henderson, 'An Aberdeen "White Paternoster"', *Scottish Studies*, vi (1962), 223–8.

[2] I am extremely grateful to the editors of *Den Arnamagnæanske Kommissions Ordbog* and in particular to Mr Hans Bekker-Nielsen for confirmation of this fact.

[3] The word has been adopted as a kind of technical term in Icelandic folk-lore collections, chiefly for superstitious prohibitions and omens. See Jón Árnason, *Íslenzkar þjóðsögur*, ed. Árni Böðvarsson and Bjarni Vilhjálmsson (1954–61), ii, pp. 521 and 546 (for terminology), i, pp. 603, 618–21, ii, pp. 521–59, v, pp. 435–41, 473–84; cf. Ólafur Davíðsson, *Huld* (1935–6), ii, pp. 148–9 (for terminology), 149–71; idem, *Íslenzkar þjóðsögur* (1945), i, pp. 325–9 (*kreddusögur*); part vii (1945) of Sigfús Sigfússon, *Íslenzkar þjóð-sögur og -sagnir* is called *Kreddusagnir*. The word *kredda* is not used of papistical relics or morning and evening prayers of the 'angel-prayer' kind, although their relationship with Þránd's *kredda* is of course recognized, cf. e.g. Jón Árnason, ii, p. 60.

[4] Dr Jakob Benediktsson, chief editor of *Orðabók Háskóla Íslands*, has kindly sent me this quotation, the oldest instance of *kredda* they have in their files, and a number of others. Björn Halldórsson, *Lexicon Islandico-Latino-Danicum* (1814), s.v., has only '*religio*, Ens Troesartikel. 2) *symbolum*, et Løsen, et Tegn, hvorpaa man kjender En' (where it looks as though Rask, the author of the Danish glosses,

pejorative sense developed after the Reformation, but we cannot be sure of this. It certainly seems safe to presume that if the word had a pejorative sense at all before the Reformation, it had a tolerant and not a condemnatory tone.

There is no doubt about the meaning of *kredda* in the passage from *Færeyinga saga*. First, used with the definite article, it means the Apostles' Creed, answering to the one use of *kredo* in the episode, the Latin form which in Þóra's mouth so beautifully points the pained orthodoxy of her reply; then it is used of Þránd's verse; and finally it seems to mean 'creed, statement of belief' in general, though always within a Christian context.

The Latin *credo* is the common literary form for 'creed' in early Icelandic and Scandinavian.[1] *Kredda* must be a more popular form, as the consonantism may suggest, and it is usually regarded as a loan-word derived orally and early from a west Germanic language, though it is hard to say which.[2] As philologists have pointed out, intervocalic west Germanic -*d*- would have to be replaced by -*ð*- or -*dd*- if the word was to conform to the Norse pattern.[3]

misunderstood *symbolum* in this context); but Hallgrímur Scheving, *Íslenskir málshættir*, i (1843), 45, quotes 'Sérhvør hefir sína kreddu', Guðbrandur Vigfússon in *An Icelandic-English Dictionary* (1874) glosses *kredda* i.a. as 'belief, fancy' and quotes what he calls the conversational expressions 'hafa sína kreddu, sitja við sína kreddu', and Sigfús Blöndal, *Íslenzk-dönsk orðabók* (1920-4), gives '1. Dogme, Læresetning. 2. Særmening, ensidig Opfattelse. 3. Overtro, Indbildning, fantastisk Paastand.' In compounds the word appears similarly to have both neutral and pejorative meanings.

[1] The word appears as an indeclinable feminine or may be declined as a weak feminine (certainly in early Swedish), see C.-E. Thors, *Den kristna terminologien i fornsvenskan* (Studier i nordisk filologi utg. genom R. Pipping, xlv, 1957), pp. 263–264. Thors can have no evidence however for his statement 'Fvn. brukar däremot oftast en form kredda . . .'; O. Höfler, *Arkiv för nordisk filologi*, xlvii (1931), 288, makes the same error; cf. p. 131, n. 2, and text above. Even in its one occurrence in an early set of *rímur* the word is *credo*, not *kredda*, see *Skáldhelgarímur*, v, st. 15 (*Rímnasafn*, ed. Finnur Jónsson, 1905-22, i, p. 140).

[2] Cf. OE *créda*, m., MLG *créde*, m., MHG *créde*, m., *crêdô*, n., early Dutch *crede*, m. and f., OFris. *kredo*, *kreda*, f. and m.(?), see Höfler and Thors, loc. cit. F. Fischer, *Die Lehnwörter des Altwestnordischen* (Palaestra, lxxxv, 1909), p. 53, gets the gender of OE *créda* wrong, and this has misled Jan de Vries, *Altnordisches etymologisches Wörterbuch* (1961), p. 329.

[3] A. Torp og H. Falk, *Dansk-Norskens Lydhistorie* (1898), pp. 40, 187–8;

Kredda then joins the group of words with mediageminata in Icelandic.[1] The words with which it is most closely associated, *an-* and *on-*stems in *-dd-*, commonly have, like so many of the other words with mediageminata, a homely, familiar or contemptuous ring, often coupled with diminutive connotation.[2] Even though *kredda* was at any rate based on a loan-word, its form would readily help it to acquire some sort of hypocoristic status: it suggests that it denotes the creed that is little, ordinary, homely. The form has in all probability played a part in ensuring the frequent contemptuous sense of the word in modern Icelandic; but as an early 'innocent' diminutive and familiar term for the Apostles' Creed, as in the passage above, it is also entirely appropriate, for this creed, to use Wyclif's words, 'is more comyn and more schortyr þan eny oþer'[3]—it is everybody's everyday creed and not as long as *Credo in unum* and *Quicunque vult*. So in Old English it can be called *se læssa créda*,[4] and in Middle English the *commune crede*, with the Nicene Creed distinguished as the *muchel* creed;[5]

D. A. Seip, *Låneordstudier*, i (1915), 36–7, 101; A. Noreen, *Vårt språk*, iv (1918), 62; O. Höfler, *Arkiv*, xlvii (1931), 276, 287.

[1] See especially Alexander Jóhannesson, *Die Mediageminata im Isländischen* (1932). Since words from *credo* do not appear to exist with gemination in other languages, *kredda* could be counted among the 'rein isländische Bildungen' listed on p. 61 of this book. It may well be that the origin of the gemination in *kredda* in Icelandic has less to do with phonemic reasons than it has with the common principle Wissmann has distinguished behind the whole group of such words, 'die Gefühlsbetontheit', see W. Wissmann, *Nomina postverbalia in den altgermanischen Sprachen* (Ergänzungshefte zur *Zeitschrift für vergleichende Sprachforschung* . . ., Nr. 11, 1932), p. 168.

[2] Wissmann, op. cit., pp. 160–8, discusses the chief classes as Lallworte, Kurznamen, Tiernamen, Spitznamen, onomatopoeic words, and notes (p. 166): 'besonders in den germanischen Sprachen . . . zeigen Bezeichnungen von wertlosen oder geringgeschätzten Dingen Geminata'; Alexander Jóhannesson, op. cit., p. 61, remarks that among the appellatives 'euphemistische oder diminutive Bedeutung waren vorherrschend'; E. Hellquist, *Några anmärkningar om de nordiska verben med mediageminata* (Göteborgs Högskolas Årsskrift, xiv, 1908), p. 6, characterizes the words as pre-eminently 'hvardagsord'.

[3] *MED*, s.v. *crede* n. (2).

[4] J. Bosworth and T. N. Toller, *An Anglo-Saxon Dictionary* (1882–1921), s.v. *créda*.

[5] *MED*, s.v. *crede* n. (2).

in Middle Low German the terms *grote* and *kleine crede*[1] are found; and it can be called *de corte crede* in early Dutch.[2] It is interesting to note that a form of the 'angel-prayer' and a couple of other rigmaroles related in kind (one of them probably to be classed with 'Mary's dream'), found in sources from the seventeenth century onwards, are on rare occasions referred to as 'Credo-le-petit', 'little Credo', 'little creed'.[3] These are linked with the so-called 'White Paternoster',[4] which is a name sometimes given to the 'angel-prayer'; and we find that both 'White Paternoster' and 'little creed' are used for what is basically the same prayer-charm.[5] A hundred years ago Maurer asked, with

[1] K. Schiller and A. Lübben, *Mittelniederdeutsches Wörterbuch*, ii (1876), s.v. *crede*.

[2] Fritzner, loc. cit. (p. 130, n. 2, above), equates this with the 'Credo-le-petit' and 'little Credo' referred to in the following, but in the source it is linked with the *Ave* and, though satirically meant, it must refer to the formal creed of the Church; see the text printed in *Weimarisches Jahrbuch*, i (1854), 125.

[3] J. Harland and T. T. Wilkinson, *Lancashire Folk-Lore* (1867), p. 114, quote 'The Little Creed' from a printed source of 1624 (its preface dated 1608); the same text from the same source is also given by W. J. Thoms in *The Folk-Lore Record*, i (1878), 153, and by G. F. Northall, *English Folk-rhymes* (1892), p. 147. A so-called 'little Credo' is given in T. F. Dibdin, *Typographical Antiquities*, ii (1812), 108 note. On 'Credo-le-petit' see R. Köhler, *Germania*, xi (1866), 443.

[4] Harland and Wilkinson, op. cit., p. 115; W. J. Thoms, 'Chaucer's Night-Spell', *The Folk-Lore Record*, i (1878), 143–54; E. Carrington, 'A Note on the "White Paternoster"', ibid., ii (1879), 127–34; R. Köhler, *Germania*, xi (1866), 444–5; idem, in *Anglia*, iii (1880), 380–1 (these reprinted in *Kleinere Schriften*, iii (1890), 340–1, 591–2 respectively); E. Martinengo-Cesaresco, *Essays in the Study of Folk-songs* (1886), pp. 203–13; W. W. Skeat, *Notes to the Canterbury Tales* (The complete works of Geoffrey Chaucer, v, 1894), pp. 105–6; F. N. Robinson, ed., *The Poetical Works of Chaucer*, p. 788; L. R. C. Yoffie, 'Chaucer's "White Paternoster", Milton's Angels, and a Hebrew Night Prayer', *Southern Folklore Quarterly*, xv (1951), 203–10.

[5] Cf. the text of the 'little Credo' with that of the 'White Pater Noster' printed by Dibdin, op. cit., p. 108 note and p. 110 note respectively, and further the 'Credo-le-petit' and the 'Petite patenôtre blanche' quoted by Köhler, *Germania*, xi (1866), 443–5. It is interesting to see that the adjective 'little' is used of the 'white paternoster' as well; it is also found, for example, in references to Danish prayer-charms of just the same kind ('denne lille Bön', 'denne liden Bön', 'den lille Bön'), see F. Ohrt, *Danmarks Trylleformler*, i (1917), nr. 1073, 1074 *f, g, i*, 1077. It is possible that the adjective in these cases is ultimately a loan from the 'little creed', although it could obviously also be an independent usage. It would be interesting to know the distinction made between 'Pater le blanc' and 'le Pater petit' referred

general reference to the name 'creed' in the *Færeyinga saga* and these modern instances, 'Woher diese Bezeichnung für Formeln, die doch mit dem wirklichen Credo nicht das Mindeste gemein haben?'[1] We see now however that what was adopted seems to have been not merely the name 'creed' but also the diminutive form of it that was otherwise specifically attached to the Apostles' Creed. (The transferred diminutive has naturally, of course, acquired a new significance.) An answer to Maurer's question may be found if we consider the place of the Apostles' Creed in the ordinary devotional life of the middle ages.

The *Pater noster* and the *Credo in deum* were obligatory learning for every Christian, joined in the course of the thirteenth century by the *Ave*.[2] (The absence of the last from the story in the saga may be taken as an indication of early date.[3]) They were the foundation of the faith, the first means to salvation, taught to every Christian child and so the essential knowledge of the godparent, the chief and ready shield against temptation and danger. On waking and on rising, on retiring and before sleeping, they are the prescribed formulas of private devotion and protection as well as features of prime and compline;[4] and this was as much the case in Iceland as anywhere else in medieval Christendom.[5] *Pater noster*

to in a seventeenth-century Provençal poem and quoted by Köhler, *Anglia*, iii (1880), 380 (= *Kleinere Schriften*, iii (1890), 591); and between the 'Paternoster pichenin' and 'Paternoster grande' of the nineteenth-century Venetians mentioned by E. Carrington, *The Folk-Lore Record*, ii (1879), 130.

[1] *Germania*, xii (1867), 236.

[2] See e.g. B. I. Kilström, *Den kateketiska undervisningen i Sverige under medeltiden* (1958), pp. 24–37; and the articles by Kilström, T. Gad, Lilli Gjerløw and Magnús Már Lárusson in *Kulturhistorisk leksikon for nordisk middelalder*, viii (1963), pp. 354–360.

[3] On this point see Ole Widding, 'Ave Maria eller Maríuvers i norrøn litteratur', *Maal og Minne* (1958), pp. 1–7.

[4] Cf. e.g. N. Gihr, *Prim und Komplet des römischen Breviers* (zweite unveränderte Auflage, 1924), pp. 56–7.

[5] The so-called *Stockholm Homily Book*, written c. 1200, contains the following injunctions: Hofom þat uphaf hversdags athæfes várs. at þa er maþr vacnar fyrst of morgoneN. syngve hann credo in deum oc signe sik áþr . . . þa er nest at miNasc miþsmorgoNs tíþar þa er vér kollom príma tíþ . . . Syngue þar .v. pater noster oc credo in deum . . . Siþarst er at miNasc natsǫngs . . . þa scal syngua eN

and *Credo in deum* were the morning, evening and going-out prayers in daily and universal use, and the transfer of their names to vernacular prayers, believed to have the same protective function and said in place of or side by side with the Latin forms,[1] seems entirely natural. The titles themselves were likely to be regarded as guarantees of supernatural efficacy.

There is nothing un-Christian about Þránd's *kredda*, but it is not surprising that Þóra the catechist finds it unsatisfactory in comparison with the *Symbolum apostolicum* itself, and she says so. But Þrándr has his explanation and justification: 'Christ had twelve disciples, or more, and each knew his own creed: now I have my own creed and you the one that you have learnt, and there are lots of creeds, and in such a thing, says he, one way has not got all the right.'

We can maybe never know for sure just what lies behind this rejoinder of Þránd's, although we may be reasonably certain that the author was not crediting him with the outlook of a modern rationalist.[2] It seems likely for one thing that the author wanted to stress the confusion and the difference between *kreddan*, the familiar but still formal Latin *credo* of the catechism and hours, and *kredda*, a name presumably already applied to popular, vernacular morning and evening prayers of Þránd's kind. It is also hard to avoid the thought that Þránd's defence contains an oblique reference to the well-known story concerning the composition of the creed by the apostles themselves, and that the author expects us to understand that Þrándr has got hold of the wrong end of the

.v. pater noster. oc credo in deum . . . oc meþ slíco credo at syngva sem of morgoNEN . . . En þa er maþr keomr i reckio. oc hann bysc til svefns. synge hann pater noster. oc credo (*Homiliu-bók*, ed. Th. Wisén (1872), pp. 109-10). Cf. the passages in *Jóns saga ens helga* (also with reference to conditions in the twelfth century) in *Biskupa sögur* (gefnar út af hinu íslenzka Bókmentafélagi, 1858-78), i, pp. 164-5, 237; and on these cf. K. Vrátný, *Arkiv*, xxxii (1916), 37-8.

[1] It is said for example in J. Harland and T. T. Wilkinson, op. cit., pp. 68-9, that it was customary in most parts of Lancashire to say at bedtime a version of the 'angel-prayer', followed by the Lord's Prayer and the Apostles' Creed, after which the 'angel-prayer' was repeated.

[2] As Niels Winther, following J. H. Schrøter, seems inclined to do in his *Færøernes Oldtidshistorie* (1875), p. 257.

stick. The tradition that the creed was the work of the apostles goes back at least to the fourth century, and it gained currency in the anecdotal form given it by Rufinus about A.D. 400 in his commentary on the creed.[1] According to this, the apostles, before going out into the world, ensured the unity of their missionary teaching by composing the *Credo in deum*. This story, later with precise but varying indications of which part each apostle composed, became well known, commonplace indeed, in Latin and vernacular expositions of the creed and could make part of the catechistical instruction concerning it; it was put into verse to aid the memory.[2] That it was certainly known in Iceland by the time the *Færeyinga saga* was written is made clear by a passage in the so-called *Stockholm Homily Book*;[3] and a knowledge of it is amply attested in later sources from continental Scandinavia.[4] The legend was also portrayed in pictorial form and all sorts of misunderstanding might arise from that. Manuscript illustrations and, more important, mural paintings show the apostles (later often accompanied by Old Testament counterparts) with bands filled with the

---

[1] *Tyrannii Rvfini Opera* recognovit Manlivs Simonetti (Corpvs Christianorvm Series Latina xx, 1961), pp. 134–5; Migne, *PL*, xxi, 337.

[2] On the development of the legend see e.g. A. Hahn, *Bibliothek der Symbole und Glaubensregeln der alten Kirche* (dritte . . . Auflage . . . 1897), pp. 52–3; F. Kattenbusch, *Das apostolische Symbol*, ii (1900), pp. 3–17; H. Leclercq in *Dictionnaire d'archéologie chrétienne et de liturgie*, xv, 2 (1951), pp. 1757–60.

[3] *Homiliu-bók*, pp. 148–50.

[4] Kilström, op. cit., pp. 168–74; a fragmentary Danish text from AM 1056 4to XIX (fifteenth century) is published by O. Nielsen in *Ny kirke-historiske Samlinger*, iv (1867–8), 154; Latin and Danish texts in *En Klosterbog fra Middelalderens Slutning* (*AM 76, 8°*), ed. Marius Kristensen (1933), pp. 22–4, 62–3. (In the last place the Apostles' Creed and the explanation of its origin form an addition to this *Lucidarius* text (see p. vi of the edition) and occur in an exposition of the mass— where the creed said is of course the *Credo in unum*. This piece of ignorance or thoughtlessness ought perhaps to make one wonder whether the miscellany really is 'en Klosterbog'.) For vernacular texts of the creed see K. Maurer, 'Das Bekenntniss des christlichen Glaubens in den Gesetzbüchern aus der Zeit des Königs Magnús lagabœtir', *Sitzungsberichte der königl. bayerischen Akademie der Wissenschaften*, Philos.-philol. Cl. (1892), pp. 537–81; F. Kattenbusch, *Das apostolische Symbol*, i (1894), pp. 199–202; Kilström, op. cit., pp. 99–101; the articles by C. I. Ståhle and Redaktionen in *Kulturhistorisk leksikon for nordisk middelalder*, ii (1957), p. 601, and the articles, ibid., viii (1963), 354–60, referred to p. 135, n. 2, above.

words of the part of the creed they are each supposed to have composed.[1] The custom seems to have arisen in Germany and the oldest certain examples are of the ninth–tenth century in Reichenau[2]—appropriately enough because St Pirminius is one of the earliest writers to assign specific articles in the creed to specific apostles.[3] The murals in Reichenau had certainly been seen by some Scandinavians and Icelanders by the end of the twelfth century,[4] although of course there is no need to look for so precise a link. Þránd's defence seems to give a rough handling to basic accepted truths. What was the conventional believer to make of 'twelve disciples, or more', and of the idea that there are lots of creeds and one is no more right than the other, when in fact it was faithfully believed that twelve apostles composed twelve articles in the *Credo in deum* to ensure that one creed and one only was preached throughout the world? We see however that Þránd's words are not so much a negation of the facts as a travesty of them, and in a travesty of this kind, as in the case of *credo, kreddan* and *kredda*, the

---

[1] See e.g. K. Künstle, *Ikonographie der christlichen Kunst*, i (1928), pp. 181–4; L. Réau, *Iconographie de l'art chrétien*, iii, 1 (1958), pp. 135–6; C. Wernicke, 'Die bildliche Darstellung des apostolischen Glaubensbekenntnisses in der deutschen Kunst des Mittelalters', *Christliches Kunstblatt* (1887), pp. 102–5, 123–6, 135–9, 155–60, 171–5, (1888), pp. 10–15, (1889), pp. 42–6, 59–64, (1893), pp. 20–7, 41–6, 72–9. For Scandinavia see Ellen Jørgensen, *Helgendyrkelse i Danmark* (1909), p. 110; B. I. Kilström, 'Den apostoliska trosbekännelsen i vår medeltida kyrkokunst', *Fornvännen*, xlvii (1952), 129–53; idem, in *Kulturhistorisk leksikon for nordisk middelalder*, ii (1957), pp. 601–2. The oldest of the known Scandinavian instances of the theme is probably that in Fröjel church on Gotland from about 1300.

[2] X. Barbier de Montault, *Traité d'iconographie chrétienne* (1890), ii, pp. 249–50, says the oldest example is in a Gallican missal 'du VIIIᵉ siècle environ', but he does not identify this book and no one seems to have done so since. On the Reichenau paintings see F. X. Kraus, *Die Wandgemälde in der S. Georgskirche zu Oberzell auf der Reichenau* (1884), p. 6 and Tafel XIII; J. Sauer in *Die Kultur der Abtei Reichenau*, ed. K. Beyerle (1925), especially pp. 906–8. Although the apostles are equipped with speech-ribbons, no words are now visible in them.

[3] Migne, *PL*, lxxxix, 1034–5; cf. H. Leclercq in *Dictionnaire d'archéologie chrétienne et de liturgie*, xv, 2 (1951), p. 1760.

[4] Cf. Finnur Jónsson and Ellen Jørgensen, 'Nordiske Pilegrimsnavne i Broderskabsbogen fra Reichenau', *Aarbøger for nordisk Oldkyndighed* (1923), pp. 1–36.

closer one can follow Þránd's pugnacious confusion to its source, the more accomplished the joke becomes. We can imagine thoughts on these lines: Twelve apostles, subtract Judas Iscariot, add Matthias, was Thaddaeus the same man as the other Judas or not, what about Paul, and Mark and Luke, the gospel-makers who often join the apostles in the litany lists? As for the creed, are we not told, have some of us not seen, how each apostle had his own article of faith?

The situation where the orthodox are shaken by some piece of literalism or by some relic of paganism or popery brought out in good faith by the ignorant has produced many amusing anecdotes, often founded on fact, but I know none in which the humour is as gentle and complex as in this story of Þrándr. Clearly enough, the author expected his audience to be amused by the inadequacy of Þránd's sacred learning, contrasted as it is with his skill in secular law, and he relied on them to recognize and appreciate the contrast between accepted Christian truths and the perversion of them that Þránd's defence is. The author's confident intimacy in his approach to his audience and his humour are fully in keeping with what we find in other episodes in the saga.[1] But we may say too that, in a way, the joke is not merely at Þránd's expense: the author is bold enough to leave him with the last word, and the sacred learning itself must seem to be at some risk. But if the author borders thus securely on the irreverent, he is surely doing so affectionately from the inside, as it were, not in mockery from the outside, and his confidence in his audience springs from his knowledge of what they share. Where this sort of comedy is permitted and enjoyed, we may not unreasonably look to find a tolerant society in which the Church is a firmly established institution and Christian devotion familiar and everyday, in which people can be broadminded with confidence and good humour, and there is no serious tension or conflict between clerical and lay. And by and large this seems to have been the condition of things in twelfth-century Iceland, where churchman and chieftain were

[1] Cf. P. G. Foote, *On the Saga of the Faroe Islanders. An Inaugural Lecture* (1964), pp. 14–21.

in close alliance, often indeed identified, where there was little social strife, where schooling was the same for everyone who had any schooling at all—and within their limits many Icelanders who grew up in the twelfth century became highly educated men, no matter whether they followed a clerical or secular career.[1] It is this background that we must bear in mind when considering, for example, the interpretative mythology of Snorri Sturluson, thoroughly leavened by Christian ideas and idioms as it has been shown to be.[2] And we must certainly assume that the author of the *Færeyinga saga* grew up in such a milieu and wrote his book about or soon after A.D. 1200. Later than that it would have been hard for him to form his story of Þrándr and the apostles in just this way.

[1] Cf. Sigurður Nordal, *Íslenzk menning*, i (1942), especially pp. 299–305, although this chiefly concerns the earlier part of the century; P. G. Foote, 'Sturlusaga and its background', *Saga-Book*, xiii (1946–53), especially pp. 207–16.

[2] Anne Holtsmark, *Studier i Snorres mytologi* (Skrifter utg. av Det Norske Videnskaps-Akademi i Oslo, II. Hist.-Filos. Kl., Ny Serie. No. 4. 1964).

9

An Early Representation
of St Olaf

DAVID M. WILSON

THE PURPOSE of this note is to suggest that a figure carrying an axe on the Irish Shrine of St Manchan is an early representation of St Olaf and that it should be dated to the early twelfth century.

The figure (see p. 142) is half-round and is of cast bronze: it was originally gilt and is 16 cm high. It portrays a man with protruding ears, large bulbous lentoid eyes, wavy hair and a forked beard. In two strap-like hands he holds an axe, his left hand clasping its blade. The upper part of the body is naked and he wears a panelled skirt-like garment which reaches to his knees, where it terminates in a zigzag hem. His legs and feet are formalized, each consisting of a simple bar with incisions to suggest toes. Between the legs is a flat plate and between the feet is a rivet hole. Another rivet hole occurs in the middle of the chest in the fork of the beard.

The figure is attached to the Shrine of St Manchan,[1] now preserved in Boher church, Co. Offaly, but originally kept in the church of the monastery which bore the saint's name at Lemanaghan, in the same county. The figure was already fixed to the face of the shrine when it was first published by Robert Travers in connection with the Dublin exhibition of 1853,[2] and it seems unlikely that it has not always been with its companion figures, of which at least another nine survive.

---

[1] The shrine has been published very fully by T. D. Kendrick and E. Senior, 'St Manchan's Shrine', *Archaeologia*, lxxxvi (1937), 105–18, and it is from this source that I have taken the details of its history and provenance.

[2] *Exhibition Expositor and Advertiser* (Dublin, 1853), no. 12, 4.

Cast bronze representation of St Olaf on the shrine of St Manchan

Scale $\frac{1}{1}$

Its date is not as clear as might at first glance appear. Miss Senior suggested that the figures on the shrine were derived from early twelfth-century crucifix-figures of continental type.[1] She was thus forced to date them to the last quarter of the twelfth century,[2] nearly fifty years after the rest of the shrine was manufactured. This, she argued, also helps to explain the clumsy manner in which the figures are set on the face of the shrine. I myself cannot accept that the figures post-date the main body of the shrine,[3] which should be dated to c. 1120–30.[4]

The decoration of the body of the shrine is very similar to that of the Cross of Cong (which is dated by inscription to c. 1123, having been commissioned by Toirdelbach Ua Conchubair, king of Connacht). Indeed their decorative techniques are so closely related that it is quite possible that they were made in the same workshop. If we are to date the figures of the shrine we can only do so by a study of their form and of the ornament with which they are decorated. The figure which I allege to be a representation of St Olaf has no incidental ornament on it; but, on stylistic grounds, it must be accepted that all the figures on the shrine were made in the same workshop. In this context it should be noticed that some of the other figures have ornament on their skirts which can be analysed.[5] This ornament can be compared, for instance, with the ornament at the top of the Aghadoe crozier,[6] which is decorated in typical Irish Urnes style of the early twelfth century; a date which agrees with that proposed by both Dr Henry[7] and myself[8] for these figures. The style of the figures themselves is paralleled to a certain extent in the roughly contemporaneous Irish stone sculpture—on the shaft of the Dysert O'Dea cross,[9] for example, or on a cross from Kilfenora.[10]

[1] Kendrick and Senior, op. cit., p. 114.　　　　[2] Ibid., p. 115.

[3] I have already cursorily argued this point in D. M. Wilson and O. Klindt-Jensen, *Viking Art* (London, 1966), pp. 158–9.

[4] Miss F. Henry, *L'art irlandais*, iii (Paris, 1964), p. 157, dates it more specifically to between 1128 and 1136.

[5] Senior and Kendrick, loc. cit., pl. xxix, 1. b, c, g, h and, possibly, i and k.

[6] Henry, op. cit., pl. 85.　　　　[7] Ibid., p. 158.　　　　[8] Loc. cit.

[9] Henry, op. cit., pl. 60.　　　　[10] Ibid., pl. 55.

Miss Senior's twelfth-century parallels have been denied by Miss Henry who has cited alternative earlier prototypes. These, taken together with the ornament and stylistic parallels quoted above, would seem to invalidate Miss Senior's arguments. The disposition of the figures on the face of the shrine remains rather perturbing. It should, however, be said that not all the figures which originally embellished the shrine survive, and it may in fairness be added that the figures which do survive are not in their original position. In their pristine state they were mounted over a sheet of metal (which was presumably gilded) and may well have formed part of a logical and balanced scheme of disposition, together with a number of, now missing, companion pieces.

There can be little doubt, then, that the figure dates to the early twelfth century and was manufactured in Ireland in a sphere of Scandinavian artistic influence.

It seems difficult to deny that this figure is that of a saint or other holy person and the iconographical association of a man with an axe would seem, particularly in this sub-Viking context, to indicate that the figure represents St Olaf. The iconography of St Olaf has been carefully investigated, in its north-western European context, by Wallem and Larsen[1] who showed that the axe is his most common attribute. The lack of the royal crown, which is an almost universal characteristic of later European representations of the saint, need not trouble us in this highly representational style, in a country where there is little or no pictorial evidence of crowns at this early period. This particular representation of the saint is, of course, completely unlike any of the other normal Romanesque or Gothic figures which abound in Scandinavian art. Only one representation of St Olaf indeed can possibly be anywhere near contemporary to the St Manchan shrine; this comes from Vernes and is dated to the late twelfth century.[2]

There seems, however, to be no reason to question the likelihood of the presence of a figure of St Olaf in the old Scandinavian

[1] F. B. Wallem and B. I. Larsen, 'Iconographia Sancti Olavi', *Det kongelige norske Videnskabers Selskaps Skrifter* (1930).

[2] Ibid., fig. 1.

kingdom of Ireland on an object which has so much ornament executed in the Viking idiom. Professor Bruce Dickins, in his study of the cult of St Olaf in Britain,[1] has pointed out that relics of the saint were apparently deposited by Donatus, the first bishop of Dublin (a Dane who died in 1074), in his cathedral church at Dublin. Professor Dickins further quotes[2] the miraculous victory achieved in Ireland by Guthormr Ketilsson over Margaðr Ragnvaldsson in 1052 as a result of intercession by Guthormr with St Olaf. Although there is little evidence of a strong late medieval cult of Olaf in Ireland, this early evidence, together with two (apparently early) dedications of churches to the saint,[3] shows that his cult had some importance in Ireland—at least in the period before the Norman conquest of that country when Scandinavian influence was still very strong.

If my identification of this strange figure is correct, and if we do have here a representation of the royal Olaf, then it would seem to be the earliest portrayal of this great Scandinavian saint so far recorded.

[1] B. Dickins, 'The Cult of S. Olave in the British Isles', *Saga Book of the Viking Society for Northern Research*, xii (1940), 71.

[2] Ibid., p. 72.

[3] Ibid., p. 71.

10

The Translator of
Mandevilles Rejse: a new name in
Fifteenth-century Danish Prose?

S. A. J. BRADLEY

OF THE four manuscripts containing Mandeville material in Danish, one is E III 6 in Karen Brahe's collection in the Landsarkiv for Fyn in Odense, Denmark; two others, SKB M 306 (formerly Cod. Holm. 55) and SKB M 307 (formerly Cod. Holm. K. 31), are in the Royal Library in Stockholm; and the fourth, an unfinished summary, is GKS 3559 in the Royal Library in Copenhagen.[1]

SKB M 307 was edited by M. Lorenzen[2] in 1882 with comparative readings from SKB M 306 and GKS 3559, but unfortunately E III 6 had been misplaced at Odense, and was not located until the book was at press, so that only the most notable variants could be listed in an addition to the Introduction.[3]

SKB M 306 contains an inscription dating it in 1584; and GKS 3559 and E III 6 are also in hands of the latter 1500's. SKB M 307 is signed by Ole Jakobsen (Olauus Jacobi),[4] a friar of the Franciscan

[1] For a survey of the Danish Mandeville tradition and the MSS, see Helge Toldberg's article 'Mandeville', *Kulturhistorisk leksikon for nordisk middelalder*, xi (1966); also M. C. Seymour and R. A. Waldron, 'The Danish Version of *Mandeville's Travels*', *N. & Q.*, November 1963.

[2] *Mandevilles Rejse i Gammeldansk Oversættelse* (Copenhagen, 1882).

[3] Lorenzen, op. cit., Indledning, pp. lxiii f.

[4] His hand is also found in the MS SKB K 46, now in Stockholm but made in Denmark and containing the Middle Danish *Dyrerim* (rhyming bestiary) and *Sagnkrønike* (legendary chronicle), reproduced in facsimile in *Corpus Codicum Danicorum Medii Ævi* (Copenhagen, 1960–), vol. iv, with comment by Dr Erik Kroman.

house at Næstved, about 50 km south-west of Roskilde, Zealand, and dated by him *anno domini mcdl nono in profesto assumpcionis virginis gloriose*. The hand well fits the date claimed,[1] and so it is clear that SKB M 307 is the oldest extant manuscript of the Danish Mandeville, dating from 1459.

But the identification of the oldest *version* of the translation is not so simple a matter, despite the fact that in each of the three complete manuscripts a specific date of translation is alleged. The sixteenth-century E III 6 says: 'nu er hun aff latine omset paa danske aar effter gudz byr mcdxliiii'.[2] SKB M 306 says: 'nu er hun af Latine omset paa Danske. Anno d. 1584.' SKB M 307, on its first leaf, says: 'nw ar effther gutz byrdh thusenne ok fæm hundredæ ok trætywe ok paa thet fierdæ wor hun seth aff lathyne ok paa danskæ aff een hedherlik clærk som hedher hær Pædhær Haræ j Roskylle bescopess dømæ'.[3] Leaving aside for the moment the obvious discrepancy in SKB M 307 between the alleged date of translation and the date of Jakobsen's copying it, we are given the impression that E III 6 is a copy of the oldest of three separate translations, made at different times. But Lorenzen's examination[4] showed that the texts of these three manuscripts are overall so close that it is impossible to regard them as being independent of each other; nor is it possible to regard one of them as being the source of the other two. They can only be copies made at various times, which all derive from a common original translation of the Latin Vulgate Version of *Mandeville's Travels*.[5] Almost certainly GKS 3559, for all its freedom in condensing, is also derived from this archetype. It at once becomes clear, then, that not all, if any, of the alleged dates of translation can be accepted at face value; but

[1] Kroman, op. cit., p. xxii.
[2] 'now is it from Latin translated into Danish, the year after God's birth 1444.'
[3] 'now the year after God's birth a thousand and five hundred and thirty and in the fourth [1534] was it translated from Latin and into Danish by a worthy priest who is called Hr Peder Hare in Roskilde diocese.' Danish text from Lorenzen, op. cit., p. 1.
[4] Lorenzen, op. cit., Indledning, p. xliv, and p. il.
[5] Lorenzen, op. cit., Indledning, pp. lxix f., and Seymour and Waldron, op. cit., p. 407.

consideration of the date discrepancy in SKB M 307 may help to restore a pattern to this confused situation.

Lorenzen[1] and Molbech[2] before him noted this discrepancy between the claim on the first leaf that Peder Hare translated it in 1534 and the claim on the last leaf that Ole Jakobsen copied it in 1459. Both scholars accepted both dates: the bulk of the manuscript did indeed date from 1459, but the first two leaves had been supplied in 1534 by Hare to replace lost or illegible leaves of the 1459 manuscript. But whilst Molbech took literally the claim that Hare had *translated* these two leaves, Lorenzen argued that the inscription *af latin omset paa danske*, found in all three complete manuscripts, was a standard formula deriving from the common original, into which the successive copyists would feel free to insert the date of their copy where formerly stood the date of the original translation. The exception is the date 1444 in E III 6, which Lorenzen accepted as authentically reproduced by the sixteenth-century copyist from his original, since it is improbable he would have invented such a date.

This line of reasoning led Lorenzen to the conclusion that the original translation existed at least as early as 1444, that Jakobsen was therefore a copyist (not, as Molbech held, the translator of his part), that Hare was a sixteenth-century repairer only, and that consequently neither name nor date can be put to the original translation.

Lorenzen's arguments in support of the notion of a two-part manuscript spanning seventy-five years between its production and its repair are persuasive only in so far as they show that the first two leaves of the present manuscript (which he designated B) may indeed constitute some kind of repair. The remainder of the manuscript (which he designated A) is characterized by red chapter headings and red initials, but B has only blank spaces for red letters never actually inserted; B also lacks the fine line-rulings which mark out the columns in A; and the text at the end of B overlaps the text at the beginning of A by three words.

[1] Lorenzen, op. cit., Indledning, pp. xlii f.
[2] C. Molbech, 'Danske Haandskrifter i Stockholm', *Historisk Tidsskrift*, iv (Copenhagen, 1843).

But for the further extension of the case, to show that there are two hands from two different periods, he was not able to present such support. The language of B is the same as that of A; but to the objection that one would expect to find differences of linguistic forms between two texts separated by seventy-five years, Lorenzen replied with the assumption that Hare copied the substitute leaves letter by letter from the damaged original leaves, or from another exemplar identical with Jakobsen's text. As for the developments in handwriting over the intervening seventy-five years, which one could have expected to be not only present, but pronounced, Lorenzen asserted that there is a difference, but felt obliged to admit that it is 'not perhaps as great as one might have expected in view of the difference of age'.[1]

But preoccupation with the fact of the 'repair' and the fact of the two conflicting dates outweighed the diffidence he clearly felt in reviewing the supporting evidence, and he finally aligned himself with Molbech in accepting both dates. The situation of stalemate thus implied over the question of date and authorship of the original translation remained as Lorenzen left it, and has been repeated without further investigation until quite recently.

Dr Erik Kroman,[2] in a footnote to a description of the other manuscript known to be in Ole Jakobsen's hand, has expressed his judgement upon the palæographical issues involved in SKB M 307: 'To judge from the character of the script, as well as from orthography and language, the two leaves [containing Hare's name and the date 1534] could not possibly have been written in 1534. Besides, there can be no doubt that they were written by the same hand as the remainder of the manuscript. Quite decisive is, finally, the fact that the watermark of one of the two leaves occurs in the rhyming beast fables [in SKB K 46, written wholly in Jakobsen's hand].' It is, of course, possible that Hare took two blank leaves from the damaged 1459 manuscript and wrote his version upon these, which would account for the watermark; but this would seem barely more probable than that Hare also imitated the hand of the manuscript he was repairing so well that

[1] Lorenzen, op. cit., Indledning, pp. xliii f.   [2] Kroman, op. cit., loc. cit.

Lorenzen was surprised to find a hand of 1534 looking so much like a hand of 1459, whilst Kroman was quite firmly convinced that the two hands were really one. In Kroman's opinion, the hand, the orthography, the language, and the paper itself are all in agreement with the date claimed in the *Explicit*, 1459. He therefore concluded that the date 1534 is an error, and suggested it should be read as 1434.[1]

Had the date been written in roman numerals, such a scribal slip would not have seemed unduly surprising: the copying of roman numerals provided opportunity for errors of reproduction and mathematical blunders, of which sufficient examples can be provided from these four Danish *Mandevilles* alone. For example, in GKS 3559, the summarizer wrote that Mandeville left England in 1322, was away for xxxiii years, and returned in MCCCLX (for 1355). However, the date 1534 is written not in numerals but in words, and it might therefore be objected that a scribal error in such circumstances is less probable.

But SKB M 307 is the only one of the four manuscripts to use words for numbers—the standard practice of the others is to use numerals—so that by gratuitously undertaking to convert the numerals of his original into words the scribe increased the chances of error arising from any idiosyncrasy in his personal mathematical ability. And in fact Jakobsen (for surely the error must be his, and not one he copied from an earlier exemplar)[2] provided ample evidence in the course of the text that he was highly and peculiarly

---

[1] Accepted by Toldberg, op. cit. Kroman's rejection of Lorenzen's view that 'translated' could be a mistake for 'copied' in the 1534 ascription in SKB M 307 is less weighty than his other arguments. He says that 'the expression *seth aff lathyne ok paa danske* can scarcely be misconstrued' (loc. cit.)—yet some such explanation is required for the parallel instance in SKB M 306, where the text is certainly a copy, though it poses as a translation.

[2] It seems a degree more plausible to me that Jakobsen could have made so gross an error under the strain of computing from roman numerals, and overlooked it in his general carelessness of revision, than that he could have overlooked it if he had found it in the verbal form in his original, of which he might be expected to have followed the sense at least sufficiently closely to observe an error of this order. But it is admittedly hazardous to distinguish degrees of plausibility in this kind of situation.

prone to making serious mistakes of conversion, even in the simpler problems of arithmetic: for example, he read LX as 40 on one occasion, but LXX as 90 plus 20 on another.[1] The degree of attentiveness with which this scribe treated his original can be measured by 'the whole list of errors' remarked upon by Lorenzen,[2] errors of misreading, misunderstanding, and incorrect expansion of the abbreviations of his Danish exemplar,[3] which led Lorenzen to comment that this was far from being what one could call a careful copy.[4] And Dr Kroman[5] noted another curious pointer to the nature of Ole Jakobsen's mind in SKB K 46, where 'as a sort of rubric or filling in of a line, there are a number of instances of Danish and Latin words which have nothing whatsoever to do with the text and which show where the scribe's thoughts really were. Words such as *kiæræ sødæ, kiæræ gadelam, sødhæ lif, myt hiertæ kæræ . . . kiæræ rosen*[6] can hardly be deemed entirely fitting, considering that the scribe was a monk.'

From such evidence of general carelessness and of mathematical deficiency in particular, it appears quite plausible that this scribe, even more than his class at large, was capable of writing 1534 in error for 1434. Nor need it be supposed that having done so the scribe would at once be aware of the absurdity of the error: examples are plentiful of scribes so unthinkingly absorbed in the mechanics of copying that they had no awareness of the sense or nonsense of what they wrote (the scribe of GKS 3559 provides an instance, in giving the dates of Mandeville's journey, quoted above). Though Jakobsen made corrections in his own text, these are random, and it has been left to a later hand, according to

---

[1] Lorenzen, op. cit., p. 197 line 6 and p. 11 line 33 respectively.

[2] Lorenzen, op. cit., Indledning, pp. xlvi f.

[3] The natural assumption that Jakobsen followed a Danish exemplar and was not himself the translator is confirmed by, among other things, certain errors which could result only from the misreading of a Danish original. Molbech, however, believed he was the translator. Lorenzen, op. cit., Indledning, pp. xlvi f.

[4] Lorenzen, op. cit., Indledning, p. li.

[5] Kroman, op. cit., loc. cit.

[6] 'dear sweet, dear pet lamb, sweet life, my dear heart . . . dear rose'—whether the object of contemplation is fleshly or spiritual, Kroman's implication is that Jakobsen's mind was too preoccupied for him to be an efficient copyist!

Lorenzen,[1] to correct still other errors missed by him. Also, the fact that the incorrect date was in words and not numerals may have obscured its incongruity from his cursory check.

But even if it is accepted that 1534 is an error for 1434, the position about dates is still not satisfactory, because there remains the conflict between the three translation dates claimed by the three complete translations stemming from the single original. One of these three can be put aside immediately: the 'translation' date 1584 in SKB M 306 must necessarily be a false claim, since the translation undoubtedly derives from the same original as the older manuscript, SKB M 307. This date can only be that on which a copyist decided for reasons innocent or culpable to replace the date he found in his original exemplar with the date of the year in which he made his copy. Apart from noting this fact, there is apparently nothing more to do with the date recorded here.

But perhaps there is something useful to be done about the dates claimed in the other two complete manuscripts, 1434 in SKB M 307 (reconstructed) and 1444 in E III 6. At the risk of seeming to persecute him beyond his deserving, attention must again be turned to the mathematical deficiency of the scribe of SKB M 307.

Of all the circumstances in which Jakobsen made blunders of computing, the one which most commonly caused him trouble was that in which the roman numeral L must have appeared in his exemplar.[2] In particular, he had a curious blind spot about the combination XL. On one occasion[3] he gave it the value X *plus* L totalling 60: but elsewhere[4] he totted it up to *trætyuæ*, 30. So, looking at it the other way, where in his copy he has written the word *trætyuæ*, there is a great probability that the number which had stood in roman numerals in his exemplar was not XXX, but XL.

The word *trætyuæ* appears in the wording of the critical date in SKB M 307, the date claimed for Peder Hare's translation. If

---

[1] Lorenzen, op. cit., Indledning, p. il.
[2] Lorenzen, op. cit., Indledning, p. xlviii.
[3] Lorenzen, op. cit., p. 19 line 2.
[4] Lorenzen, op. cit., p. 34 lines 4 and 8, 37 line 10, etc.

Jakobsen produced the sum by his usual incorrect computation, then the date which stood in his original was not 1434, but 1444.[1]

This reconstructed date now coincides with the date claimed in E III 6 for its original, which was the same original as that from which Jakobsen's copy also ultimately derives.

If the reconstructed date in SKB M 307 is accepted, the position is now that two of the three complete versions offer information about the original translation of the Latin Vulgate *Mandeville* into Danish. E III 6 preserves a date for the translation, 1444, which is confirmed by the date preserved in SKB M 307. The latter also preserves the name of the translator, Peder Hare, priest in the diocese of Roskilde. The fact that it is Ole Jakobsen, a clerical scribe writing in the diocese of Roskilde after a space of only fifteen years, who preserves Hare's name, strengthens the probability that the ascription to him as translator is correct.

On these conclusions, the following timetable may be constructed:

c. 1420	Claudius Clavus, Danish cartographer, refers to Mandeville as an authority[2]
1434	Copy of the Latin Vulgate *Mandeville* made in Denmark (GKS 445—not used, according to Lorenzen, for the Danish translation)
1444	Peder Hare translates Latin Vulgate *Mandeville* into Danish (common original of the four extant versions)
1459	Ole Jakobsen makes copy of Hare's translation (SKB M 307)
1584	Another copy of Hare's translation made (SKB M 306)
Late 1500's	Another copy of Hare's translation made (Odense E III 6)
Late 1500's	Summary of Hare's translation begun, incomplete (GKS 3559)

---

[1] Allowing also for the error of 15– for 14–.
[2] See the article 'Kartografi' in the *Kulturhistorisk leksikon*.

Whilst it is perhaps true that a translation seldom enjoys the prestige of an original composition, Lorenzen was surely justified in writing of SKB M 307: 'Certainly the translator can rightfully lay claim to praise for having by and large expressed himself in a good Danish, and in this respect stands not a little above various other translators of the middle ages.'[1] Hare's translation, as he said, 'is of most value to us as a monument of the Danish language, of correspondingly considerable importance'.[2]

Perhaps, then, it is time that Peder Hare's name should be given a place in the annals of Danish literary history, and his work more attention than it has hitherto received.

[1] Lorenzen, op. cit., Indledning, p. lxxii: 'oversætteren vistnok med rette kan gøre fordring paa den ros, at han i det hele taget har udtrykt sig paa et godt dansk sprog og i den henseende ikke staar saa lidt over flere andre middelalderlige oversættere.'

[2] Lorenzen, op. cit., Indledning, p. lxxii: '. . . for os sikkert har sit største værd om et dansk sprogmonument af forholdsvis ikke ringe betydning'.

II

Conjectural Emendation[1]

GEORGE KANE

CONJECTURAL EMENDATION as an editorial practice has a bad name in English studies. What A. J. Wyatt once called indulgence 'in the luxury of personal emendations'[2] has seemed to imply a kind of capriciously irresponsible selfishness inappropriate to a discipline dedicated to the preservation of a tradition, and for all the time that has passed since he wrote thus in 1894 there is still a feeling that such self-indulgence is, if not 'the greatest', certainly a grave 'disqualification for discharging duly the functions of an editor'.[3] Further, the suspicion of presumptuousness that attaches to all emendation falls most heavily upon the kind called conjectural, which, as I understand the term, is practised when an editor rejects the evidence afforded by his manuscripts and in defiance of this proposes as the lost original a reading for which no manuscript evidence exists. The situation that has generated this attitude (which I do not think I have misrepresented) is of some complexity: while the unsatisfactory character of received texts is generally acknowledged, and the need for good editions is manifest, the fairly extensive, but not very well coordinated discussions of the theory and practice of editing have fallen short of agreement.

One principal objection to conjectural emendation—it has also been laid against less venturesome kinds of editing—is that it includes an element of uncontrollable subjectivity. The popular conception of that subjectivity is excellently illustrated in Vinaver's

---

[1] This essay is based on a paper read to the Oxford Medieval Society on 3 March 1966.

[2] *Beowulf with the Finnsburg Fragment*, ed. A. J. Wyatt, rev. R. W. Chambers (Cambridge, 1948), p. xxvi.

[3] Ibid.

introduction to his edition of Malory: he is there writing about his own situation when confronted with the necessity of evaluating conflicting evidence from two sources, the Winchester manuscript, and Caxton's print of a lost manuscript.

The traditional method consists in selecting from each of the two texts or groups of texts the 'best' readings they can offer so as to produce what is often inappropriately called a 'critical' text . . . the value of such a text depends on the clear understanding that what is 'best' is not what seems best to the critic, but what is attributable to the author. And it so happens that it is not humanly possible for any critic, however cautious and competent, to maintain this distinction. For the more he is bent on his task, the less he can conceive of himself and the author as two distinct individuals whose ways of thinking and writing are inevitably unlike, who are both liable to err, each in his own unaccountable way, just as they are capable of choosing two equally 'good', but conflicting, forms of expression. There may be various degrees of skill in the handling of the situation, and various degrees of accuracy in the results; but the procedure proves in the end . . . disastrous; . . . the fault lies . . . with certain habits of mind inseparable from any practical application of the method, habits which broadly speaking amount to the belief that whatever satisfies one's taste and judgement must be 'good', and that whatever is 'good' belongs to the author.[1]

For anyone who agrees with him Vinaver's objection must apply *a fortiori* to the conjecturing editor, who rejects as 'bad' an actual, received, often unanimously attested reading, and prefers, would set in its place a hypothetical reading, one which he himself has invented. What wild fancies must we expect of him when even editors soberly regarding a choice of manuscript readings are incapable of sustained intellectual discipline?

For such anxieties there are undoubtedly grounds in the history of textual criticism. The capricious, or inept or misguided conjectural emendation is one of its recurrent themes. Of Bentley, for instance, 'impatient, . . . tyrannical, . . . too sure of himself', A. E. Housman wrote

he corrupts sound verses which he will not wait to understand, alters

---

[1] E. Vinaver, *The Works of Sir Thomas Malory* (Oxford, 1948), i, pp. xcii–xciii.

what offends his taste without staying to ask about the taste of Manilius, plies his desperate hook upon corruptions which do not yield at once to gentler measures, and treats the MSS. much as if they were fellows of Trinity.[1]

Bentley was not, Housman also implies, altogether intellectually honest or wholly secure against self-delusion: 'many a time when he feigned and half fancied that he was correcting the scribe, he knew in his heart . . . that he was revising the author'.[2] In the century following Bentley's, less brilliant but equally wayward, irrational and arbitrary conjecture appears to have been a common practice of editors of classical texts.[3] Two extreme attitudes can be observed: Bentley's seemingly arrogant *Nobis et ratio et res ipsa centum codicum potiores sunt*:[4] and the more romantic one expressed by Dr Johnson:

The allurements of emendation are scarcely resistible. Conjecture has all the joy and all the pride of invention, and he that has once started a happy change, is much too delighted to consider what objections may rise against it.[5]

Excessive subjectivity, an identification with the author leading to the assumption that the editor perfectly commanded his style, or a supersession of author by editor, were bound to discredit both conjectural emendation and, by association, to some extent at least the whole practice of editing. Whether this effect was altogether just has not seemed to matter; and the brilliance of many conjectures, especially in the texts of the Greek and Roman poets, some so intrinsically excellent that for most readers they own the status of received readings, has not sufficed to check it. The demonstration of the fallibility of editorial judgement had been too extreme.

If therefore a modern editor, especially of a vernacular text, professed to identify corruption when his manuscripts did not

[1] A. E. Housman, *Selected Prose*, ed. J. Carter (Cambridge, 1961), p. 29.
[2] Ibid.   [3] Compare Housman, p. 43.
[4] Quoted by A. Dain, *Les Manuscrits* (Paris, 1949), p. 151.
[5] *Johnson on Shakespeare*, ed. W. Raleigh (London, 1931), p. 60.

necessarily indicate this (that is when the archetypal reading of the manuscripts was not in doubt), and further professed confidence in his ability to restore the actual words of his author, he was behaving at best ill-advisedly, at worst with unbecoming conceit of himself. The current scepticism about conjecture extended, as it may still do, to the whole editorial process, and one form of the flight from judgement has been 'to condemn any critical treatment of manuscript material beyond a mere reproduction of the extant tradition or of one of its representatives'.[1] 'One should' (I quote a student of Bédier reporting the master's view) 'select a manuscript which is of the poet's own dialect, which is relatively old, which does not have many mechanical defects and one should reproduce this text without attempting correction unless there is a proved slip of the pen . . . . versification should not be corrected.'[2] This appeared the judicious, the laudable scholarly course: 'möglichst die lesungen der handschrift zu wahren'.[3] Housman, however, drew attention to another aspect of the conservative editor's mentality: 'an editor who wishes to be praised . . . must defend the MS. tradition not only where it appears to be right but also where it appears to be wrong';[4] and again, 'assuredly there is no trade on earth, excepting textual criticism, in which the name of prudence would be given to that habit of mind which in ordinary human life is called credulity'.[5] We have, I hope, laid aside the caustic address of Housman's generation of editors, but perhaps in textual criticism our world is still as topsy-turvy; at any rate it might seem so when an eminent contemporary editor asserts in all seriousness that 'The line of least resistance in textual studies is to declare a reading corrupt and substitute one's own.'[6]

That statement, however plausible it may *prima facie* seem, does not accurately represent the situation. It must mean, in its context,

---

[1] Vinaver, op. cit., p. xciii. Compare Housman, pp. 105, 106, and K. Sisam, *Studies in the History of Old English Literature* (Oxford, 1953), p. 30, n.

[2] U. T. Holmes, reviewing E. B. Ham, *Textual Criticism and Jehan le Venelais* in *Speculum*, xxii (1947), 469.

[3] R. P. Wülker, quoted by Sisam, op. et loc. cit.

[4] Housman, p. 105.   [5] Ibid., p. 43.

[6] Vinaver, p. xciii.

that emending conjecturally is in general easier than accounting for a received reading. But that proposition is manifestly false because, if conjectural emendation is correctly practised, it must begin with and embrace accounting for the received reading; it is thus, as the more comprehensive operation, obviously a more difficult one than any which it comprises.

Moreover the statement does not reflect general opinion. This, as I see it, has two main attitudes: one that the excesses to which conjectural emendation has been carried have made it disreputable; the other that since it is very often possible to conjecture alternative readings for a crux, none of which can be validated, the more disciplined scholarship is to refrain from the activity.

These attitudes, on the face of it, seem reasonable; moreover they should, one might think, serve to moderate speculation, to control the operation of judgement, to safeguard the desirable principle of restraint. If, however, the arguments behind them are examined they appear with less credit. For instance: conjectural emendation is an activity which has been, and thus can be, badly conducted; because of this possibility it ought to be avoided. Or, conjectural emendation is an activity at which one can make mistakes; it is thus dangerous to an editor's reputation and he should therefore avoid it. Or, conjectural emendation cannot produce results of absolute certainty; it is therefore unprofitable and should be avoided. The first and second of these lines of thinking condemn themselves as mean-spirited; the third loses force from the indisputable consideration that there are very few results of literary scholarship in general for which the claim of absolute certainty can be made. In view of this the presumptive character of the results of textual criticism, and specifically of conjectural emendation, cannot cogently be invoked as a special, arbitrarily applicable objection to these particular forms of the activity. Such arguments lack force and we dismiss them easily; but there still survives a deep-seated objection to conjectural emendation, arising from a very natural human state of mind, the instinct for security.

That instinct would be best satisfied if the texts of ancient authors were generally sound.[1] Since that is not the case the next best reassurance would be to have available a system of editing which would eliminate or at least reduce the possibility of error in that unfortunately necessary process by removing the element of judgement from the operation or minimizing it; there should be a formula whose answers would replace the irresponsible, subjective decisions of erratic editors. It was to perform this function that the system called recension was devised. The twin considerations that it seldom if ever works (because stemmata turn out to be bifid, thus affording no casting vote, or because the evidence permits no stemma to be constructed), and that some impudent critics have presumed to discredit its logic as well as its practicability, have failed to dismiss the *fata Morgana* of a mechanistic system of editing. That continues both to exert its attraction and to obscure the real nature of the situation.

To this last the great modern theorists of textual criticism (I think particularly of Maas, Pasquali and Greg) have not been blind. They recognized and proclaimed the indispensability of judgement in editing. Above all Maas, and there is irony here, for he is nowadays often invoked as the modern exponent of recensionism, emphasized the editor's obligation to the ultimate exercise of judgement, the conjectural emendation which is my subject: 'Erweist sich die Überlieferung als verdorben, so muss versucht werden, sie durch divinatio zu heilen.'[2] The eclectic treatment of his theories is like that suffered by those of Alphonse Dain, now most often followed in a relatively unimportant objection to unduly minute collation, but in fact a merciless critic of erroneous notions about editing. Dain too pronounces on conjectural emendation, in terms strikingly similar to those first of Maas, then of Housman: 'Si le texte transmis est mauvais, on n'a

---

[1] Compare Housman, p. 43: 'The average man, if he meddles with criticism at all, is a conservative critic. . . . He believes that the text of ancient authors is generally sound, not because he has acquainted himself with the elements of the problem, but because he would feel uncomfortable if he did not believe it.'

[2] P. Maas, *Textkritik*, 3., verbesserte und vermehrte Auflage (Leipzig, 1957), p. 10.

pas le droit de ne pas essayer de l'amender. . . . Ce qui est détes-
table, de toute façon, c'est de garder un texte mauvais par souci de
s'écarter le moins possible des leçons du manuscrit.'[1]

These uncompromising statements were made by critics with
wide experience, not just of the early literature of one vernacular,
but of the long history of textual transmission in two classical
languages, men thus well apprised of the hazards and difficulties of
conjectural emendation. They might seem to restore the matter
to its correct proportions. The 'line of least resistance' is not
unbridled emendation (which would in any event be quickly
subjected to ridicule) but the attitude of total scepticism about the
capabilities of editing which, abrogating decision, shifts responsibility to a manuscript and prints this—on the argument which I
have heard 'that one would at least have an authentic medieval
form of the poem, as opposed to one incorporating the dubious
hypotheses of a modern editor'. A harder course is to accept the
principle that 'the duty of an editor is to edit', and to use available
manuscript evidence for reconstructing an archetypal text. But the
hardest course of all is to recognize the axiomatic corruption of
such an archetype, and to face the implications of this condition.
Each of these stages must be a more anxious, exacting, and
challenging operation; but the second and third cannot fail to
protect the study of literature against the postulate implied in the
first: that its data are false to an indeterminate but certainly large
extent. And they avoid the unhistorical corollary of the doctrine
of passive 'editing': that the ancient or the medieval public did not
care about the quality of its texts.

If nevertheless what Maas has called the 'reprehensible fear' of
admitting that textual criticism is an operation which may not
attain completely satisfying results[2] prevails, there is a harder
argument still, which seems to create an intellectual obligation to
conjectural emendation. This was first (as far as I know) formulated by Maas: 'In the nature of things it is much more harmful
when a corruption remains unidentified than when a sound text
is unjustly attacked . . . the unsignalled corruption vitiates the

---

[1] *Les Manuscrits*, p. 159.　　　　[2] *Textkritik*, p. 13.

general stylistic impression.'[1] It has been more explicitly stated by Dr Sisam:

To support a bad manuscript reading is in no way more meritorious than to support a bad conjecture, and so far from being safer, it is more insidious as a source of error. For, in good practice, a conjecture is printed with some distinguishing mark which attracts doubt; but a bad manuscript reading, if it is defended, looks like solid ground for the defence of other readings. So intensive study with a strong bias towards the manuscript reading blunts the sense of style, and works in a vicious circle of debasement.[2]

Old and Middle English scholars will know how large this circle can be; the lexicography, the grammatical study, the notions about metre, our critical judgements and the literary history of the periods are embraced in it.

This concurrence of Maas and Sisam extends to a further conception of the function of conjecture: for Maas it is an essential part of what he calls *Examinatio*, 'Prüfung' of the quality of the received text;[3] Sisam correspondingly believes that

there would be a real gain if conjecture, instead of being reserved for the useful but disheartening task of dealing with obvious or desperate faults, were restored to its true functions, which include probing as well as healing.[4]

These considerations, which from their nature are not lightly to be dismissed, seem to define the true, ancillary function of textual criticism: an activity designed not to afford its practitioners either an outlet for self-expression or a secure and comfortable occupation, but to contribute to the right understanding and evaluation of older literature. They express the means by which

[1] *Textkritik*, p. 13: 'Natürlich ist es viel schädlicher, wenn eine Verderbnis unerkannt bleibt, als wenn ein heiler Text zu Unrecht angegriffen wird . . . die nicht bezeichnete Verderbnis schädigt den stilistischen Gesamteindruck.'

[2] *Studies*, p. 39.

[3] *Textkritik*, p. 33: 'Konjektur, 'richtig' oder 'falsch', [ist] ein wesentlicher Teil der examinatio, d.h. der Prüfung, ob der überlieferte Text der beste ausdenkbare ist oder nicht'; and p. 13: 'jede Konjektur reizt zur Widerlegung, durch die das Verständnis der Stelle jedenfalls gefördert wird'.

[4] *Studies*, p. 44.

that function will be exercised: through restoring, or attempting to restore, or indicating the damage suffered by texts in transmission, not in order to 'improve' these but to recover their historical truth, in itself and as a basis for other knowledge. Thus active editing, whether positive in establishing originality of readings, or negative in merely identifying corruption, or conjectural, in proposing hypothetical original readings which would account for putative corruptions, appears an intellectual responsibility, and one which from its character it would be wrong to abdicate or to restrict because its problems are not often or always conclusively soluble. In these terms conjectural emendation loses any character of unbridled self-indulgence and seems, rather, a valuable activity, hazardous indeed to the reputations of those who undertake it, but if correctly practised more likely to promote knowledge than to mislead.

Supposing the force of such arguments to be accepted it might seem desirable to look again at the theory and practice of conjectural emendation. In such a reconsideration the question is bound to come up how the results of the practice can be validated; to this the answer is that a conjecture can be validated conclusively only by the emergence of new textual evidence which supports it; otherwise it can appear as only more or less probably correct. That is a part of the nature of textual criticism, to which I shall recur. There is a second, related question: how the danger of 'improving the poet's work by brilliant conjecture' is to be avoided. This must be answered in terms of the degree of danger, which will depend on the nature of the text, and the quality of its author. There are, to be sure, some Middle English writers whose works invite improvement; I am not concerned with them. In the case of a major poet the danger must seem small from several considerations: first there is the intrinsic unlikelihood of any editor possessing such a capability; second, there is the extreme probability (demonstrable as such beyond reasonable doubt) that a bad reading in a great poem is scribal, not authorial, which must limit the number of occasions where the danger is real; third, the observation of a rationale in conjecture can restrain the creative impulses of an editor. There remains a further question: is the twentieth-century editor as good a judge of the originality of readings as, say, a Middle English scribe copying a near-contemporary poem? Has he any grounds for challenging a reading which, from its unanimous attestation, was evidently acceptable to many such scribes? At the risk of arrogance my answer must, with respect to a competent editor, be affirmative. He has a purpose, to recover what his author actually wrote; from all indications scribes, if they had any purpose of a comparable order, had a different one in which the concept of originality of readings was not included. And his equipment is, except in some notable cases of isolated detail, superior to that of scribes: he has the comparative evidence of his collations, which they lacked; with the advantage of print he has a better general and particular knowledge of the text than theirs; and he has access to information about the history of lexis, grammar and dialect which no scribe (at least in medieval England) could have possessed.[1]

Of the above questions the fundamental one is the first. Various opinions about the means of assessing the probable truth of a conjectural emendation are to be found in the literature of textual criticism. For instance Housman specified 'fitness to the context and propriety to the genius of the author' as 'the indispensable things'.[2] Hall in his *Companion to Classical Texts* required that a conjecture must satisfy both the two tests of 'Transcriptional Probability' and 'Intrinsic Probability', that is the conjecture and corruption must be in a palæographically explicable relation, and the conjecture must 'suit the context, the author's style and vocabulary, and any general laws which have been proved to apply to his works'.[3] Maas formulated two criteria, a primary one of the appropriate quality of the style and substance of the con-

---

[1] Compare Sisam, *Studies*, pp. 36–7: 'A defender of the manuscript readings . . . might argue that the scribes were well trained, and that they knew more about Old English usage, thought and tradition than a modern critic can. I doubt if this holds good for the earlier poetry.' Textual criticism is in debt to Dr Sisam for giving this doubt the support of his authority.

[2] Housman, p. 51.

[3] F. W. Hall, *A Companion to Classical Texts* (Oxford, 1913), p. 151.

jectural reading, and a secondary one of its likelihood to have given rise to the suspect or impossible received reading.[1] These and similar generalizations, whether satisfactory in themselves or not, might well fail, however, to allay the doubts of the sceptic, for all, ultimately, operate by the subjective judgement which he distrusts.

But if, as seems to be the case, subjective judgement is an invariable element of all editing except the most elementary, and since editing seems an indispensable activity, it is necessary to ask two questions: what justification is there for our sceptic's deep-seated distrust, and how can the dangers of subjectivity be minimized? I find the answer to both questions in the nature of the study of literature. This comprises very few activities where subjectivity in some form or other does not play a major part; we accept its presence in many cases; can we reasonably balk at it in others? Where we take the presence and function of subjectivity for granted we know how to test it. We study not the particular attractiveness of any of its conclusions, but the quality of the processes by which this was attained. We do not discard the practice of literary or interpretative criticism because bad criticism has been written; we scrutinize its assumptions, measure its affective constituents against our own responses, apply the tests of logic to its inferences, repeat its processes to better effect, thus incidentally advancing knowledge. To me it seems that the conclusions of textual criticism, and particularly of conjectural emendation, can be similarly tested, and the subjective element in them thus controlled.

As I understand editing an edited text has no absolute authority: it is as sound or unsound as the case the competent editor can make out for it. An edition constitutes an attempt to account for available phenomena in terms of what is known about the circumstances which generated them. To that extent it has the character

---

[1] *Textkritik*, pp. 11–12, esp. p. 12. His general discussion implies a third criterion, the consensus of competent judgement, 'die Übereinstimmung aller Urteilsfähigen', adding that this is 'freilich ein schwer zu umgrenzender Begriff': on p. 13 he writes, of conjectural readings, 'nur die besten werden sich durchsetzen'.

of a scientific activity. It operates by advancing hypotheses to explain data, and tests such hypotheses in terms of their efficiency as explanations. Those which pass the test it accepts as presumptively, not absolutely true; they remain subject to revision or rejection if new data come to light or more efficient hypotheses are devised. Its character implies an editorial obligation to expose its procedures and the precise extent to which their results are speculative for scrutiny.[1] In such a process conjectural emendation can represent itself as not merely legitimate, but even on particular occasions strongly indicated, and it will be directed less by Maas's *Fingerspitzengefühl*, though that must play its part, than by deductive and inductive thought. Thus viewed it resumes the character of a respectable activity, one meriting a better name than *divinatio*. We can, admittedly, seldom if ever estimate the absolute truth of its conclusions, but correspondingly we can never know absolutely of any ancient texts except autographs that their words are the words of the authors. All textual criticism except the most elementary is an assessment of relative probabilities, and the authority of ancient texts must always vary—in the last analysis indeterminably—from line to line. 'Wer sich fürchtet', wrote Maas, 'einen unsicheren Text zu geben [and one might add 'oder zu bearbeiten'], wird besser tun, sich nur mit Autographa zu beschäftigen.'[2]

I suppose that the feature of conjectural emendation logically rather than psychologically hardest to accept is its rejection of unanimous manuscript testimony. In Housman's words

The MSS. are the material upon which we base our rule, and then, when we have got our rule, we turn round upon the MSS. and say that the rule, based upon them, convicts them of error. We are thus working in a circle, that is a fact which there is no denying.[3]

In other words, we reject certain evidence on the grounds of other evidence from the same source; this strikes at the principle of

---

[1] Maas, *Textkritik*, p. 13: 'die Texte als die Grundlage jeder philologischen Forschung sollten so behandelt werden, dass über den Grad der Sicherheit, der ihnen zukommt, möglichste Klarheit herrsch'.

[2] *Textkritik*, p. 13.   [3] Housman, p. 145.

authority. But may it perhaps not be that the force of the principle of authority in textual criticism has been misconceived? Let us look on the preceding situation from another aspect. The editor of a major poet must begin with a presumption of the excellence of his author; he is also governed by an axiom that texts, including archetypal texts, are corrupt. The excellence of his author is a matter of consensus of critical judgement; the axiom is a matter of manifest fact. Further, that excellence has survived notwithstanding the axiomatic deterioration of his texts, and must thus once have been even greater than the received texts now represent it to be. Is it then such bad thinking for his editor, where the text seems inferior in particulars although unanimously attested, to impute the falling off to archetypal scribal corruption? Such an inference, as the logic of literary studies goes, might seem good rather than suspect.

It is, of course, subjective, speculative and hazardous. The subjectivity enters when, in a situation where manuscripts offer no choice of readings, the editor carries out a comparison between the received text and his *idea* of the uncorrupted poem, of how the poet would and would not write. Assessing the quality of the received text he concludes that it exhibits characteristics which, in situations where manuscript evidence was divided, were produced by scribal variation. It is speculative because the editor goes on to propose what the poet actually did write, if he did not write the words unanimously attested by the manuscripts, having regard to his performance elsewhere. It is hazardous, although more to the editor's reputation than the poet's, because of the possibilities of error. The editor may mistake in identifying archetypal corruption, from a misconception of his author's *usus scribendi*, in which I include matters of language and literary form; or from a misunderstanding of his meaning, local and general. And he may conjecture badly, either through failure to identify the causes and processes of corruption which should guide him back to the original reading, or through lack of flair, *Fingerspitzengefühl*, which is an indispensable part of his equipment. But taking full account of this situation I will assert that the editor has not so much a right as an intellectual obligation to attempt the recovery of truth. The risk is to himself; however inept he may be he will not—I invoke Maas and Sisam—injure the poet.

Assuming that an editor who accepts this obligation is competent, are there any means by which he can protect himself against the dangers of his undertaking? The answer may lie with Maas, who describes the theoretical situation in which ideal conditions for conjecture would exist. In this situation evidence would be such as to permit a classification of errors specifically likely in particular periods of history, literary kinds, and types of transcription, either from manuscripts with surviving exemplars or from manuscripts whose exemplar can be reconstructed by recension. By this means the probable incidence of any specific type of error in given circumstances could be established. In addition it would be possible to ascertain the quality of the archetype, and this could happen where such an archetype was reduced to the status of a variant text (*Variantenträger*) or even of a derivative text (*codex descriptus*) through earlier branching of the tradition, or where it appeared as a quotation (*Zitat*). In such a situation the demonstrable classes of error would also, Maas asserts, be presumable in those areas of the text where no control is available, and no means of checking the archetypal quality exists. In other words a knowledge of the incidence of the typical corruption to which any given work was exposed or susceptible, and the possibility of assessing the quality of its archetypal text, that is the exclusive common ancestor of the surviving copies, would be the ideal determinants first of the need for conjecture and second of its accuracy.[1]

The tone in which Maas describes this situation suggests some doubt on his part about the likelihood of its actually ever occurring. In fact it is instanced in *Piers Plowman*. Each version of this poem survives in many copies, and its archetypal text can generally be recovered without difficulty; thus Maas's ideal classification of typical error is abundantly possible. For long passages two, or even all three versions, correspond: where unrevised B corre-

[1] *Textkritik*, pp. 11-12.

sponds to A the B archetype has the character of a *codex descriptus*; where B corresponds to unrevised C it appears in C as a *Zitat*; where the three versions correspond B has both characters. Each revision was carried out on a copy of the immediately preceding version antecedent to the archetypal copy of that version; thus the quality of the archetypal texts can be assessed by comparing them where they correspond.

The editing of *Piers Plowman* will then afford an ideal occasion for reexamining the relation between the theory of conjectural emendation and its practice. From the reexamination it will appear that the distance between the rationale and its confident application must vary from crux to crux and can be immense. Instances of demonstrable archetypal corruption will range from those where the original can be conjectured with some assurance of acclamation to others where, while the received reading is manifestly corrupt, neither text nor context affords any indication of the words of the lost original. This situation is in the nature of the activity. The logical respectability of conjectural emendation is unassailable: the material question in any given editorial situation must be whether it was worth attempting, and this will be answered in terms of the competence of the particular editor. Criticism of conjectural emendation, as of all active editing, must bear not on the legitimacy of the operation but on the quality of its execution.

12

Saracens and Crusaders: from Fact to Allegory

BEATRICE WHITE

THE DIVIDING LINE between fact and fiction was never more lightly drawn than in the Middle Ages. This paper pretends to do no more than point to certain resemblances which indicate the narrow margin between works intended to instruct and those intended to entertain. The exaggerations of the one appeared as the distortions of the other; the recognizable contemporary persons of the one became the formalized types of the other, and developed as symbols in a moral allegory. Then, some centuries later, the original material was passed through a different alembic and reappeared in a changed form, the historical novel, to cast a more subtle and lasting enchantment.

The Crusades, 'performed by strength and described by ignorance' (Gibbon), with their complex and closely interwoven motives—materialistic, idealistic, religious—left their impact on literature from the end of the eleventh century onwards. The idea of this conflict between Christians and Saracens as a holy war was deeply engrained in the experience of Western Christendom. Balderick of Dol reports Pope Urban as saying, at the time of the First Crusade (1095): 'It is the only warfare that is righteous, for it is charity to risk your life for your brothers.' Roland and Oliver, 'proz' and 'sage' (worthy and wise, like Chaucer's knight), were dedicated fighting men and had no time for the conflicting emotions that tormented the knights errant of later literature. They were on the right side in what was considered an entirely just and holy war against infidels. Dante places his ancestor, Cacciaguida, a Crusader, in Paradise as a martyr to the faith (*Paradiso*, 15, 135), and Mohammed in Malebolge, the ninth circle of Hell (*Inferno*, 28, 31). That was the right, the inevitable place for him, the Arch-Schismatic, just as the eternal repose of Heaven was for Caccia-guida. 'Paiens unt tort e Chrestiens unt dreit' was a basic concept, and it did not change until intellectual horizons grew broader.

The word Saracen,[1] familiar in England since the time of Bede, had by 1300 extended its meaning from 'Arab' or 'Muslim' to any non-Christian, heathen, or pagan. Many of the so-called Saracens that swarm in the English metrical romances had never been any nearer to the Holy Land than the Isle of Man or Germany. In *King Horn* the Saracens are common-or-garden Viking marauders: in *Arthur and Merlin* they are plain Saxons: 'That day Gawain slough many a sarazin of the Saxons more then eny of his felowes' we are told. In the alliterative *Morte Arthure* they are vassals of the king of Rome. Vikings and Saxons were Pagans, and they were there in the romances in that category simply to be destroyed by valiant Christians. This extension of the meaning of the word to any active enemy of Christendom reflects the popular conception of Islam as a debased religion involving the worship of idols and therefore to be despised and derided.[2] There is no hint in the medieval metrical romances of the enlightened and more indul-gent attitude to the Saracens which involves the problem of the 'righteous heathen' referred to by Dante in *Paradiso*, 19, 78: 'ov'è la

[1] The word Saracen: *Saracenus* (Greek Σαρακηνός), originally the name of an Arabic tribe, was gradually applied to all Arabs, who had generally adopted the name in the time of St Jerome. He, thinking that the Arabs were thus claiming to be the descendants of Sarah, proposed to call them *Agareni* (descendants of Hagar), a name often adopted by Greek and Latin writers of the Middle Ages. (Du Cange s.v. *Saraceni*). Perhaps, says Gaston Paris, the term *Saraceni* is 'd'origine érudite, car les Arabes, qui se le donnaient au IVe siècle, semblent ne plus l'avoir employé au VIIe siècle'. Suggested medieval etymologies were that the word was a pun, *a Sarra vacuos*, or that it implied descent from Sarah, *a Sarra geniti*, or that it implied Syrian origin, *quasi Syrigenae*. But it may possibly derive from the Arabic *sharqí*, eastern; *sharq*, sunrise. (See R. W. Southern, *Western Views of Islam in the Middle Ages*, Cambridge, Mass., 1962.)

[2] In the Miracle Plays of the fourteenth and fifteenth centuries the ranting tyrants, Pharaoh, Herod, and Pilate—Egyptian, Jew, Roman—all swear lustily by Termagaunt and Mahoun, with perfect congruity. They were alike Pagan—in a word, Saracen.

171

colpa sua, sed ei non crede?'; and by the author of *Piers Plowman*, B XI, 150: 'Nouȝt þorw preyere of a pope . . . was þat Sarasene saued.' (The Saracen in question is the Emperor Trajan.) There are no interesting doubts about the fate of non-believers in the minds of the authors of the English metrical romances and not one of them would have gone a fraction of the way as far as the four-teenth-century poet, Chaucer's friend, John Gower, who, in the *Confessio Amantis*, Lib. III, l. 2485, labours the bigger question of whether it is really just and lawful to kill in the name of faith and comes to the conclusion that it is not.

'Outremer', the Holy Land of Palestine, was very far away from Western Europe, and ideas about the Saracen, biased by religious prejudice, were exaggerated by distance and inevitably by ignorance. In the twelfth century between 1137 and 1155 Walter of Compiègne, a monk of Tours, wrote a Latin poem of 1090 lines on the life of Mahomet, claiming that the 'facts' had been given, by a converted Saracen brought back by a returning Crusader, to Paganus, abbot of St Mary, Étampes, who handed them on to Warner, abbot of Compiègne:

> nam si vera mihi dixit Warnerius abbas,
> me quoque vera loqui de Machomete puta.[1]

These so-called 'facts', in reality picturesque lies, were a reflection of current distortions and became the source of later tenacious inventions and calumnies. From the twelfth century onwards the best that could be said in popular literature of fine, fanatical Saracen fighters, who were occasionally admitted to be worthy of their Christian opponents, was: 'What a pity they weren't Christians!' (*La Chanson de Roland*, l. 3135): and the worst that they were 'heathen hounds', spawn of the devil, who deserved all they got at the hands of the Crusaders.[2]

The force of the impetus that sent men 'outremer' and overrode all sentimental ties can be felt most strongly, perhaps, not in the

---

[1] *Otia de Machomete*, ed. R. B. C. Huygens (1956); *Poésies populaires latines du moyen âge*, ed. E. du Méril (Paris, 1847).

[2] See W. W. Comfort, 'The Saracens in the French Epic', *PMLA*, lv (1940), 628–59.

Chansons de geste but in the *Songs* of the Crusaders.[1] These are either calls to battle or love songs. In the *Chanson de Roland*, Aude, Roland's fiancée, is only a shadowy figure, but in 1189 the Chatelain de Coucy serves God in order first to serve his lady, and before he goes overseas he longs to hold her just once, naked, in his arms. 'Félons sont les Sarrasins' was the universal conviction, and pilgrim and Crusader, facing separation from home and the possibility of no return, were strengthened by the promise of Paradise 'od les angles de nostre Segnor'. But not all Crusaders were enthusiastic volunteers, spurred on by the hope of spiritual booty. At the time of Rutebeuf (thirteenth century) their ranks were swelled by common criminals forced to take the cross as an act of penance (*Complaint de Constantinople*), a dangerous practice which led not only to defection, but to uncontrollable acts of brutality. Others, reluctant to 'stand up for Jesus' in a strange land, recognized the plain common sense of remaining at home, like Rutebeuf's Décroisé, for—beautiful Chauvinism—if God were anywhere in the world He was most certainly in 'la douce France' (*Disputaison du croisé et du décroisé*).

It remains a debatable question how far writers of the *Chansons de geste*, as well as the authors of the much later metrical romances, were familiar with the works of contemporary chroniclers describing the Crusades, or with accounts collected first-hand from returned Crusaders. However authentic the basic narrative material was, excesses of prejudice were bound to colour it highly. William of Tyre's *Historia rerum in partibus transmarinis gestarum* (1163–83), a systematic history of the First Crusade, compiled by an author long resident in Palestine and familiar with the events he describes in Latin, was subsequently translated into English from a French version and published in 1481 by Caxton, who, years later than the recorded events, professed to regard the work as both inspiring and admonitory: 'The hye courageous faytes and valyaunt actes' which Caxton admired had admitted what he called 'grete occission and slaughter'. When Jerusalem fell to the Crusaders in July 1099, ten thousand infidels

[1] *Les Chansons de Croisade*, ed. J. Bédier (Paris, 1909).

were put to the sword within the enclosure of the Temple. 'Paiens unt tort e Chrestiens unt dreit', in a world where the fighting overseas could be thought of as *Gesta Dei per Francos*.[1]

The author of the *Gesta Francorum* (c. 1101)[2] seriously maintained the accepted view that the Christians had a right to kill as many infidels as possible, but he paid tribute to the skill, prowess, and courage of the Saracens and said it would be difficult to find better soldiers anywhere. According to this anonymous chronicler both Christian and Saracen were involved in acts of savage ferocity which non-combatant women who were with the Christian army, bringing water for the fighting men to drink and urging them on to deeds of valour, must have witnessed, and in the case of their own men, condoned. Heads of dead Saracens were cut off and brought to the Christian tents 'so that they could count the number exactly'—a sensible, if drastic, reason for decapitation. At Marra the Christians systematically ripped up the bodies of the dead, searching the entrails for gold coins swallowed in desperation by their prisoners. Some, driven by hunger, cut the dead flesh into slices, and cooked and ate it. Throughout the work there is emphatic mention of the vast multitudes of Saracens always ready for combat. This constant insistence on the inexhaustible numbers of their foes represents the Western idea of the dangerous fertility of a race committed to polygamy.

The events of the carefully organized Third Crusade (1189), resulting in the surrender of Acre in 1191, the defeat of Saladin at Arsuf, the relief of Jaffa and the arrangement of a three years' truce with the Saracens, were described at some length by Ambroise, a devoted admirer of the English King Richard I, and a humble participant in the wars he recounts in *L'Estoire de la Guerre sainte* (1190–2).[3] He has the traditional attitude towards the Saracens. They are 'cels qui Deu mescroient', 'les mescreanz', 'la gent à diable', 'la chenaille', 'la putaille', 'a hideous black race, godless and

---

[1] Guibert of Nogent, *Gesta Dei per Francos* (PL, CLVI, 679–838).

[2] *Gesta Francorum et aliorum Hierosolimitanorum*, ed. Rosalind Hill (London, 1962).

[3] *L'Estoire de la Guerre sainte*, par Ambroise. Publiée et traduite . . . par Gaston Paris (Paris, 1897).

unnatural'—'God never made more ugly beasts.' He approves of
the massacre, ordered by Richard, of two thousand five hundred
prisoners at Acre, throwing the blame on Saladin for not adhering
to the strict terms of an arranged pact.[1] But Ambroise does not
fail to do justice to the courage of the infidels. Even if they had
been Christians they could not have been better warriors. He is
very favourably disposed to Safadin, the brother of Saladin, whom
he describes as 'sage, vaillant et libéral'; he even recognizes the
great qualities of Saladin and repeats the words of the bishop of
Salisbury, later archbishop of Canterbury,[2] to the Saracen leader:
'If King Richard's virtues could be joined to yours it could well be
said that two such worthy and valiant princes could not be found
in the world' (l. 12139)—an attitude reflected in the chronicle of
Richard of Devizes (c. 1193), where Richard's story of Safadin's
visit to the Christian camp expresses the 'chivalric admiration'
which the Saracen brothers felt for the English king.

Together with the inevitable accounts of atrocities, Ambroise
has anecdotes illustrating the courage of women, who at Acre
worked side by side with the men (l. 3635), describes the effective-
ness of the light-armed Saracen cavalry with its devastatingly
successful strategy of simulated flight (they were like gnats, he
says), suggests the more thorough siege methods of the Crusaders
and sometimes provides a tantalizing detail, for example: that the
duke of Burgundy had a song composed attacking Richard, to
which Richard responded in kind (l. 10653). We could sacrifice a
lot of medieval literature for that. One instance of neat chicanery
concerns a game which plays a prominent part in the later metrical
romance of *Richard Coer de Lion*. It is the so-called 'pluck-buffet', a
challenge to an exchange of blows. A Saracen called Grair
challenged a Gallois called Marcaduc to a duel. He was to strike
the first blow, but missed his stroke. Marcaduc agreed to stand

---

[1] It appears that the necessity for guarding so large a number of prisoners
prevented Richard from carrying out further operations, and so he had them all
slaughtered except a few of the more illustrious, who were held to ransom.
(Richard of Devizes.)

[2] Hubert Walter. In September 1192 he conducted a convoy of pilgrims to
Jerusalem and it was on this occasion that he was honourably received by Saladin.

and take a second, but before the Saracen was ready he killed him, because he had violated the original agreement (l. 3733).

Contemporary chroniclers cannot be expected to present the enemy with detachment. By recognizing his fighting qualities they enhance the valour of their own soldiers and each side, Christian and Muslim, takes its individual atrocities for granted and as part of the established pattern of warfare. Both adversaries were engaged in a Holy War, a Jihád, for the defence of their religion, and the ends were held to justify the means. The great massacre of Jews and Muslims by the Crusaders after their capture of Jerusalem in 1099 (a striking contrast to the later clemency of Saladin in 1187) could hardly fail to provoke reprisals. Savagery and ferocity met with equal horrors and these find a place in Arabic chronicles.

The historian Al-Qalānisī (d. 1160) describes in his *Damascus Chronicle*[1] how, after the assault on Banyas in December 1132, the victor, Shams-al-Mulūk, took all his booty to Damascus and 'the people came out of the city to meet him and to gaze at the quantities of prisoners in ropes and of heads on lances. The spectacle refreshed their eyes and rejoiced their hearts and strengthened their loins, and they gave abundant thanks to God Most High for this glorious victory and success which He had vouchsafed.' The Crusaders, always referred to as 'polytheists', from their belief in the Trinity, defeated again in 1158, were subjected to the same sort of treatment. Prisoners and the heads of the slain were sent back to Damascus, foot-soldiers were roped together and the Frankish horsemen were set in pairs on camels, each pair with one of their own standards unfurled 'to which were attached a number of scalps with the hair'. By this time the mutual rivalries and jealousies which had distracted Islam at the end of the eleventh century had given way to a united drive against the Christian invaders, and a formidable force, adept in cavalry tactics, had been organized in mounted regiments ably supported by mercenaries and militia.

---

[1] *The Damascus Chronicle of the Crusades*, extracted and translated from the chronicle of Ibn Al-Qalānisī by H. A. R. Gibb (London, 1932).

If the Christian chroniclers distorted the picture the same tendency can be assumed in their Muslim counterparts, who found it difficult to understand the Crusaders' way of life. Al-Qalānisī's contemporary, Ousâma (1095–1188), reveals in his *Autobiography* that he is constantly puzzled by the Franks' curious mentality, their curious medicine, their curious manners, their crude sense of humour, and their extraordinary lack of jealousy in sexual matters. They seemed to care little who slept with their wives as long as the ladies were happy. They had none of the virtues of men except bravery, but that was a quality that could not be denied to distinguished Saracen women, like Ousâma's mother and sister, who were prepared to kill themselves rather than face capture, or like Bouraika, the old servant, who carried drink to the soldiers in combat, or the old woman Fanoun, who rushed into the fight against Ousâma's enemies at Shaizar, or Rafoul, the beautiful girl who drowned herself when taken prisoner.[1]

Ousâma, like many another Arab gentleman of his time, was on quite good terms with some of the older Crusaders, who had settled 'outremer' and had become, as the Americans say, 'acclimated'. But to Anna Comnena, the learned Greek princess of Byzantium, the invading Franks of the First Crusade (1095), with their murderous crossbows and fighting priests, their fickleness and impetuosity, their armour, long shields, and endless chatter, had appeared truly barbarous. From the core of her prejudice she gave a remarkable picture of a leader who at once repelled and fascinated her, Bohémund: he was tall and perfectly proportioned, closely shaved, with short yellow hair, very blue eyes and a proud nose. He was charming, but horrible, implacable, and savage in size and glance. Courage and passion 'reared their crests within him' and even his laughter caused fear.[2] It would pass as a portrait of the later Crusader, the English King Richard I.

The features of the Holy War which the contemporary Christian chroniclers, writing both in Latin and in the vernacular, are at

[1] *The Autobiography of Ousâma*, trans. with Introduction and Notes by George Richard Potter (London, 1929).
[2] *The Alexiad*, trans. E. Dawes (London, 1928).

pains to emphasize, are the deeds of reckless heroism, the practice of single combat, the vast numbers of opposing mounted forces, the sound and fury of battle, the painful calamities of sieges, and the hideous atrocities, including cannibalism, committed by the combatants. Such scenes are the inevitable concomitants of war at close range, and details of this type recur *ad nauseam* in the medieval English romances describing fights with Saracens. Many earlier parallels to these ghastly scenes, endemic in life as in literature when war is let loose, can be found in classical story in general, and in the late Latin epic in particular, a rich quarry for story and for style. In the *Thebaid* of Statius and in Lucan's *Pharsalia* there is a plethora of violent, heroic, and cruel incidents. All the shocking, repulsive horrors served up in the medieval romances are there, and no doubt Joseph of Exeter's *Antiocheis*, a Latin epic poem on the deeds of Richard I, had it been preserved (Camden, in his *Remaines concerning Britain*, has saved two fragments), would be found to have been constructed on a similar pattern and to have employed the same descriptive rhetoric. It is perhaps worth noticing that the works of Statius and Lucan, well known in the Middle Ages and abundant in the morbid, grotesque, sensational realism that typifies the *romans d'aventure*, were already marked by those strong hyperbolic tendencies which seem to be an important feature of the development from epic to romance, and which, carried to extremes, easily produce the abstractions of allegory.

The average, plodding, medieval English romance writer, quite ignorant of the classics, took his material ready-made from the French and knew little and cared less about the superior ethics, learning, and civilization of Islam. He aimed at and succeeded in producing preposterously exaggerated effects, making Christians and Saracens equally ferocious, equally fanatical, and from a modern viewpoint equally appalling. The Crusades had never become a national movement in England as they had in France, with its Mediterranean seaboard, and the majority of writers in the fourteenth century knew precious little about them and still less about Islam. It was in their traditional guise of the fiendish enemies of Christendom that the Saracens ubiquitously invaded the medieval romances compiled in England, whether those dealt with the 'matter of France', the 'matter of England', or the 'matter of Britain'.

Of all the tales concerning Charlemagne and his peers the most lasting in popularity was *Sir Firumbras*. Referred to admiringly by Barbour, alluded to by Skelton, and mentioned by Rabelais, the story survived to be turned by Schubert, in 1823, into an opera, *Fierabras*, the overture to which was later arranged for the piano in 1827 by Carl Czerny. If *Sir Firumbras* is compared with other verse tales of the same group, *The Sowdone of Babylone*, an independent work on an identical theme, *Roland and Vernagu*, and *Otuel*, certain characteristics conforming to a common design emerge. 'Félons sont les Sarrasins'; Saracens are first and foremost furious fighters, huge men skilled in single combat. When they are sensible, well-born, and worthy opponents, like Firumbras or Otuel, they become fanatical converts, or they remain fanatical infidels, like Vernagu and Laban, the father of Firumbras, who smote the baptizing bishop and spat in the holy water to show his contempt for Christianity and thus came to a violent, well-deserved end.

Such conduct as Laban's was likely to be exacerbated by a constant diet of 'beastys blood' alternating with serpents fried in oil as a sort of savoury. The hideous and abnormal army of Laban, a truly Satanic crew, consisted of:

> Thre hundred thousand of Sarsyns felle
> Some bloo, some yolowe, some blake as more,
> Some horible and stronge as devel of helle,
> (*Sowdone of Babylone*, ll. 1004–6)[1]

and its fighting power was increased by its carnivorous habits and by its addiction to curiously adventurous drinks compounded of the blood of such ill-assorted animals as tigers, antelopes, and 'camalyons'.[2]

[1] Ed. E. Hausknecht (EETS, 1881).
[2] George Ellis comments with wry humour: 'meaning probably the camelopardalis. The blood of a cameleon [*sic*] would go a very little way towards satisfying a thirsty Saracen.' *Specimens of Early English Metrical Romances* (1847).

Saracens like Laban, and like Sir Garcy in *Otuel*, lose their tempers and, when things go wrong for them, belabour their idols. Laban is much given to this kind of hysteria, and as for Sir Garcy:

> All hys goddys he gaf a cloute
> He gaf hem strokys, styf and stoute.
> 'Harawe!' they ganne to calle.
> He brake bothe legges and swere,
> And kest hem bothe into the fere,
> Mahoun, and hem all.
>
> (*Otuel*, ll. 1553-8)[1]

The Sowdan of Damas in *The King of Tars* takes the same strong line with recalcitrant gods:

> Ne holpe him nought his goddes alle
> Wel wo was him bigon,
> On Tirmagaunt he gon to grede
> 'On yow nas never help at nede,
> Fy on ow everichon!'
> He hente a staf with herte grete
> And al his goddes he gan to bete,
> And drouh hem alle adoun. . . .
>
> (ll. 608-15)[2]

The Sowdan in *Guy of Warwick* also revenges himself petulantly on his tutelary deities and so does Bradmond in *Bevis of Hamtoun*. Petty spite and futile rage at the inefficacy of their gods' protection become a regular Saracen trait, from *La Chanson de Roland* onwards.[3]

---

[1] Ed. M. I. O'Sullivan (EETS, 1935).

[2] *Ancient Engleish Metrical Romanceës*, selected and published by Joseph Ritson (London, 1802), vol. ii.

[3] In the *Jeu de St Nicolas* the author, Jean Bodel, exploits this favourite characteristic in a burlesque scene in which the King of Africa, having threatened his deity, Tervagan, is induced by his Seneschal to apologize to the god and blames his outburst on to 'malencolie'.

Such unreasonable and childish reactions in the face of adverse circumstances were naturally expected of 'heathen hounds' whose testy and uncontrolled violence could thus be contrasted with Christian resignation and dignity. In any case, Christians were supposed to have no idols to belabour, although they sometimes came perilously near the frantic conduct of their infuriated enemies. The pagans in the romances are fools as well as knaves and their ridiculous antics under stress convey most forcibly the sense of Christian contempt for the puerility of any other faith. It was by a delighted lingering on exaggerated episodes like these that the medieval romancers were able to express their scorn for Islam while revealing their ignorance of its beliefs.

The most obvious and frequent exaggeration of the fighting conditions more soberly related in the original chronicles stresses with particular energy, in the romances, the enormous size of the Christians' individual foes. Yet great size was not in this popular literature an attribute of the adversary only, but of the hero as well, as had already appeared from the story of the preservation of Hygelac's huge bones on an island in the Rhine for tourists of the day to goggle at. Charlemagne's height for instance, in medieval story, varies from nine to twenty feet, according to the fancy of the romancer. The main difference between huge heroes and their immense foes seems to be that genuine giants were not only hideous in appearance but treacherous in disposition, because of their dark origins in the race of Cain.

Very occasionally, by possessing exceptional qualities, the Saracens in the Charlemagne romances prove ripe for baptism and the transference from 'unjust' to 'just' fighting. But they are always formidable foes—powerful, malevolent, temperamental, treacherous, and battle-crazy. Bloodthirsty, they rave, they roar, and they rant, and are invariably ready for further punishment, resembling the caricatures that cartoonists produce in war propaganda. There is very little that is individual about them. They simply represent in their exaggerated description an extension, in the direction of the grotesque and burlesque, of conventional and traditional attitudes towards the enemy.

It is this conception of the Saracen—a product of exuberant Western imagination issuing in 'error taking the form of extravagance along familiar lines'[1]—which persists in romances concerning English heroes like Bevis of Hamtoun and Guy of Warwick. Guy is involved in large-scale battles with enormous Saracen armies, kills a Sowdan while acting as a messenger (such conduct is always condoned if committed by Christians) and fights successfully with a Saracen giant. His son, Raynbrun, is stolen by Saracens. This motif we meet again in *Bevis*, who was sold to the Saracens as a slave and landed up in the court of a king, Ermyn, to whose daughter Josian, after her conversion, he is duly married. During his career in Heathennesse, which involved a term in prison where:

> Rats and mice and such small deer
> Was his food that seven year—

Bevis destroys an impressive multitude of Saracens, gigantic and generally repulsive, defeats in single combat a Saracen king, and wins a Saracen kingdom.

Sir Perceval of Galles, an Arthurian hero, valiantly dispatches an astronomical number of Saracens invading Maidenland, a mysterious region ruled over by a lady with the pleonastic name of Lufamour:

> Now he strykes for þe nonys,
> Made þe Sarazenes hede-bones
> Hoppe, als dose hayle-stones
> Abowtte one þe gres.
> Thus he dalt þame on rawe
> Till þe daye gunne dawe:
> He layd þaire lyues fulle law,
> Als many als there was.
>
> (ll. 1189–96)[2]

Their Sowdan, Gollerotherame, he meets in single combat:

---

[1] R. W. Southern, op. cit.
[2] *The Thornton Romances*, ed. J. O. Halliwell (London, Camden Society, 1844).

> He hitt hym euene one þe nekk-bane,
> Thurgh ventale and pesane,
> The hede of the sowdane
> He strykes the body fra!

(ll. 1721–4)

And he follows up his success by adroitly decapitating Gollero-therame's giant brother:

> He was ane vnhende knave
> A geant berde so to schafe,
> For sothe als I say!

(ll. 2094–6)

Sir Perceval, in the true romance tradition, achieves his conquests alone and unaided. It was what was expected of him.

A much more extraordinary combat is that which takes place between thirty thousand Saracens and the Christian knight, Sir Isumbras, supported by his faithful spouse:

> Sir Ysambrace was thane fulle waa,
> He kyssede his lady and wolde furthe gaa.
>   With sorow and hert fulle sare;
> A dolefulle worde thane gunne he saye,
> 'Nowe, certis, lady, hafe now gud daye,
>   For nowe and evermare!'
> 'A! Lorde', scho sayd, 'helpe that I were dyghte
> In armours, als I were a knyghte,
>   And with the wille I fare,
> And God that made bothe see and lande,
> My saule I wyte into thy hande,
>   For I kepe to lyffe no mare!'
>
> Sone was the lady dyghte
> In armours, als thofe scho were a knyghte,
>   And had both spere and schelde,
> Agaynes thrytty thowsandez and maa
> Come there nane bot thay twaa,
>   Nyne hundrethe sone hafe thay slayne!

(ll. 723–40)[1]

---

[1] Ibid., p. 118 (*Sir Isumbras*).

Needless to say, such unshakeable devotion meets with its reward, through divine intervention, in the complete rout of the forces of Islam. Christian ladies were generally reserved for gentler roles. The female Saracen of the metrical romances could, on the contrary, prove more deadly than the male.

Romance writers show the most perverse ignorance of Muslim life. They seem almost totally unaware of the careful seclusion of Muslim women. Saracen maidens in the romances, beautiful, susceptible, and in respect of birth and beauty eligible mates for Christian heroes, are curiously forthright and likely to share the most bloodthirsty characteristics of their men. While conforming to an established convention of physical allurement they impose upon it another pattern—resolution and independence—thus creating a new one. Floripas ('Pasque Flower', a most inappropriate name for so dangerous a character), the Saracen heroine of both *Sir Firumbras* and *The Sowdone of Babylone*, must be one of the most redoubtable figures in fiction. If she has a prototype it is not Potiphar's wife, a Celtic fée, nor any of the more forceful ladies of Islam so admiringly alluded to by Ousâma, but Medea.

Since Floripas favours the Christians there is no doubt in the minds of the romancers about the propriety of her conduct, however unfilial and violent that may be. A slight altercation over Christian prisoners with her governess, Maragounde, leads her at once to violent Commando strategy:

> Floripe bythought hir on a gyle,
> And cleped Maragounde anoon right
> To the wyndowe to come a while
> And se ther a wonder syght:
> 'Loke oute', she saide, 'and see aferre
> The Porpais pley as thay were wode.'
> Maragounde lokede oute, Floripe come nere,
> And shofed hire oute into the flode.
> 'Go there', she saide, 'the devel the spede!'
> (*Sowdone of Babylone*, ll. 1571–9)

Her subsequent murder of the prisoners' jailer was comparatively easy. She had only to fetch the unsuspecting fellow a whack on the head with the 'key-cloge' to finish him off for good. It was love of the reluctant Sir Guy of Burgundy, whose religion she was prepared to embrace in order to secure his favours, which spurred her on to such deeds. The sole rival of Floripas in the field of romance is Josian, in *Bevis of Hamtoun*, who, like the Danaides, resourcefully gets rid of the unloved husband of a forced marriage on the wedding night. In fact she marries him in order to destroy him and does so quite neatly by the simple device of stringing him up on the bed-rail and leaving him to die while she slumbers peacefully.

It was the conversion and baptism of beauteous Saracen girls enamoured of Christian heroes which provided the romancers with scope for purely aesthetic effects. These accounts of strip-tease acts revealing female charms were, as might be expected, considerably truncated in English versions of French poems, and in *The Sowdone of Babylone* the interesting and exotic ceremony is tersely dismissed in a couple of lines:

> Dame Floryp was Baptysed than
> And her maydens alle.
>
> (ll. 3191–2)

But in *Sir Firumbras* the scene is more theatrical:

> She kest of her Clothys, all folke a-forne,
> And stode ther naked as sche was borne.
> The good byschope that was of grete pryse
> Crystenede the mayde & dude the seruise.
>
> (ll. 1735–8)

According to the legend of Thomas à Becket's parents, his mother, a Saracen lady, having followed his father to England, was impressively baptized in St Paul's Cathedral by no fewer than six bishops—a tale which finds its way into the Ballads as *Lord Beichan and Young Bekie*, where the persistent heroine, who rejoiced in the endearing name of Susie Pye, exhibits the same invincible resolution in landing her man as Floripas and Josian.

The only English romances known to me which present the Saracen in a more favourable light are *The King of Tars* and *Floris and Blanchflour*. In the first, the Sowdan of Damas, converted by his Christian wife, loses his ferociousness with his colour in the baptismal font, where he turns sensationally—a wonderful moment—from black to white. In the second, the beauty and constancy of the young lovers touches the Emir's heart to pity, a rare note, and he spares and unites them.

In *Partonope of Blois* the word 'Saracen' is used as it is in *King Horn* to mean heathens in general and Vikings in particular. Sornegour, described as a Saracen, is really king of the Danes. He is, we learn:

> a passynge semely knygthte,
> For and he hadde bene off Crystys lore,
> I trowe men haue neuer by-fore
> In Romaunce herd a worthyer kynge.
> He loued knythhode aboue alle thyng.
>
> (ll. 2670–4)

Such concessions to the virtues of 'heathen houndes' are seldom met with. But the romancers are ready enough to admire the architectural skill of the Saracens in passages of lavish description like that of Bradmond's palace in *Bevis*, with its gold walls, brass doors, glass windows, moat, and gold and azure tower surmounted by a golden eagle with flashing eyes made of precious stones which illuminated the whole building.

Richard Coer de Lion,[1] a robust English romance of the fourteenth century, based on a thirteenth-century Anglo-Norman original, embodies more fully than any other the popular medieval conception of the Saracens. The work has affiliations with both *Arthur and Merlin* and *King Alisaunder*, whose life, with its strange birth story and eastern adventures, shares something of the same pattern. Printed by Wynkyn de Worde in 1509 and 1528, and by

---

[1] *Metrical Romances of the Thirteenth, Fourteenth and Fifteenth Centuries*: published from Ancient Manuscripts, with an Introduction, Notes, and a Glossary, by Henry Weber (Edinburgh, 1810). (Text unreliable.) Quotations from the critical edition, *Richard Löwenherz*, by Karl Brunner (Vienna and Leipzig, 1913).

Thomas Purfoot in 1568, it was still a cherished tale in Tudor times. It has moved a good way from Ambroise and his contemporary chronicle of the Third Crusade (1189) and confronts us not only with the most ferocious brand of Christianity but with the most intractable nationalism. If the Saracens are detestable so are the French and most other Christians apart from the English, who, of course, like Sir Gawain, are to other folk as pearls to white peas. But the essential features of the Holy War which the chroniclers had stressed remain—the reckless heroism, the violence, and the atrocities, vastly exaggerated and sharpened to suit the ghoulish taste of a popular audience.

Richard, who shares this trait with other heroes, is marked for great things by the curious circumstances of his birth. He is accredited with a supernatural mother who disappears dramatically from the story when she is no longer necessary to its development. Made captive in Germany while returning from a preliminary tour of the Holy Land, Richard consents to a game of 'pluck-buffet', not unlike the one described by the jongleur Ambroise, and by a trick kills his opponent, the king's son. It is at this point that the motif of the forthright lady is introduced. She is neither fée, nor Saracen, but Margery, the German king's daughter:

> Sche louede Rychard wiþ al here myȝt. . . .
> Whenne sche sawȝ hym, wiþ eyen twoo,
> Here loue sche caste vpon hym þoo,
> And sayde: 'Richard, saue God aboue,
> Off alle þyng most j þe loue!'
>
> (ll. 884 ff.–898)

It is she who, by providing him with yards of silk to wind around his arm, saves him from the devouring lion, whose heart he tears out and eats, thus gaining his soubriquet. (One of the roof bosses in Norwich Cathedral records the incident.) But Richard, like Roland, is not really interested in love. His destiny is to lead a crusade to the Holy Land and in due time the romance gets him there to carry out his main business of slaughtering Saracens and quelling the insulting French with their irritating references to 'tailed dogs' and 'taylards'.[1]

The English king's truculent and triumphant progress eastwards is marked by signal success not only in Sicily, where he constructed his celebrated wooden castle, *Mate-Griffon* (Greek-Killer), but also in Cyprus. The self-styled emperor of this island, Isaac Comnenos, after arresting Richard's shipwrecked men and confiscating his goods, receives his messenger with the utmost contempt. According to Ambroise he had uttered the scornful expletive, 'Tproupt!' (l. 1466), an intolerable insult which at once elicited the stern reply, 'Aux armes!' This incident becomes greatly exaggerated in the English romance. The emperor, we are told, throws a knife at the messenger (Sir Murdour in *Bevis* does much the same thing) and when his steward quite properly remonstrates with him, Isaac, pretending to ask for advice, commands the wretched man to come near and suddenly cuts off his nose—a rash act which brings upon him swift vengeance and the loss of his kingdom:

> The emperoure began to rage,
> He grunte his tethe, and faste blewe,
> A knyfe after Syr Roberte he threwe. . . .
> And syth he cryed, as vncourteys:
> 'Out, taylardes, of my paleys!' . . .
>
> The stewarde on knees hym set adowne
> With the emperour for to rowne,
> And the emperour of euyll truste
> Carued off his nose by the gruste,[2]
> And sayd: 'Traytour, thefe, stewarde,
> Go playne the to þe Englysshe taylarde!' . .

---

[1] The English were said to have tails—a reference to a punishment supposed to have been bestowed on the insulting men of Kent by St Augustine of Canterbury in 597.

[2] In *OED* Weber's reading of this couplet ('trusle/grusle') is quoted under *gristle* (2). No explanation is there given of the interesting form 'trusle'. It is in fact a ghost word. The variants recorded by Karl Brunner are 'truste', 'triste' and 'gruste', 'griste'.

> The stewarde his nose hente
> (Iwys his vysage was jshente),
> Quickely out of the castell ran,
> Leue he ne toke of no man, . . .
>
> (ll. 2118 ff.–2166)

rushing, with the severed appendage clutched cautiously in his hand, straight to Richard, who takes prompt action, wins the island, great treasure, and two famous horses, Fauvel and Lyard.

Richard begins his operations against Acre with siege engines, mangonels and 'robinets', hurling very effective ammunition—beehives full of angry bees—at the enemy. But he falls ill and has a longing for pork, difficult to gratify in a Saracen neighbourhood. His resourceful cook provides him with a Saracen 'young and fat' tastefully garnished. Richard tucks in and laughs when he is shown the head of the 'swine' whose body he has demolished—'What! is Saracen's flesh thus good?' An even more gruesome banquet is offered to unfortunate ambassadors of Saladin who are served with the heads of their near relatives, properly labelled, in case cooking should have altered their features. They not unnaturally recoiled from such an alarming hors-d'œuvre and were told by Richard:

> Þer is no fflesch so norysschaunt
> Vnto an Ynglyssche Cristen-man,
> Partryck, plouer, heroun, ne swan,
> Cow ne oxe, scheep ne swyn,
> As is þe flesshe of a Sarezyn.
>
> (ll. 3548–52)

That the author and his audience relished these cannibal scenes is obvious from the repetition of the incident in all its hideous detail in a report to Saladin.

To a hero who could dine pleasantly off Saracen's flesh, the execution of sixty thousand infidel prisoners meant little except the necessary exertion, for he was cheered on by angelic choirs enjoying the carnage—a flagrant concession on the part of the author to the demands of popular taste in a context of popular faith:

189

Þere þey herden an aungele off heuene
þat seyde: 'Seynyours, tuez, tuese,
Spares hem nouȝt, behediþ þese!'
Kyng Richard herde þe aungelys voys,
And þankyd God *and* þe holy croys.

(ll. 3748–52)

At this juncture, with Richard safe in Acre, the author indulges in a seasonal headpiece sweet with the song of birds and scent of blossom in Maytime—a startling contrast to the immediate context of blood and battle.[1] There was no quarter, no ransom for Saracens. 'What scholde dogges doo but dye?' (l. 4672). The valleys are flooded with Saracen blood:

And manye off þe heþene houndes
Wiþ here teeþ gnowȝ þe groundes.
By þe blood vpon þe gras
Men myȝte see where Richard was!

(ll. 5115–18)

A vision of St George, who had appeared, according to the chronicler of the *Gesta Francorum*, at an appropriate moment in the First Crusade, was enough to rally the Christians to further violence against the Saracen host, whose numbers, in spite of every effort to exterminate them, never seemed to diminish. There they were, helmets shining, hauberks bright, banners unfurled, ready in their countless thousands of mounted horsemen in ordered ranks, to meet the next assault. The most cunning of their stratagems, a demon horse and foal sent as a present to Richard from Saladin (a legendary exaggeration of a genuine gift of horses to Richard from Safadin, Saladin's brother), could not prevail against the angelically protected English king, 'the English devil' as the Saracens called him.

In the opinion of the author there never was a fighting hero who could compare with Richard:

---

[1] A feature of epic style. Statius set the trend for this sort of thing: *Thebaid*, v, 459. See *Kyng Alisaunder*, ed. G. V. Smithers (EETS, 1957), ii, pp. 35 f.

> I wene neuere, par ma fay,
> þat in þe tyme off here day,
> Dede ony off hem so douȝty dede
> Off strong batayle *and* gret wyȝthede,
> As dede Kyng Rychard, saun fayle,
> At Jaffe in þat batayle.
>
> (ll. 6735–40)

The 'heathen hounds' in such a narrative appear worthy of such an outrageously active antagonist only by virtue of their stubborn bellicosity. They are the cruel martial enemy typified.

By a process of the elimination of all but their central traits and purpose, the writers of the English metrical romances, like St Bernard long before them, presented the Saracens as symbols of evil to be destroyed by equally symbolic warring Christians. As in the works of Statius, Lucan, and Silius Italicus we can trace the gradual drift towards allegory, a holy war of vices and virtues, to become explicit later in the *Psychomachia* of Prudentius, so the Saracens and Christians of the earlier romances, already little more than abstractions, were, by the time of Tasso, formally reduced to allegorical figures. The transition from the medieval romance to the moral allegory of the *Gerusalemme Liberata* was slow, but easy and inevitable.

'Le preux reis, le quer de lion' of the chronicler Ambroise (l. 2310) becomes in the romance of *Richard Coer de Lion* a symbol of Christian invincibility, and a sort of crude ancestor of the Red Cross Knight, blazing the trail towards allegory. Years later Richard reappeared in literature, tamed but still recognizable. In *The Talisman* Scott creates afresh, in a new idiom—the historical novel—the 'mondo cavaleresco, romanzesco, fantastico e voluttuoso' in which the Saracen, Saladin, and the Crusader, Richard, struggle heroically for supremacy in the Holy Land. They are no longer symbols but comprehensible characters of more or less human dimensions. The play of imagination on history has produced two credible beings but—last echo of the metrical romances—one significant detail obtrudes from the past. The English king is still 'of a size approaching the gigantic'.

13

Another Fragment of the Auchinleck MS

G. V. SMITHERS

THE LIBRARY of the University of London has recently acquired from Miss Winifred A. Myers, whose source was a Scots one of undisclosed identity, a bifolium[1] of a Middle English text, which was identified both by Professor D. J. A. Ross and by Miss Yeo (of the staff of the Library) as being part of the text of *Kyng Alisaunder* and as having been contained in the Auchinleck MS copy of that work. By the generosity of Professor Ross, as of the Librarian and his staff (and notably Miss Gibbs and Miss Yeo), I have been given the privilege of making the contents of this bifolium available.[2] It is hoped that the portion of the Auchinleck text that is represented in it may eventually be included in the EETS edition of *Kyng Alisaunder* when the occasion for a reprint of the latter arises. But this lies in the indefinite future. The text of the new fragment is therefore presented here, along with such evidence as it offers on two questions—the original position of the bifolium in the Auchinleck MS, and its relation as a text of *Kyng Alisaunder* to the other two copies in MSS Laud Misc. 622 (Bodleian Library) and Lincoln's Inn 150, referred to here as B and L respectively. No attempt has been made (e.g. by the use of dots) to indicate the number of missing letters in illegible passages, since in many instances this number cannot be determined. Abbreviations (other than those for numerals) have been expanded, and word-division has been regularized.

[1] MS 593 of the University of London Library.

[2] The difficulty of deciphering the only partly legible 2 v. and 1 r. has been substantially eased by the excellent photographic copies kindly made for me by the Photographic Department of the Library.

e quen candace   al   *f.* I *r.* I

Sendeþ þe greteinges   amour

Alisaunder dere s rie

Ouer al men y þe desire

Nim me to þ n owen quen   6680

Riche schal þi mede ben

Jchil charge saun faile

Wiþ bes   s aþousand c

Jchil ȝiue þe ȝim   beiȝes

  en þousand ca   rs   6685

  chil charge

Wiþ

                     en

                           mbardinges   6690

                               inges

                   sand noble kniȝt

To þi w   and

And   d

Ful of   der   6695

Gold

Nomiȝt þe   worþ

            þou   oceros

And v. c olifa

             red   6700

     þousand

Olif   pleyne

Strong   of   6705

And v. c   gold

       lond   w ld

And an hundred þousand gentil squiers

Þat   þe se ue in ich misters

6680 me: *B* me þer fore, *L* me fore alle   6680 owen: *not in BL.*
6709 ich: *B* alle

193

þousand maidens briȝt   6710
For to serue þine kniȝt
Alle erles do hters and barouones
Ful of sw   teis wones
O   Alisaunder   riche
                                                         6715

                                                         6720

Þer was cumen wiþ   þem alang   *f.* I r. 2
A queint man a metalȝete   6725
Þat coupe   in al þing
He avised þan   e king
And þo he com ho   sikerliche
He kest a fourme þe king y iche
J   face in eiȝe in nose in mouþe   6730
Jn lengþe in membres þat is selcouþ
Þe quen it bischet in hir bour
And kept it wiþ gret honour
Now rideþ alisaunder in his iurnaiing
Wiþ michel   de and singinge   6735
Jn gr   t and solasinge
Listneþ   of his meting
So þe king rode wiþ doukes and erls
He mett to hore cherls
To þe nauel her berd hing   6740
Þus aresounde hem þe king
Say me now ȝe eld   hore
Mani day is ȝe were ybore

6727 þan: *B* wel.   6732 it bischet: *B* it sette, *L* sette him   6733 wiþ: *BL* in
6743 is: *L* is seothe

Wite ȝe owhar bi ani way
Oni meruaile in þis cuntray   6745
Þat ich miȝt don in storie
Oþer men to memorie
ȝa   fa quaþen he
A gret meruaile we tellen þe
Þat is hennes an euen wey   6750
Þe mountaun of ten iurnay
Þou schalt finde trewes to
Seint and holy þai ben bo
Her and in oþer cuntres alle
Arbe sec men hem calle   6755
ȝif þou wilt þe þider diȝt
Þou miȝt wiþ þe lede xl. m kniȝt
Wiþ hem þou miȝt þe wele were
Þat non wilde bestes schul þe dere
Mo no miȝtow lede saun dotaunce   6760
Bot þe faile sustenaunce

Go to hem and aske an hert   *f. 1 v. 1*   6768
Al þatow wilt cert
Oþer of frende oþer of ken   6770
Oþer of strong men
And þou schalt here þe soþe anon
      þou wilt þider gon
Þe king bi conseil of his best

6744 ani: L þis   6747 to: B to haue of, L han in   6754 Her and: L Hyȝer þan
6755 Arbe sec: B Arbre sek, L arbeset   men: B men done   6757 miȝt wiþ þe:
L most   6758 þe: *not in L*   6759 schul: *not in L*   6761 faile: B failed.
6768 an: BL in   6769 wilt: B wilt wite, L wolt wite   6770 Oþer of: B Of
þee oiþer, L Of þe of   6771 of: B of oþer, L of oþir   6774 L by god counsaile

Di3t him þiderward on hast   6775
And sent wiþ porrus al his men
Jn to þe cite of faacen
Bot fourti þousand wiþ him he toke
So we finden writen in boke
Alisaunder so rideþ and wendeþ   6780
What he comeþ to þe trewes hende
Now þe muge and þe cetewal
On hem smelleþ and þe galingale
Þe canel and þe licoriis
Swete odour 3iueþ ywis   6785
Gelofre quibibbe and þe mace
Gingeuer comin 3eueþ odour of gras
And vnder sonne of alle spice
He 3aue odour wiþ delice
Þat lond was holy he vnderstode   6790
Þai li3t of her destrers gode
Þai 3eden on fot and men hem mett
Euerich oþer fair gret
Of lyonus and of panteren
Alle her weden certes weren   6795
Han þai no wolle to spinne
Her cloþes ben of bestes skinne
Þe bischop þat was of þe lond
Of þe kinges com haþ sond
He di3t him and went þe king o3an   6800
Hereþ now of a selcouþe man
Þe bischop hete Longis sikerliche
He was boþe blac and griseliche
And rouwe and scheldred al so

6775 þiderward on hast: *L* þider saunfaile   6779 writen: *not in BL*   6780 *L*
Forþ Alisaundre gan wende   6781 what: *B* þat, *L* til   hende: *L* ende   6782
Now: *not in BL*   6783 galingale: *L* wodewale   6785 3iueþ: *L* ymeynt   odour:
B flauour, *L* sauour   6789 3aue: *BL* hadden   odour: *BL* sauour(e)   6791 þai:
BL And   6792 And men: *B* and many, *L* men   6795 weden: *L* wodes   6796
wolle: *B* wille.   6800 di3t: *B* graiþed, *L* greyþed   6804 and scheldred: *B* and
shuldred, *L* y schuldreod

His o fot was more þan þe oþer to 6805

Þe king wel fair he gret   *f.* 1 *v.* 2   6812
Al so sone so he him mett
And þe king him seyd bi gode resoun
Of his coming þere chesoun 6815
What helpeþ it long to telle
Þe bischop him grauntèd al his wille
And schreueþ him and al þo
Þat wiþ him þider schuld gon
Now is þe sonne ygon vnder 6820
Þe bischop ledeþ þe king to þis wonder
And þre hundred kniʒtes him mede
To þe trewes wiþ him ʒede
No seiʒe he neuer so fair atour
No neuer smelled so swete odour 6825
At þe trewe of þe sonne
Her sacrifise þai bigunne
Þe bischop to þe king seyd
And to alle his felawered
King he seyd þis trewe onest 6830
Asked offring of no best
No of broches no of ringes
No of no muþe crieinges
Bot in þine hert þenk al þi wille

6805 þe oþer: *B* þe oþere, *L* oþir   6812 fair: *B* faire þere   6815 *MS*
þerechesoun *or* þenchesoun   6816 long: *BL* al it: *not in L*   6817 him: *not*
in BL   6818 him and: *L* heom.   6819 þider: *B* to þe trowes, *L* to þe trouʒh
6821 þis: *L* þe   6822 þre: *L* foure hundred: *B* þousande   6823 wiþ him:
BL after   6824 so fair: *L* suche   6825 odour: *L* sauour.   6829 his: *L* þeo
6831 *L* Ac hit spryngiþ of noblest

And þou schalt finde it ful snelle   6835
For byheld vp þi steuen
Is yherd vp to heuen
Þe king seiȝe a leyt of fer brond
Fram þe trewe in to heuen stond
On knewe he gan anon to falle   6840
And wiþ him his kniȝtes alle
And þouȝt ȝif he schuld þe warl win forþ
Est and west and souþe and norþ
ȝif he schuld to grece oȝain wende
To sen his moder and his frende   6845
Þat trewe him answerd oȝen
Jn language of Jnden
King alisaunder y telle þe cert
Of alle þe world þe þridde part
        winne and ben of king   6850

King alisaunder kneu ades   *f. 2 r. 1*
Boþe Torold and ek Phares   7215
And seyd to hem frendes onest
Telleþ on ȝour lordes hest
Ben it foly ben it wise
ȝe no schul haue bot curteisie
Torold seyd þe king wroþ is   7220
And seiþ ȝe don michel amis
Þat ȝe ȝou maken lord and sire

6835 schalt finde it ful: *B* it shalt wite, *L* schalt ywite   6836 vp: *B* vp riȝth
6837 vp: *BL* in   6838 leyt of: *BL* le(e)m so   6839 Fram: *L* And from   in to:
L astem to   6840 anon to: *L* doun   6841 and wiþ him: *B* adoune þere wiþ
6842 forþ: *L* þoruȝ.   7219 *B* ȝee ne schulle non harme haue, jwis; *L* Ne schole
ȝe me fynde bote curteise

198

Fer and neiȝe of his empire
Cites makeþ walles rareþ
He dredeþ him al to his care   7225
Ȝe han him tviis ouercome
And alle his tresour him binome
He wiþclepeþ al homage
And sendeþ ȝou bi ous sond gage
And deffiaunce bi our hond   7230
And hoteþ ȝou remu out of his lond
Alisaunder ginneþ to leiȝen smale
And þus he ginneþ to hem his tale
Jchil proue wiþ spere and sword
Þat of þis lond icham lord   7235
Porrus weneþ ich be amaid
For his gviours me han bitraid
And of mi pople haþ forlore
Jn þat cas he is forswore
Al þe lere in him ich rett   7240
Y schal ȝeld him wele his dett
Ȝete ichaue aliue saun fable
Alle min xii. constable
He haþ sponnen a þred
Þat is comen of iuel red   7245
Ȝete ichaue c. þusinde
Betters kniȝtes no ben in ynde
Redi to proue wiþ vigour
Þat he is a vile traitour
And ȝif he doþ also ich ille   7250
His no mine no schul spille
F   aqueintaunce þat haþ ben

7224 rareþ: *L* þare   7225 *L* Ȝe dreden him   7228 wiþclepeþ: *L* wiþ seiþ
7229 bi ous sond gage: *B* by sonde gage, *L* by ous saun gage   7231 hoteþ: *L* bad
7235 þat of þis lond: *BL* Of þis lond þat   7236 be: *L* am   7238 haþ: *B* haue,
L haþ   7239 cas: *not in BL*   7240 lere: *L* lore.   7241 him: *B* ful; *not in L*
7247 Betters: *B* None better   7249 vile: *not in BL*   7250 And: *L* Ac

For his barouns and for mine   *f. 2 r. 2*   7258
Þis were þe riȝtest liue
Þe to barouns he kneu baþe   7260
He schewed hem al þe cuntray
Of his folk þe pite
And þe atire of þat cite

7265

Þe messangers oȝain wendeþ
Alisaunder his barouns ofsendeþ
And þis deffiinge hem telleþ
Þai him conseild al so snelle
Wenden swiþe after hem   7270
Þat he weren at faacen
Þai trussen alle in þe daweinge
And makeþ swiþe after wendinge
Torold and phares beþ comen hom
Oȝain hem com lord and grom   7275
For to here what tiding
Þai brouȝten fram alisaunder king
Þe messangers beþ comen to halle
Bifor porrus and þe barouns alle
And seyd porrus we ben ycome   7280
Fram alisaunder þat hende gome
And haþ afong þine deffiinge
And sent þe bi ous tidinge
He nil ȝour barouns no his
Ne beren cark of alle þis   7285
Ȝete he may to bataile finde

7260 *B* Wel he knew þoo barouns tweye, *L* þeo two barouns he kneow by
eyȝe   7266 oȝain: *B* so swiþe, *L* swiþe   7270 Wenden: *B* Wendeþ, *L* To
wende   7271 he: *L* ȝe, *B* we (*corrected: from* he?)   7277 king: *BL* þe kyng
7281 þat hende: *BL* þe riche   7283 And: *B* He, *L* And

Douhti kniȝtes xx þousinde
He no wil nouȝt þine amere
No þat his þine adere
Ac ȝe to wiþ hors and scheld   7290
Comen armed in þe feld

ȝif þou miȝt him parforce aquelle
His folk wil don þi wille   7295
ȝe þat chalange al to habbe
Bitven ȝou deliteþ it wiþ dabbe
And wiþ spere and swerdes dent
Js alisaunders jugement
Prince and douke baroun and kniȝt   7300

P   stode and was   *f. 2 v. 1*
He no   nouȝt
Colour he chaungeþ sumdel for d
And   gret ire to hem he sede
Lordinges ȝif ȝe weren gent   7310
To me fel þe jugement
Ac for ȝe recheþ of me lite
Of me ȝe habbeþ now aquited
Ac naþeles ich wot þis
Strenger icham þan he ywis   7315
And more in eueri lim al so
Oȝaines him y dar me do
Falle it to nesche oþer to hard

7288 þine amere: *L* þat ȝe demere   7289 his þine: *B* þine hise, *L* his no þyn no   7292–3 *no gap in MS*   7297 deliteþ: *BL* deleþ   7313 habbeþ now: *B* habbeþ ȝou, *L* haueþ ȝou   7314 þis: *BL* jwys   7315 ywis: *BL* is   7316 lim: *BL* bon   7317 me do: *B* go.

No schal y neuer be coward
Bi þate þis was fuly sade   7320
Alisaunder was in a made
Ycomen boldliche wiþ al his
Bifor þe cite of faacen
Þer was quic mani tent sett
Mani cord to pauiloun knett   7325
Mani baner vp ypelt
And mani scheld wiþ best ygelt
Eten and drinken on aise apliȝt
And resten hem þat ich niȝt
And beþ so warded alle about   7330
Þat hem no stondeþ no dout
Amorwe as ich haue ysade
Þis couenaunt was bitven hem made
Þat þe batail schuld ben
Porrus and alisaunder bitven   7335
Who so oþer win miȝt
Jn batail wiþ strengþe of fiȝt
He schuld haue al ynde lond
And al þat folk vnder his hond
Alisaunder him gan affie   7340
Jn his owne chiualrie
He wist wel and soþ forhole
Þat he no schuld þat deþ þole
    us affied him in his strengþe

    7345

Ostage ytake and treuþe ypliȝt   *f. 2 v. 2*   7350
Now hereþ of þe kinges fiȝt
G   ere to be kniȝt
Ner t r

7342 and: *BL* in   7343 þat: *BL* þe   7344 him: *not in BL*   7351 þe: *B* þise

Wiþ me   mdes to   hende
No were aco   es at   7355
Swete is loue of da
Ac it askeþ
Better is litel han   se
Þan michel eiȝte in mal ai
Who so is of dedes vntrewe   7360
Oft it schal him sore rewe
Alisaun er   comen to   el
Wele yarmed vnder
On a stede wele ydiȝt
And suteþ to a noble kni   7365
He rit his spe e br
Þe ensel rateleþ wiþ þe
P   us also comeþ flinge
Ygraiþed als a riche   g
Y   wele on   kniȝtes   7370
Nis no nede hir armes
     oþer lete gon þe rein
      gider w   gre
         sheldes
And dassed ouer in þe felde   7375
     turn oȝan
Wiþ
    oþer leggeþ on
   þe mass   on þe
Ac as þai   to   7380
O er   h   slo   hors
Þo   mosten of   aþe
De   en her medlaye
Geteþ it   of rest to   eche
Aiþer ginneþ oþer to seche   7385
Wiþ asailinge and wiþ s   inge

7354 *three minims visible before* des.   7364–5 *L inverts*   7365 suteþ to: *B* sitteþ as, *L* syt so   7367 *not in L*   7382 aþe: *B* beye, *L* boþe   7384 Geteþ: *B* Gayneþ

And epeþ hem wiþ fair wreyinge
We e þai en on þe ple

7387 fair wreyinge: B wrieynge, L fair werryng   7388 en: B fiȝtten on, L fouȝte in

The really irrefragable evidence that identifies the London fragment as having originally belonged to the Auchinleck MS happens to be of a textual kind; and it is this that is set out below. There would thus not be much point in elaborating on purely palæographical data here. One important fact, however, calls for mention: the running number xliiij is clearly visible on the 1 recto and 2 recto of the bifolium—and this is the running number on the recto of one of the St Andrews strips, while the trimmed and therefore partly illegible running number on the Auchinleck MS copy itself (of *Kyng Alisaunder*) could be read as either xliiij or xlviij.

We must here recall that in 1949 Dr N. R. Ker discovered two fragments of the Auchinleck text of *Kyng Alisaunder* in the binding of an edition (dated 1543) of Horace, belonging to the University Library at St Andrews. The text contained in them corresponds to ll. 6856–7194 of the Laud MS. Moreover, it is continuous (apart from lacunæ of twenty lines in each column where the lower half of the leaf is missing); it covers 338 lines, and may be reckoned to have originally contained about 358 if one allows for the lacunæ in the lower part of the columns; and this latter figure is almost exactly the number of lines that would fill a bifolium, if it were written—as comparable parts of the Auchlineck MS itself normally are—in two columns of forty-four lines each on both recto and verso, i.e. with about 176 lines on each folio. It is therefore clear not only that the St Andrews fragments constitute a bifolium, but that the bifolium in question was the central one of the gathering.

The bottom of each leaf of the London bifolium has been trimmed away (no doubt in order that it might be used as the binding of a book). The sections of text that have consequently been lost correspond to ll. 6715–23, 6762–7, 6806–11, and 7253–7 of the Laud MS. The whole section of the text originally contained in it can be computed within narrow limits of error; though we must allow for the possibility that, at some stage in the evolution of this copy, the odd line or two in these passages may have been omitted—since in fact ll. 7264-5 and 7292-3 are missing from a continuous portion of text in the fragment.

Fortunately, the upper (and major) part of each column, and therefore the line at the head of each column, has been preserved intact. The portions of text contained in each of the two leaves amount to about 179 and 178 lines respectively. Moreover, each of these two blocks of text is continuous within itself (except for the lacunæ of between five and seven lines at the foot of each column). The first immediately precedes the section of text contained in the St Andrews bifolium, while the second immediately follows it. In other words (since the gatherings in the Auchinleck MS contain eight leaves each), the London bifolium contains leaves 3 and 6, and the St Andrews bifolium contains leaves 4 and 5, of one and the same gathering; and the two bifolia were immediately adjacent in the manuscript. This is perhaps the most interesting and remarkable fact about the London fragment. And it makes possible a further deduction. Since the portion of the text of *Kyng Alisaunder* that is still contained in the Auchinleck MS begins at l. 7760 (according to the numeration of the Laud MS), and the last column of the London bifolium begins at l. 7350, the London fragment must have ended at l. 7393 or thereabouts. The difference of 365 lines between 7394 and 7759 is roughly equivalent to the amount written on two leaves; these would have been leaves 7 and 8 of the same gathering as the St Andrews and London bifolia.

These facts and conclusions may be more simply displayed in the following table. In this column I refers to the text of *Kyng Alisaunder* contained in the Auchinleck MS, II to that in the St Andrews fragment, III to that in the London fragment, IV to the number of lines in each block of text, V to the number of the folio, VI to the position of the leaf in its gathering, and square brackets enclose figures that have been arrived at by deduction.

The line numbering is that of the Laud MS; and in III, the numbers separated by an oblique stroke are those of the lines at the head of columns in the London bifolium.

I	II	III	IV	V	VI
		6676/6724–6767 ⎫ 6768/6812–[6855] ⎭	179	[272]	3
	6856–[7031]		175	[273]	4
	7032–[7207]		175	[274]	5
		7214/7258–[7305] ⎫ 7306/7350–[7393] ⎭	179	[275]	6
				[276]	[7]
				[277]	[8]
7760–7803 ⎫ 7804–7849 ⎭			⎰ 43 ⎱ 45	⎰ 278 r 1 ⎱ 278 r 2	
7850–7893 ⎫ 7894–7937 ⎭			⎰ 43 ⎱ 43	⎰ 278 v 1 ⎱ 278 v 2	
7938–7981 ⎫ [7982]–8021 ⎭			⎰ 43 ⎱ 39	⎰ 279 r 1 ⎱ 279 r 2	

The general character of the London bifolium is in keeping with that of the other extant parts of the Auchinleck copy. It intermittently preserves the author's Essex-London forms in rhyme, as in *rarep* 7224: *care*, and even when the Laud MS obscures them and corrupts the rhyme, as in *sade*: *made* 7321-2. It is much superior to the Lincoln's Inn copy as a textual authority: it agrees again and again with the Laud MS when the Lincoln's Inn MS has a very inferior or preposterous reading which is palpably an independent corruption. These things, however, do not call for further illustration here. The main point at issue is the affiliation of the London bifolium with the other copies, since there is naturally not a great deal of evidence on this question to be got from the 750 lines or so that are preserved in the Auchinleck MS and the St Andrews fragments.

There are in fact not less than six passages in the London bifolium which undeniably raise the issue of the affiliation of the manuscripts. Thus no editor can afford to pass them over, even though they yield only tentative results. Though no one of them singly is decisive or unambiguous, they cumulatively point to the same conclusion: that the Auchinleck copy (as a whole) and the Lincoln's Inn may well derive from a common antecedent. They thus support in some measure the conclusions stated in the EETS edition of *Kyng Alisaunder* (vol. ii, pp. 14–15), and the stemma there constructed. They are as follows:

1. *Arbe sec* men hem calle   6755 (B *Arbre sek*; L *Arbe set*)

In this allusion to the 'Dry Tree', a corruption of *Arbre* to *Arbe* might just conceivably have taken place independently in A and L; but it is hardly likely. If the form *Arbe* is indeed corrupt (and there is no easy alternative assumption), it was probably inherited from a common antecedent of A and L.

2. Han þai no *wolle* to spinne   6796 (B *wille*; L *wolle*)

As the *lectio difficilior*, B's *wille* has some claim to be regarded as the author's word here; in that case, and if *wolle* in A and L is meant for 'wool', *wolle* is to be regarded as a 'common error' in A and L, and would imply their descent from a common antecedent manuscript. But the superiority of *wille* is perhaps not sufficiently clear-cut to justify the application of this principle without reservations.

3. Ben it foly, ben it wise,   Be he fole, be he wijs,
   ʒe no schul haue *bot curteisie*   ʒee ne schulle non harme haue,
            (7218–19)   jwis (B)

   Beon þey fole, beon þey wyse,
   Ne schole ʒe me fynde *bote corteise* (L)

The main point here is the substantial concurrence of A and L in respect of the words *curteisie* and *corteise*. In itself, this need be no more than the independent survival (from the author's version) of a word formed on this root. But the rhyme on [i:] (which is represented in all three manuscripts) rules this out: since no [i:] form is attested in *corteis* adj., both *corteis* and *curteisie* must be corrupt. If corrupt, they point in conjunction to the descent of A and L from a common antecedent.

4. Þe to barouns he kneu *baÞe*   Wel he knew Þoo barouns
   He schewed hem al Þe cuntray   *tweye,*
   (7260–1)   And shewed hem al Þe cuntreye
                              (B)

   Þeo two barouns he kneow *by eyȝe,*
   And schewed heom alle Þe contreye (L)

The L reading is likely to be one of the innumerable corruptions typical of that manuscript. But A's *baÞe* (which the rhyme shows to be corrupt) suggests that both derive from *beye* 'both' at an earlier stage. *Beye* (as a synonym of *baÞe*) makes corruption to the latter in A understandable. The alternative is that *beye* is what the author wrote, and has been independently corrupted in antecedent manuscripts of A and L (as well as B). But *beye* occurs in B 7382, in rhyme, and in a context in which it cannot be a corruption of *tweye* or any other conceivable equivalent. Thus there is no perceptible reason why B should have corrupted *beye* to *tweye* in 7260. In other words, *tweye*, not *beye*, is likely to be what the author wrote; and if this is so, the presumptive *beye*, being itself corrupt, implies that A and L derive from a common antecedent.

5. He wiÞclepeÞ al homage   He wiÞclepeÞ al homage,
   And sendeÞ ȝou bi *ous sond* gage   And sendeÞ ȝou by *sonde* gage
   And deffiaunce bi our hond   And defyaunce by oure honde
   (7228–30)   (B)

   He wiÞ seiÞ alle homage
   And sent ȝou by *ous saun* gage
   And defence by oure hond (L)

The question here is the status of *ous* in A and L. There is unfortunately no decisive criterion for a judgement. But *ous* and *sond* in immediate succession are metrically harsh, since *sond*, though a noun, would be an unstressed element, as full stresses are required on *bi* and *gage*. It seems most improbable that the author would suddenly have launched into Anglo-Norman with the word *saun*: this, at least, is likely to be corrupt in the L version. On the whole, and given the fact that B is usually the best textual authority, *ous* in A and L is probably to be regarded as suspect. If by any chance this verdict is sound, it follows that *ous* implies a common antecedent for A and L. The equivalent in the *Roman de toute chevalerie* does not really avail to give an unmistakable lead:

> Pur vous, Alixaundre, defier eimes cea esmuez. . . .
> Ore vous defyt od *ses* gages renduz.
> (Durham MS 10413–18)

6. He no wil nou3t þine amere   Ne wil he nou3th þine amere
  No þat *his pine* adere (7288–9)   Ne þat *pine hise* dere (B)
            He nul nou3t þat 3e demere
            No þat *his no þyn* no dere (L)

There is little doubt that the B reading in 7289 is the natural and appropriate one, since it provides the contrasting alternative to 7288 that seems apt, while the order of the elements *his* and *pine* in A and L gives a parallel to it (though this is admittedly not an utterly impossible kind of thing for someone to have said). This is at least a reasonably probable example of the concurrence of A and L in a corrupt reading, and, as such, points to their derivation from a common antecedent. Though there is not a complete equivalent in the *Roman*, the corresponding passage, so far as it goes, confirms the above interpretation:

> Ne volt que desore murge pur ly *sa* gent
> (Durham MS 10444)

The chance that has now thrown up separately, at an interval of fifteen years, two bifolia that were actually adjacent in the Auchinleck MS is sufficiently remarkable—but probably not quite so remarkable as it seems. The two leaves of *Richard Coeur de Lion* acquired by Laing by 1857, and the two fragments of it discovered by Mr D. L. Bushnell in 1949, all originally belonged to one and the same gathering in the Auchinleck MS, in which gathering they were respectively the second and seventh leaves (Laing's fragment) and the fourth and fifth (Mr Bushnell's).[1] The gathering was no. 48.[2] The St Andrews fragment and the London bifolium likewise come from one and the same gathering (no. 40) in

---

[1] See *Medium Ævum*, xviii (1949), 1–3.

[2] For the gatherings, see the table of A. J. Bliss on pp. 655–6 of his 'Notes on the Auchinleck Manuscript', *Speculum*, xxvi (1951), 652–8.

the Auchinleck copy of *Kyng Alisaunder*. Moreover, three of the four sets of fragments have been found in St Andrews; while the London bifolium, which is of unknown immediate provenance, is clearly likely to be from the same ultimate source as they. And all four were used as bindings; and since this was done at St Andrews itself with at least two of them, the same probably applies to the London bifolium. In fact, all four may well have been torn out of the manuscript at St Andrews by one and the same hand.

The recovery of more leaves, and the furtherance of our knowledge, might be made possible by information regarding the history of the London University bifolium; and it is very much to be hoped that anyone in a position to give it will do so.

14

Chaucer: The Prioress's Tale

G. H. RUSSELL

WE RECALL the context. The Shipman has completed his tale, ending with what we recognize as a characteristically improper pun and with a prayer to God which is little short of blasphemous:

> Thus endeth now my tale, and God us sende
> Taillynge ynough unto oure lyves ende.
>
> (VII. 433–4)[1]

It is a conclusion that befits a tale which is coldly polished in its devising, a tale which lacks the high and engaging comedy of the best of the fabliaux and which leaves us with an uneasy sense of the triumph of baseness, greed and folly. It is a tale of flesh and lucre: the tale of three people enmeshed in *cupiditas*.

The Host's response to the tale is favourable, but hardly enthusiastic, though at least its anti-clerical tone has met with his approval, and it is the baseness of daun John that makes the strongest impression upon him. But he does not linger over the Shipman's performance, and, perhaps seeking a balance or a riposte, he turns and speaks to the Prioress with elaborate politeness. At once we are aware of a change of tone. He had addressed the 'gentil maister, gentil maryneer' using the familiar singular pronoun and had expressed his opinion of his tale in what we judge to be an idiom that is deliberately colloquial in both its turn of phrase and its syntax. But now, with an almost exaggerated change of manner, 'As curteisly as it had been a mayde', he invites the Prioress to take her turn in telling a story in a speech which now employs both the formal plural of address and the elaborate

---

[1] Quotations are taken from, and line references are given to, F. N. Robinson, ed., *The Works of Geoffrey Chaucer*, 2nd edition (Oxford, 1957).

syntactic structure of formal utterance, and which is replete with deferential phrases at the farthest remove from the brusque and even provocative requests which he addresses to some of the pilgrims. She is, at the beginning and the end of the request, a 'lady' whose 'leve' is sought, in the hope that no offence is taken. The Host, not seeming to presume, takes care to say that he 'wolde demen' that she should be the next to tell a tale—'if so were that ye wolde'—and he finishes by inquiring, with some anxiety and a great deal of deference, 'Now wol ye vouche sauf, my lady deere'. And to this anxious invitation, the lady replies with a single word—'Gladly'. Her terse answer is in striking contrast to the Host's anxiously tortuous question. And no doubt the Prioress *is* glad to tell her tale. She must have listened to that of the Shipman with distaste and disapproval. Her short reply suggests that she is willing to redress the balance.

It is natural for a modern reader, perhaps hypersensitive in these matters, and warned by the apparent absurdity of the Host's adopting the 'courtesy' of a 'maid', to look for irony in this invitation. Yet the text does not seem to allow of such a reading. We are, it seems, expected to take the deliberately courteous form of address as being a genuine reflection of the Host's deferential attitude to the Prioress. It is pointless to read the text in any other way. It may be that he expected some other kind of response than that of her severe, single-word reply. But the text of the head-link does not allow us to make any such assumption. Nor does the Prologue to the *Tale of Sir Thopas* which follows the completing of the *Tale*. This, indeed, makes it clear that, whatever might have been the expectation before the Prioress told her tale, the effect of its telling was to cast something of a spell over the whole company, regenerate and unregenerate alike:

> Whan seyd was al this miracle, every man
> As sobre was that wonder was to se,
> Til that oure Hooste japen tho bigan. . . .
>
> (VII. 692–4)

The Host is obliged to break this spell and to turn to the poet him- self for 'a tale of myrthe' or 'deynte thyng' which, by implication, will balance the solemnity of the story told by the Prioress. He offers no comment. Perhaps his own participation in the sobered reaction to the story, which was experienced by 'every man', is a sufficient comment. The respect shown to the Prioress is as real at the end as it was at the beginning of her tale.

It is as we recall the terms of the portrait of the Prioress in the *General Prologue* that we look for a repetition or development of some of the ironically pointed remarks which have led critics to form a generally unfavourable opinion of her character.[1] Even if we concede some part of these earlier criticisms, it is impossible to see their reappearance at this point in the poem. If we are to look for persistence and exploitation of the alleged ironies of the *General Prologue*, we shall have to wait to see if the tale itself will offer these. If they appear in neither the prefatory section nor the tale nor the link with the succeeding tale, we might even think that we have been hypersubtle in our reading of the text of this part of the *General Prologue*, and that we have, in fact, read too much into it.

As the Prioress begins her tale, we are given a further sense of distance from the world of the Shipman. We are, at once, translated to a level of literary and spiritual experience which is far removed from those which had been explored in *The Shipman's Tale*, and this contrast is reinforced by our recalling that, at some point in the writing, this *Tale*, too, had been prepared for a woman narrator, presumably the Wife of Bath.[2] The supple couplets and the lithe, if rather chilly, movement of *The Shipman's Tale* yield now to those statuesque, formal stanzas which recall an earlier, 'courtly', phase of Chaucer's creative work and which he was to use on only three other occasions in *The Canterbury Tales*— the first in a tale told by a nun, the second in another tale told by an ecclesiastic, the Monk, who is provoked into telling a tale of monumental solemnity by the mockery of the Host, and the third by yet another churchman, the grave and idealized Clerk. It is,

[1] See, for instance, an extreme recent example in D. W. Robertson Jr, *A Preface to Chaucer* (Princeton, 1964), pp. 244 ff.
[2] See VII. 11 ff.

then, no surprise that the Prioress elects to cast her narrative in this form. She was, in any case, a woman who admired and imitated courtly demeanour and practice. But the stanzas which open the *Tale* are more than merely 'estatlich': they constitute the Prologue which, as has been noted, is in that shape of a prayerful invocation to God which forms an integral part of many of the Miracles of the Virgin, an invocation, furthermore, replete with verbal reminiscences of that part of the liturgy so familiar to a nun—the offices of the Blessed Virgin Mary. The Prioress is represented as choosing a metrical form that is at once appropriate—almost inevitable—for one of her station and sympathies, and of putting it to use in a traditional introduction to the type of narrative that she is to relate—again a type pre-eminently suited to a nun—and of casting this introduction in a language that is deeply and traditionally evocative.

The Prioress, then, is operating within an idiom that is, in important ways, sustained by liturgical reminiscences and this, in turn, recalls to us the emphasis laid by the portrait in the *General Prologue* upon the elegance and distinction of her chanting of the Divine Service, an emphasis which is now shown to have been seriously intended. It is a linguistic framework which contrives to combine deep personal involvement with a sense of detachment and deeper dimension that is, perhaps, only possible in liturgical language of the kind represented by the Office. Her respect for the most characteristic activity of her vocation enables her to use its idiom in a way that establishes at once the solemnity and the stature of the narrative that is to follow. There is here no sense of the sentimental, of the spuriously courtly, of the mincingly pretentious or indeed of the merely formulaic. The language is, of course, highly contrived and the strong liturgical underpinning gives to it a depth in which the nun's own intensely sincere involvement is placed and strengthened. We have an immediate sense of being offered a reverent introduction to the narrative, an introduction designed to assert at once the seriousness of that narrative and the relevance of it to its teller and its hearers. This conscious exploitation of the hieratic reinforces for us the contrast with *The Shipman's Tale*, the final couplet of which, as we have seen, offered the pilgrims a near-blasphemous prayer. It was the Shipman's prayer that he (and we) might enjoy a successful exploitation of sex and money throughout our lives. The Prioress's prayer, separated from this only by the brief intervention of the Host, is, in the first place, a prayer of praise to God and His Mother and then a prayer that she might obtain the guidance of the Virgin in the successful management of that narrative which is to be in honour of the Virgin, and finally an assertion that if success is to come it will come only from the 'benyngnytee' of the Virgin, in whose hands the Prioress is an unworthy agent. Her prayer is a humble and selfless prayer at the furthest remove from that of the Shipman and a fervent expression of values of an utterly different kind and dimension.

In fact, whatever our expectation might have been, the Prioress's prologue is neither narrow nor parochial in its reference. As if to emphasize this, it opens with a stanza in which the central images are those of size, value, 'dignitee' and 'bountee'. It offers a reverent attempt to evoke the magnitude and the depth of the mystery of God, a mystery which, as the second stanza recalls, is further deepened by the fact of the Incarnation's being made possible by the consent of an ordinary young woman who, by this consent, is exalted so that we may say that 'she hirself is honour, and the roote / Of bountee, next hir Sone, and soules boote'. This motif of the accessibility of the transcendent to the humble will, as we shall see, play an important part in what is to follow.

It is this paradoxical union of the human and the divine which leads to the highly contrived and witty development of the third stanza with its conceits of those conjunctions of opposites which are so characteristic of the tradition of Christian liturgical prayer and hymnology centred on the Incarnation:

> O mooder Mayde! o mayde Mooder free!
> O bussh unbrent, brennynge in Moyses sighte,
> That ravyshedest doun fro the Deitee,

Thurgh thyn humblesse, the Goost that in th'alighte,
Of whos vertu, whan he thyn herte lighte,
Conceyved was the Fadres sapience,
Help me to telle it in thy reverence!

(VII. 467-73)

And from this peak of elaboration and intensity, the last two stanzas of the Prologue lead quietly to the task in hand. They incorporate the prayer for assistance with a suggestion that just as in the Virgin humility coexisted with greatness so here, on an infinitely lower level, the humility of her devotee may enable her to transcend her limitations and to obtain the grace to offer a narrative which will, in essence, be a celebration of the glory of the Virgin, a glory beyond human comprehension. Another reference to herself as one like 'a child of twelf month oold, or lesse', the first of a series of reminiscences of the mass of the Feast of the Holy Innocents, points up the close organization of the Prologue and takes us back to its opening and suggests to us that, granted this assistance, this 'child' too may perform as notably as 'men of dignitee'. As we are to learn later, her tale is to be concerned with the transformation of a 'child' into one who is capable of going far beyond 'men of dignitee' in the work of the praise of God. But this is to look forward. For the moment the important thing is the emphasis upon the power of the Virgin to raise the humble to greatness, as she herself had been raised to greatness by her humility. Before all else, it is suggested to us that, instead of a tale of the flesh, we shall be offered a tale of transcendence, a tale in which the mysterious coexistence of nature with supernature, once and for all demonstrated by Mary's role in the Incarnation, will be offered as a testimony to the continuing presence of Christ through His Mother in human affairs. We are already far from *The Shipman's Tale.*

This is made clear as soon as the Prioress begins her story with lines not altogether unlike those which introduced *The Shipman's Tale.* It is a story placed in the world and at once it proposes to us an abrupt transition from the stainlessness of Heaven to the sordidness of the world of men. It brings to us a world quite precisely

identified and located; but it is a world within a world, a world of
the rejected who are being exploited for his own sordid profit by
one who has power over them:

> Ther was in Asye, in a greet citee,
> Amonges Cristene folk, a Jewerye,
> Sustened by a lord of that contree
> For foule usure and lucre of vileynye,
> Hateful to Crist and to his compaignye;
> And thurgh the strete men myghte ride or wende,
> For it was free and open at eyther ende.
>
> (VII. 488–94)

From the height of love and dedication we have descended into
a society so completely in thrall to the baseness of human cupidity
that it is given over to practices which, so far from winning the
love of God, cannot fail to earn His hatred. It is a 'greet citee',
'Sustened by a lord': but it is the city of men, not the city of God.
Human power, human greed and human presumption flaunt the
law of God. It is in a world of spiritual and moral bondage that
these people live for, as the Prioress in seeming naïveté and matter-
of-factness remarks, the street which traversed the 'Jewerye' was
'free and open at eyther ende'. This world within a world is, in
physical terms, totally accessible and 'free', and yet it is in fact
inhabited by a group of people who are oppressed by the weight
of evil, and, as the sequel is to show, hemmed in by hostility. It is
evil's own enclave and evil's dominion ensures that, however 'open'
and 'free' it may appear to be, it is, in fact, a place of tyranny and
fear. Physical freedom and spiritual freedom are not coterminous.

From the greatness of the city and the power of its lord mani-
fested by his ability to create and maintain a society within a
society, we pass abruptly into another world—a world of small-
ness, of innocence and of insignificance. The stanzas which follow
the opening stanza are filled with words and phrases which evoke
a world of the very young, the innocent and the defenceless—
'litel scole', 'children an heep', 'smale children', 'wydwes sone',
'litel clergeon, seven yeer of age', 'litel sone', 'sely child'. The
intention of these phrases seems quite clear. It is not that the

Prioress is sentimentalizing her narrative. It is rather that she is making an attempt to represent a world of innocence which has all the appearances of helplessness but, as her reference to St Nicholas at l. 514 reminds us, this is a world which, on a deeper and truer assessment, proves to possess a strength immensely greater than that of its apparently more powerful neighbour. It is the world of a child and his companions, a world of piety, simple and unaffected, and, for them, the world of the school of the Lord.

It seems at least possible that the recurrent images of teaching and learning which appear especially at ll. 516–29 are designed, in addition to performing their central function of identifying the child and his world, to evoke a sense of training for the service of the Lord. Not, of course, that there is question of a training in the sense that Benedict might have intended. This process is not that of patient, disciplined acquisition of a spiritual perfection which will ensure success in struggles to come. This small boy, still at his Primer, learns the opening of the *Alma Redemptoris* 'al by rote' and the Prioress makes it clear at ll. 537 ff. that this determination to master that which is beyond him is an instinctive gesture of 'reverence' and that even the older boy to whom he turns for help is unable to offer very much.

Yet he has learned. He has, in his own important way, penetrated not so much into the text of the hymn itself, as into that mystery of which it is an expression, and he has become an innocent, apparently uncomprehending, agent, an agent of God's message with whom the Prioress shares a mission since she in her Prologue had represented herself as being an agent of this very kind—a child who yet may honour God and His Mother. It is an exploration, by implication, of a traditional Christian concept of the ability of the simple to penetrate into that which, in human terms, seems beyond them.

This apparent lack of comprehension which yet masks deep, if not fully realized, perceptions is responsible for the introduction of the first admonition of death to the *Tale*. The 'felawe' represents to his young inquirer that *Alma Redemptoris* is a 'song' which will invoke the help of Mary 'To been oure help and socour whan we

deye'. In fact, as we know, *Alma Redemptoris* does not say anything explicitly about the Virgin's help at the time of death. The
idea has been gratuitously introduced and from this point in the
poem the sense of violence and death becomes more and more
obtrusive. Even in the very next stanza where the child expresses
his determination to learn the hymn *in toto* he seems to use language
of unusual force: he will be 'shent' for failing to master his Primer
and he will be beaten three times in an hour. A price is to be paid
but the heaviness of that price is not yet fully revealed. At this
point it is expressed merely in terms of a schoolboy's experience.
Despite this consciousness of a penalty to be imposed, he will learn
the hymn by the time, he says, that 'Cristemasse be went'. And,
as we know, the end of Christmas, on one reckoning, will be the
feast of the Holy Innocents.

This determination attains its immediate reward. The difficult
task is accomplished and for the moment no shadow is cast upon
the child's simple but important accomplishment which has, so
far, cost him so much. There is a sense of confidence and of
exhilaration in the boy's newly acquired ability to sing the hymn:
as a result he sings it 'boldely'. And in the following stanza this
newly found confidence sends the child through the 'Jewerye'
full of joy, his heart filled with the love of the Mother of Christ.
Again he is represented as the instrument of the praise of Mary:
now, indeed, 'On Cristes mooder set was his entente'. He is, in a
very real, almost literal, sense, an instrument in the hands of the
Virgin.

This joy, sweetness and love proclaimed by his hymn in honour
of Mary are, of course, inimical to the malignity and bitterness of
Satan, and the following stanza turns us abruptly from this world
of innocence and sweetness back to the sordidness and evil of the
opening lines of the *Tale*. But this sordidness has now assumed an
even more sinister guise. 'Oure firste foo, the serpent Sathanas' has
entered the hearts of the Jews, to build there his 'waspes nest'.
Bitterness now confronts sweetness, pride humility. Satan's appeal
is to the bitterness of pride scorned, the pride of the 'Hebrayk
peple'. In this characteristically malignant appeal, the simple,

humble act of 'reverence' offered to Mary by the boy—here contemptuously referred to as 'swich a boy'—is represented by Satan as a deliberate provocation and he asks, rhetorically, 'Is this to yow a thyng that is honest?' The boy's simplicity and uncomplicated devotion as represented by his action in walking 'as hym lest' and, allegedly, 'in youre despit' are used to inflame the latent hostility of the Jews. It is a characteristic perversion of good into evil that the humble devotion of the child should be represented by Satan as a calculated insult to the Jews. That he should 'synge of swich sentence' is offered as proof of this: but, as we know, the child scarcely comprehends. His grasp of the 'sentence' of what he sings is very insecure. His intention, of course, is quite other than Satan suggests and, as the gospel for Childermas, taken from the Book of Revelation, reminds us:

. . . et in ore eorum non est inventum mendacium, sine macula enim sunt ante thronum Dei.

As ever, Satan is using the good for his own ends and the Jews are, once more, being exploited for evil purposes as they had been depicted in the opening stanza. The exploitation has, however, become more sinister. The perversion of values by which the simple and reverent offering of the boy's tribute to the Virgin is represented as being 'agayn oure lawes reverence' is to have a sequel of the utmost violence.[1]

Very suddenly, in a manner that recalls to us the brevity and compression of the usual Miracle of the Virgin, the pace of the tale is quickened and its central, violent episode introduced. The Jews, as befits a people in thrall, are quickly and fatally duped by the appeal of Satan and determine to kill the child. As usual in such situations in medieval narrative, there is no representation of a long period of indecision. Evil manifests itself quickly because

---

[1] This is to accept, with Donaldson, the reading *oure* as against *youre* in Robinson's edition. As Carleton Brown points out in *Sources and Analogues*, p. 448, this ability of Satan to kindle the hatred of the Jews is more intelligible in those versions of the story in which the 'song' is *Gaude Maria* which is much more provocative to the Jews.

these people, inured to evil by their bondage, are the instruments of Satan and can be so used. In all this the notion of the human as controlled by superhuman powers is central, and we recall the burden of the prologue and earlier part of the tale. The boy, as he goes to his death, is no longer represented in the terms of the early part of the poem. No longer is he 'a little clergeon' or 'a sely child': now he is simply a 'child'. It is as though his stature has already grown, that he is no longer thought of in the purely human terms in which he had first appeared. At this point there is no attempt to evoke the sense of the pity of the child's violent death, and the Prioress does not linger over the details of the murder.

A child has been murdered in the most sordid of circumstances. But for the Prioress this is no matter for lamentation. There is, it is true, a brief display of indignation. She at once places him with those other innocents, the victims of Herod, and ll. 572–9 are heavy with prognostications of punishment in prospect, a punishment suggested in the last solemn line of the stanza with its reminiscence of Genesis iv. 10 and all that this implies. The text of the Tract of the mass of the Holy Innocents is also in our minds and we catch the irony of its application:

Effuderunt sanguinem sanctorum, velut aquam, in circuitu Jerusalem. Et non erat qui sepeliret. Vindica, Domine, sanguinem sanctorum tuorum, qui effusus est super terram.

These thoughts are not further developed at this stage. There have been death and violence, but with them has come the glory of martyrdom as their reward. The Prioress breaks into a deeply felt expression of joy at the translation of one who now has been raised from the lowliest of human situations to become one of that heavenly host celebrated in the Book of Revelation. His simple singing of a hymn barely comprehended has now yielded—indeed has led—to his participation in that celebration of the glory of God by the choir of the martyrs without stain. He who was first presented to us as pathetically helpless and weak is now one of the elect of God. The child's uncomprehended song of praise has, as it were, now become the 'song al newe' eternally offered in honour of God.

For all this, the child's disappearance and death, in human terms, remain both tragic and pathetic, and they are surrounded by the normal human reactions. From the height of the contemplation of his newly-won glory we are brought abruptly back to the world of human experience, in a deliberate juxtaposition of the supernatural and the natural. His mother is a 'poure wydwe' still and for her he is 'hir litel child': she is filled with fear and anxiety to the point of distraction as she searches for her lost child. Hers is a 'moodres pitee' and, appropriately, she invokes—as others before have done in the course of the Prioress's narrative—the assistance of 'Cristes mooder meeke and kynde'. The glory of the martyr's triumph is not lessened, but neither is the agony of the concomitant human situation. For the moment it is the purely human that engages us. Yet as the mother's search continues and as, under Divine guidance, she approaches the place in which the body is concealed, the Prioress again allows the sense of weakness and helplessness to recede. Once more the diminutives are dropped and, as the discovery of the body is made, he is 'hir child' and 'hir sone'. But he is far more than this and the following stanza offers a solemn celebration of the power of God which is able to transform this weakest and humblest of humans into 'This gemme of chastite, this emeraude, / And eek of martirdom the ruby bright . . .' (ll. 609–10). And it is in accord with this renewed sense of his glory that his voice, miraculously sustained, is heard with a strength so great that 'al the place gan to rynge'. This voice which had once been the voice of a child now masters the place as befits the voice of a saint proclaiming the glory of the Mother of God in a place of evil. The small has become very great: and we recall the words of the Introit for the mass of the Holy Innocents:

Ex ore infantium, Deus, et lactentium perfecisti laudem propter inimicos tuos. Domine, Dominus noster: quam admirabile est nomen tuum in universa terra.

With this discovery of the body we are returned to the world of human affairs. The 'provost', not forgetting to offer his praise to Christ and His Mother, quickly exercises his legal authority. The body of the child is carried, with appropriate ceremony, to 'the nexte abbay'. The mother whom we had last seen distraught and fearful is now the new Rachel, grieving indeed, but raised in stature by the glory of her son, Once more the Prioress recalls the liturgy of Childermas where both the Gospel and the Communion verse, taken from Matthew xi, recall the lamentation of Rachel for her lost children.

Alongside of this, curtly disposed of, is the display of savage and summary justice by the provost. It offers a chilling intervention of a brutal but, to most medieval minds, just process of legal revenge. The child, as the Gradual of the mass tells us, is 'free'. The Jews, who have always been in bondage, go to a death which is represented as the return of evil for evil. And this death itself is evil; unlike that of their victim, it is not the gateway to glory.

But this is not dwelt upon. The Prioress, as we would expect, makes no comment. Nor does she display any tendency to indulge in further recriminations. The dead child is the centre of her preoccupation and she moves now to the final phase of her tale, the paying of appropriate honour to a saint in the ceremonies of burial. The holy abbot,[1] rather obtusely it seems, fails to grasp the greatness of the miracle that is being witnessed, and he addresses his questions to the child in terms that recall those of the earlier part of the tale: for him, he is a 'yonge child', a 'deere child'. But when the child replies he speaks in a manner that is very different from that which he had used in that early part of the poem. There is now nothing of the simplicity and artlessness of childhood in

---

[1] He, at least, is holy. The Prioress seems to offer what is, to the modern reader, a rather unexpected and perhaps jarring comment on monastic spirituality when she remarks:

> This abbot, which that was an hooly man,
> As monkes been—or elles oghte be— . . . (VII. 642–3)

In her this is simply matter-of-fact. There is no reason, I believe, to press the significance of the remark, far less see it as any kind of comment on the Monk of the pilgrimage.

what he says. His response to the abbot's gentle questioning is magisterial and he speaks with an authority which makes the abbot's mode of address look foolish. He is now the very reverse of the uncomprehending innocent, and he looks back to the experience of his human existence as one who has totally transcended it, and is now able to judge it with calm authority. The anxious and bewildered child of the first half of the *Tale* makes no appearance in a passage like the following:

> 'My throte is kut unto my nekke boon',
> Seyde this child, 'and, as by wey of kynde,
> I sholde have dyed, ye, longe tyme agon.
> But Jesu Crist, as ye in bookes fynde,
> Wil that his glorie laste and be in mynde,
> And for the worship of his Mooder deere
> Yet may I synge *O Alma* loude and cleere.'
>
> (VII. 649–55)

Following this and the child's death by the abbot's removal of the 'greyn', the fullness of the mystery of the events penetrates the minds of the onlookers. The abbot and his community are deeply moved, not now by the human pathos of the situation which had produced the earlier 'pitous lamentacioun', but by the greatness of the miracle that the Virgin has wrought. They now grasp the child's having transcended his human limitations and having become a saint of God. While it is still a 'litel body sweete' that is enclosed in the 'tombe of marbul stones', and while the Prioress still reminds us that the martyr was a child of the tenderest years, as his small body proclaims, all this is now irrelevant for he has been taken into the company of martyrs with whom there is question neither of age nor of size, nor of life nor of death.

As she had begun with a prayer for help in telling her tale, the Prioress closes with another prayer for assistance. This time the prayer is not addressed to Mary, but to the martyred Hugh of Lincoln whose fate had, in some ways, paralleled that of the child of the *Tale*. Her prayer, again at a far remove from that of the Shipman, is for him to intercede for us 'synful folk unstable' that

God will 'multiplie' His grace in us 'for reverence of his mooder Marie'. It is a characteristically sober and reverent end to the story.

The Prioress's Tale is, then, in face of the portrait of its teller given in the *General Prologue* perhaps a little surprising. It is not in the least a mannered narration; it is not in the least a sentimental story. Whatever the apparent ambiguousness of her behaviour and attitudes as represented by the *General Prologue*, whatever the apparent tepidity of her dedication to the rigours of the religious life, the tale that the Prioress tells would seem to show that her spirituality, even if not necessarily deep and highly developed, is neither feeble nor histrionic, and it would seem to suggest further that some of his commentators have far outstripped Chaucer in pointing up the Nun's weaknesses.

Her election to relate a Miracle of the Virgin is, for a nun, a natural enough decision, and the miracle that she chooses to recount is, in its kind, restrained, tasteful and moderate. It contains nothing of the exaggerations and absurdities which so often disfigure this *genre* in its medieval forms. The Prioress reveals herself as a person who, while having little of the obvious strength of the central ecclesiastical members of the pilgrimage, is yet capable of relating a story which, while participating in a tradition that so often displays a naïve and crude spirituality, is able to avoid its pitfalls and turn it to distinguished artistic account. It is a performance which must lead us to think that her critics have read into her portrait too much that is unflattering. This decisively sensitive rejoinder to the Shipman leaves an impression of quiet and assured maturity.

Her assurance is displayed in the economy and skill with which the fiction is organized and in the easy mastery of the verse of a mature tradition handled with unusual sensitivity. Its basic mode is tempered, gentle and unemphatic. As such it bears the narrative along without strain and without display. As befits its story, its staple vocabulary is apparently simple and undemonstrative; it is, in fact, the assured language of a tradition of Christian writing that is venerable and rich:

Thus hath this wydwe hir litel sone ytaught
Oure blisful Lady, Cristes mooder deere,
To worshipe ay, and he forgat it naught,
For sely child wol alday soone leere.
But ay, whan I remembre on this mateere,
Seint Nicholas stant evere in my presence,
For he so yong to Crist dide reverence.

(VII. 509–15)

Chaucer has given to the Prioress a verse which, in his best manner, is deceptively easy and simple, with a total control over a demanding rime scheme and a rhythmical pattern attuned to respond sensitively to the needs of the narration. Its use of language is unaffected and unobtrusive, deriving its hidden strength from the command of a series of words that are resonantly strong and evocative in his hands—*blisful, deere, sely, reverence*. Words like these recur through the poem and serve to remind us of the depth and the density of the verbal complex that the best late-fourteenth-century religious poetry in England has achieved. It embodies a mature management of language which enables the fullness and richness of a series of recurring words and phrases to suggest the depth and mystery which underlie this simple and otherwise merely pathetic story. Its success is intimately involved with this coexistence in its language of the apparently simple and that which is conceptually and emotionally rich and dense.

By casting the staple of the *Tale* in this tempered, disciplined mode, Chaucer is enabled, as he wishes, to raise the tension. He had, in fact, caused the Prioress to open with an invocation that is highly wrought and deliberately impressive in its movement, as a kind of proclamation of faith and a decisive assertion of a change of tone in the poem. At important moments through the narrative—at the moment of the temptation of the Jews by Satan, in the celebration of the death of the virgin martyr, after the discovery of the body in the pit, in the child's reply to the abbot and in the invocation to St Hugh of Lincoln—he is able to rise to a kind of verse that is much more ceremonial than is that of the narrative staple. And here, perhaps in more obvious ways, the assured strength of the verse is proclaimed. For this is the area of late Middle English verse which is notoriously exposed to the temptation to display the merely decorative and the merely formulaic, as much of the verse in, say, the Carleton Brown collections demonstrates.

Instead of the idle and repetitive gesturing of verse of this kind Chaucer offers a highly wrought and deeply felt poetry which draws much of its strength from its sensitive use of liturgical and biblical reminiscence and which attempts to sustain the level of expression of heightened religious experience for only short periods. There is throughout the poem a persistent and pervasive apprehension of the significance of the story but it is only at climactic points that the mystery of the intervention of Christ and His Mother is allowed its full ceremonial expression. It is then that Chaucer causes the muted, restrained verse to enkindle into a moment of fuller revelation of that mystery to the expression of which language allows him only partial access. Yet the closing lines of the *Tale* remind us that it is, after all, in the gentle and simple that the mystery of this story is captured. It is fitting that these lines should bring the Prioress's narrative to an end in a mood of deep and reverent acknowledgement of the power of God:

> Preye eek for us, we synful folk unstable,
> That, of his mercy, God so merciable
> On us his grete mercy multiplie,
> For reverence of his mooder Marie.

For the poem's concern is with the humble and the simple, but not with these as types of human weakness. Humility and simplicity are, in fact, capable of access to sources of strength which enable them not merely to triumph over their apparent human superiors, but to transcend all human limitations. And this is also the message of the liturgy of Childermas.

15

The Nine Unworthies

BRUCE DICKINS

Les Neuf Preux, in Latin *Nouem Probi* and in English *The Nine Worthies*, are grouped in threes. The Pagans are Hector of Troy (since medieval sympathy was with Trojan rather than with Greek), Alexander the Great (prominent in the Matter of Rome the Great, which comprehended all classical antiquity) and Julius Caesar (ideologically, though not in blood, the parent of the Roman emperors). The three Jews are Joshua (who led the Israelites into the Promised Land), King David, and Judas Maccabaeus (the hero of Jewish resistance to the Syrians in the Apocryphal Books of Maccabees). The three Christians are King Arthur (the chief figure in the Matter of Britain), Charlemagne (the centre of the Matter of France) and Godfrey de Bouillon (elected chief of the Christian state in Palestine established by the First Crusade).

This triple grouping was popularized, though not devised, by Jacques de Longuyon in *Les Vœux du Paon*, c. 1310. It soon became fashionable in art as well as in literature. As an example one may recall the considerable remains of a splendid late-fourteenth-century French tapestry believed to have been made for Jean, duc de Berry, and now in New York.[1] Here five of the tapestried Worthies survive—Joshua and David, Alexander (probably) and Julius Caesar, and lastly King Arthur.

From this side of the Channel a number of Middle English passages dealing with the Nine Worthies are conveniently collected in Sir Israel Gollancz's Appendix to his edition of *The Parlement of the Three Ages* (Oxford, 1915). When the Middle Ages were

[1] J. J. Rorimer, *The Metropolitan Museum of Art: The Cloisters* (New York, 1951), pp. 47–55, and the same and Margaret B. Freeman, *The Nine Heroes Tapestry* (New York, 1960).

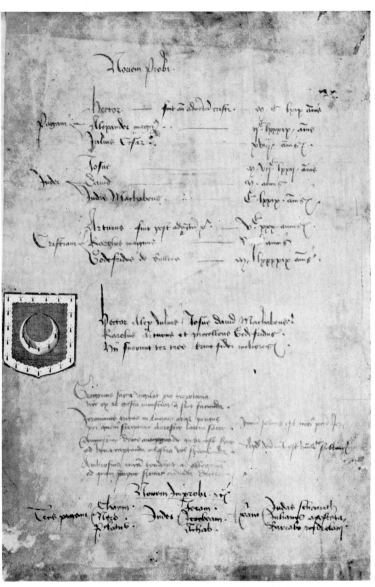

The Nine Unworthies. MS Trinity Hall Cambridge 10

over (if in England they ever were till the middle of the seventeenth century) the Worthies were affectionately, if humorously, remembered in literature. In *Love's Labour's Lost*, Act V, the whole concept is burlesqued. Hector of Troy is presented by Don Armatho the fantastical Spaniard, Alexander the Great by Sir Nathaniel the Curate, Judas Maccabaeus by Holofernes the pedant. Pompey the Great and Hercules, played by Costard the Clown and the minute page Moth, are interpolated, and the remaining Worthies are promised but not presented.

In contemporary art the Nine Worthies are taken rather more seriously. At Montacute House, Somerset, the east front of this very late Elizabethan house, originally the main entrance front, has between the windows of the top storey clumsily carved but attractive statues of the Nine Worthies in classical dress; one and a half of these are figured on the plate facing p. 9 of the guide.[1] Again there is in the Victoria and Albert Museum, South Kensington, part of a panelled room (248–1894) that can be securely dated to 1606.[2] This comes from 'The Old Palace' at Bromley-by-Bow, now demolished, which was a hunting lodge of James I. On the plaster work of the ceiling are circular medallions with busts of Hector, Joshua and Alexander derived from plates issued in 1597 by Nicholas de Bruyn.[3] There were also figures of the Worthies in the Jacobean hall at Blickling, Norfolk. The earl of Buckinghamshire (died 1793), who had determined to make drastic changes in his hall, wrote in November 1767: 'Some tributary sorrow should, however, be paid to the nine worthies, but Hector has lost his spear and his nose, David his harp, Godfrey of Boulogne his ears, Alexander the Great his highest shoulder, and part of Joshua's belly has fallen in. As the ceiling is to be raised, eight of them must have gone, and Hector is at all events determined to leave his niche.'[4] To multiply examples would be

---

[1] National Trust, *Guide to Montacute*, p. 6.

[2] M. Jourdain, *English Decorative Plasterwork of the Renaissance* (London, 1926), figs. 14–17, and the V. and A. booklet now unhappily out of print.

[3] James Lees-Milne, *Tudor Renaissance* (London, 1951), p. 92.

[4] Quoted by Lord Suffield in *My Memories* (London, 1913), pp. 89–90.

tedious, especially as Miss Patricia M. Butler, M.A., of the Ipswich Museum, who has been most helpful, has in mind a comprehensive study of the Nine Worthies. But I cannot refrain from noting the set of twelve silver spoons of the apostle type bearing the date-letter of 1592 and once owned by the Tichborne family. This presents eight of the Nine and Guy of Warwick (a native hero of romance who takes the place of Godfrey de Bouillon), all in 'artist's armour' such as never was worn unless upon the stage. The dozen is made up by the Master spoon (Christ), St Peter—and Queen Elizabeth I bearing the orb. After all her ancestor Robert Bruce was, in Scotland, acclaimed as the Tenth Worthy; so was Henry VIII in England.[1]

In Scotland *Les Vœux du Paon* was well known from the Scots translation in *The Buik of Alexander*, ll. 9897–10012,[2] and the Nine Worthies are represented in art as well as in literature, notably at Crathes Castle, Kincardineshire. They are dated 1602 and are painted on the ceiling of the Chamber of the Nine Nobles, where they are accompanied by Late Middle Scots verses describing them in turn. These latter were clumsily repainted after they had been uncovered in 1877 and the text printed in the Guide can scarcely be accurate.[3]

The corresponding *Nouem Improbi*, who may be called the *Nine Unworthies*, are only listed, so far as I know, on the first pastedown of a Cambridge manuscript, Trinity Hall 10 (M. R. James's *Catalogue*, p. 11). This is a not much later addition made in England to a collection of historical material compiled in Bruges towards the end of the fifteenth century. The *Improbi* are of course the anti-types of the *Probi* and as such may suitably be compared with (the remains of) a row of persecutors in glass (Windows

[1] Charles Oman, *English Domestic Silver*, 3rd ed. (London, 1949), pp. 71–2.

[2] It is edited along with the French original (ll. 7484–7575) by R. L. Græme Ritchie in the Scottish Text Society's *Buik of Alexander*, IV, 402–6. Reference should also be made to his Introduction (I, xxxv–xlvii).

[3] *A Guide to Crathes Castle and its Gardens*, published by the National Trust for Scotland, 4th ed. (Edinburgh, 1963), is well illustrated in black and white: a coloured card of part of the ceiling is also available.

xxv–xxviii) who face a row of saints (Windows xxi–xxiv) across the nave of Fairford church, Gloucestershire.[1]

The significant parts of the paste-down (reproduced facing p. 228 by the kindness of the Master and Fellows of Trinity Hall) may be transcribed as follows:

Nouem Probi.

Pagani	Hector—fuit ante aduentum cristi. —— M.C.lxix annis
	Alexander magnus ———————— ij^c.lxxxix annis
	Julius Cesar. ———————— xviij annis.

Iudei	Josue ———————— M.vij^c.lxxij annis
	Dauid ———————— M. annis
	Iudas Machabeus ———————— C.lxxix annis

Cristiani	Arturus fuit post aduentum christi V^c.xxx annis
	Karolus magnus ———————— Viij^c annis
	Godefridus de Bulleine ———————— M.lxxxxix annis

Hector Alex. Iulius / Josue Dauid Machabeus.
Karolus Arturus et precellens Godefridus.
Hii fuerunt ter tres / trine fidei meliores.

. . . .

Nouem Improbi. viz

Tres pagani	Chaym.	Iudei	Joram.	christiani	Iudas Scharioth.
	Nero.		Ieroboam.		Iulianus apostata.
	Pylatus.		Achab.		Barnabo Mediolanj.

Chaym is a medieval form of Cain, and *Nero* and *Pylatus* need no explanation; nor do *Ieroboam* (Jeroboam I), *Achab* (Ahab) and *Iudas Scharioth* (Judas Iscariot). The name *Joram*, the Vulgate form of Jehoram, was borne by ninth-century kings of Israel and Judah, both of whom did evil in the sight of the Lord. The king of Israel is perhaps to be preferred as having been the son of Ahab and Jezebel. Julian the Apostate was Caesar from 355 and Emperor from 361 to 363 and tried to re-establish the cult of the ancient

---

[1] O. G. Farmer, *Fairford Church and its Stained Glass Windows*, 8th ed. (1965), pp. 35–9.

gods of Rome. The only character from medieval history was Bernabò Visconti (1323–85), lord of Milan, who achieved a bad eminence even among Italian tyrants of the fourteenth century. On 5 May 1385 he was seized by his 'double allye' Gian Galeazzo Visconti and, conveniently, died in prison a few months later.[1] Lionel, duke of Clarence, married Violante, niece of Bernabò, and Chaucer, who had once been in Lionel's service, used Bernabò's fall as a 'tragedie' in his Monk's Tale (C. T. VII. 2399–2406 = B², 3589–96):

De Barnabo de Lumbardia

Off Melan grete Barnabo Viscounte,
God of delit, and scourge of Lumbardye,
Why sholde I nat thyn infortune acounte,
Sith in estaat thow cloumbe were so hye?
Thy brother sone, that was thy double allye,
For he thy nevew was, and sone-in-lawe,
Withinne his prisoun made thee to dye,—
But why, ne how, noot I that thou were slawe.

[1] E. R. Chamberlin, The Count of Virtue (London, 1965), pp. 63–91.

16

A Middle English Version of the *Epistola Luciferi ad Cleros*

ROBERT R. RAYMO

AMONG the manuscripts of the Henry E. Huntington Library is an early-fifteenth-century miscellany, HM 114, containing copies of *Piers Ploghman*, *Troilus and Criseyde*, *The Pistill of Susan*, Mandeville's *Travels*, a portion of the *Legend of the Three Kings*, and, on folios 319a–325b, a unique and hitherto unedited Middle English version of a celebrated burlesque Latin satire known as the *Epistola Luciferi ad Cleros*. A colophon on folio 325a identifies the work for us: *The lettre of the infernall emperour Lucifer, prince of the potestates of the gehennall regyon, Duke of Derkeness, sent to his dere, leef and entierly bylovid speciall childryn and frendis, the forlost childryn of the moderne cherche*. Unfortunately, the *Letter* survives in an imperfect state. A portion of f. 324 has been torn away with the result that we lack in whole or in part sixteen lines of the text. The entire manuscript is written on vellum and paper in an English vernacular bookhand by the same scribe who wrote Harley 3943.[1]

The author of the *Epistola Luciferi* was Peter Ceffons of Clairvaux, a controversial Cistercian theologian of the mid-fourteenth century with an avid interest in humanism.[2] He wrote the *Epistola* in 1352. The following year he renewed his attack upon the higher clergy in a much longer work entitled *Centilogium Domini Nostri*

---

[1] For a fuller description of HM 114, see R. K. Root, *The Manuscripts of Chaucer's Troilus* (1914), p. 35. The manuscript was formerly Phillipps MS 8252. The paper bears watermarks in use between 1383 and 1437: *Briquet* 7514, 3975, 3978, and 11872.

[2] The most detailed account of the life and work of Peter Ceffons is by D. Trapp in *Recherches de Theologie Ancienne et Medievale*, xxiv (1957), 101–54.

Jesu Christi or *Epistola Jesu Christi ad Prelatos* which purported to refute the charges contained in the *Epistola Luciferi*, but, in reality, only restated them more strongly and in greater detail. It has been argued by Father Damasus Trapp, O.S.A., that Ceffons, who liked 'to appear as moral philosopher in the gown of the ancients', had 'no personal feud with the bishops or the pope. If he castigates them in the *Epistola Luciferi* and the *Centilogium* . . ., we feel that he only wants to get the opportunity to follow the ancient models of a *commendatio priscorum* and *damnatio modernorum*'.[1] Be that as it may, the *Epistola Luciferi* achieved immediate success as a fierce protest against the venality and extravagance of the Avignon papacy and it soon outstripped in popularity and influence all the other anti-clerical Höllenbriefe that had circulated throughout Europe from the twelfth century onwards.[2] It was known in England at least as early as the first decade of the fifteenth century when it appears in the *Reply* of Friar Daw Topias to the Wycliffite attack on the friars, *Jack Upland*:

> But good Jak, your grace, where be ye foundid?
> Not in Goddis gospel but in Sathanas pistile.[3]

The Middle English version of the *Epistola Luciferi* is very far from a straightforward translation of the Latin original. The scope of the satire has been extended to include possessioners (ll. 63–4) and friars (ll. 229–48). Significantly, the activity of the friars is contrasted to 'the busy worchyng of the prechyng of the servauntes of Ihesu . . . for many now in these dayes agens us aryse, the lawes of that Ihesu Crist prechyng and with all her myghtes and strengthes enhauncyng, the fortheryng of our magiste to hyndre noght shamyng ne dredyng' (ll. 251–56). In view of these additions to the original text it is difficult to avoid the suggestion that the *Letter*

---

[1] Ibid., 116–17.
[2] For the popularity and influence of Ceffons's *Epistola*, and a general history of the form, see P. Lehmann, *Die Parodie im Mittelalter* (1922), pp. 85–95 and G. Zippel, 'La lettera del Diavolo al clero, dal secolo XII alla Riforma', *Bulletino Dell'Istituto Storico Italiano per Il Medio Evo*, lxx (1958), 125–79.
[3] T. Wright, *Political Poems and Songs Relating to English History* (1861), ii, p. 111. I am indebted to Mr P. L. Heyworth for this reference.

as it now exists reflects the Wycliffite outlook. What, perhaps, is more interesting is that the *Epistola* has been recast in a style that is evidently intended to ridicule the bloated and adorned prose, with its inexhaustible pile-up of epithets, 'colours' and quotations, which was sanctioned by medieval books of *dictamen* and cultivated most diligently by ecclesiastical chanceries. The present parody, however clumsy, may be taken as yet another protest, so often voiced in the late fourteenth and fifteenth centuries, against the preciosity of much official and clerical composition both in Latin and in the vernacular. Unhappily, the translator's inadequate command of both Latin and English thwarts his purpose. Inaccuracies frequently mar his work and occasional felicities of word and phrase are lost amidst the wild profusion of sprawling and structureless sentences.[1]

LUCIFER'S LETTER TO THE CLERGY

[319a] Lucifer, lord and prince of the depe donion of derke- 1
nes, rewlour of the regne of the infernall empyre, kyng of the
contre of cumbryd, caytifs iustise and iuge of all gehennall
subiettes, duke of the dale of dysesse, heer of the erytage of
hell, to all our dere, leef and worthi to be lovyd felawes, 5
bretherin and childryn of pryde, universall and singuler, with
the froyte of all falsnes fulfillyd of this dayes cherche, as the
feute of your obediens to our ymperial magnificens and
infernall sovereynte to which evereyet we fynd yow obey-
saunt and trewe lieges and subietes, helthe, welthe and gret- 10
yng, which as to ourself and oures we coveyte and desire,
while ye are to our willes, preceptes and maundementz

Lucifer, princeps tenebrarum, tristicia profundi regens Acherontis imperia, dux
Herebi, rex Inferni rectorque Gehenne, universis sociis regni nostri, filiis superbie,

---

[1] The *Letter* is reproduced by the kind permission of the Henry E. Huntington Library, San Marino, California. The punctuation and the use of capitals are modern, and abbreviations are expanded. þ has been transcribed as *th*, ȝ as *y* or *g*. There is no title in the manuscript. The text of the *Epistola Luciferi* is taken from Zippel, pp. 163–6, who edited it from the author's holograph, Troyes MS 930, ff. 67a–68a.

obedyent, redy and wele willyng, and as to us plesauntly of
your lyst bygonne and long lastyngly contynuyd to the lawes
15   of our lordship everlastyngly enduryng and fulfillyng, of
wham our adversare, thilk Ihesu Cryst, by his prophete
sometyme seyde, *Odivi ecclesiam malignancium*, 'I have hatyd
the chirche of mysdoers'. Somtyme some of the vikers,
subiettys and disciples of that Ihesu Crist, folowyng his
20   steppis and the tracys of his weyes, stablid in the signes of his
vertues, perfourmyng his will in her worchynges, lyvyng
undur a pore manere lyf, by her prechynges and werchynges,
ynto moost illusion of our tartariall regne / [319b] and iurisdiccion and contempte of our infernall magestee, alle the
25   world from the yok and servitute of the excellence of our
tyrannye turnyd to her doctryne, conversacion and lyf and
into grete preiudice, grevaunce and hyndryng of our iehennal
iurisdiccion, noght dredyng ne shamyng to hurte, defoyle and
greve our fereful powere and to offende the mageste of our
30   infernale estate. In tho dayes, thurgh her wrongful destour-
blyng, we were violently precludid from the tribute of the
dwetes of our subiettes, and to our wepeful paleys of the
gehennall empyre concours of our peple was than wrecchidly
lettyd and stoppid, and the brode light wey *que ducit ad*
35   *mortem*, 'that ledith to the dethe', without eny prees or steppys
of wrecches of our subiect peple, lay forletyngly undefoulyd,
unhauntyd and unusyd. Wherfor al the cravvyd court of our

precipue moderne ecclesie principibus, de qua noster adversarius Jhesus Christus
per prophetam predixit 'Odivi ecclesiam malignantium' salutem quam vobis
optamus, et nostris obedire mandatis ac prout incepistis legibus parare Sathanae ac
nostri iuris precepta iugiter observare. Dudum quidem Christi vicarii sequentes
eius vestigia signis et virtutibus coruscantes, degentes sub quadam paupere vita per
ipsorum predicationes et opera quasi totum mundum a nostre tirannidis iugo ad
suam converterunt doctrinam, et vitam in nostri tartarei regni illusionem maxi-
mam et contemptum, nec non in nostre iurisdictionis non modicum periudicium
et gravamen, non verentes nostram ledere potestatem et terrificam nostri principatus offendere maiestatem. Illo namque tempore nulla recipiebamus a mundo
tributa, nec concursu solito catervatim ruebat ad nostri baratri limina animarum
flebile vulgus. Sed via declivis et lata que ducit ad mortem sine ullo strepitu
manebat, nullis miserorum gressibus conculcata et tota nostra vacante curia

caytif cumpanye with all wepely compleyntes waylid,
mornyd and sorowyd, so pytously dispoylid of the right of
our rufull regyon, yn so myche that the impacient wodenes 40
of our brest no lenger myght bere hit ne the hard unpite of
the herte of our heer and our sorowful subiettes no lenger
furthermore myght suffre hit. But now, with forseying from
hennys forwarde to mete with our circumspeccion with all
suche like perelis, we have avisely / [320a] purveyd us of an 45
opyn remedy, and in the place and stede of tho our harmeful
adversares, that Ihesu Cristes apostles and al her folowers in
doctryne or maners, by our myghtfull powere and sotyl
boldenes, we have now in thes dayes and moderne tymes
made yow which, in the moderne cherche, be presidentes, 50
prelates, and potestates fyctely srutede ynto her place ocupyng
substitutes, as thilk Crist Ihesu of you seyde, *Regnaverunt sed
non de me*, 'Thei have regnyd but not of me'. Onys yet we
behette hym, that Ihesu, al the kyngdoms of the world yf he
fallyng on kne had wurshipyd our ryal myght, but he wold 55
noght, seying, *Regnum meum non est de hoc mundo*, 'My
kyngdom is not of this world', fleying and voydyng whan
the peple wold chose have hym into eny temperall kyng-
dome or lordship. In yow, which of the grees, steppes and
state of grace and trouthe be falle and slyden and to us and to 60
our preceptes, conceils and persuasions in the erthe trewly and
continuelly serve, is fulfillyd the promission and byheest, and
now by us and of us al that ye of possessioners which we into
continuaunce of your trewe servise have geve ye withholde.

ululabat infernus gemens, anxius, spoliatus. Et nostri ferrei pectoris impatiens
feritas ferre non valuit, neque dira Ditis inclementia potuit amplius tolerare. Sed
precaventes in posterum, obviando periculis de remedio providimus opportuno et
loco istorum nobis adversantium apostolorum et ceterorum Christum sequentium
moribus et doctrina, per nostram scientiam atqua potentiam succedere fecimus
vos, qui modernis temporibus ecclesie presidetis. Sic ille de vobis predixit:
'Regnaverunt et non ex me'. Semel sibi promisimus omnia regna mundi si
cadens nos adoraret: ipse vero noluit, quia dixit, 'Regnum meum non est de hoc
mundo' et fugit quando turbe voluerunt ipsum in regem eligere temporalem. In
vobis autem qui de statu gratie cecidistis, et nobis ministratis, in terris impleta est
promissio et iam per nos a nobis tenetis terrena quae vobis contulimus imperia.

65 Thilk Ihesu of yow, as ye wyte wele, thus seyde, *Venit enim*
princeps mundi huius et super omnes superbie filios voluit vos
regnare, 'The Prince of this world ys come and ovir al the
childryn of pryde He will that ye regne'. But tho our adversares forseyde, thilk Cristis apostlis and her fo / [320b] lowers,
70 to the princes of the world were subiettis, as thei so taght,
Subiecti estote omni humane creature propter deum: sive regi quasi
precellenti etc., 'Be ye subiettis to all humane creature for God
to the kyng as precellent', and in another place, *Obedietis*
prepositis vestris, 'Ye shul obey to your sovereynes'. So here
75 maystre, that Ihesu, dede and bade him do, seyng, *Reges*
gencium dominantur eorum et qui potestatem habent benefici
vocantur; vos autem non sic, 'Kynges and princes of peple have
power overe hem and tho that be potestates be callyd good,
but do ye not so'. And evere thes our adversares forsaide led a
80 pore, dispyteful and wrecchid lyf, but ye, as hit best likth us,
done noght so, but of the venymouse elacion of pride, which
we sometyme geete and hieldid in yow, be utturly enflawuryd
in yow and blowyn into fulfillyng of pleasaunce with our
iehennall maieste. To the first fadris forseyd noght only unpier
85 but utturly contrare bothe in lyf and yn maners, above all
othere elate and erecte yn pryde, all that ye may kecche and
gete havyng and yn possession kepyng, and neither *Que sunt*
Cesaris Cesari nec que sunt dei deo, 'Delyveryng or yeldyng to
Cesar that hym byfallith ne to God that to him longith', but
90 aftir the will and entent of our conceils, preceptis and

Ille enim de nobis dicit, ut scitis: 'Venit enim princeps mundi huius et super
omnes filios superbie voluit vos regnare'. Subiiciebantur itaque principibus huius
seculi in temporalibus nostri adversarii antedicti et hoc docebant, dicentes:
'Subiecti estote omni creature propter Deum sive regi tamquam perexcellenti' et
cetera. Et rursum: 'Obedite prepositis vestris'. Sic enim magister eorum fecerat
atque preceperat, dicens 'Reges gentium dominantur eorum qui potestatem
habent benefici vocantur'; vos autem non sic et sicut prediximus despectabilem et
inopen vitam gerebant in continuis laboribus et erumnis et nos vobis dicimus: vos
autem non sic. Venenum diu effudimus, iam estia inflati. Nam ipsis primis
parentibus non solum dispares sed penitus contrarii moribus et vita super omnes
elati et omnia possidentes, nec redditis quae sunt Cesaris Cesari, nec que sunt Dei

decrees, iurisdiccion and power of either swerd of temperalte
as wele as of spiritualte ye excercise, of all worldlynes medlyng
undur our conduyt / [321a] of al manere secular ocupacions
and nedys entremetyng, from the wrecchidnes and al manere
grevaunce of poverte evermore fleyng, to the hyest coppes 95
of astates and worshippes hyingly by all infynite wordly
prudences and wittis, subtiltees, fallaces, glosynges, lesynges,
forswerynges, deceytes, tresons, bygylyngis, symonyes, dis-
simulyd and othir peyntid ypocrisye, and al other manere
wordly wikkidnes, whiche unnethe al the incomprehensible 100
gehennal wyttis and conceytes kan undurstonde or bythenke
without grely ordre ascendyng. And whan ye to tho profites of
worshippes so bene erecte and elate ye be smyte with more
houndship hungre than byfor, the pore and al your lower
unpitously with an houndisshe rage oppressyng, al that ye 105
cacche and hold ravisshyng, al thing out of his kynd, as yt
may best lyke us, pervertyng with inflacion of all manere of
pryde, the curis and thoghtis of your hertys pyttyng yn all
lustis of lecherous lyvyng, in all delices and bodyly lustys,
confortes and fedynges your dayes of this lyf leding and 110
expendyng, takyng on you on erthe names of goddis, and
holy under dissimulid face of holynes and visage of goodnes
the privehyd supersticious pride as our predilecte childrin of
wikkidnes with all the craft of our cautels curiosly and
ypocrytly coveryng, the world but noght that Ihesu decey- 115
vyng, and the wele willyng of our / [321b] tartareal mageste
pleasauntly and continuelly fulfillyng. The yeftes of the
chirche which othir ye violently ravisshyn or abusyn,

Deo, imo secundum nostra decreta utriusque gladii iurisdictionem exercetis vos
mundanis immiscentes, vos militantes secularibus negotiis implicati ac de pauper-
tatis miseria gradatim ascenditis et ad culmen honoris et ad summa fastigia
dignitatum per astutas practicas et fallaces fabricas per ipocrisim, adulationes,
mendacia, periuria, proditiones, fraudes, simonias, ceteras nequitias ampliores
quam excogitare possent sorores nostre, furie infernales. Cum autem illic raptastis
non sufficit, sed estis famelici, plusquam antea pauperes opprimitis, omnia rapitis,
totum pervertitis inflati superbia, luxuriose viventes in deliciis et fruitionibus
corporalibus ducitis dies vestros. Vocatis vobis nomina in terris, vos deos sanctos
et sanctissimos appellando, bona etiam que aut violenter capitis aut per abusiones

ocupyen or falsly holdyn, or by fals title as our wele bylovid
120 childryn tirauntly kepyng, and tho goodis whiche for
sustentacion of the pore peple of that ilk Ihesu Crist which
we have and ever have had in hate were somtyme distribute
and ordeynyd ye into your uses to our moost bodyly
acordyng and likyng, as ye shold, spendyn and consumyn,
125 strumpetes, iapers and ianglers, harlotes, hores and her
haunters norisshyng and susteynyng, with him as princes of
our infernal paleys prowdely goyng and ryding and your
dayes voluptuously, as ye shold, ledyng, noght as that pore
caytif the peple of that Ihesu and of his first chirche. Ye bylde
130 your bildynges as palayces with al manere delices and wordly
delicacyes spectable, with al manere delicate metys your
bodies fedyng, al curiouse wynes in plente drynkyng, infinite
tresours unsaciably gedryng and hidyng, noght as thilk Petir
that seyde, *Argentum et aurum non est michi*, 'Silver and gold is
135 not to me'. O ye our levest felawship, to us dukes of dethe
sumtyme by the prophetes worthily and deservingly byhet,
and of hem of old tyme reprevyd, whil that ilk Ihesu clepid
yow the Sinagoge of Sathanas and prefigurid yow by the
comen strumpet whiche dyde fornycacion with the kynges
140 and princes of the erthe, turnyd from a modir to a stepmodir,
from Cristes spouse to a strayed strumpet, from chaste / [322a]
to a comyn hore, thin olde clennesse and virginite thow hast
broke and distroyed, thin olde charite thow haste lost, to us

dolose subripitis et fallaciter extorquetis et falso titulo possidetis, que pro substen-
tatione pauperum Christi, quos odimus, fuerunt antiquitus erogata, in usus nobis
placitos expenditis. Unde meretrices et lenonum ac latronum turbas nutritis, cum
quibus equitantes pompatice veluti magni principes inceditis, aliter quam illi
pauperes sacerdotes ecclesie primitive. Vobis edificastis palatia omni amenitate et
pulchritudine spectabilia, comedetis cibaria et bibitis vina omni curiosa lecacitate
exquisita, thesauros coacervatis infinitos, non sicut is qui dicebat: 'Argentum et
aurum non est mecum', vos aurea secula reparastis. O societas gratissima demoni-
bus, nobis olim per prophetas promissa et ab ipsis priscis temporibus antiquitus
reprobata, dum te Johannes vocatur sinagogam Sathane et te designavit per
meretricem magnam, que fornicata est cum regibus terrae, facta de matre
noverca, de sponsa Christi adultera, de casta meretrix: 'confracte sunt mamme
pubertatis tue' caritatem tuam primam reliquisti, nobis adhesisti. O dilecta nostra

diligently thow hast drawyn and geve the. O ye our worthily bylovid citezeins of our bylovid Babyloyne, worthily we 145 love yow, hertly we ioy in yow, for ye, as our bylovid childryn, to the plesaunt lawys of Simon Magus, as it likth us, evermore yow submyttyng and in opyn boldely hit usyng and exercysyng, al spiritual thinges in the chirche bysily bying and sellyng, and agen the preceptis of that Ihesu 150 benefices and states of the cherche delyng and departyng other for prayer or paying or servise or favour, the ecclesiastical offices and degrees now holy subvertyng, the worthy able and kunnyng refusyng and the unworthy hertly anouncyng as your own childryn cosyns and other to yow 155 bylovid your clerkis and gromys into the heritage of that goddis seyntuarie callyng, to a child many provendres unworthily wytyngly gevyng of which the leest to an able pore man denyng, the persone and noght his abylite or unablete acceptyng and concidering, the cure of the pecunie and 160 noght of soules receyving. The hows of that Ihesu ye have made a den of theves, all manere abusions, extorcions, wronges and unrightes an hundridfold in your iurisdiccion and court excersisid than among eny seculere tyrauntes lawes among yow ordeynyng and hem your self in no wyse 165 holdyng and aftyr your will for the tyme dispensyng, the wikkid and the trespassour for mede / [322b] and giftis iustifying, the rightwis for hate and lak of mede condempnyng, and al manere of evels aftir the balaunce of your wil ye

Babilon, et o cives nostri qui huc de Ierusalem transmigrastis, vos merito diligimus, vobis applaudimus, qui leges Simonis Petri negligitis, et legibus Simonis Magi amici nostri penitus adherentes, ipsis tenetis ad unguem et publice exercetis in templo Dei vendentes et ementes spiritualia et contra Christi precepta distribuitis beneficia et honores, aut prece vel pretio aut pro turpi servicio seu favore; et ad ecclesiasticas dignitates reprobando dignos, indignos promovetis indigne, utpote ganeones, lenones, aut megaros vestros nepotes aut filios proprios, ut hereditarie possidoatis sanctuarium Dei; et uni puero multas confertis prebendas, quarum minimam probo pauperi denegatis, personas accipitis et munera, curam habetis pecuniarum non animarum, domum Christi fecistis speluncam latronum, omnis abusus, omnis unquam extorsio in foro vestro plusquam centies exercetur, tenetis et totum vestra dispensatione ad libitum dissipatis; 'Justificatis impium pro

170 wey. And so incessably in our servise whereof hertly we
thonk you travaillyng and moost principally as to the
destruccion of the cristyn feith in which the lay peple stont in
hesitacion and dout for whan eny of the lawe of that Ihesu, al
seldyn thogh and neglygently, be prechid to hem thei be
175 sette in no ful byleve therof, seyng eche of yow shewith
on yn prechyng, the contrarie fulfill in wurchyng, seyng on
and another doyng; wherfor thei folowyng your steppis in
wurchyng which go byfor hem yn ensaumple yevyng, the
rewles of our custumes and decrees continnuelly usyng,
180 irremedyably slydyng and fallyng into the depe vale of vices
and so to the derk desolacion of the careful comete of the
contre of derknes copiouse multitude of hem plentevously
drawyng and comyng. So myche multitude of al manere of
peple now adayes ye sende us that we ne mowe hem receyve,
185 but that the insaciable mansioun of our derk region in the
indefinent hunger and thirst of swolowyng more and more
also that evere ther comith plentevously and ungrucchyngly
myght herburgh, receyve and devoure, and so by yow the
plentevous recours of our subiettes of which by the pore
190 caytifs servauntes of that Ihesu we were sumtyme violently
precludid from the wey and steppis toward the habutacion
of dominacion and principilte of the empire of our tartariall
regyon ys now by your bysines and lastyngly labour / [323a]
plenerly refourmyd, and our olde importable harmes and
195 losses fully restoryd. Wherefor we have yow menyfold

muneribus et iustitiam iusti aufertis ab eo'. Et breviter, omnia genera scelerorum
prout volumus perpetratis et multum vestri gratia in nostro servitio insudatis,
potissime ad destructionem fidei christiane. Iam enim laici de fide hesitant, et si
predicatis quandoque, licet non nisi tantum negligenter et raro, non tamen
credunt, quoniam manifeste vident quod quisque vestrum contrarium operatur;
et sic ostenditis vos credere aliud quam dicatis, unde et ipsi vos sequentes, qui sibi
estis in exemplo, iam ut plurimum nostris utuntur regulis, irruentes in pelagus
vitiorum, et ad funereas edes baratri assidue confluit ipsorum maxima multitudo.
Et enim ex omni hominum genere nobis cotidie transmittitis, quod capere non
possemus, nisi quia nostrum chaos insatiabile mille faucibus avidis innumerabiles
animas deglutiret: et sic per vos nostri inperii principatus extitit refornitus, et
damnun nobis importabile restitutum. Unde vos habemus multipliciter commen-

recomended ynfinite thonkynges yeldyng to yow prayng
yow nevertheles on your love and sure hope of our full
rewarde, charchyng that of your longe so bygynnyng and
contynuyng ye hold yow to us in trewe perseveraunce as ye
done and have done so evere ferther procedyng, for by yow   200
we fully purpose and hope the unyte of al the world undir
the iurisdiccion of the emperiall court and our iehennall
region revoke and rewle. Nowadayes we from day to day for
the multitude and aboute hem and her comyng whiche ye to
us everyday sende and transmytte bysily ocupyed, wherfor   205
we may not come for our lastyng bysynes to visite yow.
Therfor we commytte to yow on the erthe yn continuance
of the bysynes of your forseyd ocupacions our power,
wyllyng yow to our vykers in this partie and mynistres,
remembryng us mych in thoght of the ny coming of Ante-   210
crist to whom at the beste as trewe precursours ye make redy
way, noght as Iohn Baptist that come byfor that Ihesu, seyng,
Ego vox clamantis in deserto, but as our trewe servauntes,
taking evermore the recours of your counceile as the wele
wyllyng servauntz of our infernal courte to whos suggestions,   215
conceils and doctrines yncessably ye take kepe and confourme
yow. Conceylyng yow also whiche we sette in the coppe of
astates and dignytes as for a wysdom that evere more bytwene
the potestatis and princes worldly ye procure and meve
fyghtly by the pees, prively / [323b] nevertheles all maters of   220
discorde bytwene hem norisshyng as ye sometyme the ruyle
of the empire of Rome boldly distroyed, no regne ne regyon

datos atque grates magnas referimus, nihilominus exhortantes quatenus perseveretis
sicut facitis semper ulterius procedendo, quia per vos intendimus et speramus
totum mundum sub nostra iurisdicione iterum revocare. Iam enim pro multitudine
quam nobis destinatis, his obscuris recessibus multipliciter occupati, vobis in
terris superius committimus vices nostras, et volumus vos esse nostros vicarios, et
ministros etiam esse de missione propinqua Antichristi cogitamus, cui viam
optime preparatis. In vestrum tamen consilium atque auxilium de stigiis eminenti-
bus et satrapis Inferni aliquos deputamus, quorum suggestionibus acquiescere et
dolosis inventionibus etiam addere vestra calliditas consuevit et novit. Insuper
vobis, qui summum tenetis apicem, consulimus ad cautelam ut inter principes
seculi pacem ficte procuretis, sed occulte causas discordie nutriatis, et sicut astute

243

suffryng yn the ruyle of pees or tranquillite dwellyng or
restyng, lest tho temperal princes fortified longe undir the
225 ese and pes of tranquyllite oppresse you revyng yow than
your possessions, tresours and temperal lordshippes which
we have put in your kepyng and warde for store agen the
nye comyng of anticrist afor whom bysily ye make wey.
Wherfor forthermore to your protection and power of all
230 iehennall dominacion utterly we commende al universale
and singuler that in eny ordre or secte we constitute and
chefly and principally our hyly bylovid childryn, the four
beggyng ordres, which about espleyte and bysinnes of our
nedis and your be yndesessably labouryng as we by opyn
235 experience have lernyd, prayng yow that ye for her good
desertes have hem so in cherysyng and favour, comfortyng
hem with such mede as thei may reioyce him to have so
labourid for you and for us and with the gladder spirit to be
redy in continuyng of her bysy labour to comyng. For
240 thurgh diligence of her bysenes meny be discordyng from the
chirch fey and led into meny errours. Wherfor hertly we prey
yow undur ful retribucion of mede of our infernall mageste
and tartareall dominacion and for our love that ye leve noght
of the puttyng to hem your hondis of your help and / [324a]
245 supportyng, and hem at the lest in all her cursyd werkys
uttirly ye defende and maynteyne so that thei may knowe
hem to yow and us for her entier and speciall frendis many-
fold boundyn, holdyn and yn dette, understondyng hertly
that we be passyngly in herte pertourblyd and with hevy
250 hepyd sorow woundid that ye with the blyndenes of derkenes
erryng concider noght what the bysy worchyng of the
prechyng of the servauntes of Ihesu axith, for many now in
these dayes agens us aryse, the lawes of that Ihesu Crist prechyng and with all her myghtes and strengthes enhauncyng,
255 the fortheryng of our magiste to hyndre noght shamyng ne

Romanum imperium, ita ne permittatis aliud regnum nimium ampliari, ne forte
multum fortificati et pacem habentes vellent deprimere statum vestrum et a nobis
auferre thesauros, quos apud vos in deposito Antichristi diximus reservari. Com-

244

dredyng. Wherefor with our best conceill in this partie
manly us withstondyng as ye the indignacion of our infernall
mageste which ye with your merytis noght unworthily have
deservid may make to yow more seure as hit byhovid noght
to our infernall powere, dominacion and mageste undur 260
dissimulacion such reprefe, despite and wrong suffre to passe
without lettyng sethe the offence thereof goth . . . to our
herte. Prayng yow . . . ye inhibite and forbede that fr . . .
chyng and to us to execrabl . . . and if ye fynd eny in contr . . .
riall mageste agen our . . . / [324b] contempte thurgh auc- 265
torite of our ryal iurisdiccion and powere so fervently ye
punisshe hem so that thei for drede of your censures and our
mowe evere be ferde to atempte agen our forbode or yncurre
into our and your indignacion heraftir and that thei have
pleyne cause to remember hem evere aftir her lyf of your 270
vengyng and ponysshyng for her offence forseyd, havyng
evere yncessantly to your hertly cherisyng utterly recomen-
did our derrest and best bylovyd doghtris, pryde, covetise,
envie, ire, lecherye, fraude, deceytis, accidie, glotonye and all
other universall and singulere, namely, among al othere, our 275
speciall doghtir, simonye, which ye with your owne pappes
have norisshed, mylkyd, and broght forth, noght callyng our
dere doghter, symonye, synne sethe all is youres. Nothing
may it be seyd that ye selle, for youres is payed al that is payd,
and prowd may ye not be seyd, howevere ye do, for such 280
magnificens requirith worthily your astate. Ne to calle yow
coveytous reson will not . . . gadre ye kepe for the patri-
moyne . . . the chirche and of Seynt Petir . . . and anounce
youres as that Ihesu . . . and kynnysmen callid to the . . . thei

mendatas habete nostras carissimas filias Superbiam, Avaritiam, Fraudem,
Luxuriam et alias: precipue dominam Simoniam, que vos fecit ac propriis lactavit
uberibus et nutrivit. Ipsamque non vocetis simoniam seu peccatum quia omnia
vestra sunt, vel ergo potestis vendere, quia de vestro proprio solvuntur: nec vos
estis superbi, quia talem requirit magnificentiam status vester; nec avari, quia pro
sancto Petro est quicquid congregatis et thesaurus ecclesie seu patrimonium
crucifixi. Promoveatis vestros sicut Christus ad apostolatum vocavit cognatos et

285 natheles were called to . . . despiteful, but ye as we . . . to
state of pryde and to the coppis . . . hesses and worshippes
they / [325a] also lost all. Ye to your ynfynite plente gadre
more copiouse multitude, and so consequently as best ys and
moost liketh us ye excercise custumably all hauntyng of vices
290 and synne undur the hid coveryd mantell and coloured visage
of virtue. And whoevere agen your and our iurisdiccion
preche or teche cursyng with our censures fervently ye
chastise hem and violently oppresse and as for eretikes and
transgressours of our lawe and iurisdiccion condempnyng.
295 And so in the mynysterye of our servise bysily ye swete and
laboure that ye may worthily deserve to reioyce that place
which we have for yow made redy and preparat undur the
seurest condite of abydyng in the habitacion of our tartariall
region which also we have to yow preservid wher none of
300 oures hath eny assignement of enhabytyng but if it be the
principal officers or mynistres of the regne of our iehennall
lordship. Ye neither hope the future rewarde or premyacion
of that ilk Ihesu ne drede the eternal retribucion of our
wepely turmente and therfor reioyce yow yn the usyng of
305 the felicite of this present lyf that in digne recompensacion of
your merites ye may deserve the retribucion of eternal dethe
which was to yow preparate from the original constitucion
of the world, hopyng this sikerly while ye lede your dayes of
this lyf, no creature on the erthe dredyng ne yet that ilk
310 Ihesu. Farith now wele ledyng your dayes in that felicite
which your bodily lystes and confortes may moost renovele

notos; taceatis quod ipsi vocabantur ad statum pauperem et vestri ad divitias, quod
reliquerunt omnia et vestris tribuitis infinita et sic de aliis, sicut melius nostis,
propterea vitia sub virtutis specie palliata. Et allegetis pro vobis et glosetis pro
scripturis distorte et advocatis ad propositum indirecte; et si quis contra vos
predicet aut doceat, ipsum excommunicantes violenter opprimite et a vobis
tamquam hereticus condemnetur. Tantum inde faciatis, quod locum valeatis
habere, quem vobis paravimus sub nostri habitaculi secretissimo fundamento et
quem vobis singulariter reservamus, ubi nondum quisquam novit accedere,
exceptis maioribus satrapis regni nostri. Vos enim nec speratis ut beati futurum
premium nec eternum supplicium formidatis: ideoque nec vitam quam non
creditis habebitis, sed nobiscum post mortem obtinebitis quam dum vivitis non

and encrese and with plenere hope of that ilk retribucion whiche we from the / [325b] originall and prymytif tyme of the constitucion of our tartareall dominacion have willid and plenerly purposid to geve yow yn fynall and lastyngly 315 durable privacion. Datum at the centre of the erthe yn our tenebrouse paleys yn presence of ynfynite legions of the princes, potestates, mynistres, and subgites specially cityd to our dolorouse concistorie yn testificacion of the dominacion of thes present lettres prynted and empressid.   320

timetis. Valete illa felicitate quam vobis desideramus et intendimus finaliter premiare. Datum apud centrum terre in nostro palatio tenebroso, presentibus catervis demonum propter hoc specialiter vocatorum ad nostrum concistorium dolorosum, sub terribili signeti caractere in robore premissorum.

NOTES TO THE TEXT

3. *Cumbryd*, perhaps 'Care/Heaviness' or 'Evil' (*MED*, s.v. *combraunce, combrement*). The form is not in *OED* or *MED*.
3. *Gehennal*: the form not in *OED*.
4. *Dysesse*, 'Death' (*OED*, s.v. *decease*).
17–18. *Psalm*. 25. 5.
23. *Tartariall*, 'Infernal' (*OED*, s.v. *tartareal*: earliest reference given is 1602).
34–5. *Prov*. 12. 28.
36. *Forletyngly*, 'Contemptuously' or 'Neglectfully' (*MED*, s.v. *forletyng*).
42. *Heer*, 'A host of devils' (*MED*, s.v. *here* 1b).
51. *Fyctely*, 'Feignedly' (*OED*, s.v. *fictly*: earliest reference given is 1677). *Srutede*, 'Shrouded'.
52–3. *Osea* 8. 4.
54. Cf. *Matt*. 4. 9.
56–7. *Ioan*. 18. 36.
65–8. *Ioan*. 14. 30 and *Iob* 41. 25.
71–3. I *Petr*. 2. 13.
73–4. *Hebr*. 13. 17.
75–9. *Luc*. 22. 25.
82. *Geete*, 'Produce', 'Beget', (*MED*, s.v. *geten* 7). *Hieldid*, 'Pour', 'Shed' in figurative sense (*OED*, s.v. *hield* 7). *Enflawuryd*: earliest reference given in *OED* is 1523.
84. *Unpier*: MS *umpier*: the form not in *OED*.
87–9. *Marc*. 12. 17 and *Matt*. 22. 21.
93. *Conduyt*, 'Guidance', 'Provision' (*OED*, s.v. *conduct*).
94. *From*: MS *fron*.
96. *Hyingly*: the form not in *OED*.

102. *Grely*, perhaps 'Proper', 'Careful', 'Due' (*MED*, s.v. *greithli*). The meaning of the phrase, however, remains obscure.

104. *Houndship*: the form not in *OED*. *Lower*, 'Inferiors' (*OED*).

109. *Bodyly*: MS *body*.

132. *Drynkyng*: MS *drynkyg*.

134-5. *Act. Ap.* 3. 6.

137-40. *Apoc.* 17. 1-6.

142. *Thow*: MS *thow thow*.

157. *Provendres*, 'Prebends'.

161-2. *Matt.* 21. 13.

167. *Isa.* 5. 23.

170. *Our*: MS *your*.

171. *Travaillyng*: MS *travaillyg*.

174. *Neglygently*: MS *newlygently*.

186. *Indefinent*: the form, if correct and not a scribal error for *indefinet*, not in *OED*. The earliest reference to *indefinite* given in the *OED* is 1561.

213. *Ioan.* 1. 23.

217. *We*: MS *ve*.

233. *Espleyte*, 'Exploit', 'Endeavour', 'Performance' (*OED*, s.v. *exploit*).

276. *Ye*: MS *the*.

302. *Premyacion*, 'Reward': the form not in *OED*.

17

The Epistolary Usages
of William Worcester

NORMAN DAVIS

KNOWLEDGE of English usage before printing can most accurately
be built upon the detailed study of autograph writings of identifiable persons about whose origins and conditions of life we have
some information. A group of fifteenth-century documents which
meet these conditions, but which have not been as much regarded
as they deserve, is the score of letters written by the amateur
antiquary and minor author William Worcester, who called
himself also, from his mother's name, Botoner. He is a rewarding
subject for such a study because, though obviously far from being
intellectually distinguished, he was a man of some education and
of lively curiosity who showed throughout his life a keen interest
in books as well as in astronomy, topography, and antiquities. His
writing is thus good evidence of what might be expected of a
literate layman of modest competence a few years senior to
William Caxton.

The outlines of Worcester's career have often been described,
notably by James Tait in *DNB* and most recently by A. B. Emden
in his *Biographical Register of the University of Oxford to A.D. 1500*
(1959),[1] and his work has been admirably investigated by K. B.
McFarlane,[2] whose knowledge of the period was unparalleled.
The essential points are these. Worcester was born in Bristol in
1415, was an undergraduate at Hart Hall, Oxford (attached to

---

[1] Since this was written a new edition of Worcester's *Itineraries*, edited with an
introduction by John H. Harvey, has been announced by the Clarendon Press for
publication in 1968.

[2] 'William Worcester: a Preliminary Survey', in *Studies Presented to Sir Hilary
Jenkinson* (Oxford, 1957), pp. 196–221.

Balliol College) by 1432, and remained there for some years but did not take a degree. By 1438 he was in the service of Sir John Fastolf as a kind of confidential secretary, occupied with all manner of estate business as well as writing a great many of Fastolf's letters, and he remained in this post until the old knight died in 1459. Despite his long and important work for Fastolf he was never given the position in the household that he thought he deserved. He wrote to John Paston I soon after Fastolf took up residence in his new castle at Caister (near Yarmouth) in 1454, complaining that he had no secure position or salary but received only 'wages of housold in comune *entaunt comme nows plaira* . . . and so I endure *inter egenos vt seruus ad aratrum*';[1] and though he passed this off as a joke—'foryefe me, I wryte to make yow laugh'—later events, and other letters such as that printed below, show that he had reason to feel that his work was insufficiently appreciated or rewarded and that he did resent this. He remained a layman, and married the niece of Thomas Howes, a priest also in the service of Sir John Fastolf—evidently rather late, for he wrote of women in 1478, 'I was kept froo her company xxx yeres or ony such were of my councelle, I thank God of yt.'[2] During Fastolf's lifetime he was on good terms with the Pastons. He was made one of Fastolf's executors, and on Fastolf's death he went up to London with William Paston II to attend to the disposal of the estate. It was then, on 12 November 1459, that William Paston wrote to his brother John:

As for Wyllyam Worceter, he trustythe veryly ȝe wold do for hym and for his avayll in reson; and I dowthe natt and he may ueryly and feythefully vnderstand ȝow so disposyd to hym ward, ȝe schall fynd hym feythefull to ȝow in leke wysse. I vnderstand by hym he will neuer haue oder master but his old master; and to myn consaythe it were pete but iff he schull stand in suche casse be myn master that he schuld neuer nede seruyce, conse[de]ryng how myn master trustyd hym, and þe long ȝerys that he hathe be wyth hym in and many schrew jornay fore his sake, &c.[3]

[1] *The Paston Letters*, ed. J. Gairdner (Westminster, 4 vols. 1901; London, 6 vols. 1904), no. 214/258.
[2] Ibid., xcii/927.   [3] Ibid., 338/391.

But no more than two months later, as the letter printed below eloquently shows, relations were strained; and soon afterwards, disappointed that he was still unrewarded and believing that Fastolf's wishes were not being carried out, Worcester joined Sir William Yelverton in contesting the Paston claim to the Fastolf inheritance. It was not until after John Paston I's death in 1466, when a compromise was reached which led in 1470 to the assignment of administration to William Wainfleet, bishop of Winchester, that he resumed friendly relations with Margaret Paston and her sons. He continued to concern himself with the problems of the Fastolf estate under Wainfleet, but he also travelled and wrote. He died in or soon after 1482.

He had early made a hobby of antiquarian studies, in which he was helped by the researches into pedigrees which were part of his duty in establishing titles to land, and by the 'many shrewd journeys' which he had to undertake on Fastolf's business. These led, among other fruits, to his Latin *Itinerarium*;[1] and he also composed *The Boke of Noblesse*,[2] revised the translation of *The Dicts and Sayings of the Philosophers* made by Stephen Scrope, Fastolf's stepson and ward,[3] and translated Cicero's *de Senectute* from the French version by Laurence de Premierfait. Of this last he wrote in his *Itinerary*: '1473 die 10 Aug. presentavi W. episcopo Wyntoniensi apud Asher librum Tullii de Senectute per me translatum in anglicis, sed nullum regardum recepi de episcopo.'[4] There should be no doubt that this was the text revised and printed by Caxton in 1481 as *Tullius of Olde Age*; but a good deal of confusion has arisen because Caxton printed in the same volume a translation of the *de Amicitia*, of which he said, 'which book was translated by the vertuous and noble Erle therle of wurcestre in to our englyssh tongue' (and essentially the same in slightly different words in three other places, in the Prologue and Epilogue, and in

---

[1] Ed. J. Nasmith, *Itineraria Symonis Simeonis et Willelmi de Worcestre* (Cambridge, 1778).
[2] Ed. J. G. Nichols (Roxburghe Club, 1860).
[3] Ed. C. F. Bühler (EETS 211, 1941).
[4] Ed. Nasmith, p. 368.

the Epilogue to *The Declamacion of Noblesse*).[1] As long ago as Leland this attribution was extended to the preceding translation of *de Senectute*.[2] A remarkable complication was introduced by John Fenn, the first editor of the Paston Letters. In printing the mutilated inventory of John Paston II's books, one of which was 'in quayers Tully or cypio de Ami . . . leffte w^t Will'm Worcest'', he remarked, 'It is a curious circumstance that this book should be here mentioned as left with William Worcester, who, with the assistance of John Tiptoft, Earl of Worcester, and John Phrea, or Free, a Monk of Bristol, translated it.'[3] There appears to be no evidence of such collaboration between the two Worcesters, and in principle it is unlikely that the powerful Tiptoft would have assisted an obscure clerk such as Botoner. The circumstance is, none the less, certainly 'curious', for it proves that William Worcester was strongly interested in the *de Amicitia*—to which, indeed, he had referred in a letter of 1460.[4] Both Dr Bühler[5] and McFarlane[6] are willing to entertain the possibility that he, not Tiptoft, was the translator of Caxton's text; but since Caxton so often repeated that it was the earl's this cannot be accepted without stronger reasons than any so far advanced. For *de Senectute* the position is quite different. Worcester says that he translated it; Caxton says that his text was translated 'by the ordenaunce and desyre of the noble Auncyent knyght Syr Johan Fastolf of the countee of Norfolk banerette'; and Worcester was Fastolf's 'servant'. The natural conclusion is that Caxton printed Worcester's translation; and this has been accepted by many,[7] but by some only with reservations. Even McFarlane says that Caxton printed this text 'as from the pen of John Tiptoft, Earl of Worcester',

---

[1] *The Prologues and Epilogues of William Caxton*, ed. W. J. B. Crotch (EETS 176, 1928), pp. 43, 44, 45, 46–7.

[2] See H. B. Lathrop, 'The Translations of John Tiptoft', *MLN*, xli (1926), 496–501, and C. Clark in *TLS*, 22 Aug. 1952, p. 549.

[3] *Original Letters, Written during the Reigns of Henry VI, Edward IV, and Richard III* (London, 1787), ii, p. 302.

[4] Gairdner 347/401.   [5] *Dicts*, p. xlvi n. 2.   [6] *Studies*, p. 216.

[7] See Gairdner, Introduction, p. clxxiv/153, and H. Susebach, *Caxton: Tulle of Olde Age* (Studien zur engl. Philologie 75, Halle, 1933), pp. xv-xvi.

though he thinks he was probably wrong, and Emden says essentially the same thing. Yet this misrepresents Caxton, who nowhere claims *Olde Age* for the earl. He makes the statement about Fastolf's 'ordenaunce and desyre' just quoted, and adds that he himself had 'dilygently aftir my litil vnderstandyng corrected it'. There is no reason to associate Tiptoft with this text at all.

In addition to these complete surviving works Worcester is known to have written an *Antiquitates Anglie* in three books and *de Agri Norfolcensis familiis antiquis*; and several notebooks of his exist, one of them containing extracts from a French historical compendium and from the works of Alain Chartier.[1] As McFarlane observed, the existence of this evidence of extensive reading in French in 1453 destroys the suggestion, first made by Sir George Warner in his edition of Scrope's *Epistle of Othea to Hector*,[2] that Worcester knew no French until 1458. The ground for this belief was a letter written from London by Henry Windsor, another of Fastolf's employees, to John Paston I probably in 1458, in which the following passage occurs:

William hath goon to scole to a Lumbard called Karoll Giles to lern and to be red in poetre or els in Frensh, for he hath byn wyth the same Caroll euery dey ij tymes or iij, and hath bought diuers boks of hym. . . . I made a mocion to William to have knoen part of his besines, and he answered and seid that he wold be as glad and as feyn of a good boke of Frensh or of poetre as my maistre Fastolf wold be to purchace a faire manoir.[3]

Obviously this testifies to Worcester's enthusiasm for poetry, French, and books in general, and does not imply that he was a beginner in French.

[1] McFarlane in *Studies*, pp. 216, 212; and M. S. Blayney, 'Fifteenth-Century English Translations of Alain Chartier's *Le Traité de l'Esperance* and *Le Quadrilogue Invectif*' (Oxford D.Phil. thesis, 1966), p. xxi: 'William Worcester copied French passages from both *Le Quadrilogue Invectif* and *Le Traité de l'Esperance* in his notebooks in November and December 1453. He mainly copied historical examples used in the French works to illustrate Chartier's general commentary. In B.M. Royal MS 13 C I, ff. 136–138v, the extracts are from *Le Quadrilogue*, and on ff. 138v–141 from *L'Esperance*.'
[2] (Roxburghe Club, 1904), pp. xlv-xlvi.   [3] Gairdner 318/370.

Worcester, then, a Bristol man educated at Oxford, living for a long time in Norfolk but travelling extensively, experienced in estate management and litigation, reading Latin and French and writing voluminously in both Latin and English, should present a fair example of the usage of a man of varied connections and accustomed to written language of many kinds. The total volume of his writings, and of papers in his hand written for or on behalf of Fastolf, is very considerable; but among the *Paston Letters* there are 22 letters by him which form a fairly compact specimen of his own independent writing. Gairdner numbers them, in his two editions, as follows, and assigns dates which are all acceptable: 206/247, 208/249, 214/258—1454 (the last uncertainly); 252/297, 259/305—1455; 267/314, 268/315, 269/316, 273/320, 296/346—1456 (269/316 approximately, 296/346 uncertainly); 304/355, 305/356—1457; 313/364, 314/365, 320/372—1458; 345/399, 347/401—1460; 498/577—1465; 582/681—probably 1468; 639/744, 640/745—1470; xcii/927—1478.[1] Of these no. 347 is a copy in the hand of Richard Calle, John Paston I's head bailiff (not of John Paston himself as Gairdner says), and the manuscript of no. 582 has been lost; so that these two can be used only with caution for linguistic study. The other twenty, all of which are in the British Museum except nos. 639 and 640 which are in Magdalen College, Oxford, are autograph. Not all of them are printed in full by Gairdner—of the two Magdalen letters he gives only abstracts, and no. 345 he prints only in part, following Fenn.[2] Nor is his text minutely accurate, especially when copied from Fenn. To give only a few examples, in 304 'as ye now' should read 'as ys now', in 305 'streng' should read 'strenger' and 'them' should read 'after', and in the date of 252 'the noneday, vij day Jullet' (which Fenn, followed by Gairdner, annotated 'The day of the Nones'!) should read 'the Monday . . .' . The forms I give below are taken from the manuscripts or from photographs, and I have used also an additional

[1] Henceforward I simplify reference to the autograph letters by giving only the number in the earlier edition.

[2] The manuscripts of Fenn's first two volumes were not available to Gairdner. For the relation between the editions see 'The Text of Margaret Paston's Letters', *MÆ*, xviii (1949), 12–13.

letter not printed by Gairdner: MS Guton 290 in Magdalen College, which is also autograph and is dated 21 August 1474, so that it usefully fits into the long gap between 640 and xcii; I denote this letter by 'M'.[1] Of this total of twenty-three letters, twelve are addressed to John Paston I and another (259) to him jointly with John Bocking; nos. 313 and 314 are to Fastolf, 345 to John Berney, 582 to Margaret Paston, xcii to John Paston II, 640 and M to Wainfleet; the other three (347, 498, 639) are to unknown recipients.

Worcester differs from many of his contemporaries in his method of dating his letters. The commonest practice during most of the fifteenth century was to refer to the nearest saint's day or other church festival. Worcester does this occasionally—304 is dated 'the Wensday in Esterweke', 498 'on Passyon Sonday', M 'the Sonday before seynt Bertillmeu'—but the rest of his letters which are dated at all (four are not) are assigned to day and month: 206 is 'viij day of June', 252 'the Monday vij day of Jullet', and so on. The year of most of them has to be inferred from the content. The earliest to specify it is 313, which is dated, by the commonest method of the time, 'the fyrst day of Feuerȝere A⁰ 36 R. H vj', i.e. 1458. The unusual feature of this is Worcester's use of Arabic numerals in '36'; and still more unusual is his use of them in three later letters to give the year of grace instead of the regnal year: 345, 'the Monday after I departed from you 1459 Cristi'; 640, 'the xvij day of Maij A⁰ 1470 Cristi'; M, 'the Sonday before seynt Bertill-meu 1474 Cristi' (in which *Cristi* in the first two is abbreviated *x* with raised *i*, in the third *xpi* with stroke above).

Worcester's signatures are very individual. Ten of the auto-graph letters, including both the earliest and the latest, are signed with some form of *Botoner* or *W. Botoner*, six *W. Wyrcestre*, one *W. Worcestre*, one *W.W.*, one *W. Botoner dit Worcestre*, and one *W. Botoner called Wyrcestre*. The remaining one (320) is signed

[1] I am much indebted to the late K. B. McFarlane and to Mr N. R. Ker for looking out the Magdalen manuscripts for me and allowing me to copy them. For the use of the manuscript which I print below I am obliged to the Trustees of the British Museum.

THE EPISTOLARY USAGES OF WILLIAM WORCESTER

only with the mysterious monogram that he often used in conjunction with his signature—in 206 it is written between *Bote* and *nere*, in 259 between *Wor* and *cestre*, in 267 after *Botonere*, in 345 above *Wyrcestre*, and in 304 it follows *Boto* which is not completed. The composition and meaning of this sign remain obscure. It has hitherto been read as *H.R.*, and sometimes thought (improbably enough) to be an abbreviation of *Hibernicus*, an epithet applied to Worcester by Friar John Brackley for unknown reasons (e.g. Gairdner XLII/404, XLV/417).[1] But the letters, or characters, are not *H.R.* The first is quite distinct from the shape of Worcester's *H*, and resembles his Arabic figure 5; the second looks most like a *þ*, with the bow extended to form a flourish across the tail. I can make no sense of this, and can suggest only that it might be a kind of merchant's mark or brand (perhaps Worcester's father's) similar to Caxton's well-known device between his initials.

To exhibit a characteristic Worcester letter I give the complete text of no. 345 (B.M. MS Add. 43488 f. 49), written in January 1460—that is, some two months after Fastolf's death—to John Berney, another dependant of Fastolf who was still living at Caister. The month is fixed by the satirical reference to Denham's capture of Rivers at Sandwich. Fenn printed only the salutation, the final blessing, and the two short paragraphs preceding it,[2] and Gairdner, who had no access to the manuscript, perforce followed him in this. I italicize expanded abbreviations, enclose interlineations in half-brackets, and punctuate.

To the Ryght Worshypfull S*er*, John Berneye, scuier, at Castre beyng

Ryght worshypfull s*er*, I reco*m*maund me to yow; and the cause of my co*m*myng and taryeng yn London ys forasmoch as I obliged me by my *lettre* to be here now and to reken wyth all the credytours that I caused my maist*er* frendes, God blesse hys soule, to be seurtee for me for the cloth I made be bought for my maist*er* entierme*nt*. I dyd but hald the candell among*es* you yn Norff*olk*, for I was ⌐not¬ put yn fauour ne

---

[1] See further Bühler, *Dicts*, p. xxiii n. 2.
[2] *Original Letters*, i, pp. 182–5.

trust to co*m*maund *and* yeve yn my maist*er* name *and* for hys sake a goune cloth to none of hys frendes, *seruauntes* or almesfolk*es*, but most beg *and* pray as I were a str*a*ung*er*. Yff I caused maist*er* Paston *and* myne oncle the p*ar*son that they hafe such autorite as they hafe, they ought be the fayner *and* desyrouse of the contyn*au*nce of myne autorite, that ys as grete as theyrs or grett*er*, whate so evyr Frere Brakle or they sey, and so it ys to opynly knowen of record.

S*er*, I am the same man as ye left me, vpryght and yndyfferent for to wille *and* do for my maist*er* asmoch as my symple power may, and hafe made no promysse to no man, ne thus avysed shall not tille I speke wyth the p*ar*son myne oncle, that myne affecc*i*on ys to sey my hert moste vntoo rather then to such as wold str*a*unge me from my maister ⌜ys⌝ frendes *and* from the gode wille *and* fauour of my gode maist*er*s. Tho that I hafe holp to be cherysed w*yth* my maist*er* be now myne adu*er*saryes; there shewyth no gentlenesse of blode ne noble condic*i*on yn that poynt namely, &c. S*er*, who ought more halde wyth me yn reson more then my wyfys oncle yn all maner caus*es* be reson of myne alliaunce w*yth* hym, and namely yn my maist*er* cause that he ys bounde to me and I to hy*m* for the trouth we owe to our maist*er* and the grete trust he hath put yn hym *and* me, and obliged ws by othe? A, allas that he or onye such shuld be so nakedly disposed to me where I nevyr gafe cause. All myne adu*er*syte, trouble yn my spyrytt*es*, thought, and hevynesse that I susteyn, ye know well whom I do *and* may wyte it. Suppose ye that such yefft*es and* grauntes my maist*er* made to me for my relieffe yn recompense of my s*er*uyce, that I wille let it passe, and my maist*er* *seruauntes*, w*yth* hys pore kynnesfolk*es*, so sy*m*plye rewarded? I shall be for hem to my symple power as my maist*er* charged me. S*er*, at reu*er*ence of God, and for the verray *and* faythfull lofe ye hafe to my maist*er* yn the yeer*es and* dayes that ye dyd hym s*er*uyce yn the werr*es*, suffred prysonment *and* manye a sherp day for hys sake not rewarded, yhyt meove ye myn oncle the p*ar*son, and othyrs havyng autorite w*yth* hym, to peyn hem to do that at ys moste nede for the helth of my maist*er* soule *and* for the relieve of all Cristen soules, and namely for the susten*au*nce and encresyng of a comyn weelle. Hyt ys not a comyn proffyt to gefe manye blak gounys to such as nede none of yeft, and namely yff they be yoven to my maister ennemyes as som seyn there been, &c. I confesse me to yow, &c.

As to tydyng*es* here, I sende som of hem wreten to you *and* othyrs, how the Lord Ryuers, S*er* Antonye hys son, *and* othyrs hafe wonne

Calix be a feble assault made at Sandwych by Denham squyer wyth the nombre of viij c. men on Twyesday betwene iiij and v at clok yn the mornyng; but my lady duchesse ys stille ayen returned yn Kent. The Duke of York ys at Devylyn strengthed wyth hys erles and homagers, as ye shall see by a bille. God sende the Kyng victorie of hys ennemyes and rest and pease amonges hys lordes.

I hafe remembred Cristofer of your mater and hafe do hym wryte to you by the brynger hereoff. And after ye hafe spoke wyth myne oncle I pray you hertly of a lettre of gode confort and stedfastnesse ⌈of hym⌉. I am ryʒt gretly hevyed for my pore wyfe for the sorow she takyth, and most leefe hyr and hyr contrec. Y shall no thyng take from hyr more then a litill spendyng money tille better may bee.

And the blessed Trinite kepe and sende you helth. Wret ⌈at London⌉ hastly the Monday after I departed from you 1459 Cristi.

Your W. Botoner called Wyrcestre

In the conventional opening and closing phrases Worcester used comparatively simple formulas: 'Right worshipful sir, I recommend me to you' is a standard type in ordinary polite use. In addressing Fastolf he was more obsequious, as 313, 'Ryght worshypfull ser and my ryght gode maister, I recommaund me to yow yn my full humble wyse', and even to John Paston in 206 he wrote, 'Worshypfull ser and my gode maister, after dewe recommendacion wyth all my trew seruyce precedyng . . .'; but M opens plainly, 'My lord'. The transition to the matter of the letter he mostly made by some variant of 'please yow to wete', or 'please your (gode) maistershyp to wete'. In 304, omitting the salutation, he combined this with 'recommendation' and the otiose 'it is so that': 'Please yow to wete that after dew recommendacion hyt ys so that . . .'.[1] In the two early letters 206 and 208, but never afterwards, he used instead 'lyke you wete', without the 'to' which is regular after 'please'. The most noticeable feature of these transitions is the absence of the participial constructions so much favoured by many, perhaps most, letter-writers of the time.[2] In

---

[1] For the prevalence of this expression in fifteenth-century letters see 'Style and Stereotype in Early English Letters', *Leeds Studies in English*, n.s. i (1967), 7–17.

[2] For examples see 'The *Litera Troili* and English Letters', *RES*, n.s. xvi (1965), 233–44, and the article mentioned in the preceding note.

introducing reports of news, in the manner of 'As to tydynges here' in 345, two of Worcester's uses are individual—'nouueltes' for 'news' in 206, 305, and 313 (*OED*'s first comparable quotation is from a Plumpton letter of 1475), and 'couth' for 'known' in 252, 'As for tydyngys be none couthe', and 305, 'As for nouueltes, none couth'. In the closing formulas, up to 305 Worcester used variants of 'Lord kepe yow' (206) or 'Our Lord be wyth yow' (267, 305), and only from 313 regularly replaced these by invocations to the Trinity, sometimes elaborated as in M, 'And the blessed Trinite you prosper yn all felicitee', or 640, with a participial transition, 'besechyng the blysfull Trinite yow preserf yn prosperous helth long to contynewe'. Such appeals to the Trinity were favoured by many contemporaries.

Even in his day Worcester is conspicuous for the frequency of his oaths and asseverations. 'At reuerence of God', as in 345 above, he used again in 269, and 'at reuerence of Jesu' in xcII. Another favourite turn appears in 267, 'so wold Jesus ye were here', 269, 'so wold Jesus one of yow iij . . . myʒt hang at hys gyrdyll dayly', similarly in 305 and 582, and 347, 'wolde God I kowde plese bothe Maister Paston and my oncle in reson, who preserue you'. In 314 he wrote, 'there shall be sent yow, I trust to God, the somme of xl li.', and at the end of the same letter he interlined the words 'to God' to make the following concluding sentence: 'Y hope to God ye wille hald you ryʒt well pleased, who hafe yow yn hys blessed gouernaunce.' In 320 the form is 'I ensure yow by my soule', which is expanded in 347 to 'by my sowle, that is the grettest othe that I may swere of my silff', but fortified by 'be the blissed sacrament that I receyued at Pasch'. Milder protestations of sincerity appear in xcII, 'I mene faythfullye, and soo I pray yow take yt', and 498, 'for how so evyr I wryte I meene well, and so shall'.

The construction in the last quotation, with the auxiliary at the end without either subject pronoun or infinitive complement, may serve to introduce other uses of auxiliaries, some simple, others with far-reaching implications. Simple co-ordination appears in 252, 'Y doubt he shall and most obbey', and M, 'whych maters wille and most discourage me'; a loose use of the negative distorts that in 267, 'a generallte shall ne may be so gode as a particuler declaracion'; a free use of uninflected *be* as both past participle and infinitive in 347, 'on that hath and euermore schal be next of my knowlege'. A correctly logical pairing, but with *do* instead of a second auxiliary, appears in 345 (above), 'ye know well whom I do and may wyte it'; an illogical one in 296, 'I hafe and do purchasse malgre' (where *do* is interlined). In these cases *do* contrasts modally with *may* and temporally with *hafe*. Worcester rarely used it to form a periphrastic indicative without such contrast, but there are one or two examples: 296, 'he doth make maters to my maister', and, in the past negative, 267, 'my maistre dyd not graunt it', and M, 'dyd not gefe'. The use in 345, 'I dyd but hald the candell', is a special development of an originally negative construction.[1] These are significant stages in the evolution of 'auxiliary *do*'. Beside them the causative use of *do* survives in 304, 'to do hys audytours cast and make rollys of hys accomptys', 345, 'I . . . hafe do hym wryte to you', and probably 268, 'the parson wyth yow shall do well sort my maister evidensys'. But in addition *make* is used causatively in the phrase quoted above from 214, 'to make yow laugh', and with a following passive infinitive in 345, 'the cloth I made be bought';[2] and *cause* is used in the opening paragraph of 345 constructed both with infinitive and with a *that*-clause.

Another construction in which *do* appears in a different function may conveniently be noticed here. In 267 and 639 Worcester wrote 'whate ys to be do(o)n', compared with 268, 'yff ye thynk to don', which evidently means 'if you think it is to be done'; the latter of the same type as 267, 'he seyd hys wille was for to make'.

After certain verbs Worcester used, abnormally, an infinitive without *to*: 273, 'I cast duelle yn my contree'; 320, 'Fen desyred me abyde'; 498, 'it meovyth me wryte to yow the rathyre'. This is

---

[1] For contemporary usage see A. Ellegård, *The Auxiliary Do* (Gothenburg Studies in English 2, Stockholm, 1953), esp. pp. 124–5, 134–6. On p. 66 Ellegård quotes some of Worcester's forms, but wrongly says 'Botoner . . . was from Worcester'.

[2] For parallels see Ellegård, pp. 105–6.

most conspicuous with *help*: 214, 'to help pay for bonettys'; 273, 'to help ghete ayen a pore gode of myne'; 320, 'whych to my power wold help make it knowen'; 347, 'I that helped gete my maister goode and brynge it to gedre'; 498, 'whate proffyt, ease, and avaylle I may help stand hem'; 639, 'that a waraunt be made to help shyt vpp and make the see bankys'. The only example of an infinitive with *to* after *help* seems to be in 345, 'tho that I hafe holp to be cherysed'. *OED*, under *help* v. 5.a, notes that 'the infinitive has normally *to*, which however from 16th c. is often omitted: this is now *dial.* or *vulgar*'. The H volume of *OED* was of course written before the reversion to the construction without *to* which, apparently under American influence, has been widespread in the last twenty years or so. But its date in the sixteenth century is too late: Mustanoja notes four cases in Chaucer and one as early as the Cambridge manuscript of *Horn*.[1] The other verb after which Worcester normally used the plain infinitive is *ought*, as 345, 'they ought be the fayner', M, 'I ought hafe a grete amendys', xcii, 'your discrecion ought not loth'; but this was a common alternative throughout the Middle English period.[2]

In word order Worcester favoured certain turns which were proportionately less frequent among his contemporaries. It is not always easy to detect the currency of particular forms. For example the order in 252, 'it shall be to hym a singuler pleaser', looks abnormal until we find it in other writers from John Paston (1454) to Thomas Betanson (1486).[3] For constructions with a verbal noun and its object Worcester often used the order in 208, 'Gressam qwyt hym well yn your erandys doyng'. This is common in earlier Middle English,[4] but is not frequent in fifteenth-century letters though there are occasional examples—Windsor in 253/299 (1455) has 'of the whiche excuse makyng', and the

---

[1] T. F. Mustanoja, *A Middle English Syntax*, pt. I (Helsinki, 1960), p. 532.

[2] Ibid., p. 533.

[3] See the article in *Leeds Studies* mentioned on p. 258, n. 1. Cf. 'It is to me a ryght gret joy', R. H. Robbins and J. L. Cutler, *Supplement to the Index of Middle English Verse* (Lexington, 1965), no. 1637.2.

[4] Mustanoja, pp. 574–5. See also *Caxton's Blanchardyn and Eglantine*, ed. L. Kellner (EETS, e.s. lviii, 1890), p. lxxv.

anonymous writer of 179/217 (1452, the draft corrected by John Paston I), 'in evel exaumple gevyng'; this last so resembles Margery Kempe's 'be good exampyl ʒeuyng' that it must have been to some extent formulaic. Other examples in Worcester are 273, 'yn hys causys spedyng'; 296, 'of hys accomptys apposyng'; 347, 'in viagys makyng' (but 'spedyng the seid paymentys' in the same letter). In certain set phrases he preferred to place an adjective after its noun, as 206 'causys criminall' (first recorded in Lydgate), even with an adjective of English origin as 'his (your) councell lerned' in 259, 273, 296, XCII, and in M beside 'your lerned councelle'—this also known elsewhere since about 1400 (*MED* under *counseil* 4.(b), and Margaret Paston in 529/610 (1465)).

A characteristic of Worcester's noun syntax is his frequent use of possessives or genitives without ending, both in proper names and in common nouns denoting persons: 305, 'Herbert partye', 'the Kyng wyffe and chylde', 'the erle yonger broþere'; 313, 'Dygon the parson chylde'; 314, 'at Maister Paston commyng'; 320, 'ayenst my maister wille'; 347, 'for my maister sowle heele'. In a few places where the end of the noun is expressed by an abbreviation, as it is in *maister* in the last example, the genitive ending might be taken to be comprehended in the abbreviation; but there are many other cases in which the same words are written in full and still have no ending, as 345, 'my maister ennemyes'. Yet this usage is far from universal: 305, 'Richard the parson ys seruaunt of Blofeld'; 345, 'my wyfys oncle'; and it is remarkable that in one place in 345, 'my maister ys frendes', the *ys* is interlined. The genitive without ending is held to be mainly northern,[1] but Worcester's frequent use of it shows that it was more widely accepted. It is fairly common in some Norfolk writers, but his language does not seem to have been affected in any other significant way by his Norfolk residence. (A form of related interest is the relative *at* in 345, 'to do that at ys moste nede', which again is held to be northerly.[2])

A minor eccentricity of Worcester's is a leaning towards double

[1] Mustanoja, p. 72.   [2] Ibid., p. 191.

comparative adverbs: 259, 'that he may be more rypelyer groun-ded yn the seyd mater' (*OED* quotes one other example of 'the more rypliere', from the Rolls Series *Wars of the English in France*[1] —and this comes from the Prologue to Worcester's own Collec-tions, which has also 'more fervientlier'); 305, 'hyt ought be [*read* 'the'] more redelyere be doon'; 314, 'more speciallyere'. A final detail of syntax not common among the letter-writers is 268, 'that ys one the grettist thyng nedefull'.

I turn now to a number of words and phrases Worcester's use of which is in some way noteworthy—usually in being an early record. The collection is exceedingly miscellaneous, and for convenience of dictionary reference I italicize the relevant word in each quotation and list them in alphabetical order.

M. 'myne long *absentyng* from my pore loggyng'. *MED* quotes *absenting* only once, from Bokenham; *OED* only twice, later.

313. 'Barker wrytith to yow more *along*', i.e. 'at length'. *OED* quotes this sense first from a letter by John Russe, another of Fastolf's servants, in 1461, and next from Caxton (who used it often). *MED* has no other exactly like it.

259. 'My maister *carpyth* so oft *on* it dayly'. No other example of *carp on* appears in the dictionaries; perhaps it is affected by *harp on*, first recorded *c.* 1450.

M. '[I] was *coherted* ['compelled'] to fynde hym new sewrtee'. The dictionaries treat this word differently. *OED* enters it under *cohert*, with the first quotation from *The Boke of Noblesse* (by Worcester) and the second from Hawes's *The Conversion of Swearers* (printed 1509). *MED* gives *coherted* (from *Rolls of Parliament* 1450) under *coarten*, and has an entry *cohercen* with only two quotations, one of them from *The Boke of Noblesse*. The latter *OED* also records, under *coerce*, which otherwise does not appear until 1659, and suggests that it may be a misprint for *coherte*. In view of the common difficulty of distinguishing *c* and *t* in hands of the time (including Worcester's sometimes), of Worcester's undoubted use of *coherted* in two places, and of the confirmation of the form *coherte* by Hawes's rhymes on *herte* and *conuerte*, *OED* is

[1] Ed. J. Stevenson (1861–4), ii, pt. 2.

evidently right—though *coherced* is no doubt rather an editorial misreading than a 'misprint'.

640. 'They [the tenants] seyden that they had delyuered vpp the *culettys* of chepe and beestes . . . that they had ghedered to pasture vppon the mershes. And were bestowed vppon othyr pasturys yn othyr lordshyppys that they coude hafe no *culettys* to lay the pasture wyth beestys.' *OED* has *culet* (OF *cueillete*, etc.) from 1550 in the sense of 'a sum collected from a number of persons chargeable an assessment, a rate'; *MED* has only *colet(te)* as a variant of *collecte*. This seems inappropriate here; some such sense as 'selection', hence 'group', 'small flock' is required.

305. 'in *debursyng* hys money'. *MED*'s only quotation; *OED* from 1529.

640. 'the infynyte processe of the *decysyng* of my maister Fastolf testamentys'. *OED* quotes *decise*, meaning 'decide', first from 1538. *MED* quotes only Chauliac, where it is evidently an error, and an unpublished work by Capgrave dated 1440.

313. 'the kyng of Hungerye whych had the *descomfytur* vppon the Turkys'. *OED* records *discomfiture* only in the sense of 'defeat', etc. *MED* quotes Mannyng and Lydgate for the sense 'overcoming', and one other example besides the present one of the use with *upon* meaning 'victory over'. That other example is from *The Boke of Noblesse*, and so is Worcester's again; and there are at least two more examples in the same book—a particularly good one is: 'his eldest sonne Edward prince of Walis . . . had a gret discomfiture afore the cite of Peyters vppon John callyng hym King of Fraunce' (p. 13).

498. 'yff he or hys frendys set littille by it I may not *do wyth all*'. *OED* under *do* v. 54 gives examples of *do withal* in negative and interrogative sentences from Malory to Chapman meaning 'to help it', which is the appropriate sense here. This therefore is the earliest by a few years.

206. 'that ye wolle *hald your hand* well yn the seyd mater'. *OED* gives 'hold (one's) hand' first from the Towneley Plays, '*c*. 1460'.

305. 'manye opere accomptantys that maken lyvere of provysyons . . . can not approve theyr *liberatz* just tille the seyd housold

bokes be made vpp'. *OED* gives *liberate*, from the sixteenth century, only as a name of various writs. Here it apparently means 'receipts for delivery'.

296. 'hyt shall be ymagyned . . . that he doth *make maters* to my maister'. This seems to mean 'intrigue'. *OED* does not record this sense, but under *matter* sb.[1] 20.b gives 'to make a matter to' in the sense of 'quarrel' from the sixteenth century.

582. 'but for gelosye and *mysdemyng* of peple' . . ., 'the world ys to *mysdemyng*'. These are *OED*'s first records of *misdeeming* as both noun and adjective.

347. 'all the worlde woll *mysreporte* of hem and litel truste hem'. *OED* first records this sense of the verb from More.

305. 'of such chafre takyng he shall neuere be *monyed*'. *OED*'s first record.

345. 'allas that he . . . shuld be so *nakedly* disposed to me'. *OED* has no example of *nakedly* exactly in this sense; cf. 347, 'som of hem haue seid ful nakedly of you'. (Cf. also 'righte nakedly provided' in the Prologue to Worcester's Collections, meaning 'poorly', which *OED* gives from 1589.)

267. 'he . . . came by hym at *ny3t lyeng*', evidently meaning 'bedtime'. *OED* records only here.

'allwey new to constrew and *oppynable*', i.e. 'disputable'. *OED*'s first example.

305. 'seth it hath be kept *ordynarylye*', i.e. 'regularly'. *OED* records first from More (1532).

206. '*Pentecost Sonday*' is not recorded. In attributive use *OED* has first *Pentecost week* (1568).

M. 'the blessed Trinite you *prosper*'. The transitive use of *prosper* is recorded from 1530.

269. 'he *questioneth* and desputyth wyth hys seruauntys'. *OED* has *question* in this sense first in Malory.

M. 'and so hath caused hym *renne* hys dayes of payment', i.e. overrun, miss. This use of 'run' is not recorded.

269. 'I had but litille thyng to done when I *scrybled* thys bille.' This is evidently the first use of *scribble* so far noticed. *OED* quotes first from a Plumpton letter of about 1465 and certainly before

1477, and there are at least six other cases in the Plumpton correspondence, all substantially later—*c.* 1500. They are all in much the same tone, of hasty and rather careless letter-writing, all but one specifically 'scribbled in haste'.

'whych both Hygham and Jermyn hath suffred my maister hafe, savyng your reuerence, tweyn *shrewde tornys*'. This use of *shrewd turn* is a few years earlier than *OED*'s first quotation, which is from John Pamping, one of John Paston's clerks, in 1464. The apologetic 'saving your reverence' suggests that the expression was felt to be less than correct.

498. 'yff onye thyng falle *sinistrely*'. *OED*'s first example.

314. 'Frute of figes and reysyns be dere here at xviij *s.* the *sort.*' (Gairdner read 'croc (?)'.) The reading is clearly *sort*, *OED*'s sb.³—'some measure or weight of figs and raisins', sparsely recorded from the fifteenth century only.

273. 'one Haryngton of Doncastre, a besye *soule*'. This is earlier than any quotation in *OED* under *soul*, 13, where it belongs. (It may be a reminiscence of the phrase *besy goost* which occurs in *The Legend of Good Women* 103 and *The Kingis Quair* st. 173.)

345. 'a litell *spendyng money*'. *OED* quotes first from 1598. But it occurs again in an inventory of John Paston I's dated 1462 (B.M. MS Add. 39848 f. 50 v, not yet published).

252. 'the parson most nedys *vp* to London', and again 273, 'yff he most nedys com *vpp*'. This use of *up* (to London) *OED* records, under *up* adv.¹ 26.c, first from 1516; but Margaret Paston used it in 1460 (365/427) and later, John Paston I in 1465 (LIII/535 and LIX/575), and William Paston II in 1467 (LXXI/664).

345. '*vpryght* and yndyfferent'. *OED* records this sense first from Palsgrave (1530), who glosses it 'indifferent'.

320. '*yersten efe*'. *OED* records *yester-eve* from Ben Jonson, *yester-even* from the fifteenth century, but *yersten-eve* not at all. *Yersten* is Worcester's regular form of this element, as in *yerstenday* 214.

Worcester was fond of sententious remarks, proverbs, and sayings, of which the following are typical: 268, 'he þat wille dysseyve hys seruaunt yn maryage for so litell a thyng, he wold dysseyve another frende yn a gretter thyng'; 296, 'he that takyth the tolle most take the charge'; 304, 'a peny yn seson spent wille safe a pounde', 'taryeng drawyth parell'; 345, 'I dyd but hald the candell'; 347, 'A very frende at nede experience will schewe be deede, as wele as be autorite of Aristotle in the Etiques that he made of moralite'—the earliest recorded example of this proverb with the rhyme between *need* and *deed*;[1] 582, 'better ys a frende unknow then knowen'; xcii, 'yt ys seyd yn a vers, "Gutta cauat lapidem non vi set sepe cadendo"', 'to remembre a thyng yn seson ys gretely to commend and of a spedy auauntage'. In 296 Worcester used the proverbial 'barking at the moon' in a punning jibe at his rival William Barker—'my felow Barker, as of such othyr berkers ayenst the mone to make wysemen laugh at her folye'.

Related to his liking for expressions of this kind is the little jingle in xcii, in the manner of many similar things in fifteenth-century letters:[2] 'for now thys vacacion to spede, or nevyr shall stand yn yow no stede'. It is likely that a play on words is intended also in 273, 'ye have nede fare fayre wyth hym'. Though *fare* and *fayre* would not normally be homonyms they already were in some dialects; but in any case a play of this kind does not require complete identity of sound. The phrase 'fare fayre' was used also by Margaret Paston in 1462 (436/505), by John Paston I in 1465 (519/600), and, with the old use of *ferd(e)* as the past of *fare(n)*, also in William Lomnor's letter on the murder of Suffolk in 1450 (93/120), 'he shuld be faire ferd wyth'.

I conclude with some comments on Worcester's spelling and grammatical forms, in which he is for the most part undistinguished in his time but shows a few notable eccentricities. His spelling is unusually—not, of course, completely—consistent and shows no important development or revision in the period covered by these letters. Since he was nearly forty years old when

---

[1] See *The Oxford Dictionary of English Proverbs* (2nd ed. 1948), p. 227.

[2] See the article in *Leeds Studies* mentioned on p. 258 n. 1. Cf. also the 'Englishe billes rymed in partye' threatening William Paston I, posted on various gates and other places in Norwich in 1424 (Gairdner 4/6).

the earliest of them was written it is not surprising that his habits should have been well established.[1] His long residence in Norfolk did not lead him to adopt such characteristic local spellings as *x* for *sh* in *shall*, *qh* or *qw* for *wh-*, *-t* or *-th* for *-ght*. When there were alternative spellings for certain sounds he generally used the later one, so that much of his writing has a fairly modern look; of the spellings just mentioned, *sh-* and *wh-* are regular, without alternative *sch-* and *w-* which some writers used. Initial ʒ appears only in the name *Ʒeluerton* 269, 313; otherwise *y* is regular. After *ou* (occasionally written *o*) ʒ is not used before *t* but always *gh*: *boght* 320, *broght* 305, *bought* 345, *doughter* 313, *ought* 305, 345, *thought* 304. After *y* and before *t* the usual spelling is also *gh*, but ʒ is occasional throughout the series: *myʒt* 267, 498, *nyʒt* 267, 269, *ryʒt* 273, 304, 313, 314, 345, XCII. In other positions ʒ is very rare, as *Feuerʒere* 313. Worcester used *þ* very seldom, only in association with abbreviations except for an isolated *þat* in XCII: *þ^t* occurs once in 268 and twice in 273, *broþere* 304, 305, 313, *wheþere* 304, *oþere*, *raþere* 305. Elsewhere *th* is regular in all positions. Though it is not merely a matter of spelling, this is a convenient place to note that words ending in *-der* in earlier Middle English are always still spelt with *d*—*thedre* 206, 640, *hedre* 208, *hederto*(*o*) 498, M, *to gheders* 267, *to ghedre* 304, 305, *ghedered* 640, *to gedre*, *fadre*, *modre* 320—and those with historical *th* are not spelt with *d*—*whethyr* 305, *othyrs* 206 (and often).[2]

Among these examples those with *gh-* are one of Worcester's conspicuous eccentricities. In addition to the four cases of *gheder*, *ghedre* there are two of *ghete*(*n*) in 208 and 273, so that the spelling appears at intervals from 1454 to 1470; but it is only in these words—cf. *gefe* 268, 296, 305, M, XCII. The spelling *gh* is remarkable in view of the general belief, as expressed by *OED*, that the modern spelling of *ghost* is due directly to Caxton's adoption of the

---

[1] For examples of writers who did alter their habits see 'A Scribal Problem in the Paston Letters', *English and Germanic Studies*, iv (1951-2), 31-64, and 'A Paston Hand', *RES*, N.S. iii (1952), 209-21.

[2] Some different contemporary scribal habits can conveniently be seen in the extract from William Paston II's letter on p. 250 above.

gh of Dutch *gheest*.[1] Though Worcester used *gh-* only before *e*, he did so well before Caxton and with no apparent models in English. *MED* under *gete(n)*, an entry 8½ columns long, gives only two examples spelt *gh-*: one is in Worcester's letter 208, the other in a letter from Fastolf to Howes (132/162), which is in Worcester's hand. Presumably he too learnt it from Dutch.

The example of *gefe* introduces Worcester's other principal, and much more widespread, abnormality of spelling. He used *f* instead of *u* or *v* in the great majority of occurrences of such words as *gefe* (including the past *gafe* 345 and the alternative *for-yefe* 296), *hafe*, *lofe*, *meofe*, *prefe* (and *preffe* 268), and even without *-e* in *preserf* 640, *serf* XCII. The commonest of these in occurrence is naturally *hafe*, which appears over 40 times from the earliest to the latest of these letters. Such forms are not without exception—cf. *yeve*, *meove* 345—but they are plainly the normal ones; *lyve* for 'life' in 252 and 259 is a curious reversal. H. Kökeritz has noted that they are also common in Sir Thomas Wyatt's poems and in Machyn's diary.[2] Perhaps related to these in origin, though remarkable because of its uniqueness, is Worcester's spelling of 'feel' as *vele* or *veele* in 259, 305, 498, and also evidently in the original of 347 where Calle, failing to recognize the word, wrote *wele*. This looks like a vestige of Worcester's Bristol origin strangely persisting; a voiced initial *f* could have led to the use of *f* for *u/v* in other positions. Another singular spelling is *yhyt* for 'yet' in 208, 296, 305, 313, 345—presumably a spelling device to avoid writing *yyt*, since in Worcester's system ʒ- was not available and he much preferred *y* to *i*.

Three other spelling features of quite different kinds may be noticed. The digraph *ea* is strikingly regular in the words *please*, in almost every letter from 214 to XCII, *pleaser* 252 (but *plees* 'pleas' 304), *ease* 269, 296, 498, M, XCII, *pease* 269, 305, 314, 345 (*pese*

---

[1] For Caxton's use of *gh-* see H. Römstedt, *Die englische Schriftsprache bei Caxton* (Göttingen, 1891), p. 34, and H. Wiencke, *Die Sprache Caxtons* (Leipzig, 1930), p. 70.

[2] 'Dialectal Traits in Sir Thomas Wyatt's Poetry', in *Medieval and Linguistic Studies in Honour of Francis Peabody Magoun, Jr.* (New York and London, 1965), p. 296 and n. 5.

once 269), *appease* 269. Other words containing slack *ē* are spelt in the more usual way, as *grete, speke, leefe* 345. The digraph *ie* is common in words of French origin: *chieff* 259, 305, *chiere* 267, *entierment, relieff/relieve* 345, *papier* 640. And *b* is regular in *debt(ys)* 268, M, *doubt* 252, XCII, in which again Worcester was more modern than most of his contemporaries.

Of spellings which presumably have a bearing on pronunciation, the following are the most important. OE *a* before *ld* is commonly *o*, as *holdeth* 269, *holden* 314, *boldyth* 273, *Oldhale* 252; but usually 'hold' is *hald(e)*, as 206, 208, 345, 639. OE *a* before *nd* is usually *a*, as *stand(yth)* 268, 304, 498, 640, *vndrestand* M, *hand, land* 206, *sand* 639; but in 639 and 640 there are eight cases of *lond(-)*. OE *ĭ* is lowered to *e* in *hedre* 208, *hederto(o)* 498, M, *thedre* 206, 640, and the past part. *wret* 314, 345, XCII. In view of these last this is probably the significance also of *wrete* 313, *wreten* 273, 345. These are the only clear cases, and *wete* 'know', which is Worcester's only form of the word and occurs in nearly every one of the letters, is therefore more likely to indicate a lengthened vowel in the open syllable. Minor features are the regular *sylf*, 206, 273, 305, 320, 640, and the occasional *hyre* 'hear', 296, 313.

Of inflexional forms the following are characteristic:
Nouns. The ending of the pl. and the gen. sg. (except in the personal nouns without ending; see p. 262 above) is represented by both *-es* and *-ys*, with a slight preponderance of the latter not large enough to be statistically significant. In the gen. the ending is often written separately, as *man ys* 208, *maister ys* 252, 259, 305, 345, *parson ys* 296, *lord ys* (4×) 639, *Paston ys* 640. After *-r* and *-n* generally but not only in French words, the pl. ending is usually only *-s*, as *aunsuers* 269, *maters* 296, 305, M, *audytours* 304, *sqwyers, fermours* 639, *mayntenours, maners, willers* M, *mocions* 269, *reysyns* 314; and abnormally *bayllyfs* 305. A few French words ending in *-t* indicate the pl. by *-z*, as *seruauntz* 273; *liberatz* 305 has the same ending, and it is extended to *frendz* 273, *londz* 639, 640 (3×). In these English words the *z* could be intended as an abbreviation of *-es*, but this seems unlikely because *londez* is also used in 640. Words ending in a vowel vary, as *aduersaryes, ennemyes* 345;

nouueltes 305, *nouueltees* 313, *nouuelteez* 206. The use of *-s* in the pl. is extended to the pronoun *othyrs*, which is frequent and regular—e.g. in 206, 214, 345, 639. This is another feature in which Worcester is more advanced than many contemporaries, who continued to use the uninflected *other*; *OED* has no examples of *others* between Wyclif and 1535.[1]

Verbs. In the 3 sg. pres. indic. the consonant ending is nearly always *-th*, preceded predominantly by *y* except in verbs with stems ending in a vowel or diphthong, as *hath, seyth*. There appears to be one genuine exception—*syt* in the phrase 'it syt not me' 267. In 208 the editors read *qwyts*, but the *s* is an expansion of a flourish on the *t*. I believe that the supposed flourish is in fact a cancellation of a miswritten curl on the cross of the *t*, and that the correct reading is *qwyt*—that is, a past tense, which in any case gives the required sense. To indicate the vowel of the ending *y* is strongly preferred throughout the whole series of letters except when the verb stem ends in *y* as *taryeth* 268, 313, *noyeth* 273, *prayeth* 313, *occupyeth* 313, 498. Apart from these only a few have *e*, as *questioneth, haldeth* 269, *wryteth* 313, compared with over 50 in *-yth*. It is evident that in the forms in *-yeth* the *e* is written to avoid the inconvenience of a second *y*, in the same way as the present participle and verbal noun ending is spelt *-eng* in *lyeng* 267, *taryeng* 345, 639, *tryeng, varyeng* 640, and commonly elsewhere in ME.

The ending *-(y)th* is sometimes used with a plural subject: *passyth* 267, *hath* 269, *menyth* 296. It is not certain that Worcester intended this, for he sometimes used singular forms ambiguously elsewhere, e.g. in 296 'such maters as was lykyng to hem' (presumably impersonal), and 313, 'or the spousells was made' (which Fenn misread *spouselle*); and he quite frequently lost track of the construction of his sentences. There is one clear case of imperative pl. *beyth* 269.

In the past tense and past participle of weak verbs the spelling of the vowel contrasts sharply with that of the pres. indic.—it

---

[1] According to H. Spies, *Studien zur Geschichte des englischen Pronomens im XV. und XVI. Jahrhundert* (Studien zur engl. Philologie 1, Halle, 1897), §83 n. 2, '. . . sind die Formen ohne *s* noch während des ganzen 16. Jahrhunderts üblich'.

is with very few exceptions *e*, not *y*. In 206 *passyd* occurs beside *passed*, in 498 *enformyd* beside *enformed*, but there are some 50 with -*ed* only. A few verbs with *r* at the end of the stem have no vowel: *fard*, *aunsuerd* 320. (In 214 *lettet* may owe its -*t* to a writing slip rather than a phonetic assimilation.)

In inflexional syllables, then, Worcester observed more distinctions of spelling than might be expected. In noun endings *e* and *y* are more or less equally frequent, but in verbs *y* is the normal vowel of the 3 present and *e* of the past, and the numbers of both are large enough to ensure that this is not accidental. It can hardly have any phonetic basis, but it is worth notice as a well-marked spelling convention.[1]

The other significant variation in verbal endings at this date concerns the state of -*n* in infinitive, present plural, past plural, and strong past participle.[2] In this feature Worcester is in general modern for his age, with one or two surprising vestiges. In infinitives he very seldom uses forms in -*n*. In 268 and 269 he has *to don*(*e*), evidently as a descendant of the inflected infin. in 'yff ye thynk to don' (268); *lyven* 640 and *owen* cxii are the only others, with the possible exception of *sowen* 640 which is more likely to be past pl. Since the total number of infinitives in the autograph letters is about 425 the occurrence of only these four or five in -*n* is remarkable, and still more so is the appearance of two of them in the late letters 640 and cxii. In the present pl. forms in -*n* are also infrequent, but there are occasional examples at different periods: *comen*, *maken* 208, *maken* 305, *commen* 314, *seyn*, *been* 345, *trustyn* 639, *ben* M. There are about 80 without -*n*, and the few doubtful cases of -*th* noticed above. In the past pl. total numbers are small—some 50—and the only certain case with -*n* is *seyden* 640, with *sowen* in the same letter also probable. It is again remarkable that these should appear so late. In the past part. the situation is naturally more complex, and the numbers are more even—a total of 27 forms with -*n* against 51 without it. (There are two

---

[1] For differing treatment of these syllables see 'Scribal Variation in Late Fifteenth-Century English' in *Mélanges Mossé* (Paris, 1959), pp. 95–103.

[2] See especially 'A Scribal Problem' mentioned on p. 268 n. 1.

cases of *born*, but this was certainly already a set form functioning as an adjective and is not comparable.) No regular line of development over the series in the use of one or the other type can be discerned; numbers in each letter are small, and much depends on the particular verb which the topic happens to demand. This can be seen from the distribution of forms with and without -*n* according to verb. Those with -*n* but no corresponding *n*-less forms are *broken, holden, sworn, seen, slayn, goon*, which occur once each. Those with no *n*-forms are *ryd, holp, bounde, founde, wonne, vnderstand* (once each), *spoke* (3×), *be* (6×). Those which have both types (including verbs related though not identical) are *wreten* (2×), *wryt(e), wret(e)* (16×); *comen* (1×), *com* (6×); *gheten* (1×), *for-yete* (2×); *yoven* (2×), *gefe, gofe* (once each); *taken, take* (once each); *knowen* (5×), *knowe* (1×); *do(o)n* (9×), *do(o)* (8×). Some trend can be observed here towards the modern position in which -(*e*)*n* is lost by dissimilation after a nasal consonant in participles like *bound, found, won, come*, and kept in those like *seen* and *gone*. But even *done*, which is the most frequent of all the verbs concerned, is only half-way to this position, *wreten* is much in the minority, and *be* does not appear with -*n* at all.

Pronouns. Though his normal form of the neuter pronoun was *it/yt*, Worcester used *hyt* repeatedly, mainly in introductory function, as 320, 'hyt fortuned that . . .', 639, 'hyt were expedyent that . . .', 640, 'hyt was promysed me and graunted xxv mark lyfelode', but also xcii, 'hyt was not of verray certeyn tolde me, but as a dreme'. The plural pronouns of the third person show a little, but not much, evolution during the series. The oblique form is *hem* throughout, from 206 to M, but there is an isolated *theym* in 305. In the possessive the relation is different: *her* occurs in 296, 305, 313, 640, xcii, but *theyr* in 296, 305, 320, 498, 640, and slightly exceeds *her* in total numbers. A single *theyrs* appears in 345, but since Calle's copy of 347 has *theris* it probably occurred there also. There is thus a slight move towards *th*- forms from about 1457, which is substantially earlier than John Paston III's move in the same direction.[1]

---

[1] See 'The Language of the Pastons', *Proc. Brit. Acad.*, xl (1955), 127.

A number of other details might be cited as characteristic of Worcester, but enough has been said to show that his particular blend of spellings and forms is distinctive, and that there is often something individual and novel in his use of words. His hand can be detected even from a printed text—for instance, Gairdner's 132/162, a letter in Fastolf's name dated 1450, can be seen to have been written by Worcester from spellings such as *ghete*, *to ghedyr*, *hafe*, *vele*, *yhyt*; and from constructions like 'the day of thys lettre wrytyng', 'it ys and woll be', 'whyche have and wold dayly labour', 'they doo not attaine', 'I ought take' and the proverb 'taryeng drawth perell' (used seven years later in 304; see p. 267) it appears to have been at least largely composed by him as well. The manuscript of that letter survives to prove the identification of the hand; it is equally sure that the lost original of 582/681 was autograph—*yhyt*, *meofe*, *hafe*, *gefe*; *sylf*; *othyrs*; *Wold Jesu*, *Maistras*, *that my gode maister*. . . . The same kind of examination ought now to be applied to Caxton's texts of *de Senectute* and *de Amicitia*, to see whether, after the revision that Caxton avowedly made, Worcester's hand can still be detected in the former, and possibly discovered in the latter as Dr Bühler and McFarlane have suggested. But that must await another occasion.

18

Martinus Polonus and some later Chroniclers

WILLIAM MATTHEWS

THE *Chronicon Pontificum et Imperatorum* that Martinus Polonus compiled in the 1270's is scarcely a record to which modern historians habitually resort. But during the fourteenth and fifteenth centuries it enjoyed great popularity. Weiland[1] records numerous continental copies of it for that period, and it also seems to have been a standard item in the major monastic libraries of Great Britain—Ker,[2] for example, records surviving copies from Bardney, Boston, Canterbury, the London Austin Friars, Norwich, Syon, and York.

The reason for its popularity seems obvious. A product of the later medieval fashion for reducing large bodies of narrative into more comfortable compass, it presents the outstanding facts of world history, as recorded by the chief Christian chroniclers (and an occasional classical one), with notable brevity and most systematically. In bare, note-like statements, it first summarizes the Creation and the history of the ancient empires, then presents a comprehensive account of the topography of Rome and the history of the Roman state down to Augustus, and completes its

---

[1] Martinus Polonus's *Chronicon Pontificum et Imperatorum* is most conveniently available in Ludwig Weiland's edition, *Monumenta Germaniae Historica, Scriptorum*, Tomus xxii (Hannover, 1872), pp. 377–475 (reprinted Stuttgart and New York, 1963). Martinus was a native of Troppau in Silesia, although he is sometimes said to have been a Pole, a Scotsman, or a Frenchman. He spent most of his life in Rome, where he was penitentiary to John XXI and Nicholas III. In 1278 he was appointed archbishop of Gnessen in Silesia, but died at Bologna on 27 June on his way to take up his new post. Copies of his chronicle are said to be numbered by the hundred.

[2] N. R. Ker, *Medieval Libraries of Great Britain*, 2nd ed. (London, 1964).

survey with notes on each of the popes, and then the emperors, down to 1277. Rarely exceeding a dozen lines or so, the entry for each pope and emperor lists, succinctly and baldly, the precise length of the reign and its chief religious, political, and literary events. Admirably no-nonsense and businesslike, the survey, both in its contents and style, is a medieval equivalent of the College Outlines that American undergraduates resort to for their final joustings with fact-minded examiners. In the seventy-eight folio pages of Weiland's edition, it handily presents to an elementary medieval scholar all the facts of history he really needs to know.

The chronicle moreover also seems to have been popular among vernacular historians, particularly some of romantic inclination. For these, Martinus's clear design and precisely stated facts formed a reassuring framework for what livelier details and fancies they might wish to load upon it. The present paper proposes to give a few instances of the kind, chosen for their English interest.

I. Andrew of Wyntoun's *Original Chronicle of Scotland*[1] (written before 1424) is a verse chronicle which extends from the Creation until recent times. For its earlier stages, the chronicler frankly and frequently refers to Frere Martyn as his major authority. For the pre-Christian period, he amplifies Martinus's record with incidents from the Bible, but for the truly historical matter of the huge Book v (5844 octosyllabic lines), which deals with human affairs from the birth of Christ to the early part of the eighth century, his reliance is mostly upon the Latin chronicle. There he records major happenings during the reigns of the popes and emperors in the same format and with essentially the same detail as his source, and, allowing for the diction of poetry, much the same style—the fact may have something to do with Wyntoun's low reputation as a poet. Here, in brief example, is his 88th chapter in Book v:

> Dyonyse, till Sixt nixt successour,
> Sat twa winter in þat honour,
> Aucht monethis and dais thre.
> First kirkȝardis ordanit he,

[1] F. J. Amours, ed., *The Original Chronicle of Andrew of Wyntoun* (STS, Edinburgh, 1903-14), 6 vols.

> And till þe kirk parochis;
> And ilk preist of his office
> He ordanit to serve the parochy
> Till him ordanit distinctly,
> And hald him of his part content,
> Usurpand nocht oure his extent.
>
> (v, 2467–76)

And here is the entry in Martinus from which it is translated:

Dionisius ex monacho, cuius genus non invenitur, sedit annis 2, mensibus 3, et cessavit episcopatus diebus 8. Hic parrochias et cimiteria divisit et unicuique ius proprium statuit, mandans, ut singuli terminis suis contenti essent et alienos non usurparent. Hic in Urbe divisit parrochias, singulis singulos dans presbiteros. (414)

This type of chapter, with emperors and popes linked in chronological order, forms the staple of this part of Wyntoun's work. But there is also a noteworthy adaptation to Scottish interests and to the less scholarly audience which the Scottish chronicler had in mind. Into this Book v, for example, he slips very skilfully brief notes concerning the Pictish and early Scottish kings, and these serve as introductions to the specialized history of Scotland which begins in Book vi, not long before the accession of Kenneth McAlpine. In accordance with his more romantic taste, Wyntoun also expands the story somewhat in the way that Jean d'Outremeuse did a little earlier in his *Myreur des Histors*.[1] At appropriate points in Book v, he introduces the legendary origins of Scotland and Britain, and for Martinus's two brief references to Merlin and Arthur, he substitutes a lengthy account of Arthur and his conquests, drawn either from the *Brut* or from that historical romance, the *Gret Gest of Arthure*, which for the confusion of Arthurian scholars he ascribed to Huchown of the Awle Ryal.

II. John Capgrave (1393–1464) is perhaps best known now by his *Chronicle of England*.[2] It is fragmentary, and for a history of

---

[1] A. Borgnet et St Borgnet, eds., *Li Myreur des Histors* (Bruxelles, 1864–87), 7 vols.

[2] John Capgrave, *The Chronicle of England*, ed. Francis C. Hingeston (Rolls Series, London, 1858).

England it is organized rather strangely. The first quarter contains the story of Genesis and of the ancient empires; the second, beginning with Christ and going down to the Norman conquest, is concerned almost entirely with the popes and emperors; only the second half is an English chronicle, reporting happenings from William I to Capgrave's own time (1417). For this second half the sources are simple: according to Kingsford,[1] the material is taken chiefly from Walsingham's *Historia Anglicana*, although Hingeston affirms that Capgrave drew from the English *Brut*, Higden, and his continuator, the Author of the *Vita Regis Ricardi*. For the earlier half, Hingeston, possibly motivated by both Capgrave's references and his early reputation for being the most learned Augustinian ever produced in England, suggests a wide study: 'the writings of Isidore, S. Jerome, Eusebius, Methodius, Hugo de Sancto Victore, and others, whom he not unfrequently refers to by name' (xxii). In fact, these authorities are cited only in connection with odd details and most of them are taken from the one principal source (unmentioned by either chronicler or editor), namely, Martinus Polonus.

Martinus's entries, as has been stated, are succinct in the extreme. But occasionally he writes in what, for him, seems almost a loquacious style. This is his account of Augustus:

Post nativitatem domini nostri Ihesu Christi, Octavianus Augustus imperavit annis 14, Romanus genere patre Octaviano senatore, maternum genus ab Enea ducens, Iulii Cesaris nepos adoptione quoque filius, totum mundum in unam redigens monarchiam. Neque vir tantus viciis caruit, serviebat enim libidini [*usque ad probrum vulgi*]. Nam inter 12 chatamitos totidemque puellas accubare solitus erat. Hunc populi Romani videntes esse tante pulcritudinis, quod nemo in oculis eius intueri poterat, et tante prosperitatis et pacis, quod totum mundum sibi tributarium fecerat, dicunt ei: *Te volumus adorare, quia deitas est in te: sic hoc non esset, non omnia tibi succederent prospere.* Qui rennuens inducias postulavit et ad se Sybillam Tyburtinam sapientem vocavit, cui quod senatores dixerant recitavit. Que spacium trium dierum peciit. Post tercium diem respondit imperatori hoc modo:

[1] Charles Lethbridge Kingsford, *English Historical Literature in the Fifteenth Century* (Oxford, 1913), p. 169.

Iudicii signum tellus sudore madescet,
E celo rex adveniet per secla futurus

et cetera que sequuntur. Illico apertum est celum et nimius splendor irruit super eum et vidit in celo quandam pulcherrimam virginem stantem super altare, puerum tenentem in brachiis, et miratus est nimis, et vocem dicentem audivit: *Haec ara filii Dei est*. Qui statim proiciens se in terram adoravit. Quam visionem senatoribus retulit, et ipsi mirati sunt nimis. Hec visio fuit in camera Octaviani imperatoris, ubi nunc est ecclesia sancte Maria in Capitolio, ubi nunc fratres sunt Minores. Ideo dicta est ecclesia sancte Maria ara celi. (443)

At the same point in Capgrave's chronicle appears the following passage, a fairly close translation of Martinus save for a couple of minor omissions and one small addition transferred from the rest of the account of Augustus in the Latin chronicle:

Anno 5157. Octavian began to regne the ȝere of the world V. thousand a hundred and sevene and fifty. Before the Nativite of Criste he regned xii. ȝere, and after the Nativite of Criste xiiii. ȝere. He was bore in Rome: his fader hite Octavian, a senatoure. His moder was of the kyn of Eneas, a Trojan. Cosyn he was onto Julius Caesar, and, be choys, his son. This man browt al the empire into o monarchi. And ȝet as worthi as he was, he wanted not vices; for he wold never rest with oute grete noumbir of women and maydenes. The puple of Rome, for his grete beute, prosperity, and pees, wold worchip him as a god. But he wold not receyve it, but asked leisir to gyve hem a answere. Than called he to him sibill Tiburtine, and rehersed onto her the desire of the Senate. Sche asked the space of thre dayes avisement, in whech sche, and he, and many mo fasted and prayed. And at the thre dayes ende, they sey Hevene open, and a grete brithnesse schining upon hem; and thanne sey thei a faire ymage of a mayde upon a auter, and a child in hir armes. And whan he merveled gretly he herd a vois fro Hevene crying in this manere—'This is the auter of Goddis Son.' Than felle he down onto the erde, and reverently worchipid that site. The next day he went onto the Capitol, and told hem al this visione, and refused her profir. This same vision was seyn in the Chambir of Octavian, whech is now a Cherch and a Covent of Freres Menouris. It is cleped now, 'Ara Celi'. (57–8)

From this point until the end of the tenth century, Martinus's work is in effect the only real source for the English chronicle, although here and there a small detail is brought in from elsewhere. Capgrave combines the material that Martinus presents separately under popes and emperors, omits details that he may have thought rhetorical or unimportant, such as catalogues of conquests, and translates the rest literally and in similar style. The following parallel exemplifies almost completely his various procedures:

Adrianus imperavit annis 21. Iste rebelles Iudeos secundo subiugavit, urbemque Iherosolimam restauravit, non Iudeos sed alias gentes in ea locando. . . . Adrianus etiam restaurata Iherosolima precepit, ne cui Iudeorum daretur licencia intrandi, sed tantum christianis. . . . Sub Adriana passa est Rome beata virgo Serapia, Antiochena genere, manens in domo nobilissime femine Sabine, quam sua doctrina converterat. . . . Floruit etiam hiis temporibus Secundus philosophus qui philosophatus est omni tempore silencium servans. Causa autem silencii in suo libro demonstratur. Hoc tempore Aquila genere Ponticus secundus interpres Mosayce legis floret. (446)

Alexander I. . . . Hic constituit aquam aspersionis cum sale benedici, et in habitaculis hominum aspergi . . . Hic etiam statuit, ut vino aqua in missa misceretur ad designandam unionem Christi et ecclesie. . . .

Sixtus I. . . . Hic constituit ut diceretur: *Sanctus, sanctus, sanctus dominus deus* et cetera in missa, et ministeria sacrata non tangerentur nisi a ministris. Iste foris portam Apiam decollatus fuit, ubi Dominus apparuit Petro. *Domine, quo vadis?* Sepultus est in Vaticano iuxta corpus beati Petri. . . .

Thelesforus natus ex Anachorita. . . . Hic constituit . . . ut missam ante terciam nullus canere presumeret. Et constituit canere hymnum angelicum ante sacrificium, et in natali Domini cantari tres missas cum *Gloria in excelsis Deo*. Hic martirio coronatur et in Vaticano iuxta corpus beati Petri sepelitur . . . . (410–11)

Anno 5317. 119.—Adrian regned xxi. ȝere. He went to Jerusalem, and punchid there the Jewis that were rebelles, and repaired the Tempull, put oute Jewis and put in hethen men, and sette there his ymage as a god. He mad eke a precept, that no Jew into Jerusalem schuld entre; but Cristen men he forbade not the entre. Undir him was martired the holy mayde Seraphia, that cam fro Antioche and dwelled with anothir mayde thei cleped Sabine. In this tyme was a Philosophre cleped Secundus, that kept silens al his lif, and answered evyr be writing.

And in this tyme was Alisaundre Pope, that ordeyned hali water, and that wyn schuld be put in the chalis, and water thereto. In this tyme lyved on Aquila that translate the Elde Testament out of Hebrew into Grek.

In the x. ȝere of Adrian was Sixte the first mad Pope. He ordeyned that Sanctus schuld be sunge at Sacri, and no man schuld handel the chales but ministeris of the auter. He was hedid withoute gate that is cleped Appia and biried in Vaticano.

In the xix. ȝere of Adrian was Thelophorus mad Pope, whech was first a ancorite. He ordeyned there schul no man say masse before that he had seid the Ters, that is to sey, 'Legem pone'. He ordeyned tho iii. masses on Cristmas morow. He deied a martir, biried in Vaticano. (65)

Some authorities for British and English history that may be expected in almost any late medieval monastic chronicle are completely lacking from Capgrave's. It seems to make no use of Geoffrey of Monmouth, for example, its only allusions to the history and kings of Britain being brief mentions of Hengist and Horsa and of Arthur, both taken from Martinus—and it even omits the few lines about Merlin that make up the second of Martinus's two references to the Arthurian story. And as for Bede's history, it is cited in relation to the date of Christ's birth, but apparently nowhere else: even the account of Augustine's conversion of England reproduces Martinus's brief note.

For the first Christian millennium, Capgrave's concern is almost solely with the emperors and popes, and his procedure is to give a slightly shortened word by word translation of what Martinus writes. From another source, probably the *Brut*, he occasionally inserts some matters of more strictly English interest, and these begin to be fairly frequent in the tenth century. A two-page list of the kings from Hengist to Æthelwold is inserted into the account of Constantine's papacy (708–15), and Alfred, Edward the Elder, Athelstan, Edmund, Æthelred, and Edmund Ironside are accorded half a page, sometimes even a little more. But it is not until

Capgrave reaches William the Conqueror that he gives over his chronicle to English affairs and moves to Walsingham as his major source. But even then the framework continues to be a regular listing of the popes and emperors, and the very last entry in Martinus's chronicle, describing the treachery of the Soudan of Babylon towards Prince Edward of England in 1271, is repeated almost word for word by Capgrave. Nor does the influence stop there. Under the year 1393, Capgrave records his own birth: 'In this ȝere, in the xxi. day of Aprile, was that Frere bore whech mad these Annotaciones.' The information is scarcely from Martinus, but the idea for it and the style in which it is stated follow his pattern; this is the way in which he habitually records the births and the deaths of emperors and popes.

III. In some ways, Capgrave's most interesting book is *The Solace of Pilgrimes*,[1] 1450, a full and detailed guide-book to Rome. In ample detail and with pleasant autobiographical gusto, it describes one by one the secular monuments of Rome and then the religious. To considerable extent it is the product of Capgrave's own observations in the holy city—'a smal pypyng of swech straunge sitis as I haue seyn and swech straunge þingis as I haue herd'. In his preface, the author states that he went on pilgrimage under the protection of his special master, Sir Thomas Tudenham (1399–1461), a gentleman who lived near King's Lynn. Internal evidence indicates that the material for the book must have been gathered between 1447 and 1452, and so it seems likely that the pilgrimage was undertaken in connection with the Jubilee of 1450.

Although Capgrave's guide-book is largely original, it too is considerably indebted to Martinus's chronicle. At one point, the debt is acknowledged. The account of *archus prici tarquini* (cap. xix), of which Capgrave says 'in uery suyrte I wot not where it standith', is frankly stated to be drawn from Martinus. The debt is more general however. Part of the introductory matter in Martinus's chronicle is a summary report on the origins of Rome and a headline description of its principal classical monuments: its gates,

[1] John Capgrave, *Ye Solace of Pilgrimes*, ed. C. A. Mills (Oxford, 1911).

its palaces, its temples, each item in the listing accompanied by a very brief note. At the beginning of his book Capgrave translates and slightly expands Martinus's notes, citing the same authorities. Thus:

Modum autem constructionis et dispositionis Romane urbis demon-strat Escodius sic dicens: Postquam filii Noe edificaverunt turrim confusionis, Noe cum aliquibus ratem ingressus venit in Ytaliam et non longe ab eo loco, ubi nunc est Roma, civitatem construxit nominis sui, in qua laboris et vite terminum dedit. Ianus vero filius una cum Iano filio Iaphet, nepote suo, et Camese indigena civitatem Ianiculum con-struens regnum accepit. Hic cum iam dicto Camese apud Transtyberim palacium construxit, quod Ianiculum appellavit, in eo loco ubi nunc ecclesia sancti Iohannis ad Ianiculum sita est. Eodem tempore Nemroth qui est Saturnus, a Iove filio eunichizatus, ad predicti Iani regnum per-venit eiusque iuvamine fultus construxit civitatem ubi nunc est Capi-tolium. Illisque diebus Ytalus rex ad Ianum et ad Saturnum cum Syracusanis veniens, construxit civitatem iuxta Albulam fluvium, qui post Tyberis dictus est. Hercules quoque filius ipsius post hoc cum Argivis veniens, ut Varro scribit, fecit civitatem Valeriam sub Capitolio. Post hunc rex Tyberis ab origine cum gente sua veniens, edificavit civitatem iuxta Tyberim. Demum Evander rex Archadie cum suis fecit civitatem in monte Palatino. Similiter rex Coriban cum exercitu veniens construxit civitatem iuxta in valle. Glaucus quoque filius minor filii Iovis veniens, civitatem et menia construxit ibidem. Post quem veniens Rome filia Enee cum multitudine Troianorum civitatem ibidem construxit. Aventinus quoque rex Albanorum in monte Aventino civitatem et mausoleum sibi construxit . . . . (399–400)

is rendered in this expanded form in Capgrave's book:

Ther was a cronicaler in elde tyme whech þei called *Estodius* whos book is not now redyly founde but he is rehersid in þe newer bookis as for a trewe auctour. Thus writith he that aftir þe tyme þat noe had seyn who his successioun had bilid þ^t hy tour of babilon & ueniaunce taken on þe puple in confusioun of tungis þat same noe with certeyn of his frenschip in a litil schip seyled in to itayle dwelt and deyid in þat same place whech we clepe now rome. Aftir him dwelt yere *ianus* his sone othir cronicles calle him *ionicus* and þei sey of hym þat he was a grete astronomer for he taut þat sciens on to nembroth he eke prophecied of þe regnes þat wer deryued fro þe sunnys of noe. For of *cam* was he belus born afterward kyng of surry. Of *sem* spronge þei of mede þei of perse and þei eke of grece. And of *iaphet* come þe romaynes. These þingis wrote þis ionicus and many othir. Neuyr þe lasse for I am not sykyr wheythir þese too names longyn to o man or to too þerfor I write what cronicles sey of janus. Ianus þey say with janus his son & his neue tamese biggid þe cite whech þei called *janiclye* and eke ouyr tibur he mad a palcys whcch he clepid *janicle* in þat sam place wher seynt peter cherch stant and þe paleys as I suppose for þis cause for þe hill a boue þese too hith ȝet *mons janiculus.* Sone after þis tyme *saturne* whech was of his owne son gelt and fled fro his cuntre he cam to þe same place and þer aftyr many bataylis he bylid a cyte wher now stant the capitole. In þoo same dayis þe kyng of itaile cam to þe same saturne with all the strength of the siracusanis whech is a cyte of cicile and he bylid eke a grete part of rome fast by the flood þat was þann clepid *albula* and now is it cleped *tibur.* Hercules eke his son as uarro writith mad a cite undir þe capitol whech he clepid ualery. Than cam a kyng þat dwelt up on tybur and mad þer a cyte. Euander after þis kyng of archadye bilid him a cite in þe mount palantine. This same man fled his cuntre as summe men seyn for he had kyllid his fadir at instauns of his moder whech hith hym grete þingis for þe dede and aftirward fled with hym on to rome. Of þis same Euander spekith uirgil in þe uiii book eneydos. Aftir him to men on hith *coroboam* an othir hith *glausus* bylid mech þing in rome. And þann as writith solinus cam a fled woman fro troye whos name was *romen* sumtyme it is seid þat sche was dowtir to eneas and summe tyme it is seid sche was but cosin but sche ȝaue þe name to the cyte as we seide be for longe or remus and romulus wer bore. Wherfor writith þis auctour þat it was for bodyn in her sacraries yat no man schul name þis woman but only put all þe honour on to romulus aftir tyme he had take þe reule. Auentinus eke the kyng of albany mad him a cite in þat hill þat is ȝet called auentyn . . . . (3–4)

The procedure indicated by these passages, of translating Martinus's text and amplifying it, is followed in much of Capgrave's account of classical Rome. He tours the city in the same order, dwelling on the same tourist spots, repeating the information given in his source, but enriching it with a considerable amount of picturesque etymology, anecdote, description, and general information drawn from his further reading, his own observation, and probably oral report. Martinus's introduction (and possibly the *Mirabilia*, the standard medieval guide to Rome) was the inspiration for Capgrave's guide-book for English pilgrims, and what he drew from it was its organization and its brief recital of basic information concerning the holy city.

IV. The author of that thoroughly remarkable polychronicon, *Li Myreur des Histors*, Jean d'Outremeuse of Liège (1338–1400), is also heavily indebted to Martinus Polonus's chronicle of the popes and emperors: it provides him with the slim framework of verifiable fact upon which to stitch the rich embroidery of legend and fiction which he derives from livelier chronicles than Martinus's, from romances of Charlemagne, Ogier, Arthur, Huon of Bordeaux, his own fertile imagination, and his sense of the appropriateness of crediting heroic behaviour to heroes well known rather than to the museum worthies of formal history.

This essay is no place to track down the complicated ways by which the Belgian chronicler perverted Martinus's simple statements into such surprising declarations as that King Arthur fought triumphant campaigns in Africa and established his rule in Persia, the Holy Land, Egypt, and Rome. Instead, we shall illustrate his procedures and indicate what value he put upon Martinus Polonus, by describing his handling of an incident crucial in the study of *Beowulf*.

In the course of his nightmarish account of western Europe in the Dark Ages, Jean has occasion to mention the raid into the Low Countries which is referred to four times in the English poem. This is what he reports of it:

Item, l'an IIII^c et LXXIII, assemblat ly roy Julin de Dannemarche ses hommes, et entrat en la terre de Turinge, qui apartinoit a roy Theoderich d'Austrie, car Julin l'avoit donneit son fis Chlochelais et ly avoit enconvent de conquere; mains ly roy Theoderich li defendit et le corut sus, et là oit fort batalhe, mains les Danois furent desconfis, et Julin et Clochelais ochis. Si fut fais roy de Dannemarche Ector, li autre fis Julin qui astoit ly anneis, qui regnat LVI ans. *Tome* ii, 170.

The Thuringia referred to here is probably the second area known by that name in the Merovingian period, the territory of the Salian Franks in north-east Belgium; while Austrie represents Austrasia, the eastern part of the Frankish kingdom, with Metz as its centre.[1]

Jean's starting-point for this episode, like most of the stories he tells about the Franks, is probably not Gregory of Tours's *Historia Francorum*,[1] but its derivative, the anonymous *Liber Historiae Francorum* (*c.* 727).[2] His lengthy account of the terrifying Frédegonde, for example, contains details of her upbringing and her relations with her lover Landeric which appear in the anonymous chronicle but not in Gregory's. But although it may be the basis for Jean's account of Hygelac's raid, the *Liber* does not provide all the details:

In illo tempore Dani cum rege suo nomine Chochilaico cum navale hoste per alto mare Gallias appetent, Theuderico paygo Attoarios vel alios devastantes atque captivantes, plenas naves de captivis alto mare intrantes, rex eorum ad litus maris resedens. Quod cum Theuderico nuntiatum fuisset, Theodobertum, filium suum, cum magno exercitu in illis partibus dirigens. Quid consequens eos, pugnavit cum eis caede magna atque prostravit, regem eorum interfecit, preda tullit, et in terra sua restituit. (274)

Neither the anonymous chronicle nor Gregory of Tours, however, knows anything of Julin of Denmark, even though Jean has remarkable achievements to relate about him, among them a siege of Cadiz, the conquest of Hungary and other mid-European regions, defeat of the Romans near Pérouse, a battle against Clovis, and this expedition against Theuderic.

But what is most interesting in Jean's story of the raid is of course the precise date he gives for it. The less assured information given by Gregory, the anonymous *History of the Franks*, Fredegar's *Chronicle* and so on, has led *Beowulf*-scholars into not a little puzzlement, for the raid provides the *terminus a quo* for dating

[1] O. M. Dalton, tr., *The History of the Franks by Gregory of Tours* (Oxford, 1927), i, p. 89.

[2] Conveniently published in *Monumenta Germaniae Historica, Scriptores Rerum Merovingicarum*, Tomus II (Hannover, 1888).

the composition of the poem. The estimates remain rather vague. 'All the evidence', writes R. W. Chambers, 'points to Hygelac's raid having been after 516 and probably before 530, although perhaps before 522 and certainly before 531.'[1] Klaeber is even less assured than this: 'The exact date of this event (the all-important starting point of our historical computations in regard to *Beowulf*) cannot be made out. It has commonly been placed at or about 516 A.D.'[2] Jean d'Outremeuse has no such doubts: plain and flat, the raid took place in the year 473.

Unfortunately, this promise of settling once and for all a basic problem in *Beowulf*-studies is completely delusory. Exact as he may seem, Jean is here, as he is so often, perversely inaccurate. Theuderic (Thierri), eldest son of Clovis by a concubine, did not succeed to the throne until 511. And since at his death in 534 he was only fifty-one,[3] in 473 he was scarcely available to deal with a Danish invasion.

The date is spurious, but why Jean should have given it is worth some consideration. So far as can now be judged, he had no special information nor any scholarly reason for preferring that particular year or even for giving any date at all. At a period that would have been more appropriate however—fifty years later—he was absorbed with the astonishing triumphs of King Arthur and his remarkable friend Paris, founder of the capital of France. For Jean's narrative design apparently, Danes were better dealt with elsewhere, and a good spot was when he was telling of Frédegonde, Clovis, and the other formidable personages whose stories he embroidered from the *Liber Historiae Francorum*. And as for the year 473, Jean, like Daniel Defoe and many another prevaricator-historian, was sensitive to the confidence that precise dates inspire: on occasions, to promote belief in his dubious histories, he will even dispute a rival chronicler's accuracy in such matters. And

---

[1] R. W. Chambers, *An Introduction to Beowulf* (Cambridge, 1932), p. 381. See also Dorothy Whitelock, *The Audience of Beowulf* (Oxford, 1951), Chapter ii.

[2] Fr Klaeber, ed., *Beowulf* (New York, 1950), p. 268 note 2.

[3] See entry under Thierri I[er] in Michaud, *Biographie Universelle*, Tome XLI. Dalton, op. cit., i, pp. 100–3; see also Jean d'Outremeuse, op. cit., Tome II, pp. 166–7.

since the chronicle of Martinus Polonus provides him with a back-bone of verifiable history, it is also likely that his dating practices are the inspiration for Jean's. 'Johannes I, nacione Tuschus ex patre Constantino, sedit annis 2, mensibus 8, diebus 18, et cessavit episcopatus diebus 8.' That is Martinus's manner, and nothing could be more reassuring as to the accuracy of everything else. Jean is no less generous: almost every one of his pages is sprinkled with exact-seeming dates, and sometimes he outdoes even Martinus by inventing the very day of the week when something occurred.

Martinus Polonus was a man of worth, faithful servant to two popes for much of his life. As an author he is a man of accurate facts and few words, respectable as a bookkeeping-machine. He is remarkable more for his progeny than for himself. Those we have mentioned here are but a sample; there were others besides. And since his solidity seems to have been a strange inspiration for historians more imaginative and romantic than he was, a more extended study of his influence might prove entertaining.

19

Pre-Conquest Historical Themes in Elizabethan Drama

GEOFFREY BULLOUGH

ON THE WHOLE the medieval chroniclers accepted the legends which had grown up in previous centuries round the lives of ancient kings and saints; but the sixteenth century with a new liking for truth to fact, comparative textual study, and a protestant mistrust of monkish superstition, introduced a certain scepticism into historical studies, sometimes for sectarian reasons, sometimes for more rational motives.

Polydore Vergil had more than a glimmering realization of the importance of evidence when he rejected most of the legends about Brut and Arthur as told by Geoffrey of Monmouth and others, and, although his scepticism was attacked by Leland and Sir John Price, later English historians became cautious in their handling of variant accounts and improbable stories. So John Foxe (though his motives were not entirely scientific) showered contempt on the superstitious lies of Catholic hagiolaters and historians. He told their stories, but only to mock at them, and while regarding Arthur as a historical figure who gave some peace to Britain, he declared the tales of his victories to be 'more fabulous, then that any credit shuld be geven unto them, more worthy to be joyned with the *Iliades* of Homere, then to have place in any Ecclesiasticall hystorie' (*Actes*, 1593, p. 113). Often he gave several versions of a story (e.g. of Earl Godwin's cruelties) without committing himself to any of them.

This attempt at balance appears also in Holinshed, who began his Chronicle by declaring it quite uncertain 'what manner of people did first inhabit this our country'. He showed some humour in discussing the name Albion, and its giants ('none other than a tall kind of men') and 'their beastlie kind of life unto the arrivall of the ladies' (maybe the daughters of Danaus, maybe not); but he did not 'doubt of Brutes comming hither', and followed Geoffrey in his account of early kings of Britain such as Locrine, Lear and Gorboduc, though he mentioned the doubts about their chronology and right names and devoted Chapter 8 to discussing the disagreements among authorities. He was sure that many stories about Arthur and other princes were fictitious reports forged by British bards, 'so unlike to be true, as the tales of Robin Hood, or the gests written by Ariost the Italian in his booke intituled "Orlando Furioso"' (Bk. IV, Ch. 32).

He moved on quickly, 'letting all dissonant opinions of writers passe, as a matter of no such moment that we should neede to sticke therein as in a gluepot'.

Other Elizabethan historians also had some notion of the responsibilities and difficulties of a true history. As Abraham Fleming wrote, introducing his computation of years in Holinshed's book, 'it is not a worke for everie common capacitie, naie it is a toile without head or taile even for extraordinarie wits, to correct the accounts of former ages so many hundred yeares received, out of uncerteinties to raise certeinties, and to reconcile writers dissenting in opinion and report' (I, p. 426).[1]

I have laboured this point because so many literary scholars have accused Elizabethan dramatists of entirely lacking historical sense, any discrimination between the provable, the probable and the impossible. The recent chroniclers whom many of them consulted however made it clear that there were various degrees of credibility. Moreover they showed that pre-Christian civilization in Britain had its own religion, customs and laws; that each of the invaders who followed Brut had a different way of life; and that the Norman Conquest brought radical changes in social organization and culture. If therefore the dramatists retold ancient legends as true, and if they disregarded historical differences, they did so deliberately; and, indeed, many of them, being purveyors of

[1] For Holinshed, see 1587 ed. or ed. H. Ellis, 1807–8.

entertainment rather than educationists, must have rejoiced that the reports of British bards and medieval monks were comparable to Homer, Robin Hood, or *Orlando Furioso*. They asked for nothing better in their source-material.

In fact however the extant plays on pre-Conquest themes fall into four groups, which are not always distinct:

A. plays in which the chronicle-stories of rulers and events are taken as authentic and are utilized mainly for their political and moral teaching, in accordance with the common contemporary view of history as essentially a didactic art, and concerned with statecraft;

B. plays taking their material mainly from the chronicles, and emphasizing less its political implications than the patriotic, domestic and private passions involved;

C. plays which introduce historical figures in situations taken from chronicles, ballads or folklore, and use them as subsidiary material in romantic plots;

D. plays which use historical names in fictitious incidents in romantic plots without reference to the chronicles.

The first two groups fall together by their more serious treatment of history and legend; the second two by their relegation of historical 'fact' to a subsidiary or negligible role. Even in the first two the predominant intention of presenting the past truly does not prevent the introduction of anachronistic scenes, of comic, satiric or fantastic figures. As Professor Irving Ribner points out, the romantic play 'grew up alongside the history play from the very beginning', and its prevalence in the nineties foreshadowed the decline of the history-play proper. But he is inclined to limit the term history-play to the play with a definite didactic intention; and 'when it ceased to serve the didactic functions of history, [it] lost the unity of purpose and design which made it significant as drama'.[1]

This is certainly a tenable view, but Elizabethan dramatists seem not to have had a strict sense of dramatic genres. For them history

[1] *The English History Play in the Age of Shakespeare* (Princeton, 1957), p. 271.

afforded a vast storehouse of exciting incidents and stories about great men, and they often subordinated overt political and moral ideas to the pleasures of strong sensation and laughter. The didactic element in *Henry V* or *Macbeth* is only one ingredient in a wider pattern of action, ethics, and psychology. The Inns of Court men used drama to exemplify political theory; the popular playwrights went to history mainly for its 'human' interest. As Professor Ribner says, they probably cared little for scholarly controversies about historical truth, but it is noticeable that (like Shakespeare himself) they handled the remoter legends with more freedom than recent history. Indeed they were forced to do so, for whereas Hall and Holinshed gave many details about Henry IV, etc., Geoffrey of Monmouth gave only a skeletal plot for *Lear*.

The chroniclers pointed out that Britain had been successfully invaded five times, by Brut, the Romans, the Anglo-Saxons, the Danes, and the Normans. Each of these crises afforded striking dramatic material and it is not surprising that many plays were written about them. In addition the periods in between invasions offered good subjects. Thus the line of Brut to its end in the strife of Ferrex and Porrex, and the legends surrounding Uther Pendragon, Merlin and Arthur, were circles of interest in the reign of a queen who rejoiced to trace her lineage back through King Arthur to Brut and the heroes of Troy. Surprisingly few plays have survived dealing with the Anglo-Saxon kings. There is not even one on King Alfred (although a Latin play *Alvredus* by William Drury was performed at Douai in 1619).

2

If we allot the extant pre-Conquest plays in English[1] to their appropriate groups we get the following scheme:

Group A

Gorboduc, by Sackville and Norton, 1561 (Line of Brut); *The*

---

[1] There were also plays in Latin, including *Fatum Vortigerni* (BM. MS Lansdowne 723) by Thomas Carleton, played 1619 at Douai (Britons v. Saxons); *Fuimus Troes*, by Jasper Fisher, 1633 (Britons v. Romans).

Misfortunes of Arthur, by R. Hughes, 1587/8 (King Arthur); *Locrine*, 1588–91 (Line of Brut).

Group B

Edmond Ironside, Anon. *c.* 1595–1600 (English v. Danes); *King Lear*, by Shakespeare, 1605–6 (Line of Brut); *Macbeth*, by Shakespeare, 1606 (English and Scots); *Bonduca*, by John Fletcher, 1609–14 (Britons v. Romans); *The Valiant Welshman*, by R.A. (Robert Armin?), *c.* 1615 (Britons v. Romans); *Hengist of Kent, or The Mayor of Quinborough*, by Thomas Middleton, 1616–20 (Britons v. Saxons).

Group C

The True Chronicle History of King Leir, Anon. *c.* 1594 (1605) (Line of Brut); *A Knack to Know a Knave*, Anon. 1594 (Edgar and Dunstan); *Cymbeline*, by Shakespeare, 1609–10 (Britons v. Romans); *Nobody and Somebody, with the true Chronicle Historie of Elydore*, Anon. *c.* 1606 (Line of Brut); *The Birth of Merlin*, by W. Rowley, 1620 (Origins of Arthur).

Group D

Old Fortunatus, by T. Dekker, 1599 (Athelstan); *The Welsh Ambassador*, Anon. *c.* 1620? (Athelstan); *The Love-Sick King*, by A. Brewer, *c.* 1604? (pubd. 1655) (Canute); *The Shoemaker a Gentleman*, by W. Rowley, *c.* 1610 (pubd. 1638) (Britons and Romans); *Grim the Collier of Croydon; or The Devil and his Dame, with the Devil and Saint Dunstan*, by I.T., *c.* 1600–20 (pubd. 1662) (St Dunstan).

Much has been written about the Elizabethan history-plays both severally and as a form, and it is difficult not to duplicate what Professor I. Ribner, J. W. Cunliffe, and F. Schelling[1] have said, but I shall illustrate briefly the characteristics of the four groups. Group A was the first to emerge, under the mingled influence of Bale's *King Johann*, *The Mirror for Magistrates*, and Senecan tragedy. *Gorboduc* and *The Misfortunes of Arthur* were written by men trained at the Inns of Court and for performance before an

[1] I. Ribner, op. cit.; J. W. Cunliffe, *Early English Classical Tragedies* (1912); F. E. Schelling, *The English Chronicle Play* (New York, 1902).

audience of lawyers, scholars and courtiers. The Inns of Court dramatists were innovators in technique and (when serious) preachers of law and order and statecraft. They made lavish use of Dumb Shows, the Chorus, a formal balance of scenic presentation, and Senecan revenge motives, and expressed in stylized rhetoric and stichomythia a diversity of passions in an atmosphere of doom. Early British history in the hands of Norton and Sackville (who contributed to *The Mirror for Magistrates*) became a vehicle for political and moral lessons.

So in *Gorboduc* the story of the old king who divided his realm between his two sons Ferrex and Porrex, causing strife, murder, and the collapse of his dynasty, was used to demonstrate the dangers of division in the modern state and the need for a ruler (such as Queen Elizabeth) to name, with help of Parliament, a suitable successor. These themes, of the 'divided land', and of the need for a strong monarchy to prevent the rise of ambitious factions and popular unrest dominated Elizabethan political drama.

The Misfortunes of Arthur, played before the Queen in February 1588, a composite work by members of Gray's Inn, was more Senecan, owing much to the *Agamemnon* and *Thyestes*, and it is a mosaic of Senecan quotations.[1] The plot gives an unusual view of Uther Pendragon and Arthur, for in order to bring early British history into line with the classical family curse, the misfortunes of Arthur are represented as due to Uther's sins and his own. Uther has seduced the wife of Gorlois, king of Cornwall, and had him killed in battle. Gorlois's ghost demands vengeance. Arthur, offspring of a crime, is also said to have committed incest with his sister Anna, and the product of this sin is Mordred (as in Malory's romance), who rebels against his father and brings the line of Uther to an evil end.

Mordred's philosophy of tyranny anticipates Macbeth's practice:

> The Sworde must seldome cease. A Soveraignes head
> Is scantly safe, but whiles it smites. Let him
> Usurpe no Crowne, that likes a guiltles Life.

[1] See J. W. Cunliffe, op. cit., pp. 326-42; I. Ribner, op. cit., pp. 228-36.

The play has less political debate than *Gorboduc*, but the perpetual lesson of history is suggested by Conan, as he and Gildas in IV.3 mourn the death of the nation:

> Or when perhaps our Childrens Children reade,
> Our woefull warres displaid with skilfull penne,
> Theyll thinke they heere some sounds of future facts,
> And not the ruines old of pompe long past.

We do not need to see the tragedy as a *roman à clef* about Scottish affairs[1] or even regard the Mordred-Arthur relationship as an intentionally close parallel to that between Mary Queen of Scots and Elizabeth.[2] Yet the play is much concerned with 'the king's relation to the law, a subject perhaps of particular concern to the members of Gray's Inn',[3] and it must have had topical relevance when performed soon after Mary's execution:

> No worse a vice then lenitie in Kings,
> Remisse indulgence soon undoes a Realme, etc.

The 'divided land' recurs in *Locrine*[4] (S.R. 20 July 1594, Q. 1595), another play in the *Gorboduc* tradition, in which the dying Brutus (Brut) partitions Britain among his three sons, Albanact, Camber, and Locrine, and betrothes the last to Gwendoline, daughter of Corineus. The main plot embroiders the story in Geoffrey of Monmouth, with material from John Higgins's supplement to *The Mirror for Magistrates* (1587 edition), and it shows how Albanact is slain defending the north against Scythian invaders, and how Locrine falls in love with the captive Estrild (IV.1), and abandons his wife, keeping his mistress in an underground palace for seven years before making her his queen (V.1). Gwendoline raises an army and defeats Locrine, who commits suicide, as does Estrild. There are two ghosts in this play, that of Albanact which cries 'Revenge! revenge for blood!' and '*Vindicta,*

---

[1] As did Miss E. H. Waller in *JEGP*, xxiv (1925), 219-45.

[2] G. Reese, *RES*, xxi (1945), 81-9.

[3] I. Ribner, op. cit., p. 231.

[4] On the tangled problems of its authorship see B. Maxwell, *Studies in the Shakespeare Apocrypha* (1956).

vindicta', and that of Corineus; and there are Dumb Shows, presented by Ate, symbolizing what is to happen in each Act. The play differs from *Gorboduc* in having comic scenes in which the Clown Strumbo plays several distinct parts. Political lessons are drawn, but they are less important than the intricacies of plot and passion. The play therefore makes a transition to those in Group B.

In editing the anonymous *Edmond Ironside* (probably before 1600) for the Malone Society, Miss Eleanore Boswell called it 'the most important extant dramatization of Anglo-Saxon history' (p. xii) for its attempt 'to present historical material in dramatic form'. It does so without subordinating events to theory. Both Miss Boswell and Irving Ribner regard the source as Holinshed (Bk. VII, Ch. 8–10); but the play may owe something to Grafton (Pt. VII, pp. 129–37). It gives a fair picture of the struggle between the Saxons and the Danes in a sprawling episodic manner, placing incidents from the reign of Ethelred into that of Edmund, and emphasizing (as did most English chroniclers) the arrogance and cruelty of the Danes, e.g. when Canute kills in cold blood two earls' sons whom he holds as hostages. The Danish counsellor Uskataulf urges Canute to be mild.

> for they are Englishmen, easye to rule
> with lynitie, soe they bee used like men,
> patient of right, impatient of wrong.
>
> (198–200)

Holinshed made much of the treacherous manœuvres of Edrike de Streona, who nevertheless may finally have brought about peace between Canute and Edmund. In the play Edricus is a Machiavellian upstart, glorying in his trickery:

> They cannot so dissemble as I can,
> Cloak, cozen, cog and flatter with the king, etc.
>
> (278–315)

He wants Canute to win because he hates to remember that Egelred raised him from the plough 'to be a duke for all my villainy'. When his parents come to see him he refuses to know them (II.2). He shifts his allegiance from side to side, but Edmond is not deceived, and after he persuades the two kings to fight in single combat he is furious when peace is made. Edricus, like Tresilian in *Woodstock*, is given a sinister comic henchman, Stich.

Edmond Ironside is a play not of ideas or political morality but of patriotic sentiment and busy plotting. Instead of Emma's marriage to Canute (as in Holinshed) we are shown him falling in love and marrying Egina, daughter of Southampton, an invention which leads nowhere.

The piece needed a sequel, for it ended with thwarted enemies demanding revenge. Maybe this was provided by the Henslowe *Kanewtus* of 1597 (see below). Plays showing the Danes as formidable foes finally reconciled to the English were probably popular in the late nineties for two reasons: first, because James VI, the likely heir to Queen Elizabeth, had a Danish wife, and second, because there was a dispute between England and Denmark about dues which the Danes claimed were payable by English merchants sailing into Danish ports. This culminated in the Danish king's assertion that England owed him annual tribute and had done so ever since the Danish Conquest! No doubt we should see the exchange of ambassadors and the references to tribute in *Hamlet* in this context.

Contrast with this loose play the much later and better organized *Bonduca* of John Fletcher (1609–14), which sought to compress into one tragedy the efforts of Bonduca (Boadicea) and Caratack (Caratacus) to beat back the Roman invaders. It presents also a vivid contrast between British and Roman attitudes to life. Most of the material came from Holinshed (Bk. IV, Ch. 6–7 for Caratack, Ch. 10–13 for 'Voadicia' or 'Boudicia'), but although Caratack was of the Silures and Bonduca of the Iceni tribe, and Caratack was captured some years before the Iceni revolted, Fletcher brings them together, suggesting that he may have been the brother of her dead husband Prasutagus.

Their association makes an admirable contrast, for whereas Caratack is generous to a fault and admires the Romans ('I love an enemy'; 'I am married to the man that woundes me'), Bonduca is ruthless and vengeful, as is natural in a woman whose kingdom has been despoiled, her daughters ravished, and she herself beaten by Roman soldiers. Whereas she and her chiefs sacrifice to their gods before battle (III.1), Caratack scorns these ritual petitions ('The gods love courage armed with confidence') and he can admire the Romans as they line up for battle (III.3).

In addition, drawing on Holinshed's description of difficulties and dissension among the Romans, Fletcher introduces motives reminiscent of *Troilus and Cressida* and *Antony and Cleopatra*.[1] The Roman troops, short of supplies, have lost their wonted discipline, and Fletcher invents the incident (II.3) when Judas and his company, while out foraging, are captured, tormented by Bonduca, but fed by Caratack—a kindness ill repaid later when Caratack and the boy Hengo are betrayed by Judas when they in turn are starving among the rocks. The Roman general Penius refuses to take part in a battle (II.1), and then (like Enobarbus) commits suicide in remorse.

A love interest is invented when a young Roman officer falls in love with Bonduca's younger daughter (cf. Achilles with Polyxena), and is trapped by her with his troop. Saved by Caratack, he recovers from his infatuation, and (like Troilus) becomes 'Dead to all folly and know my anger only' (1728).

As a history-play which tries to communicate not so much the precise details of the past but its spirit as seen by a Jacobean court-dramatist, *Bonduca* is a successful work, with its respect for the high courage of the British women, the chivalry of Caratack, the generosity of Suetonius, and the fine rhetoric that pervades it.

Turning to the old *King Leir* and Shakespeare's transmutation of it, we see how the same basic material could be made to serve very different aims. Neither *King Leir* nor Shakespeare's play is a play primarily of political didacticism, though there is much more attention to problems of state in the latter. In the older play the legend descending from Geoffrey of Monmouth is romanticized and made domestic. Leir's test on his daughters is merely a trick to get Cordeilla, who is unwilling to marry except for love, to prove

[1] Cf. I. Ribner, op. cit., pp. 264–5.

her affection for her father by marrying someone he chooses. The other daughters swear that they will marry as he wishes, knowing well the choice he has made for them. Cordeilla's marriage is made romantic, for the king of Gallia and his friend Mumford come over disguised as pilgrims to inspect 'the gallant British Dames'. He falls in love with the woeful Cordeilla, and reveals himself when she returns his love.

In addition the anonymous author makes Ragan suborn the Messenger to kill Leir and his faithful old servant Perillus, but the murderer is affected by their pleading and warned against murdering them by thunder and lightning, Heaven's admonition out of a clear sky. Since they receive no answer from Leir to their letter asking him to come to Gallia, Cordeilla and her husband start for Britain disguised as a country couple, and meet Leir and Perillus who have crossed the Channel, paying for their passage by exchanging clothes with two mariners. There is an affecting recognition-scene, after which the sisters are defeated in battle and Leir is restored to his throne.

This is, as Ribner declares, 'a sentimental fairy story' and as such has been placed in Group C, but it is also a play about the bad sisters' breach of 'nature's sacred law'. Cordeilla is bound 'by nature' to love her father and to lament his ill-will to her, and Leir comes to realize his 'unkindness'.

In rehandling the story Shakespeare has cut out most of the fairy-tale stuff and vastly increased both the political and the moral implications, insisting on Lear's twofold folly in abdicating and in trusting the hypocritical daughters. Keeping closer to Geoffrey of Monmouth's outline of events he adds new characters to a picture of a feudal society in disruption, emphasizes the turmoil in Lear's mind, and makes the power of evil over aged folly more potent by adding the story of Edmund, Edgar and Gloucester (from Sidney's *Arcadia*), until the naïve tragicomedy of the earlier piece becomes a great cosmic tragedy in which the goodness of the Universe is questioned and the beauty of individual virtue shining in the naughty world is barely enough to make life endurable.

We may take as typical of Group C a play which may have been a *riposte* to Fletcher's piece, namely *The Valiant Welshman* (1615) by R.A. (possibly the comedian Robert Armin). The Address to the Reader refers to Tacitus, *Annals*, Bk. xii, which tells how Publius Ostorius defeated Caractacus, who was then betrayed by Cartamanda, queen of the Brigantes, to the Romans and pardoned by Claudius (Ch. 33–7). The play however owes much also to Holinshed, and follows the events there told more closely than did Fletcher.

But the play is really a romantic medley. Caradoc (Caractacus) captures the Emperor Claudius, lets him go free, and is recognized later by means of the armlet Claudius gave him. Cartamanda is made wife of Venusius, governor of York. Caradoc's sister Voada narrowly escapes the lust of the Roman Marcus Galericus in a *Rape of Lucrece* scene. Other fantastic adventures are added. A witch raises a serpent to slay Caradoc, who is told how to defeat it with herbs (iv.2). The witch's son is converted to white magic and helps to free Voada by using a spell of invisibility. In a comic scene modelled on the Gravedigger scene in *Hamlet* a coroner's quest is held to decide whether Gloucester committed suicide. The whole play is framed by a Presenter, a Bard raised by Fortune from his tomb, with the help of four harpers who sing the praises of Wales —no doubt because the piece was performed before the Prince of Wales.

Long before this *A Knack to Know a Knave*, played by Lord Strange's Company in 1592, had presented an example of minimal history combined with numerous other elements. The play is set in the reign of King Edgar and the 'historical' plot tells how he sends Earl Ethenwold of Cornwall to woo Alfrida for him, and how the earl, falling in love with her, reports that she is ill-favoured. The king lets him marry her but discovers the deceit, pretends to forgive him but resolves to kill him. In the legend as told by Grafton (i.125), Holinshed (Bk. vi, Ch. 24) and Foxe (p. 155) the king actually murdered Ethenwold while out hunting, and St Dunstan put him to seven years' penance for this and other sexual crimes. In the play however Dunstan makes him spare

Ethenwold and repent. For the rest the piece is mainly a Morality with modern social comment, for we see the four sons of the Bailiff of Hexham, a courtier, a priest, a conny-catcher and a farmer, all behaving badly, till they are exposed by Honesty, the king, or Dunstan, and there are other incidents including the mad men of Gotham and a scene in which Dunstan raises the Devil, and the episode of an unkind son whose father, forced to act as his judge, is all for lenity as his parent, but for severity speaking in the name of justice.

Nobody and Somebody combines quaint allegory of the kind beloved of Elizabethan popular satirists, with the story of Elidure, the gentle soul who was king of Britain three times. *The Birth of Merlin* mingles the legends of Merlin's supernatural birth and prophecies, and the wars between British and Saxons under Aurelius, and Uther, with the (fictitious) plots of a Saxon woman Artesia who captivates Aurelius and alienates his faithful friends. There is a saintly Hermit Anselm whose white magic conquers the Saxon wizards. He takes part in another set of incidents concerning two maidens, Constantia and Modestia, who finally refuse marriage and retire into a nunnery 'Secluded from the world of men for ever'. It is an attractive play where the pretence of history is completely overborne by grotesque comedy and romance.

The plays in Group D need not detain us long, since they merely use historical names in entirely fictitious incidents. Thus Dekker's *Old Fortunatus* (1599) was based on a German folk-tale which had been dramatized by Hans Sachs. The tale had nothing to do with England, but Dekker's play brings one of Fortunatus's sons, Andelocia, to the court of King Athelstane, who is shown as greedy for the secret of Andelocia's wealth. There is no history in this piece. Rowley's *The Shoemaker a Gentleman* (taken like Dekker's *Shoemaker's Holiday* from Deloney's *Gentle Craft*) is set in Roman times, and tells how, when the Emperor Maximianus ravaged Britain, the fugitive princes Crispine and Crispianus served as apprentices to a shoemaker at Feversham. The *Love-Sick King* is a farrago of pseudo-history in which Canute (d. 1035) is represented as falling in love with an English nun, who agrees to be his queen, but is killed by a Danish noble to save the king from his folly ('Let not a Strumpets love, work all our ruine'). Canute is defeated by Alfred (who died in 901). The play also celebrates the rise to fortune of a northern Dick Whittington, Roger Thornton, first Mayor of Newcastle (d. 1430). In *Grim the Collier of Croydon* St Dunstan is introduced (from the Golden Legend) into a piece which combines Belphegor from Machiavelli's comedy, Malbecco from *The Faerie Queene*, III.9, and the indigenous folk-hero Grim who overcomes his rivals for the hand of a modest country maid.

Such plays show that in presenting unhistorical stories popular dramatists felt at liberty to set them wherever they liked in the past and to use historical figures without respect for time, place, or probability.

3

In addition to the plays which we can still read there were many more now lost whose existence we know of from contemporary references. For those performed by the several acting companies with which he had business connections between 1591 and 1602 as pawnbroker, moneylender, or banker, the *Diary* of Philip Henslowe gives the titles and often the authors' names. It is not an idle pastime to speculate what the lost plays contained. I therefore give below a list of the Henslowe plays with pre-Conquest titles, with the first-noted date of performance in his theatre,[1] and suggestions about the probable historical material used in them as provided by some of the chief chroniclers used by Elizabethan playwrights.[2]

1. *Constantine* (*Diary*, p. 17). Played 21 March 1591 only.

---

[1] References to pages in the *Diary* are to the ed. by R. A. Foakes and R. T. Rickert (Cambridge, 1961). W. W. Greg's ed. (1904–8) briefly discusses possible themes.

[2] Works consulted include: Geoffrey of Monmouth (Everyman ed.); R. Fabyan, *New Chronicles* (1516); R. Grafton, *Chronicle at Large* (1569), 1809 ed.; R. Holinshed, *Chronicles* (1587), 1807 ed.; J. Foxe, *Actes and Monuments* (1593 ed.); J. Stow, *Annales* (1592); *A Mirror for Magistrates*, ed. L. B. Campbell (1938); *Parts added to Mirror for Magistrates*, ed. L. B. Campbell (Cambridge, 1946).

Presumably not a new play. There were several British and also Scottish kings of this name. Greg suggested that Constantine would be Uther's father. 'Of this Constantine [says Grafton] is little written', except that he was the father of Constancius (whom he made a monk), Aurelius Ambrosius, and Uther Pendragon, and that a Pict whom he had favoured 'by a secret means slue the King in his Chamber' (1.73). Holinshed took from Geoffrey of Monmouth the story that he drove back the Picts and Scots after Britain was abandoned by the Romans (Bk. v.1).

It seems more likely that the play was about Constantine the Great, who had near connections with Britain. His father Constantius, 'a senatour of Rome, began to reigne over the Britains, in the yeere of our Lord 289. . . . This Constantius had to wife, Helen the daughter of the [British] king Coel, of whome he begat a sonne named Constantinus, whiche after was emperour' (Hol. IV.28; cf. Grafton, 1.68–9).

An English play would probably include some of the following features:

(i) references to his mother Helena, 'which Helen was very beautifull and fayre, and therewith had learninge and many other vertues' . . . and 'which Elyn . . . founde the Crosse at Jerusalem, on the which our Saviour Christ suffered his passion, and three of the Nayles wherewith his handes and feete were pierced' (Grafton);

(ii) the struggle between Constantine and Maxentius, 'the worst of men . . . and persecuted the Christians with all kindes of torments' (Grafton). Constantine defeated Maxentius three times after crossing the Alps, the last time near Rome (A.D. 312);

(iii) Constantine's conversion during this campaign. Previously under the influence of his wife Fausta, he had worshipped idols (Foxe). But 'he saw in the night season, the signe of the Crosse shining in the Element lyke a fyre, and an Angell by it saying on this wise: In this signe thou shalt overcome. Wherefore receyving great comfort thereby, he gathered such a courage that shortly after he vanquished the armie of *Maxencius*, and put him to flight, who in the chase was drowned in Tyber' (Grafton, 1.69). After

303

his conversion he delayed his baptism because he hoped to be baptised in the River Jordan; he was christened on his deathbed.

Possibly the play would allude also to (iv) the troubles in Britain during his absence, owing to the ambition of his lieutenant Octavius. Polydore Vergil however asserted that 'the Realme was in good quiet all the tyme of Constantine'. 'Whereby [Grafton comments] it may apere what great varietie there is even among the . . . most approved story writers.' Holinshed too discounted the story, claiming that Octavius ruled Britain long and well (IV.29).

2. *A Knack to Know a Knave* (*Diary*, p. 19). 'ne' on 10 June 1592.[1] It was registered on 7 Jan. 1593/4 and published in 1594. (See above.)

3. *William the Conqueror* (*Diary*, p. 20). Played by the earl of Sussex's men on 4 Jan. 1593/4. Not a new play; possibly a revival of *Faire Em the Millers Daughter of Manchester, with the love of William the Conqueror* (*c.* 1590). But the conquest of England and the Conqueror's previous and subsequent life offered excellent material for drama.

4. *King Lud* (*Diary*, p. 20). Played 18 Jan. 1593/4. Apparently a revival by Sussex's men. This would be very much a play for Londoners, since Lud (who began to reign about 72 B.C.) was famed as a great builder. 'He . . . repayred olde Cities and townes, and specially the Citie of Troynovaunt, where he caused many buildings to be made, and also made about the sayde Citie a strong wall. And in the west part of the sayde wall, he erected and made a strong and fayre Gate, . . . which at this day is called Ludgate. And for that he loved this City, he used much and often to lye therin, by reason wherof it was called Caerlud, or Luds towne, and after by corruption of speech, it was after called, and is so named at this day, London' (Grafton, 1.51).

Grafton (but not Holinshed, or Stow's *Annales*, 1592) would provide some conflict for the play's action, since he relates (after Bale) that 'there fell great dissension between Lud and his brother

---

[1] 'ne' in the *Diary* apparently meant that the play was new, or new to the company, or newly revised or licensed.

Nennius . . . about the chaunging of the name of Troynovaunt into Luddes towne, or London, because it might be the occasion that the memorie of Troy and the worthie deedes there done, should thereby be buried in oblivion, and be forgotten'. Lud was a good soldier, 'also bounteous and liberall and kept a great houshold', so that he was greatly beloved. When he died he was 'buried in his gate called Ludgate', leaving two young sons under the protection of his brother Cassivelan. Nennius later died fighting against Julius Caesar, and Cassivelan, after repulsing the invader, was forced to become a tributary of Rome.

5. *King Lear* (*Diary*, p. 21). Played 'by the Quenes men and my lord of Susexe to geather' 6 April 1593/4. Entered in S.R. 14 May 1594, but probably not printed till 1605 after another entry on 8 May, 'As it was latelie Acted'. This would be Shakespeare's source-play (see above, p. 298f.).

6. *Cutlack* (*Diary*, p. 21). Played by 'my lorde admeralls men', 16 May 1594; then 'At Newington, my lord Admeralls men and my Lorde chamberlens men': 6 June 1594.

The life of St Guthlac (673?–714), subject of a fine Old English poem, would afford excellent material for a play, for after being a warrior he turned hermit at Crowland, was tormented by demons and nearly murdered by his own scholar, held converse with an angel, and foretold his own death. But it is unlikely that a story so full of miracles and piety would find much favour in the nineties. More probably this play was an offshoot of the saga of Belinus and Brennus (about whom Sir John Harington had one or perhaps two plays in his library).[1]

According to Grafton (as usual summarizing Geoffrey of Monmouth's more artistic narrative), Belinus and Brennus divided Britain after the death of their father Mulmutius Dunwallow, Belinus having the south, Brennus the north. They quarrelled and fought, and Brennus, being defeated, sailed to Norway where he married the daughter of King Elfung. Learning that Belinus had seized his lands, he sailed towards Britain with a great force of Norwegians.

[1] See his list of plays in 1610: 'Belynus, Brennus' (7 *N. & Q.*, ix, 382).

And as he was keeping his course upon the sea, he was encountered with Guilthdacus King of Denmarke, the which had lyen in awayte for him, for love of a Damsell that he had maried which before tyme was promised unto the saide Guilthdacus by the saide Elfunge her father. When these two Navies were met, strong shot and fight was upon both parties: But finally the Danes overcame the Norwayes, and tooke the ship by strength, wherein the yong Damsell was, who was quickly brought unto the ship of Guilthdake . . .' (1.42).

Unfortunately for the Danish king, he was driven back by a storm, and 'was enforced to land in Northumberland, where at that tyme was Belyn making of preparation of defence against his brothers coming'. So Guilthdacus and the girl were captured.

Brennus then demanded his wife, and his patrimony, from his brother, and when Belinus 'plainly and shortly denied' him, he landed in Albany and fought him in a 'mortall and terrible battayle'. The Britons won, and Brennus fled to Gallia.

Belinus then held a council at York; 'In the which counsayle it was concluded, that the aforesayde Guilthdacus should holde and do homage to the King of Briteyn for the land of Denmarke, and yerely pay unto him a thousand pound for a tribute: which beyng done with suretie and hostages, the sayd Guilthdacus with his woman, was set at libertie, and returned into his owne Country' (Grafton, 1.42–3; cf. Holinshed, III.2).

This story, which also formed an episode in the long 'complaint' of Brennus in the 1587 *Mirror for Magistrates* (Campbell, pp. 259–79), had much to commend it: the Divided Land, the victory of Britons over foreigners, a double love-story with the Norwegian maid at the centre, scenes set in several countries, with battles and councils.

Henslowe's *Diary* shows little sign of early themes between November 1594 and January 1595/6.

7. *Fortunatus* (*Diary*, p. 34). 10 Feb. 1595/6. This was probably the play on which Dekker based his play of the same name in 1599 (see below).

8. *Vortigern* (*Volteger*) (*Diary*, p. 49). It is probably the play 'henges' performed on 22 June 1597, and it may have formed the

basis of *Hengist King of Kent, or The Mayor of Quinborough*, written by Thomas Middleton between 1616 and 1620 but not printed until 1661. But this cannot be proved, and Middleton certainly refashioned any source he used.[1] In any case, this would be necessary in shifting the emphasis from Vortigern to Hengist.

The story of Vortigern, as told by Geoffrey and retold by Ranulph Higden, Fabyan, Grafton (I.73–80) and Holinshed (v. 1–8), falls roughly into the following sections on which a play might be built:

(i) Vortigern's seizure of the throne. The British king Constantine left three sons, two young children, Aurelius Ambrosius and Uther Pendragon, and an older son Constans, a weakling and a monk. The cunning Earl Vortigern persuaded Constans to be king, with himself as his adviser, and crowned him himself (Middleton's I.I covers this). Vortigern then got the royal treasure and power into his own hands and filled Constans's retinue with drunken Picts whom he tricked into killing the king. (Middleton eliminated most of this but showed the murder in a Dumb Show. II.I.) Vortigern then punished the killers and seized the throne. Constans's two brothers escaped by leaving the country. (This also is in the Dumb Show and Chorus iii.)

(ii) The introduction of the Saxons into Britain. Vortigern feared the vengeful Picts and also the return of the two brothers. Accordingly, when the Saxon chieftains Hengist and Horsa (Hersus) landed in Britain he retained them in his service and they soon defeated the Picts in the north. They were rewarded with a 'hide' of land which they increased by dividing the hide into a thong (*Hengist*, II.3).

(iii) Vortigern's infidelity. He fell in love with Rowena, Hengist's daughter, and forsook his wife and three sons for her. (Middleton makes Roxena Hersus's mistress and by a wicked trick has Hengist's wife Castiza condemned as unchaste. II.3, III.I, 2, IV.I.) Angered by Vortigern's welcoming the Saxons and making a pagan woman his queen, the Britons revolted and made his son

[1] See the edition by R. C. Bald (New York and London, 1938), Introduction.

Vortimer king. Rowena poisoned the young man and Vortigern was restored to the throne on condition that he expel the Saxons (*Hengist*, Dumb Show iii).

(iv) The murder of the British nobles. At a feast to celebrate peace the Saxons came hiding long knives in their boots, and at a given signal murdered the British lords, but spared Vortigern, and freed him after he had given them lands and privileges. (Middleton omits the bloody banquet but shows Vortigern seized and forced to make Hengist king of Kent, Norfolk and Suffolk. IV.3.)

(v) Vortigern's tower and the coming of Merlin. Geoffrey of Monmouth now moves into magic and folklore as he tells how Vortigern, going to Wales, began to build a strong tower, but as fast as it was erected it sank into the earth. Being told that the spell could be undone only by a boy who had never had a father, after a long search they found Merlin, whose mother declared that she had been loved by a supernatural being 'in the shape of a right comely youth'. Merlin disclosed that the tower had been built over a pool, and that under the pool slept two dragons. He also foretold that Vortigern would soon be attacked both by the Saxons and by Aurelius Ambrosius and Uther Pendragon, and that he would perish by fire in a Welsh castle. These things happened. (In Middleton Merlin has no part, and Vortiger and Hersus stab each other and perish with Roxena in the burning castle.) This material was used in *The Birth of Merlin*.

(vi) The accession of Aurelius Ambrosius. Aurelius battled long against Hengist, aided by Eldol, duke of Gloucester, and in the end defeated the Saxon chief in single combat. He ruled Britain wisely and was succeeded by Uther Pendragon, whose son was Arthur.

(vii) The coming to Britain of St Germanus, sent to combat the Pelagian heresy. (In *Hengist* Germanus helps Vortiger to persuade Constans that it is his duty to become king in 1.1.)

It seems likely that the Henslowe *Vortigern* followed the chronicles fairly closely, perhaps with the appearance of Merlin (who is ignored here by Grafton and discredited by Holinshed). Most of

Middleton's comic material, the plot against Castiza and Hersus's intrigue with Roxena, were probably his own invention.

9. *Uther Pendragon* (*Diary*, p. 58). Some four and a half months after the production of *Volteger* the Admiral's men put on what was probably a sequel, 'ne' on 29 April 1597. Receipts were high and it was performed seven times in all by 13 June. On 22 June *Henges* (which may well have been *Volteger*) was revived, with poor receipts.

With the reign of Uther we are deep in the conflicting reports of Welsh legends and English chronicles, which make Grafton and Holinshed doubtful about both facts and chronology, so different were the accounts given by Geoffrey of Monmouth, Hector Boethius, Polydore Vergil, etc. Since Geoffrey's is the fullest and most dramatic story, and made much of the wonders which were still associated with Uther's name in the sixteenth century, the following summary follows his account (Bk. VIII, Ch. 14–22).

(i) The accession of Uther. After Vortigern's death Aurelius Ambrosius fought doughtily against the Saxons, and by Merlin's advice and help shifted a great circle of stones from Ireland to Stonehenge. The Irish King and Vortigern's son Pascentius invaded Britain when Aurelius was ill, and they craftily sent a Saxon disguised as a British doctor, who poisoned Aurelius. When he died a bright star appeared over Britain with a ray in the likeness of a dragon. Merlin, who was on the march with Uther in Wales, interpreted this portent, and Uther henceforth called himself Pendragon.

(ii) Uther's crime against Gorlois. In a great battle against Hengist's kinsmen Octa and Eosa Uther was assisted by Gorlois, duke of Cornwall. Octa and Eosa were captured and taken to London. At his coronation Uther saw Igerne, Gorlois's beautiful wife, and fell madly in love with her, so obviously indeed that Gorlois became jealous, took her away from the court, and refused to return. The king thereupon ravaged Cornwall. Gorlois placed Igerne in the almost inaccessible castle at Tintagel, and himself was besieged at Dimilioc. Learning where she was, Uther asked Merlin's advice. The magician thereupon changed the king into the likeness of Gorlois, and accompanied him to Tintagel, where they were welcomed by the unsuspecting Igerne. Uther lay with her, and that night Arthur was conceived. During the king's absence the beleaguered Gorlois sallied out and was slain. The messengers arriving at Tintagel to announce his death were amazed to see him apparently there sitting with his wife. Uther went out, regained his own shape, took Tintagel, and married Igerne, by whom he had not only Arthur but a daughter Anna.

(iii) The return of Octa and Eosa. After many years Uther fell ill; the imprisoned Saxon chiefs suborned their gaolers, escaped and went to Germany, then invaded Britain with a great army. Against them Uther sent Lot of Leicester, to whom he had given Anna as wife. Lot however could not drive out the Saxons, for the British lords were lukewarm and disloyal.

(iv) Uther's last fight and death. Although Uther was very ill, he upbraided his lords and said that he would lead them into battle. So he had himself carried in a litter and laid siege to Verulam, where the Saxons (scorning the sick general) had not troubled to close the gates. However they withstood the British attack and were not defeated until after two days' hard fighting. They sent spies into the British camp and these poisoned the spring whose waters alleviated the king's sickness. So Uther died and was buried at Stonehenge, and his son Arthur reigned in his stead.

10. *Hardicanute* (*Diary*, p. 60). 19 Oct. 1597. And (11.) *Canutus* on 3 Nov. Were they the same play?

The reign of this son of the great Canute was not very dramatic, but he was the last Danish king of England, and his reign ushered in the period before the Norman Conquest during which Earl Godwin was powerful (Grafton, 1.141–2; Holinshed, VII.14–15). The play may therefore have been a prologue to the Godwin plays which followed.

The piece may well have begun with the dispute about the succession when Canute died. He had two illegitimate sons (Harold and Sweyn) by his concubine Alvina (or Ælgina), before he married Emma, Egelred's widow, who bore him a son, Hardicanute. The dispute was between the friends of Harold, led by Leofric, and those of Hardicanute, led by Godwin. Harold (Harefoot) was chosen and proved a bad ruler. He banished Emma and her two eldest sons and reigned ('with little fruite, and lesse profite to the land, nor yet of the Subjectes' (Grafton)), and died after three years. Hardicanute, who was king of Denmark, succeeded and brought back Emma from Bruges. He took revenge on Harold by having his body disinterred and thrown into the Thames. According to Ranulph Higden 'he caused first the dead head of his brother to be smitten off and then thrown into the River'. (Cf. the head of Cloten in *Cymbeline*, IV.2.151–2.) The body was found by a fisherman and buried in St Clement Dane's.

Views about Hardicanute differed. For Polydore Vergil he was a hospitable monarch, 'no less gentle than liberal, and especially in banquet . . . oftentimes feasting of the people and such as would eat, three sundry times a day'.[1] For Grafton he was a prodigal tyrant, levying Danegeld and giving it 'unto Mariners and Shipmen and to sundry lewde persons' (I.142). He burned the city of Worcester when one of his agents gathering Danegeld was killed, and he gave control of the country to Emma and Godwin, 'by whom many things were disordered, and specially by the subtilty of the Erle Godwin'. After two years he died suddenly at a marriage feast in Lambeth, 'not without suspicion of poison'.

After Hardicanute's death the nobles made Egelred's son Alfred king, and drove out the arrogant Danes, and 'by common consent a decree was made, that never hereafter any Dane should be elected King of England' (P. Vergil, p. 283).

Grafton however relates that when Emma returned she brought over not only her two sons but also 'a great number of Normans'. Godwin wished to marry his daughter Goditha to one of the brothers and, realizing that Alfred 'would disdain that marriage', he chose Edward, and resolved to get rid of Alfred so that Goditha might become queen. Getting powers from the nobles, he massacred many of the Normans, and put out Alfred's eyes, but Emma sent Edward overseas again. This may have occurred

[1] *Polydore Vergil's English History*, ed. Sir H. Ellis (Camden Soc., 1846), i, p. 281.

before Hardicanute's death, and would strengthen an otherwise weak plot.

12. *Earl Goodwin and his Three Sons* (*Diary*, p. 88). On 25 March 1598 Henslowe lent the company £4 to buy the book of this play from Drayton, Dekker, Chettle, and Wilson. Apparently they had read the piece in a tavern (probably the Sun) in Fish Street, and he paid 5s. 'for good cheare'. On 30 March he lent another 40s. in final payment, and on 11 April 24s. to buy taffeta 'to macke a Rochet for the beshoppe in earlle goodwine'.

13. *The Second Part of Earl Goodwin* (*Diary*, p. 89). Henslowe lent Chettle and Dekker 20s. on 6 April towards this playbook. On 6 June he lent Drayton 10s. Four days later he advanced 50s. as final payment. On 26 June he lent £5 for satin to make two doublets, and on 27 June provided 30s. for various things for the production.

It is impossible to be sure at what point in Godwin's life the first play began; but since the Admiral's men had recently performed *Hardicanute*, it seems likely that it started after his death and the accession of Edward the Confessor in 1043. Holinshed accepts the usual view that Godwin was glad of Edward's gentleness and piety because it let him increase his own power. His general opinion of the earl is less favourable than that expressed by William Harrison in the *Description of England* printed in Holinshed's first volume—for Harrison he was a stout defender of the English against the Norman menace. Some of the following were probably included in the plays (cf. Grafton, 1.143–6; Holinshed, VIII.1–2):

(i) Edward's accession and marriage. The new king forgave any part Godwin had had in the death of Alfred, and married Godwin's daughter Goditha (Editha), though he probably 'never had to do with hir in fleshlie wise. But whether he abstained because he had haply vowed chastitie, either of impotencie of nature, or for a privie hate that he bare to hir kin, men doubted' (Holinshed).

(ii) The ordeal of Queen Emma. Edward seems to have blamed her for marrying Canute, 'the publike enemie of the realme', and for not helping her sons while they were in exile. She was despoiled of her property. Worse: she was accused of misconduct with the bishop of Winchester, and forced to undergo the ordeal by walking barefooted over nine red-hot ploughshares; which she did unharmed. Edward then restored her to favour.

(iii) The banishment of Sweyn. Godwin's son Sweyn had a mistress, the abbess Edgiva, and proposed to forsake his wife to marry her. For this and other misdemeanours he was banished. He returned to seek pardon, but in a fit of malice he slew one of his chief supporters, his cousin (some say his half-brother) Bearn. He fled to Flanders and later was allowed to return.

(iv) The banishment of Godwin and his sons. In about 1051 Eustace, earl of Boulogne (father of the hero Godfrey), who had married Edward's sister Githa, came on a visit; but at Canterbury (some say Dover) one of his harbingers was killed while rudely demanding lodgings, and Eustace retaliated by killing about twenty townsmen. A riot followed, and the earl narrowly escaped death. The king ordered Godwin, as earl of Kent, to punish the townsfolk, and when he refused to do so unless they were proved in the wrong, the king called a council at Gloucester to consider the matter. Godwin was afraid and refused to go unless with a large force. Soon civil war was imminent. The king gathered a large army; Godwin and his sons did the same, Sweyn from the West Midlands, Harold from the East Midlands. According to some authorities, the king's army refused to fight against Englishmen on behalf of foreigners; so a truce was made and then Godwin was ordered to appear before him in London. This Godwin feared to do, and when his soldiers began to desert in large numbers he fled to Flanders, with Sweyn and Tostig, while Harold went to Ireland.

The end of the first play may have come either with their departure into exile or with the truce patched up when the royal forces refused to fight. The second part was probably largely concerned with events during the exile and after until his death, and may have also included material about the sons which occurred later (Grafton, i.146-50; Holinshed, viii.3-7):

(i) The ill-treatment of Queen Editha. Afraid maybe of her

influence, the king put her away from him and had her rigorously confined to an abbey. Some historians asserted that she was no better than she should be, but later she swore that she had always lived chastely.

(ii) The visit of Duke William of Normandy. During Godwin's exile the bastard William, duke of Normandy, visited King Edward, who loaded him with gifts, and (some said) made him 'heire to the realme of England, if he chanced to die without issue' (Holinshed).

(iii) Godwin in exile. Godwin and his sons became sea-rovers and preyed upon the southern coasts of England. Godwin even sailed up the Thames and under the bridge at Southwark, where he had an army waiting on the south bank. There was grave danger of a battle, but 'they were loth to fight one against another', and negotiations followed.

(iv) Godwin's return. Godwin regained his possessions, and his daughter was restored to Edward's palace. The Norman Robert, archbishop of Canterbury, an old enemy of Queen Emma's and of Godwin, was banished, and went to Rome, where he was the first English subject to make complaint to the pope against his lawful king. His successor Stigand was 'nothing learned', but covetous and worldly. (This would give good opportunity for satire on the Church.)

(v) Earl Godwin's death. This would make a good scene, if the playwrights regarded him as guilty of Alfred's death. For at a banquet, when his guilt was hinted at, he 'tooke a piece of bread, and did eate it, saying: "God let me never swallow this bread downe into my chest, but that I may presentlie be choked there-with, if ever I was weeting or consenting unto Alfred's death!" and immediatlie therewith he fell downe starke dead' (Holinshed VIII.4).

(vi) Very probably the play included the deeds of the three sons. Sweyn was said to have remained a rebel and a pirate, until, repenting of the murder of Bearn, he 'went on a pilgrimage to Hierusalem, and died by the way, of cold which he caught returning homeward (as some write) in Licia: but others affirme, that he fell into the hands of Saracens that were robbers by the high waies, and so was murthered of them' (ibid., VIII.3).

Tostig quarrelled with Harold, who struck him in the king's presence. Tostig took a horrible revenge, for, going to Hereford, where Harold's household was preparing for a visit from the king, he slew the servants, dismembered them, and put the limbs into the tubs of food and barrels of wine and cider, 'sending the King word that he had provided against his coming good plentie of sowse and powdred meat, whatsoever he should find beside' (ibid., VIII.7). Later he joined Harald Harfager in the north and was defeated by Harold.

Harold succeeded Edward the Confessor, but before that he had been over to Normandy, either shipwrecked or voluntarily, and had been forced to swear an oath to help William become king of England. These incidents, which occurred after Godwin's death, may well have been placed before it by the dramatists.

(vii) There is also a possibility that the play contained reference to Macbeth, for Holinshed mentions that Scottish writers told how 'Siward the noble earle of Northumberland with a great power of horssemen went into Scotland, and in battell put to flight Mackbeth that had usurped the crowne of Scotland, and that doone, placed Malcolme surnamed Camoir, the sonne of Duncane, sometime king of Scotland, in the government of that realme, who afterward slue the said Mackbeth, and then reigned in quiet' (VIII.5).

14. *The Life of King Arthur* (*Diary*, p. 89). On 12 April 1598, Henslowe advanced £4 in payment for this play by Richard Hathaway. On 2 May he lent £3 for a robe to be worn in it.

It is impossible to say what parts of Arthur's adventurous life were represented in this piece.

15. *The Conquest of Brute, with the first founding of the Bath* (*Diary*, p. 96). On 30 July 1598, Henslowe lent the company 40s. to buy the book of this (probably old) play. It seems that Chettle was employed either to rewrite it or to compose a sequel, for the needy playwright was lent various sums 'in earnest' of it; and on three dates in October he was advanced (in all) £6 in payment for

the playbook. There were giants in this piece, for on 12 December Henslowe lent 24*s.* to make 'cottes for gyantes in brutte'.

If, as the title suggests, there was one play covering both the conquests of Brut and the founding of Bath, it must have been a very episodic piece.

Brut, great-grandson of Aeneas, having accidentally killed his father while hunting, went to Greece, where he met other Trojans, defeated Pandrasus, king of the Greeks, and married his daughter Innogen. Sailing to Leogitia he visited the Temple of Diana, where he was promised kingship in an island beyond Gaul. Passing Gibraltar, they landed and found more Trojans under Corineus, very wise and strong. With his aid Brut defeated King Goffarius in Aquitaine, then proceeded to Albion, at that time a land of giants. 'Among these giants (as Geoffrey of Monmouth writeth) there was one of passing strength and great estimation, named Gogmagog, with whome Brute caused Corineus to wrestle at a place beside Dover' (Holinshed, II.4). Corineus threw Gogmagog over the cliff, and was rewarded with the sovereignty over Corn-wall. Brut built Troynovant by the River Thames and before he died called the whole island Britain and divided it among his three sons (see under *Locrine* above).

The play may have summarized the reigns of Locrine, Mem-pricius, and others until Bladud, who built the city of Bath and 'fashioned hot baths therein, meet for the needs of men' (Geoffrey). Obviously this was a major ingredient of the piece. Bladud was a craftsman, a student of magic and a lover of learning. He founded a university at Stamford, and made wings with which he tried to fly, but fell and was dashed to pieces on the altar of Apollo in Troynovant. He was succeeded by his son King Lear. The 1574 *Mirror for Magistrates* stressed the varied learning of Bladud, the medicinal nature of the Bath springs, and Bladud's death in the temple he had built to Apollo.[1]

The Conquest of Brute must have been a successful play, for Hens-lowe followed it with three other plays on early British history:

[1] This poem in octosyllabic quatrains was rewritten in rhyme royal for the 1584 ed. (Campbell, pp. 132–43, 228–34).

16. *Mulmutius Dunwallow* (*Diary*, p. 99). This seems to have been an old play by William Rankins, a moral writer who published *Seven Satires* in 1598, and in 1601 collaborated with Richard Hathaway in three plays (two of them histories). On 3 October 1598, Henslowe lent the company £3 to buy 'a book of Mr. Ranckenes called Mulmutius Donwallow'; maybe because the *Seven Satires* (S.R. 3 May 1598) was having some success.

Mulmutius Dunwallow, son of Cloten of Cornwall and father of Belinus and Brennus, was celebrated for his achievements in peace. He 'made many good lawes, the which long after were called Mulmucius lawes' (Grafton, 1.41). (These laws Gildas translated into Latin and King Alfred turned them 'into English, or the Saxon tongue'.) Mulmutius 'erected temples, wherein the people should assemble for praier; to which temples he gave benefit of sanctuary' (Harrison). 'He made the law for wager of battell, in cases of murder and felony, whereby a theefe . . . should for his purgation fight with the true man whom he had robbed, beleeving assuredlie, that the gods (for then they supposed manie) would by miracle assigne victorie to none but the innocent partie' (ibid.). A roadmaker, he 'began the foure highe wayes of Britaine' (Grafton) which Belinus finished. He unified Britain from the four chiefdoms into which it was divided, and then 'by the advise of his Lordes ordeyned him a Crowne or Diademe of Golde, and caused him selfe to be crowned with great solempnitie after the usaunce of the Pagan law. And for this cause, after the opinion of some writers, he was called the first king of Briteyn' (Grafton). He also restored 'the science of Chivalrie, wonderfully decayed before his tyme, and in maner cleane extinguished' (ibid.) Violent action could have been added by material from the 1587 *Mirror for Magistrates* telling how he destroyed the usurper Pinnar, King Stater of Scotland, and Rudack of Wales (Campbell, pp. 250–8).

This may not have made a good play, but it must have been more genial and positive than most plays on British themes.

17. *Conan Prince of Cornwall* (*Diary*, p. 100). This was a joint work by Drayton and Dekker, for on 16 October 1598 Henslowe

laid out 30s. in part payment to them for the book, and also 10s. to the actor Bradshaw at their request; on 20 October he paid £4 to Drayton and Dekker for the work.

Conan Meridoc, duke of Cornwall, lived in the time of Maximianus, the successor of Constantine the Great in Britain. Between him and Maximianus there was great strife for a time, but then they made peace. When Maximianus became emperor of Rome he took 'all the chosen youth of this land' over to France where he subdued Armorica, which he gave to Conan, changing its name to Little Britain.

Conan began to colonize his new territory, driving out the old inhabitants and 'peopling that countrie onelie with Britains, which abhorring to joine themselves with women borne in Gallia, Conan was counselled to send into Britaine for maids to be coupled with his people in marriage' (Holinshed, IV.30). He therefore sent to Dionethus, duke of Cornwall, governor of Britain, asking for 11,000 maidens, '8000 to be bestowed upon the meaner sort of Conans people, and 3000 to be joined in mariage with the nobles and gentlemen' (ibid.). Dionethus sent the maidens together with his own daughter Ursula, who was to be married to Conan.

Unfortunately there was a great storm in the Channel, and many of the maids were drowned, while others fell into the hands of Guanius, king of the Huns, and Melga, king of the Picts. Ursula was among those who perished.

The two incidents—the conquest of Armorica and the tragedy of the 11,000 virgins—would make an interesting plot for Drayton and Dekker.

18. *Brute Greenshield* (*Diary*, p. 106). Towards the end of March 1599, the Master of the Revels was paid 7s. fee for licensing this play.

Of this descendant of the great Brute Polydore Vergil wrote that he 'was greatlie renowned neither at home nor in warfare'. Neither Geoffrey nor Grafton had much to say of him, but Holinshed took from Harrison the assertion that he invaded France and took the southern part of Armorica and called it, and a city which he founded there, Britain. So this play, like the previous one, may have celebrated the British hold on north-west France.

19. *The Whole History of Fortunatus* (*Diary*, p. 126). Between 9 November 1599 and 31 November Dekker received £6 for 'the altrenge of the boocke of the wholl history of fortewnatus'. Henslowe provided £10 towards production costs. Probably the *Fortunatus* of 1596 was one part of a two-part play which Dekker was set to revise and condense into one piece. It was entered in the Stationers' Register on 20 February 1600 and published in the same year 'As it was plaied before the Queenes Majestie this Christmas by the Right Honourable the Earle of Nottingham, Lord high Admirall of England his Servants'. Dekker had received an additional payment of 40s. on 12 December for 'the end of Fortunatus for the Court'. The theme has already been described.

20. *Ferrex and Porrex* (*Diary*, p. 132). In March 1600, Henslowe lent William Haughton 32s. towards the price of a playbook; in April he paid the balance, £3 3s. The play was licensed in May. It was probably a reworking of the material in *Gorboduc* with some academic Senecanism removed, a less didactic tone, and more action (e.g. with the murder of Porrex by his mother represented on the stage). It is not likely to have taken much from the complaints of Forrex and Porrex in the 1574 *Mirror for Magistrates*.[1]

21. *Malcolm King of Scots* (*Diary*, p. 199). On 18 April 1602 on behalf of the earl of Nottingham's men Henslowe paid Charles Massey £5 'for a playe Boocke called Malcolm Kynge of Scottes'. Massey had a long career (1597–1635?) as an actor.

The play may have dealt with Malcolm III's accession; more probably however with later events in the reign of Malcolm, who was the first real king of Scotland and a thorn in the side of the Normans in England. In 1067 he married Margaret, granddaughter of Edmund Ironside and sister of Edgar Atheling. She did much to civilize and Christianize Scotland and was later declared a saint. There were many stories about Malcolm, e.g. how he protected Edgar; how he challenged and then forgave a treacherous noble who would have slain him; his ravaging of Northumbria; and

[1] See L. B. Campbell, *Parts added to the Mirror for Magistrates*, pp. 167–79.

how he made peace with William the Conqueror in 1072 'and became his man'. He quarrelled violently with William Rufus and was treacherously slain near Alnwick in 1093.[1] This play may have had some connection with Shakespeare's *Macbeth*.

Of the twenty or so relevant plays in Henslowe's lists seven were on the ancient British kings before the Romans came, two (*Constantine* and *Conan*) on Roman Britain, three on the Britons and Saxons, four on Saxon England until the Danish conquest, three on Saxons and Normans, and one on early Scottish history. We do not know how the lost plays treated their historical material nor what other plots were introduced for comic or moral effect. They probably provide only a sample of the plays on early history performed in London between 1592 and 1602. We know little about the repertory of companies with which Henslowe had no concern, e.g. of the Lord Chamberlain's Company which was the chief rival of the Admiral's men after 1594. R. B. Sharpe asserted that Henslowe's appealed to a lower class of audience than the Chamberlain's men.[2] There is no evidence of this,[3] nor that interest in legendary history was confined to unsophisticated theatregoers. No doubt the Lord Chamberlain's men put on plays of all kinds, and pre-Conquest themes provided one strand among many of popular dramatic material in the nineties and later.

Analysis of Henslowe's notes on his share of the takings[4] for these plays shows that (compared with the outstanding success of Marlowe's *Dr Faustus*, which ran for twenty-four performances and brought Henslowe 72s. on the first night, when prices may have been high) most of the pre-Conquest plays were not remarkably profitable. A good first night usually brought him over £3, but his receipts normally declined at a second or third performance to under £2, and anything above 30s. was a reasonable amount. A poor 'house' would bring in less than 25s.

---

[1] These incidents were told in Holinshed's *Historie of Scotland* (1587), 1808 ed., pp. 277–83.

[2] *The Real War of the Theatres* (Boston, 1935).

[3] Foakes and Rickert, op. cit., pp. xxv–xxvi.

[4] Probably one-half of the gallery proceeds.

and if a play produced less than 20s. it was not repeated unless the circumstances were unusual. *A Knack to Know a Knave*, which contained little history, brought 72s. on its first night as a new play on 10 June 1592. It was performed three times in that month (52s., 27s.) and four times in the following Christmas season, averaging 27s. *Cutlack*, probably not new, lasted for ten performances in the summer of 1594. On 16 May 1594 it produced 42s., but when moved to Newington in the new season it made Henslowe only 11s. on 6 June (better than *Hamlet*, 9 June, 8s.). Within a fortnight however things looked up, and it averaged 31s. for four performances; then attendances fell off and in September it achieved only 11s. and 13s. in two performances. *Vortigern*, put on fourteen times between 4 December 1596 and 2 April 1597, varied between 50s. on the first night and 4s. 1d. on the last (one of the smallest sums received).

Many revivals of old historical plays did not attract large audiences, and the less popular (*Constantine*, 11s., *William the Conqueror*, 22s., *King Lud*, 22s., the older *Fortunatus* (five performances, 40s. to 14s.) and *Hardicanute*, 16s.) were dropped when this became obvious. The plays on pre-Conquest themes were on the whole part of the 'bread-and-butter business' of Henslowe's theatre, but although they did not loom large in the repertory or the profits, they were in sufficient demand for a steady trickle of them to be commissioned or revived. Henslowe's records suggest that the trickle became quite a stream between December 1596 and December 1599 when ten new plays were bought and put on besides some revivals. It is possible that this investment was to counter the popularity of Shakespeare's histories played by the Lord Chamberlain's men. But it is hard to believe that Burbage did not supplement *King John*, *Henry IV* and *Henry V* with plays looking further back into English history. Shakespeare himself however seems to have held off until, having made a foray into ancient Rome (with *Julius Caesar*) and rivalled Dekker's *Troilus and Cressida* with one of his own, he at last magisterially invaded Henslowe's pre-Conquest territory with *King Lear*, *Macbeth* and *Cymbeline*.

20

'Eng. Lang.': English Language and Medieval Literature as University Studies

A. C. CAWLEY

THE STORY of Eng. Lit.—the academic study of modern English literature (mainly at Oxford and Cambridge)—has been told by Potter, Tillyard and Palmer.[1] But the story of Eng. Lang.—the academic study of the English language and of early English literature—receives less attention from these authors, and the convulsions that have racked the body of Eng. Lang. over the past thirty or forty years go unrecorded. The purpose of this article is to add a few details to the more recent history of Eng. Lang.

Eng. Lang., as the term is used here, includes not only the history of the English language but Old and Middle English literature and Old Icelandic literature.[2] Thus used, 'Eng. Lang.' is considerably wider in meaning than '(English) language', which

[1] Stephen Potter, *The Muse in Chains, A Study in Education* (London, 1937); E. M. W. Tillyard, *The Muse Unchained, An Intimate Account of the Revolution in English Studies at Cambridge* (London, 1958); D. J. Palmer, *The Rise of English Studies, An Account of the Study of English Language and Literature from its Origins to the Making of the Oxford English School* (London, 1965).

[2] Limitations of space have made it impossible for me to comment on the teaching of Old Icelandic (for which, see the 'Report on a colloquium on the teaching of Old Norse (Old Icelandic) in University schools of English, held under the auspices of the Viking Society for Northern Research in University College, London, on 25 February 1966') or to say anything about the tremendous impact of American universities on the study of medieval literature. Where would we be without oral-formulaic theories, patristic exegesis and medieval rhetoric?— to mention only a few of the fashionable studies of recent decades which American scholars have initiated.

is the label given by first-year students of English to the phonetics/ history of English/Old English group of studies. (This student label is accurate in so far as first-year English is concerned with phonetics and the history of the language, or with the elements of Old English grammar. But it can also be misleading because it takes no account of the efforts which are often made nowadays to teach Old English literature as literature—even to first-year students—and to relate this literature to the history and art of the Anglo-Saxon period.) Eng. Lang. is, then, a convenient shorthand term to describe the counterpart of Eng. Lit.; nor need it be misleading if it is not taken too literally but is understood to refer to a whole group of language and literature studies, closely related to the medieval and early modern periods.[1]

It will be noticed that Eng. Lang. does not include the study of Linguistics: the amazing success story of Linguistics (whether General or not), with all its academic and political ramifications, lies outside the scope of this article. Eng. Lang. is apparently not in any immediate danger of being swallowed up by Linguistics; but the older discipline is bound to be influenced by this new and vigorous growth, and would do well to seek useful ways of co-operating with it in the hope of influencing as well as being influenced.

After these preliminaries I wish to put forward the proposition that Eng. Lang. is moving gradually, if unsteadily, in the direction of self-survival—which must surely be the right direction for all those who believe Eng. Lang. to be a worthwhile group of studies.

To begin with, it is clear that a modern School of English provides a much wider range of studies and a much larger measure of freedom than were available to the students of Walter Raleigh or R. W. Chambers. At first glance, the School of English at Leeds, for example, might seem to be a free-and-easy, study-

[1] Eng. Lang. at Leeds also finds room for Medieval Welsh and other Celtic studies, as well as for Anglo-Saxon Art and Archaeology, English Dialectology, and Gothic and Germanic Philology. All these subjects are optional, even for those Special English Studies students who choose to follow the Scheme B course (with an emphasis on language and medieval literature) in their second and third years.

what-you-most-affect School where almost any road leads to a degree in English. But in truth there are still restrictions left, and students are sometimes heard to complain that the traditional zoo has been replaced by a Whipsnade, Dartmoor by an open prison. One of the most obvious restrictions is the retention of Eng. Lang. as a component of all first-year English courses. In making some Eng. Lang. compulsory during the first year of English studies Leeds is following the standard practice of most British universities, at least as far as Special Studies (i.e. single honours) in English are concerned. Without this amount of compulsion few first-year students would give themselves a chance to find out if they are interested enough in Eng. Lang. to want to go on with it in the later years of their course.

So far, so good; the philologist and the medievalist should surely be given a year and a day in which to prove themselves. But the problem remains of devising a first-year course which is both a satisfactory introduction to the more advanced study of Eng. Lang. by a minority of students and a satisfactory course for the majority who will later concentrate on modern literature and/or linguistics. This problem is a difficult one, and no solution is likely to win general acceptance; and yet the future of Eng. Lang. as an undergraduate study may largely depend on what is done in the first year to present the subject as interesting and valuable in its own right and, at the same time, in some degree relevant to modern literary and linguistic studies.

One of the most violent convulsions suffered by Eng. Lang. during the past forty years has almost completely transformed the historical study of the English language. Gone, except as an optional specialist study, is the narrow approach to philology criticized in the Report on *The Teaching of English in England* (1921).[1] No longer are undergraduates required, except with their willing consent, to hunt for what Sir Walter Raleigh called

---

[1] 'The magnificent report of the Board of Education in 1921 . . . examined clearly and at length the problems which beset the teachers of English; this document was, and indeed still is, of fundamental importance, and it should be far more widely known today'; see *The Teaching of English*, ed. R. Quirk and A. H. Smith (London, 1964), p. 2.

'hypothetical sound-shiftings in the primeval German forests'.[1] English philology has become more forward-looking and much more diversified: dialects, place-names, personal names, dictionaries have all been given house-room. At its best, the historical study of English is now related to literature and implies 'an awareness of changes in meaning, of uses of syntax, and above all of those changing attitudes to the language in its relations with literature';[2] it also takes account of colloquial English and tries to bring the history of the language up to the present day.[3] In fact, English philology now has all the potentialities of a humane study. This enlarged concept of philology must inevitably influence the first-year teaching of English language, however sketchy and superficial the treatment of it is compelled to be.

Old English (which some people still call 'Anglo-Saxon') has been near the centre of the Lit.-Lang. storm for as long as anyone can remember. Nevertheless a recent survey[4] shows that most British universities still require students who are taking English as a single honours subject to study Old English for one year or more. The only exceptions mentioned are Cambridge,[5] Sussex and East Anglia.

[1] *The Teaching of English in England*, p. 218.

[2] Palmer, op. cit., p. 157.

[3] *The Times Literary Supplement* leader of 23 June 1966 rightly praises Professor Quirk's Survey of Educated English Usage and the new English Language series of which he is general editor. But it is wide of the mark in stating that 'The study of English language in the universities is older than that of English literature. But whereas in the 1920s and 1930s the study of English literature had its revolution, the study of language has got rather stuck—somewhere before 1400.' Rather the *TLS* leader-writer himself has got stuck—somewhere in the 1920s. (Professor Peter Ure challenged the same statement in a letter to the *TLS* of 30 June.)

[4] L. Harty, 'Notes on the Teaching of Old English to Students of English Literature', *Medieval Studies Newsletter* (University of Sydney), no. 3, September 1964, pp. 1–6.

[5] Concerning Old English at Cambridge, one of the gems of Dr Tillyard's book referred to above is the account of his dismay upon hearing of Chadwick's proposal that Anglo-Saxon should be transferred to the Faculty of Archaeology and Anthropology: 'I was amazed and depressed. While sympathising with his belief that Anglo-Saxon culture should be associated with Germania at large and that archaeology should reinforce literature, I could not see it in the company of totem-poles, *rites de passage*, and Cro-magnon man. Actually Chadwick's motives were personal and political, and scarcely academic at all' (op. cit., p. 112).

The attitudes to Old English range from Professor Alistair Campbell's dictum that 'Anglo-Saxon is the best part of the English course and the backbone of it'[1] to Professor Daiches's 'We do not teach Old English at all in this University [Sussex] and have no intention of introducing it, certainly at the undergraduate level. We do not believe that Old English is a necessary or even important part of the course for students studying English literature.'[2]

There are of course more moderate attitudes lying between the two extremes. But before looking at these it is worth noting what Professor Daiches has to say about 'Anglo-Saxon' in his excellent essay on 'The Place of English Studies in the Sussex Scheme'.[3] It is plain that he remembers Anglo-Saxon as a mainly linguistic exercise. At Sussex the study of English language and literature begins with the Renaissance—'apart from some work on Chaucer' —because he is convinced that 'the additional insight which it [Anglo-Saxon] will give to the modern student is marginal' (p. 98). But, on his own showing, a study of Anglo-Saxon made the Edinburgh student of the thirties 'aware of certain native strengths in the English language' (p. 84); and, concerning his own study of Anglo-Saxon, he writes, 'I myself never regret having studied it and feel that my understanding of the nature of the English language has been deepened by my doing so' (p. 97). After reading this one cannot help thinking that for the 'modern student', unless he is fundamentally different from the students of Daiches's generation, the study of Old English may still have more than a marginal value. It is also arguable that this value may be increased if Old English is made a genuine literary study and is not simply taught as a linguistic aid to the historical study of the English language.[4]

---

[1] *The Times*, 4 November 1965. On the same side of the fence is the anonymous scholar who told his students: 'When a new book is published, read an Old English one.'

[2] Professor D. Daiches, quoted by Harty, op. cit., p. 5.

[3] Chap. 5 of *The Idea of a New University, An Experiment in Sussex* (London, 1964), pp. 81–99.

[4] It is a sobering thought that if Professor Daiches had studied only at Cam-

Somewhere between the two extremes described above is the position taken up by Professor Knights, who (while he was still at Bristol) demanded 'a modest competence in Old English' for three reasons:

so that all students shall have some sense of the origins of a language which has grown by such complicated ways into the rich and expressive instrument it is; so that they shall be introduced to a literature that some will wish to study more intensively in an 'advanced' course continuing into the third year; and so that all will have a foundation for the study of the great literature of the fourteenth century.[1]

To these three good reasons for requiring some study of Old English by all students of English, at least in their first year, should be added Professor Merchant's: 'that they may have the chance of reading the poetry of some distinction in Old and Middle English which they are not likely to master in any other circumstances'.[2] This is an amplification of Professor Knights's second reason, but an important one because it emphasizes that some Old English literature is worth reading by all first-year students of English for its own sake, and not simply by the minority who will continue with it as a specialized study in the later years of their course. First-year students have to be persuaded—by teachers who are themselves persuaded—that the language of much Old English poetry is already a 'rich and expressive instrument', and that 'In its poetry oral poetic methods, a pre-Christian heritage, are assimilated with literary rhetorical methods . . . to produce literature which is not paralleled in style at any later time.'[3] This process of

bridge or Sussex he might never have been able to write the first chapter ('Anglo-Saxon Literature') of his book *A Critical History of English Literature*, 2 vols. (London, 1960).

[1] L. C. Knights, 'English at Bristol', in 'The Idea of an English School', *The Critical Survey* (Autumn, 1963), p. 182. Professor Knights (with deliberate faint surprise) observes: 'Strange as it may seem to those who reacted against the older forms of philological grind, there are always some students—and those not the least able—who find intellectual and imaginative nourishment in Old English and (a tiny minority these) in Old Norse Literature.'

[2] W. Moelwyn Merchant, 'English at Exeter', in 'The Idea of an English School', p. 186.

[3] Professor J. E. Cross, quoted by Harty, op. cit., p. 5.

persuasion must begin in the first year: all students should learn that English poetry was a splendid affair even before Chaucer, and that poems like *The Battle of Maldon* and *The Dream of the Rood* 'are all good things, *perfect* things, in that they do, in a way which cannot be bettered, what they set out to do'.[1] The difficulties are formidable and a recent *TLS* review has indicated two of them:

First, Old English has to be learnt. Most of us, with no time for this, must have recourse to translations; and what translations we have, with a few exceptions, are incredibly bad. Secondly, although every inch of Old English poetry has been subjected to close textual attention, it has received singularly little sensible critical evaluation.[2]

But perhaps it is possible to turn the second of these difficulties into an advantage: students can still be encouraged to evaluate for themselves, unburdened by the load of criticism which weighs so heavily on the student of modern literature.

Like Old English, Middle English is slowly but surely establishing itself as a literary study—though not without difficulties and convulsions of its own. Potter has amusingly described the first entry of Middle English on the academic stage. With reference to the founding of the Early English Text Society by F. J. Furnivall in 1864, he writes:

The excitement of Gold Rush days again, as the extent of the unpublished, or only hitherto sketchily published material was realised. There will never be again so much unfingered English Literature. It was not so much the Anglo-Saxon classics which made the mouth water; the most thickly filled veins lay in the transition period between this earlier writing and modern English. 'Middle English' it was called: and this phrase *Middle English* in itself held excitement, with its atmosphere of being above such irrelevancies as authors, with its scientific coolness, with its evolutionary emphasis.[3]

[1] R. W. Chambers, *The Teaching of English in the Universities of England.* English Association Pamphlet no. 53 (1922), p. 27. (As an old student of R. W. Chambers and A. H. Smith, I do not underrate the importance of Old English prose; but I recognize that for a majority of students the poetry is the exciting part of Old English literature.)

[2] Review (23 June 1966) of *The Earliest English Poems,* translated and introduced by Michael Alexander (Penguin Books).

[3] Potter, op. cit., p. 174.

There was a time, not so very long ago, when the approach to English literature of the thirteenth and fourteenth centuries was mainly philological: when textual study and translation were the only things that mattered and literary values were almost entirely ignored. This state of affairs is no longer tolerated by either staff or students. Attitudes have changed since the days when Chadwick 'despised the Gothic frothiness of the medieval allegory [and] thought *Pearl* "bloody nonsense" '.[1] But there is still a longish way to go before medieval literature is commonly studied as literature and not as something else. Undergraduate students of modern literature who are required to do some work on Chaucer and the fourteenth/fifteenth centuries are the most vociferous critics of the lingering philological attachments of medieval literature. It is probably impossible to satisfy this group of students; but they do happen to be in a majority, and some of their suggestions are worth attending to.

The study of Middle English literature will no doubt progressively become a more self-conscious literary activity as more texts of literary interest are edited for the undergraduate,[2] as the methods of practical criticism are made more use of, and as more scholarly work of a critical, evaluative kind is published. There will be further progress in the same direction as the social and intellectual history and the visual arts of the Middle Ages are more actively pressed into service as aids to a fuller understanding of the literature.

I am not suggesting that any of this is easy to do, or that it can be done by any one department or even by any one university. Indeed, at postgraduate—if not at undergraduate—level, it is essential that an association of medievalists should exist to give the student of medieval language, literature, or history a greater

[1] Tillyard, op. cit., p. 43. Chadwick's opinion of *Pearl* would be a fair enough comment on some of the criticism of the poem.

[2] I am not thinking here of definitive editions like Professor Kane's *Piers Plowman: The A Version* but of texts chosen and presented with undergraduate needs in mind, e.g. the Manchester series of Old and Middle English Texts, the York Medieval Texts, the Clarendon Medieval and Tudor Series, the Cambridge editions of Chaucer, and Nelson's Medieval and Renaissance Library.

breadth to his studies.[1] If the postgraduate student cannot get this broader view of medieval studies in his own university, he should be encouraged to go somewhere else where he can.

The overriding problem of the English School at Leeds, and presumably of any large school of English that shelters many diverse studies, is to make the whole thing cohere: to give the parts a livelier sense of belonging to the whole. As Professor Jeffares has put it:

> The School of English in Leeds is intended as an organisation, to symbolise the desire of its members to bridge the old gaps between language and literature and to prevent new ones growing up between linguistics and literature . . . plans are in preparation for the erection of a building for the School which will embody the union of its diverse activities: in English literature, in American literature and in Commonwealth literature; in philology; in folk-life; in linguistics.[2]

On an administrative level the work of keeping the Leeds School of English together is done by a Chairman, with the help of a Board of Studies to which all teachers of the School belong, and (more recently) of a staff-student committee for the discussion of academic matters of common concern. On a curricular level there are already courses 'which bring together some of the different elements within the school'.[3] Another step in this direction has lately been taken by making three new courses available to Special Studies students of English in their second year:

(1) *The uses of spoken English*, which places an emphasis on English speech, its varieties and uses. This course is not designed specifically for future teachers; it will provide opportunities for

[1] Such as the Graduate Centres for Medieval Studies at Reading and Toronto. A similar centre has been set up at Leeds, one function of which will be to provide ancillary studies for the postgraduate who is specializing in medieval history or in one of the medieval vernacular languages or literatures for the purpose of a higher degree.

[2] A. Norman Jeffares, 'English at Leeds', in 'The Idea of an English School', *The Critical Survey* (Autumn, 1963), pp. 183, 185.

[3] Jeffares, op. cit., p. 183.

the study of spoken English in all kinds of situations, formal and informal.[1]

(2) *English language and literature in the Renaissance*, which is concerned with Renaissance attitudes to language and their effect on literature.

(3) *English and Scottish literature 1400–1590*, which aims at bringing together the literature of the fifteenth and sixteenth centuries.

These courses are made possible by the co-operation of members of staff from different sections of the School. They will be taken by many students who, though not committed to Eng. Lang., are interested in second-year courses which combine linguistic and literary studies. A logical extension of courses of this kind will be the introduction of postgraduate studies which link language and literature, medieval and modern, Eng. Lang. and Eng. Lit.

Despite all our efforts, the Utopian school of English—where all knowledge is valued for its own sake, where all lecturers have something valuable to say, and all students are diligent and intellectually adventurous[2]—will continue to elude us. Yet some Utopian vision is necessary, so that we shall be intelligently discontented with what is and be moved to try for something better. As a brief statement of the Utopian aim it would be difficult to improve on Professor Daiches's words—'to enable our students to achieve the fullest possible awareness of the human relevance of works of literature'.[3] But it must be understood that

[1] 'English students tend to be inarticulate, compared with students in France or America. The chief reason for this difference is that in England both schools and universities treat writing as important but speech as unimportant'; see G. L. Brook, *The Modern University* (London, 1965), p. 71.

[2] F. R. Leavis, *Education and the University* (London, 1943), p. 59, gives the best description known to me of the sort of student that many of us would like to have a share in making: 'We should make our dispositions with an eye to producing neither the scholar nor the academic "star" (the "high-flyer")—the mind that shines at academic tests and examination gymnastic; but a mind equipped to carry on for itself; trained to work in the conditions in which it will have to work if it is to carry on at all; having sufficient knowledge, experience, self-reliance and staying-power for undertaking, and persisting in, sustained inquiries.'

[3] Daiches, op. cit., p. 99.

English literature begins with *Beowulf*, and that literature is unavoidably written in language.

Thus glossed, the above statement of aim would no doubt have been acceptable to Professor Garmonsway, whose very human approach to language and literature has been constantly in my mind.

Index